GLOBAL POLICING AND
TRANSNATIONAL LAW ENFORCEMENT

Criminology and the study of criminal justice are rapidly growing areas of scholarship internationally. The **SAGE Library of Criminology** series serves this important and expanding field by providing definitive, multi-volume collections of the most influential classic and contemporary works relating to the study of crime and criminal justice. Edited by some of the world's foremost criminologists, the collections in this series map out the study of criminology and criminal justice, providing the most authoritative overview available.

Ben Bowling is Professor of Criminology and Criminal Justice at King's College, London. His research examines practical, political and legal problems in policing and the connections between local and global police power. Relevant publications include *Policing the Caribbean*, Oxford University Press 2010 and *Stop and Search: Police Power in Global Context* (with Leanne Weber) Routledge, 2012. Ben Bowling and James Sheptycki are co-authors of *Global Policing*, SAGE 2012.

James Sheptycki is Professor of Criminology, York University, Toronto, Canada. He is widely published on topics related to transnational crime and policing. Relevant publications include *Issues in Transnational Policing*. London: Routledge 2000; *Crafting Transnational Policing* (with Andrew Goldsmith), Hart 2007, *Transnational Crime and Policing*; Selected Essays Ashgate 2012. Ben Bowling and James Sheptycki are co-authors of *Global Policing*, SAGE 2012.

GLOBAL POLICING AND TRANSNATIONAL LAW ENFORCEMENT

VOLUME I

Theorising Global Policing and Transnational Law Enforcement: Interdisciplinary Perspectives

Edited by

Ben Bowling and James Sheptycki

⑤SAGE reference

Los Angeles | London | New Delhi
Singapore | Washington DC

Los Angeles | London | New Delhi
Singapore | Washington DC

SAGE Publications Ltd
1 Oliver's Yard
55 City Road
London EC1Y 1SP

SAGE Publications Inc.
2455 Teller Road
Thousand Oaks, California 91320

SAGE Publications India Pvt Ltd
B 1/I 1, Mohan Cooperative Industrial Area
Mathura Road
New Delhi 110 044

SAGE Publications Asia-Pacific Pte Ltd
3 Church Street
#10-04 Samsung Hub
Singapore 049483

Editor: Natalie Aguilera
Assistant editor: Colette Wilson
Permissions: Swati Jain
Production controller: Prasanta Barik
Proofreader: Vijaya Ramachandran
Marketing manager: Teri Williams
Cover designer: Wendy Scott
Typeset by Diligent Typesetter, Delhi
Printed and bound by CPI Group (UK) Ltd,
Croydon, CR0 4YY [for Antony Rowe]

MIX
Paper from
responsible sources
FSC
www.fsc.org   FSC® C013604

At SAGE we take sustainability seriously. Most
of our products are printed in the UK using FSC
papers and boards. When we print overseas we
ensure sustainable papers are used as measured
by the Egmont grading system. We undertake an
annual audit to monitor our sustainability.

Library of Congress Control Number: 2015931252

British Library Cataloguing in Publication data

A catalogue record for this book is available from the
British Library

ISBN: 978-1-4739-0804-8 (set of four volumes)

Contents

Volume I: Theorising Global Policing and Transnational Law Enforcement – Interdiciplinary Perspectives

The Idea of Transnational Policing

History

Theory: Sociology, Politics and International Relations

The Future of Global Policing

Volume II: The Structures of Global Policing and Transnational Law Enforcement

The Architecture of Global Policing

Overseas Liaison Officers

Security Assemblages: High-Low/Public-Private/Surveillance-Coercion

Volume III: Spatial Dimensions of Transnational Policing

Policing Ports and Airports

Policing Seas and Oceans

Policing New Transnational Spaces: Cybercrime and Mega Events

Volume IV: Policing Transnational Problems

Policing Transnational Organised Crime, Drugs and Guns

Appendix of Sources

1. 'Policing the World: The Background', *Malcolm Anderson*
   *Policing the World: Interpol and the Politics of International Police
   Co-operation* (Oxford: Clarendon Press/Oxford University Press, 1989),
   pp. 12–34.
   Reprinted by permission of Oxford University Press.

2. 'Introduction from *Cops Across Borders*', *Ethan Nadelmann*
   *Cops Across Borders: The Internationalization of U.S. Criminal Law
   Enforcement* (Pennsylvania: Pennsylvania State University Press, 1993),
   pp. 1–14.
   Copyright © 1993 by The Pennsylvania State University Press.
   Reprinted by permission of The Pennsylvania State University Press.

3. 'Transnational Policing and the Makings of a Postmodern State',
   J.W.E. Sheptycki
   The British Journal of Criminology, 35(4) (1995): 613–635.
   Reprinted by permission of Oxford University Press via Copyright Clearance
   Center's RightsLink service.

4. 'The Role of Enforcement of Law in the Establishment of a New
   International Order: A Proposal for a Transnational Police Force',
   Robert C. Johansen and Saul H. Mendlovitz
   Alternatives: Global, Local, Political, VI(2) (1980): 307–337.
   Published by SAGE Publications, Inc. Reprinted with permission.

5. 'Transnational Policing: The Globalization Thesis, a Typology and a
   Research Agenda', *Ben Bowling*
   Policing: A Journal of Policy and Practice, 3(2) (2009): 149–160.
   © The Authors 2009. Published by Oxford University Press on behalf of
   CSF Associates: Publius, Inc. All rights reserved. Reprinted by permission
   of Oxford University Press via Copyright Clearance Center's RightsLink
   service.

6. 'The International Campaign against Anarchist Terrorism, 1880–1930s',
   Richard Bach Jensen
   Terrorism and Political Violence, 21(1) (2009): 89–109.
   Copyright © Taylor & Francis Group, LLC. Reprinted by permission of
   Taylor & Francis Ltd, http://www.tandfonline.com via Copyright Clearance
   Center's RightsLink service.

7. 'Bureaucratization and Social Control: Historical Foundations of
   International Police Cooperation', *Mathieu Deflem*
   Law & Society Review: Journal of the Law and Society Association, 34(3)
   (2000): 739–778.
   © 2000 by The Law and Society Association. All rights reserved.
   Republished with permission of John Wiley & Sons – Journals; permission
   conveyed through Copyright Clearance Center, Inc.

8. 'The Emergence of the Police – The Colonial Dimension', *Mike Brogden*
   The British Journal of Criminology, 27(1) (1987): 4–14.
   Reprinted by permission of Oxford University Press via Copyright Clearance
   Center's RightsLink service.

9. 'The Global Cops Cometh: Reflections on Transnationalization, Knowledge
   Work and Policing Subculture', *J.W.E. Sheptycki*
   The British Journal of Sociology, 49(1) (1998): 57–74.
   © London School of Economics 1998. Published by Wiley. Reprinted with
   permission.

10. 'Reasonable Force: The Emergence of Global Policing Power', *Barry J. Ryan*
    Review of International Studies, 39(2) (2013): 435–457.
    © British International Studies Association, published by Cambridge
    University Press, reproduced with permission.

11. 'International Policing and International Relations', *B.K. Greener*
    International Relations, 26(2) (2012): 181–198.
    Published by SAGE Publications Ltd. Reprinted with permission.

12. 'The Possibility of Transnational Policing', *Alice Hills*
    Policing & Society: An International Journal of Research and Policy, 19(3)
    (2009): 300–317.
    © 2009 Taylor & Francis. Reprinted by permission of Taylor & Francis Ltd,
    http://www.tandfonline.com via Copyright Clearance Center's RightsLink
    service.

13. 'Past, Present, and Future Trajectories', *Peter Andreas and Ethan Nadelmann*
    *Policing the Globe: Criminalization and Crime Control in International
    Relations* (USA: Oxford University Press, 2006), pp. 223–253 and 313–318.
    Reprinted by permission of Oxford University Press, USA.

14. 'Conclusion: The Global Cops Have Arrived', *Ben Bowling and
    James Sheptycki*
    Global Policing (London: SAGE Publications Ltd, 2012), pp. 128–136
    and 168.
    Published by SAGE Publications Ltd. Reprinted with permission.

15. 'The Global Policing Architecture', *Ben Bowling and James Sheptycki*
    Global Policing (London: SAGE Publications Ltd, 2012), pp. 53–77,
    147–153.
    Published by SAGE Publications Ltd. Reprinted with permission.

24. 'Police, Policy and Politics in Brussels: Scenarios for the Shift from
    Sovereignty to Solidarity', *Monica den Boer*
    Cambridge Review of International Affairs, 27(1) (2014): 48–65.
    Copyright © Centre of International Studies. Reprinted by permission
    of Taylor & Francis Ltd, www.tandfonline.com on behalf of Centre of
    International Studies via Copyright Clearance Center's RightsLink service.

25. 'Squaring the Circle with Mutual Recognition? *Demoi*-cratic Governance in
    Practice', *Julia Sievers and Susanne K. Schmidt*
    Journal of European Public Policy, 22(1), Special Issue: Demoi-cracy in the
    European Union (2015): 112–128.
    © 2014 Taylor & Francis. Reprinted by permission of Taylor & Francis Ltd,
    http://www.tandfonline.com via Copyright Clearance Center's RightsLink
    service.

26. 'Strategies of Police Cooperation: Comparing the Southern Chinese
    Seaboard with the European Union', *Saskia Hufnagel*
    Crime, Law and Social Change, 61(4), Special Issue: Policing the Southern
    Chinese Seaboard (2014): 377–399.
    © Springer Science+Business Media Dordrecht 2013. Reprinted with
    kind permission from Springer Science and Business Media via Copyright
    Clearance Center's RightsLink service.

27. 'Police Cooperation in the Southern African Region: Politics and
    Practicalities', *Elrena Van der Spuy*
    Crime, Law and Social Change, 51(2), Conflicts and Cooperation in Security
    and Policing (2009): 243–259.
    © Springer Science + Business Media B.V. 2008. Reprinted with kind
    permission from Springer Science and Business Media via Copyright
    Clearance Center's RightsLink service.

28. 'International Policing in Russia: Police Co-operation between the European
    Union Member States and the Russian Federation', *Ludo Block*
    Policing & Society: An International Journal of Research and Policy, 17(4)
    (2007): 367–387.
    © 2007 Taylor & Francis. Reprinted by permission of Taylor & Francis Ltd,
    http://www.tandfonline.com via Copyright Clearance Center's RightsLink
    service.

29. 'Borders as Information Flows and Transnational Networks', *Peter Shields*
    Global Media and Communication, 10(1) (2014): 3–33.
    Published by SAGE Publications Ltd. Reprinted with permission.

30. 'The (In)Securitization Practices of the Three Universes of EU Border
    Control: Military/Navy – Border Guards/Police – Database Analysts',
    Didier Bigo
    Security Dialogue, 45(3), Special issue on Border Security as Practice
    (2014): 209–225.
    Published by SAGE Publications Ltd. Reprinted with permission.

31. 'Policing across a Dimorphous Border: Challenge and Innovation at the French-German Border', *Detlef Nogala*
European Journal of Crime, Criminal Law and Criminal Justice, 9(2) (2001): 130–143.
© Kluwer Law International. Reprinted with permission from Koninklijke Brill NV via Copyright Clearance Center's RightsLink service.

32. 'Police Cooperation across the Irish Border: Familiarity Breeding Contempt for Transparency and Accountability', *Dermot P.J. Walsh*
Journal of Law and Society, 38(2) (2011): 301–330.
© 2011 The Author. *Journal of Law and Society* © 2011 Cardiff University Law School. Published by Blackwell Publishing Ltd. Reprinted with permission from John Wiley and Sons Ltd.

33. 'Establishing Cross-Border Co-operation between Professional Organizations: Police, Fire Brigades and Emergency Health Services in Dutch Border Regions', *Sebastiaan Princen, Karin Geuijen, Jeroen Candel, Oddy Folgerts and Ragna Hooijer*
European Urban and Regional Studies (2014).
doi: 10.1177/0969776414522082
Published by SAGE Publications Ltd. Reprinted with permission.

34. 'Governmentalities of an Airport: Heterotopia and Confession', *Mark B. Salter*
International Political Sociology, 1(1) (2007): 49–66.
© 2007 International Studies Association. Published by Blackwell Publishing. Reprinted with permission from John Wiley and Sons Ltd.

35. '"Port of Call": Towards a Criminology of Port Security', *Yarin Eski*
Criminology & Criminal Justice, 11(5) (2011): 415–431.
Published by SAGE Publications Ltd. Reprinted with permission.

36. 'Policing the High Seas: The Proliferation Security Initiative', *Michael Byers*
The American Journal of International Law, 98(3) (2004): 526–545.
Republished with permission of American Society of International Law; permission conveyed through Copyright Clearance Center, Inc.

37. 'Conceptualizing Maritime Environmental and Natural Resources Law Enforcement – The Case of Illegal Fishing', *Klas Sander, Julian Lee, Valerie Hickey, Victor Bundi Mosoti, John Virdin and William B. Magrath*
Environmental Development, 11 (2014): 112–122.
© 2013 The World Bank. Published by Elsevier B.V. All rights reserved. Reprinted with permission from Elsevier via Copyright Clearance Center's RightsLink service.

38. 'Floating Carceral Spaces: Border Enforcement and Gender on the High Seas', *Sharon Pickering*
Punishment & Society, 16(2) (2014): 187–205.
Published by SAGE Publications Ltd. Reprinted with permission.

39. 'Developments in the Global Law Enforcement of Cyber-Crime',
Roderic Broadhurst
Policing: An International Journal of Police Strategies & Management, 29(3)
(2006): 408–433.
© Emerald Group Publishing Limited all rights reserved. Reprinted
with permission from Emerald Group Publishing Limited via Copyright
Clearance Center's RightsLink service.

40. 'Global Policing and the Case of Kim Dotcom', *Darren Palmer and
Ian J. Warren*
International Journal for Crime, Justice and Social Democracy, 2(3) (2013):
105–119.
© The Author(s) 2013. This work is licensed under a Creative Commons
Attribution 3.0 License.

41. 'Spectacular Security: Mega-Events and the Security Complex', *Philip Boyle
and Kevin D. Haggerty*
International Political Sociology, 3(3) (2009): 257–274.
© 2009 International Studies Association. Reprinted with permission from
John Wiley and Sons Ltd.

42. 'The Organization of 'Organized Crime Policing' and Its International
Context', *Clive Harfield*
Criminology & Criminal Justice, 8(4) (2008): 483–506.
Published by SAGE Publications Ltd. Reprinted with permission.

43. 'Transnational Drugs Law Enforcement: The Problem of Jurisdiction and
Criminal Law', *Juan G. Ronderos*
Journal of Contemporary Criminal Justice, 14(4) (1998): 384–397.
Published by SAGE Publications, Inc. Reprinted with permission.

44. 'The "Drug War": Learning from the Paradigm Example of Transnational
Policing', *James Sheptycki*
James Sheptycki (ed.), *Issues in Transnational Policing* (First Edition)
(London: Routledge, 2000), pp. 201–228.
Reprinted with permission from Taylor & Francis Group.

45. 'Guns, Crime and Social Order in the West Indies', *Biko Agozino, Ben Bowling,
Elizabeth Ward and Godfrey St. Bernard*
Criminology & Criminal Justice, 9(3) (2009): 287–304.
Published by SAGE Publications Ltd. Reprinted with permission.

46. 'Money Laundering and Its Regulation', *Michael Levi*
The ANNALS of the American Academy of Political and Social Science, 582(1)
(2002): 181–194.
Reprinted by permission of SAGE Publications via Copyright Clearance
Center's RightsLink service.

54. 'Conceptualising and Combating Transnational Environmental Crime',
    Glen Wright
    Trends in Organized Crime, 14(4) (2011): 332–346.
    © Springer Science+Business Media, LLC 2011. Reprinted with kind
    permission from Springer Science and Business Media via Copyright
    Clearance Center's RightsLink service.

55. 'International Criminal Investigations of Genocide and Crimes against
    Humanity: A War Crimes Investigator's Perspective', *John R. Cencich*
    International Criminal Justice Review, 19(2) (2009): 175–191.
    © 2009 Georgia State University Research Foundation, Inc. Reprinted
    by permission of SAGE Publications via Copyright Clearance Center's
    RightsLink service.

56 'Global Policing and Transnational Rule with Law', *Ben Bowling and
    James Sheptycki*
    Transnational Legal Theory (2015).
    http://dx.doi.org/10.1080/20414005.2015.1042235
    Reprinted by permission of Taylor & Francis Ltd, www.tandfonline.com via
    Copyright Clearance Center's RightsLink service.

Foreword

This four-volume Major Work is a most impressive intellectual achievement by two authors whose earlier work, separately and jointly, has established them as leading experts on globalisation's impact on policing. Ben Bowling and James Sheptycki's standing as leaders in the burgeoning field of police studies was consolidated by their 2012 monograph on *Global Policing*. Compact, clear, readable yet scholarly, that book rapidly established itself as the key text on the subject. This comprehensive collection of theoretical and empirical papers on global policing and transnational law enforcement offers the definitive resource for students, academics and practitioners. It includes key examples from the editors' own extensive empirical research projects on transnational policing as well as their sophisticated theoretical analyses. It includes a wide-ranging assortment of other scholars' work, and is a must-have for anyone in the policing field, around the globe.

These four volumes provide an authoritative compendium of research and theory on global policing, and add much to our theoretical understanding of policing. The book covers the history of global law enforcement and theoretical analyses of it in Volume I; an array of articles probing and charting the architecture and practices of transnational police in Volume II; a third focusing on the various kinds of transnational spaces policed by such organisations, illustrated by valuable case studies; and a final volume on the problems responded to and raised by the globalisation of policing, addressing issues of effectiveness, accountability, legitimacy, inequality, and ethics.

Globalisation is a mixed blessing. Breaking down communication, cultural and spatial barriers between people is, in itself, a general good. But its neoliberal incarnation brings with it huge bads. Neoliberal globalisation is to some extent a new name for an old beast – imperialism – and this has far-reaching implications for the police and community. This impressive and important collection offers the definitive guide and the analytic tools required for a thorough knowledge and understanding of global policing.

Robert Reiner
Emeritus Professor of Criminology
Law Department
London School of Economics and Political Science

Editors' Introduction: Global Policing and Transnational Law Enforcement

Ben Bowling and James Sheptycki

Policing is globalising. The tasks of maintaining order, enforcing law, investigating crime and myriad other aspects of social control – which have historically been based almost exclusively within local communities – now stretch far beyond national boundaries. Many police agents spend most of their time communicating and collaborating with colleagues abroad. Worldwide, thousands of police officers have been dispatched to locations far from home to work in United Nations peacekeeping missions or as overseas liaison officers. Detectives from domestic police forces fly frequently to other countries or are in day-to-day contact with their foreign counterparts by telephone or through computer networks. This policework might be in pursuit of a fugitive criminal, gathering witness statements and forensic evidence, tracking the proceeds of crime, or retrieving stolen property. It could involve any of the myriad problems to which the police are thought of as a solution. It might simply be making one of the 3.3 million Interpol database searches that reportedly happen *every day*. Some policework – such as investigating cybercrime, trafficking and money laundering – is entirely concerned with cross-border criminal activity. As international travel has become easier and more frequent, and as people, goods and services flow faster and further across international boundaries, so transnational policing has grown in complexity and geographical extent.

Transnational law enforcement is, in many ways, as old as policework itself. Since the nineteenth century origins of modern police forces, officers have collaborated with their foreign counterparts. From the earliest days of policing, exchanges of ideas, techniques, methods as well as collaborative investigations and overseas travel were common, albeit nowhere near as frequent as today's globally mobile police. During the age of empire, police officers across the globe were linked to one another and to metropolitan police forces through colonial policing systems. In recent years, however, policing has undergone a step-change in the process of globalisation. International collaboration, which was once intermittent, sporadic and *ad hoc,* has become sustained, continuous and institutionalised. Since the early years of the twentieth century, and particularly since World War II, international law enforcement treaties have been signed, global databases and communication systems have been devised and new policing networks

have come into being. In less than a century, a number of new police organisations have been created and are growing in power, scope, ambition
and financial cost. Policing, still rooted in locality, has become far more
connected transnationally.

The study of policing practices that transcend national boundaries has
become a vibrant and growing area of academic interest for scholars in a
wide range of disciplines as well as among police officers themselves. This
four-volume Sage Major Work explores key themes in the study of global policing and transnational law enforcement. Its goal is to describe and explain
the emergence of new forms of policework and to explore the theoretical,
normative and substantive issues emerging in this rapidly developing field. It
brings together the most important peer-reviewed journal articles, developing theoretical perspectives on this topic from a wide range of disciplines and
presenting empirical case studies illustrating the forms, functions and effects
of the new transnational policing.

Volume I examines the history of ideas concerning global policing and
transnational law enforcement. These ideas did not emerge fully formed
into the world and various arguments have been made in developing them.
The volume lays out an interdisciplinary field drawing on police studies,
criminology and criminal justice, security studies, sociology, political science, international relations, geography, area studies, ethnic and migration
studies, public administration, information sciences, government and law.
Volume II contains essays delineating the emerging organisational architecture of transnational policing and the law enforcement, order-maintenance,
surveillance, information sharing and other practices that constitute it.
Volume III examines forms of policing developing in response to phenomena
defined as problems of security and order in what may be called transnational spaces. Border zones, for example, are the shared spaces between nations;
cyberspace is a computer generated 'virtual place'; oceans, outer-space and
so-called failed states are beyond the control of any national sovereign authority. Yet the transnational 'space of flows' requires regulation and control as
much as so-called national territories. Perhaps even more so! Articulating
fears of crime and insecurity in a 'borderless world', police leaders are increasingly vocal in advocating forms of policing that operate across national
boundaries. Transnational policing is hailed as the solution to a wide range
of global problems. This is addressed in Volume IV which contains essays
considering the police response to transnational organised crime, drug and
gun trafficking, international terrorism, money laundering, people trafficking, cybercrime, transnational environmental crimes and genocide. Each of
these problems raises important practical, political, ethical and legal issues.
Consideration of transnational policing practice confronts the issues of legitimacy, accountability and control of borderless policing.

The overarching aim of this four-volume collection is to provide the reader with a guide to the contemporary understanding of transnational policing

and law enforcement. The contributions found herein seek to articulate the activities and practices, individuals and organisations, principles and prospects that are invoked, in explaining global policing and transnational law enforcement. The title and scope of this work deliberately includes law enforcement agencies beyond conventional police forces. As well as exploring the work of global policing agencies (such as Interpol and United Nations Police), it also examines the work of customs and immigration officers, border guards, port- and airport-security officers, secret intelligence agents, private security and military forces and a range of other law enforcement and regulatory agencies involved in policing broadly defined. The study of the forms of policing and law enforcement carried out by what we might call the 'extended police family' draws on theory and research evidence from a range of disciplines and examines key issues ranging from crime, justice and security to human rights, migration, diplomacy, democratic accountability and global governance.

The study of transnational policing is a growing multi-disciplinary subfield. But, as yet, there have been only a small number of authored texts and edited collections that provide readers with anything approaching comprehensive scholarly discussion of the issues.[1] *Global Policing and Transnational Law Enforcement* makes links across a wide range of disciplines and draws on diverse theoretical models and policy debates. An important goal of this collection is to provide scholars, students, policy-makers and practitioners with a compendium of the strongest examples of existing research organised with an appreciation of the inter-disciplinary depth of field required for full conceptual understanding. The work illustrates the extent, and limits, of existing scholarly knowledge. On one hand, we could not include everything of relevance that has been written. On the other, there are global policing practices that are more or less entirely un-researched. We point to such topics in our introductions to each volume.

The transnational practices of policing are rapidly expanding and changing, with far-reaching consequences. Important social goods, such as safety, justice, liberty and democratic governance, are at stake. There is an on-going need for new theoretical tools and empirical research to describe, explain and evaluate the world of global policing. Hopefully this collection will provide a useful foundation in that continuing effort. In our view, policing provides a window into the emerging transnational state system and is its most general characteristic. There can be few fields of study that offer more fertile ground for fascinating theoretical and empirical research to flourish. As David Bayley observed, for scholars with 'sense enough to recognise the importance of the police ... the field offers almost unlimited possibilities for making a contribution'.[2] This collection is not an end point. It is the beginning, we believe, of a vibrant and exciting interdisciplinary research agenda for a new generation of scholars interested in understanding fundamental aspects of global governance.

Notes

1. See for example, James Sheptycki (ed.) (2000) *Issues in Transnational Policing*. London: Routledge; Andrew Goldsmith and James Sheptycki (eds.) (2007) *Crafting Transnational Policing*. Oxford: Hart Publishing; David Brown (ed.) (2008) *Combating International Crime*. London: Routledge. Frederic Lemieux (2010) (ed.) *International Police Cooperation; Emerging Issues, Theory and Practice*. Cullompton, Devon: Willan; Ben Bowling and James Sheptycki (2012) *Global Policing*. London: Sage.
2. David H. Bayley (1979) Police Function, Structure, and Control in Western Europe and North America: Comparative and Historical Studies. *Crime and Justice,* 1: 109–143.

Introduction: Theorising Global Policing and Transnational Law Enforcement – Interdiciplinary Perspectives

Ben Bowling and James Sheptycki

The articles in Volume I explore the concepts of global policing and transnational law enforcement. Written from various academic perspectives, the articles explore the ways in which contemporary policework extends across national boundaries. Although scholarly research in this field is relatively new, transnational policing is not. The volume covers important historical questions concerning the early origins of transnational policing: Where did the idea come from? Who developed and promoted it? How has it changed over time? It is also concerned with more abstract theoretical questions such as: How does policing relate to the nation state? How is police power shaped by state sovereignty? How does it configure a transnational system of states? The articles also explore the possibilities and pitfalls of transnational policing and consider the question of whether this development is necessarily a good thing. This volume examines these questions and considers the evidence available that helps to answer some of them and, by way of conclusion, helps us to contemplate the future of global policing and transnational law enforcement.

Policing and Law Enforcement

Policework involves more than protecting life and property and enforcing the law.[1] Police organisations enforce the law, but many police officers spend little time on law enforcement and many people who enforce the law are not police. Police officers do a bewildering variety of things from the most obvious street patrols, investigating crime and maintaining public order to the less obvious tasks of licensing, background checks on employees, guarding government offices and protecting diplomats, regulating automobile traffic, investigating crime on the Internet, dealing with accidents and emergencies, looking for missing people and responding to sudden death. Egon Bittner, the noted policing scholar, famously defined the role of the police as finding 'an unknown solution to an unknown problem'.[2] More colourfully, Bittner said that the police function is to respond to *situations* definable as 'something-that-ought-not-be-to-happening-and-about-which-someone-had-better-do-something-now'.[3]

This extremely broad definition – based on empirical observation of what the police do in practice – points to the difficulty that scholars face in theorising the role, function and capacity of the police in either domestic or global context. Barry Ryan, in his article 'Reasonable Force: The Emergence of Global Policing Power', cites Walter Benjamin's description of policing as a ghostly presence that can move through boundaries like a ghost moves through walls. It has an 'everything and nothing' quality that is 'everywhere and nowhere'. Police are charged with coordinating all aspects of order and their powers cannot be confined in space nor limited by law. Policing, Ryan argues, is limited only unto itself, based on claims to act on behalf of the commonwealth to enforce the law but also to establish and reinforce the norm, to secure peace, good order, happiness, welfare and hygiene. As Markus Dubber has expressed it, 'among the powers of government none is greater than the power to police and none less circumscribed'.[4] This point becomes even sharper as the power to police moves into the transnational realm.

Among the many and various policing strategies, some never invoke the law; they are instead geared to the collection and management of information or directed at preventing or disrupting crime and disorder. Nonetheless, a crucial aspect of policework involves the use of legal tools to get things done; this is what is known in the vernacular as law enforcement. We define law enforcement broadly as the processes, systems and actions through which compliance with the law is compelled or imposed by public and private agents through the authorised use of powers of surveillance or physical force. This is carried out by a variety of means concerned with the investigation and discovery of violations of law; the collection of evidence, efforts to stop, search and arrest law breakers; interdiction of law breaking and preparation of cases for court.

Many organisations are involved in transnational policing and law enforcement. Therefore this collection extends its gaze beyond 'blue uniformed' police to include the organisations from the 'extended police family' who are geared towards the protection of territory and surveillance of suspect populations. This includes the policing functions of immigration and customs, secret intelligence, private security, coastguard, military and a wide range of other public and private bodies. Our working definition of transnational policing includes any form of order maintenance, law enforcement, peacekeeping, crime investigation, intelligence sharing or other form of policework that transcends or traverses national boundaries. In his seminal book, *Policing the World*, Malcolm Anderson observes that the contact between police forces has been intensifying to the point where there is a qualitative shift in its nature. By the end of the 1980s, it was clear that it had become so extensive, intensive and routine that an international professional community of police officers had emerged. This raises the question of how policing, traditionally a local matter, has become so extensively a transnational phenomenon. In order to understand this shift, we must first explore the historical origins of policing beyond borders.

The Historical Emergence of Transnational Policing

The articles by Bach Jensen and Deflem show that police officers have travelled internationally since the birth of the police occupation. Shared concerns about travelling criminals and 'international anarchist terrorism' in the nineteenth century inspired *ad hoc* police cooperation on individual cases and overseas intelligence postings. For example, there were dozens of foreign police agents present at London's 1851 Great Exhibition including those from Berlin, Brussels, Paris, Vienna and New York.[5] By the 1880s, transnational policing was well established. This included overt political policework abroad, ad hoc bilateral and multilateral contacts between police officials and the distribution of information on suspects wanted overseas. These activities created new friendships among police chiefs and fostered the idea that they were fellow members of an international fraternity of police officers, expert in law enforcement with a sense of mission and moral purpose that should be performed for the good of society. At the heart of this relationship was a shared professional police culture based on a depoliticised criminological knowledge.

Early international police congresses sought to collect information about international criminals with a common system of criminal identification. Because police bureaucracies are similar across nations, their formal congruence is a condition for inter-organisational cooperation. Organisational autonomy is crucial to understanding the development of transnational policing. In his article on the historical foundations of international police, Deflem argues that police organisations became able to cooperate transnationally when they achieved bureaucratic independence from the political centres. The extent of cooperation grew when police institutions established specialised systems of expert knowledge on the 'fight against international crime'. Once crime became a 'technical problem' the logical result was that it could, and should, be managed by bureaucratic experts. Police institutions could cooperate with similar bureaucratic agencies from other nation states because of their relative autonomy from national governments from which, paradoxically, they derive their authority. It is fragmentary but coherent. As Sheptyki explains in his article, 'Transnational Policing and the Makings of a Postmodern State', 'the pattern of the patchwork quilt emerges from the folk devilry it seeks to order'. The emerging transnational state system is a free-floating form of governance beholden to no identifiable source of legitimised political power.

The 1898 Conference of Rome for the Social Defence Against Anarchists was a watershed in the development of international policing. Here, diplomatic agreements operated in conjunction with a web of bilateral accords that encouraged the development and implementation procedures at the operational level among police officers sharing a common culture and shared expertise. This was also related to the emergence of new domestic policing practices such as a more 'scientific' approach to the protection of senior political figures which became 'bureaucratic, systematic and official' during this period. The conference was an opportunity to introduce systems of international exchange of information about criminals including classifications of suspects based on the Bertillon system. This period also saw the emergence and growth of the British Special Branch, the US Secret Service and the Italian secret international force to monitor anarchist activities.

The importance of organisational autonomy is clear in the creation of the International Criminal Police Commissions in the late nineteenth and early twentieth century. The idea that would become Interpol was mooted in 1914 at the International Criminal Police Congress in Monaco which brought together police, lawyers and magistrates to discuss a range of issues from arrest and extradition procedures, the sharing of identification techniques and the creation of a centralised international criminal records system. The idea of a supranational police agency with operational powers carried out by an 'international mobile force' was discussed by police chiefs in Monaco, but this was rejected in favour of a system based on information sharing and international police cooperation. Formalised in 1923 and headquartered in Vienna, Austria, the ICPC was established without an international treaty or legal document and was, from the outset, quite independent from national politics, with activities planned and executed by participating police officials without input or control from their respective governments.

Once the structural conditions were in place, in the early twentieth century, transnational police cooperation successfully developed a common organisational interest in the fight against international crime that police officials claimed had grown into a major crime wave. They argued that a new class of 'international criminals' – including cross-border thieves, swindlers, forgers, white slavers and traffickers – took advantage of the modernisation of social life and greater geographical mobility after World War I. In much the same way that it is suggested that technological developments drive transnational organised crime in our late modern age, it was argued in the 1920s that rapid social change, new technologies and especially mobile criminals capable of transgressing and transcending national borders required new forms of transnational police cooperation.

Transnational Policing: The Colonial Dimension

Understanding the emergence of transnational policing requires an analysis of the colonial model.[6] This, as Sheptycki observes, 'reveals policing to be, in a sense, transnational from the outset'.[7] The Dublin Metropolitan Police was, arguably, the first modern police force created in Britain's first colony in 1796, 33 years prior to the London Metropolitan Police. By the mid-nineteenth century, British colonies in the Caribbean, Middle East, Mediterranean, Africa and Southeast Asia had established police forces along the 'Irish model' with a strong military ethos and direction from the colonial authorities. The policing model also involved 'policing by strangers' – senior officers were recruited and trained in Britain or Ireland before being posted overseas or transferring between colonial forces while constables were drawn from the local population. In 1936, a British Colonial Police Service was consolidated under an Inspector General in order to standardise imperial police forces and mould it to the British model. During decolonisation imperial police power was asserted through development of police intelligence systems and counter-insurgency units. Extensive links existed among British metropolitan and colonial police forces because members of the Colonial Police Service were able to transfer locally between territories and this fostered many informal officer-to-officer networks.

In 'The Emergence of Police – The Colonial Dimension', Brogden highlights the relationship between the origin of the English police system and the development of colonial institutions. These served to shape policing, administration and law through colonial practices with the effect of delegitimising indigenous customs, imposing centralised social control and incorporating local society as a branch of imperial society. Brogden also illustrates the links between colonial policing and the spread of the Metropolitan model to the British shires. As well as being related to the specific problems of crime and disorder and the need for vigilance, this was also related to protecting the commercial interests of an expanding capitalism searching for new markets and resources. Brogden shows how colonial government sought to legitimise its authority externally and internally using a variety of devices, principally, through images of law. The elements evident from the colonial origins of policing continued through decolonisation, for example in the role of police advisers in Africa, the Caribbean, Indian subcontinent, Palestine and Malaya. British colonial policing offers an interesting precursor to contemporary transnational policing in which the colonies were used as sites of experimentation.

Nadelmann's book, *Cops Across Borders: The Internationalisation of US Criminal Law Enforcement*, shows that the USA also played an imperial role in the development of transnational policing. From the earliest years, the US Customs Service, Treasury Agents and the Federal Marshalls' Service travelled abroad to cooperate with foreign police in neighbouring countries such as Canada, Mexico, the Bahamas and Cuba. In later years, it extended its sphere of influence across Latin America, Eastern Europe, the Middle East and elsewhere. The origins of US overseas capacity lie in the apprehension of fugitive slaves in the mid-nineteenth century and the controlling of alcohol production and importation during the prohibition years. The dominance of the USA law enforcement agenda and policing techniques are evident from the formulations of international agreements that have often been shaped by US officials. Such developments have led to expansion in the scope of criminal law towards US innovations such as asset forfeiture and counter-money laundering as well as methods such as undercover policing, the use of informers and electronic surveillance. For Nadelmann, this process amounts to the promotion of US criminal justice norms in the transnational realm. The linked processes of regularisation, accommodation and homogenisation have led foreign governments within the US sphere of influence to a US federal model of international policing. From this perspective, the development of transnational policing can be defined in a word: Americanisation.

The development of transnational police cooperation must also be seen in the context of an emerging national policing capacity in many places around the world. The overall direction of travel is towards increasingly centralised national control of policing organisations. This has been brought about either through the creation of national police forces, national organisations for certain specialist activities (such as organised crime or terrorism) or the creation of central coordination services, databases, training programmes and suchlike. An important insight here is that the creation of Federal agencies only began in earnest in the USA at the beginning of the twentieth century and was fiercely resisted by municipal police and opposed by the general public. Nadelmann's work in this area demonstrates that overseas policing capacity tends to be pursued very firmly in the sending state's own national interest.

Towards an International Police Force?

An entirely separate source of ideas about transnational policing can be found in discussions during the middle years of the twentieth century about how the international community should respond to problems arising from civil conflict around the world. Investigating war crimes and genocide, prosecuting perpetrators of crimes against humanity and keeping the peace in the aftermath of civil war, required some kind of policing and law enforcement function that could not be provided by weak or non-existent states in war-torn regions. The debates among scholars of international relations and public international law and officials in the nascent international organisations such as the United Nations revolved around the idea of an International Police Force (IPF). In her article on 'International Policing and International Relations', Greener notes that during the inter-war years, Lord David Davies lobbied for the creation of robust forms of international institutions, including the creation of an impartial tribunal with its own police force to enforce international justice. Drawing on a liberal 'domestic analogy', Davies argued in his influential book *The Problem of the Twentieth Century* that international justice could be upheld and order maintained by the courts and the police in much the same way that the criminal justice systems operate at the national level.[8] The idea of an IPF became a staple of discussions of global justice after World War II. For example a 1948 UN Secretariat Working paper argued that an 'IPF' was required 'for the maintenance of law and order in a territory for which the international society was responsible', the pressing case at the time being Palestine.[9]

Just over a decade later, the idea took its first steps towards reality when a contingent of Ghanaian riot police was deployed to the Congo in 1960 to support UN peacekeeping troops and to assist the local police in maintaining civil order. A few years later, in 1963, UN Secretary General U Thant declared that he had 'no doubt that the world should eventually have an international police force which will be accepted as an integral and essential part of life in the same way as national police forces are accepted'.[10] Thant did not see this as a realistic proposition at the time, however. In addition to the practical problems of selecting personnel and the burdensome financial implications of such a force, he knew it would be politically unacceptable to many world governments who would naturally be concerned about interference with national sovereignty.

In their 1980 article, peace scholars Johansen and Mendlovitz consider the role of law enforcement in the establishment of a new international order, and set out a specific 'proposal for a transnational police force'. They discuss the arguments for and against such an organisation and explain how it might be created and function. Johansen and Mendlovitz argue that individual nations often require a means to supplement national self-help in law enforcement. They insist that a standing transnational constabulary police force can 'transcend narrowly defined national interest and respond more effectively to the global human interest'. They argue that only transnational law enforcement can realise the values of peace and security in keeping peace in border areas, provide humanitarian aid to innocent victims caught in the crossfire of war, and restrain state violence. Such a force, they suggest can go far beyond this to provide justice, economic wellbeing and ecological balance. They envisage that such matters as nuclear arms reduction inspected by the International Atomic Energy Agency would be better guaranteed with the assistance of global enforcement officers, as would the protection of the oceans from environmental destruction. They argue that a transnational police force, accompanied by political and moral support would enable practical engagement with critical problems that are planetary in scope including food, energy, non-renewable resources, toxic waste, human brutality and collective violence.

In each of these areas, Johansen and Mendlovitz argue that a permanent police force acting on behalf of the world community could act as a valuable supplement for domestic policing. The authors claim, optimistically, that a 'global police force can increase justice by strengthening the weak and discouraging the strong from yielding to the temptation to intervene outside their territories and to ignore callously the norms of justice and fair play'. Acknowledging the difficulties in achieving this goal and the potentially 'irrelevant theorising and impractical advocacy' of their proposals, the authors make specific recommendations about the size, recruitment and training, funding and control. They propose that the force be under UN control via Security Council Chapter VII powers or under a semi-autonomous body to authorise operations. They foresee the need to build a tradition of trustworthiness and impartiality. The authors supplement their thinking with a proposal to create, through private effort, a small force of well-educated, multilingual, disciplined people skilled in mediation, peace observation, and nonviolent direct action for the purpose of upholding international norms already enjoying wide consensus as well as supporting disaster relief or responding to humanitarian crises.

There is today no IPF as envisaged by Davies, Thant, Johansen and Mendlovitz, or the many other pundits who have called for such a force. However, in her 2012 article on this topic, Greener argues that we are witnessing the emergence of a kind of international policing that is entirely new in terms of its scale, institutional arrangements, roles and expectations. International police deployments are very extensive and based increasingly on international norms and values, institutionalised through the development of a common doctrine and training. In her view, liberalism's 'domestic analogy' resonates with international actors and is becoming increasingly plausible. Hills' article on the 'possibility of transnational policing' shows that a style of policing claiming to transcend territorial boundaries has become highly influential, especially in the rich liberal democracies of Australasia, Europe and North America. She is sceptical, however, that there is a 'common policecraft' or set of norms capable of fulfilling the requirement of what Sheptycki calls a 'transnational constabulary ethic'. Largely because there is a lack of consensus on what is required for effective policing. For Hills, the reality is that policing is essentially a 'sub-state practice' and therefore definitions of effective policing and appropriate levels of force are determined by the officer's home environment rather than by international pressure.

Theorising Transnational Policing

Reading the articles presented in the later volumes in this collection, it becomes very clear that from the seedling ideas set out above, a mature and flourishing field of transnational policing has emerged. This leads us to ask why this rapid development has occurred and what economic, political and technological forces drive it? One potential answer can be captured neatly, if oversimplistically, by the word 'globalisation'. As set out by Bowling in his article, 'Transnational Policing: The Globalisation Thesis, a Typology and a Research Agenda' the thesis proposes that rapid developments in transport and information communications technologies, the integration of global economic systems, and the emergence of a new political order – the transnational state system – has led to an intensely interconnected 'world society'. This development is driven by the twin pressures of globalisation from below – the unpredictable and unplanned integration of systems of human communication and exchange – and 'globalisation from above' – the more purposive integration of formal systems of governance and regulation promulgated by state actors. The former is exemplified by the emergence of transnational communities, groups of people connected by family, national origin, ethnicity, politics or in a myriad other ways, who communicate with one another on a routine and daily basis and exchange goods, services and money. The latter is exemplified by the emergence of governmental structures such as the United Nations or the European Union, financial institutions such as the IMF and World Bank and policing institutions such as Interpol, EUROPOL and the World Customs Organisation.

A key effect of the step-change in the extensity, intensity, speed and impact of global interconnectedness is a greater demand for, and possibilities of, connections among the world's police. These connections take many and various forms and the emergent architecture of global policing and transnational law enforcement is described and explained in Volume II of this work. What is important to note at this juncture is that although police officers have made connections with their counterparts throughout history – especially in certain contexts, such as the colonial policing system – the nature and extent of transnational policing that emerged in the second half of the twentieth century, and is now characteristic of contemporary police practice, is quite new. This presents new challenges for scholars, policy makers and police officers themselves, who seek to understand policing, how it is done and how it is regulated through legal and political structures.

In his article, 'Transnational Policing and the Makings of the Post Modern State', Sheptycki shows that in the late modern age, global capital has become unfettered from states to such an extent that governments can no longer control or direct its flows. Information and communications technologies play a key role in stitching together the transnational policing system. In the movement towards a global criminal intelligence system, the processes that record, store, analyse and transmit information between individuals and organisations become integrated across national organisations. Flexible, accurate, immediate, voluminous and complex, information serves to restructure operations and changes the nature of control. Sheptycki shows that a new transnational space has opened up within the system of hitherto individual nation states in the informationalised interstitial space between governed territories.

The contemporary policing landscape is made up of organisations of many overlapping sizes and shapes, from those that cover nation states, to those that cover a province, a region or a municipality. There is no real 'system of policing'. Instead, there is a 'hodgepodge of autonomous police forces' operating at various levels of government made of 'patches on patches rather than tailored to fit'.[1] Sheptycki draws on this metaphor to argue that in the European theatre, transnational policing is 'patchwork quilt of agencies stitched together by the efforts of transnational liaison officers'.

Scholarly research on these topics has laid the theoretical foundations for this subfield. We have sociological insights about the nature of social control. Legal scholars have contributed to discussions about the nature of the legal and regulatory frameworks. International relations draws our attention to questions about relations between nation states, sovereignty and the increasingly important role played by sub-state actors in the global system. As Anderson makes crystal clear in *Policing the World*, sovereignty is no longer an axiom of political life. The emergence of transnational policing illustrates that the state is no longer the exclusive fount of all powers and prerogatives of rule; it is no longer the final and absolute authority within a given territory. It is not that sovereignty is entirely irrelevant since many aspects of policing are at least partly shaped by criminal offences which are rooted in national laws.

Barry Ryan theorises that the emergence of global policing power is related to universalism and the codification of reasonable force. This, he argues, emerged as a form of international administration, a kind of 'global arterial power' to serve the populace, state and transnational state system that emerged from the colonial system to link the metropolis with the periphery. Ryan argues that the move of policing into the transnational realm is to construct a global *raison d'état* into what might be called a *raison de planète*. This implies that police power reinforces the reason and rationality of the transnational state system to pursue the global interest with specific global ambitions that are politically superior to moral or even legal considerations. Policing is the nexus of legal and military power which is directed inwards to the domestic sphere but also increasingly outwards into transnational spaces such as the oceans, cyberspace and the domestic territories of other states, especially those deemed to be weak, fragile, failed or failing.

Sheptycki explores the relationship between the development of transnational policing and the 'globalisation of the social system'. He argues that 'transnational folk devils require a transnational police effort, but this removes policing form its nesting place in the state and situates it in the realm of transnational practices'. Transnational policing, therefore, is a harbinger of the emergence of a post-modern transnational state system. It is the posting of overseas police liaison officers, (to which we return in Volume II) that provides transnational policing with operational capacity. Although transnational policing is grounded in intergovernmental agreements, a thick web of relations constitutes transnational control networks binding sovereign states to each other and bolstering their collective solidity.

The Future of Global Policing and Transnational Law Enforcement

We end this first volume by pondering on the current state of the world of transnational policing and contemplating what the future holds for the next stage of its development. In their book, *Policing the Globe*, Andreas and Nadelmann point to the increasingly transnational reach of law enforcers. The articles in this four-volume collection illustrate this trend clearly. Witness the creation of new policing organisations, bilateral and multilateral agreements, training programmes and overseas stationing of liaison officers all of which seek to regularise and homogenise transnational law enforcement and minimise friction when sovereign law enforcement systems interact. Although there are possibilities for change and adaptation, at present Western transnational moral entrepreneurs play a dominant role in developments. We are witnessing the emergence of a transnational law enforcement community with distinct expertise, understandings and subculture that has the power to override political differences and formal procedures originating in individual nation states. This transnational police culture, in Andreas and Nadelmann's evocative phrase, 'provides the oil and glue of international law enforcement'. All the authors excerpted in this collection are agreed that transnational policing has reached unprecedented levels. Andreas and Nadelmann see this as an 'international crime control industrial complex' driven by the dominant forces of Americanisation and Europeanisation of policing and crime control.

Although there is no global sovereign to claim universal policing authority, the UN does come close to this. This of course creates a significant tension with issues of national sovereignty and also problematises the notion of a national police force. UN Secretary General Thant predicted fifty years ago that international policing would be seen as an integral and essential part of life, and accepted 'in the same way as national police forces are accepted'.[11] On this point, it is worth remembering that the idea of a *national police force* is, even today, a highly contested idea in many places including highly developed nations such as the USA and UK. Interestingly, it is the pressure to develop an overseas policing capacity that has led many national governments to the conclusion that a centralised national policing capacity is required. In many places where fully integrated national policing does not exist, there are moves to consolidate local police forces and debates about national police forces continue to be a hardy perennial of political discussions about police.

The major global policing agencies – especially Interpol and UNPOL – are growing in numerical strength, operational capacity and ambition. Although Interpol General Secretariat, Regional Bureaus and Liaison offices employ a small force of 650 people, their networks extend deeply into the local police forces of the 190 member nations. Interpol is increasingly working in partnership with the United Nations, the World Customs Organisation, World Health Organisation and the private sector. The relationship between the UN and Interpol goes back to 1949 and was formalised in a Cooperation Agreement in 1997 after which the two organisations have cooperated and collaborated on numerous projects. An important development was the 2004 opening of an Office of the Special Representative of

Interpol at the UN Headquarters in New York. This ensures that Interpol concerns are represented in the work of the UN, including in initiatives, declarations and policy decisions. In October 2009, Interpol and the UN Police Division hosted a meeting of justice and foreign ministers from 60 countries in New York, announced as a step towards a 'global policing doctrine' that would see the two organisations becoming 'partners in fighting crime by jointly grooming a global police force'. This force would combine the UN's peacekeeping role with Interpol's role in responding to organised crime, arms and drug trafficking.[12] Their 'shared vision' is a well-equipped, trained and resourced global policing capacity linking operational capability with global databases. As is clear from these four volumes, transnational policing is extensive and varied in form. It is set to expand and is seeking power to do whatever is required working primarily through the bonds of trusted officer-to-officer contact. This is a major theme running through the articles in later volumes of this major work.

The sceptical conclusion of our book *Global Policing* is that there is little convincing evidence of the effectiveness of transnational policing. There is, to be sure, good evidence of successful investigations and prosecutions of some of the world's most serious criminals – the perpetrators of genocide and crimes against humanity, people traffickers whose actions have led to multiple deaths. But systematically collected evidence of the overall effectiveness of this gargantuan policing effort is thin on the ground. On the contrary, many of the articles in this collection show that transnational police do not always solve the problems that they set out to solve and their efforts are sometimes counter-productive. The most pessimistic conclusion is that prohibition and criminalisation regimes have failed in their own terms.

Conclusion

There is no doubt that the global cops have arrived. Despite the vision and ambition of many commentators in this field, there is no global police force; but there is global policing. Policing extends in a worldwide web of surveillance of suspect movements and the use of coercive power to disrupt, arrest and control. There is a complex architecture of organisations and agencies, mutual legal assistance treaties, regional arrest warrants, expedited extradition processes and other forms of transnational law enforcement. Today's police are globally connected by phone, email, computer databases and personnel exchanges. Transnational policing is a specialism with its own unique subculture that is gradually forming amongst the thousands of officers who are globally mobile or stationed overseas.

Policing concerned with the maintenance of social order through surveillant and coercive practices in the transnational realm is not entirely new, but it has expanded massively and changed shape dramatically in recent decades. In our view, this development requires continuing close empirical and theoretical scrutiny. The shift from policing the local beat to the novel transnational policing practices of customs, immigration, airport security, financial intelligence and private security agencies opens up a new empirical research agenda on police powers that transgress and transcend the boundaries of the nation-state. This volume explores the origins of the global policing idea, and seeks to develop a theoretical framework within which it can be understood. The challenge now is to investigate its complex forms, structures and practices as it develops in the decades ahead.

Notes

1. David H. Bayley (1979) 'Police Function, Structure, and Control in Western Europe and North America: Comparative and Historical Studies'. *Crime and Justice,* Vol. 1, 109–143; Robert Reiner (2010) *The Politics of the Police*, 4th Edition. Oxford: Oxford University Press.
2. Egon Bittner (1967) 'The Police on Skid Row', *American Sociological Review,* 32(5): 699–715.
3. Egon Bittner (1990) *Aspects of Policework.* Boston, MA: Northeastern University Press, p. 249; cited by Peter Manning (2013) 'The Work of Egon Bittner', *Ethnographic Studies,* 13: 51–66.
4. Markus Dirk Dubber (2005) *The Police Power: Patriarchy and the Foundations of American Government.* New York: Columbia University Press, p. xi.
5. Mathieu Deflem (2004) *Policing World Society: Historical Foundations of International Police Cooperation.* Oxford: Oxford University Press.
6. David Anderson and David Killingray (1991) *Policing the Empire: Government, Authority and Control, 1830–1940.* Manchester: Manchester University Press; David Anderson and David Killingray (1992) *Policing and Decolonisation: Nationalism, Politics and the Police, 1917–1965.* Manchester: University of Manchester Press.
7. James Sheptycki (1998) 'Policing, Post-modernism and Transnationalisation'. *British Journal of Criminology,* 38(3):485–503, at p. 496.
8. David Davies (1930) *The Problem of the Twentieth Century: A Study in International Relationships.* London: E. Benn Publishers.
9. Relationship between the United Nations Palestine Commission and the Security Council – Working Paper Prepared by the Secretariat for the Commission. February 3 1948.
10. U Thant, UN Secretary General, June 13 1963, cited by; B. K. Greener (2009) *The New International Policing.* London: Palgrave Macmillan, p. 1.
11. U Thant, *op cit.*
12. 'Interpol and UN back 'Global Policing Doctrine', *New York Times* (11 October 2009), our emphasis.

The Idea of
Transnational Policing

Policing the World: The Background

Malcolm Anderson

In the three decades following the Second World War international police co-operation was regarded by all but a tiny minority of people as a low-level technical-administrative exercise which raised few, if any, general political questions. Since the middle of the 1970s an agenda of issues and controversies has been established; some of these have become matters which are of direct interest to governments and to well-informed members of the public. The aim of this chapter is to set out the fundamental themes which underlie this agenda.

Certain basic factors create barriers to international police cooperation: varying state traditions, different levels of economic and social development, ideological and foreign-policy conflicts. There are political, legal, and psychological barriers to the development of improved co-operation. But there are also factors tending to break down barriers, such as the convergence of methods of policing in the highly industrialized democracies and a growing awareness of common problems of crime control; these influences are reinforced by a process of learning from the experience of other countries in the field of law enforcement. The development of co-operative attitudes and practices depends on the seriousness with which particular forms of criminality are regarded. But governments do not always give effective support to police co-operation. Although, in principle, they strongly support crime control and crime prevention, they often do not seriously press for the abolition of the thicket of legal rules and administrative procedures which slow down the investigation and prosecution of offences with international dimensions. At worst, governments sometimes appear to collude in crime, as, for example,

Source: *Policing the World: Interpol and the Politics of International Police Co-operation* (Oxford: Clarendon Press/Oxford University Press, 1989), pp. 12–34.

in cases where intelligence services, particularly the CIA, have co-operative associations with drug dealers.[1] Considerations of political advantage as well as the pressure of powerful economic interests often work against the effective suppression of drug trafficking and other types of serious crime. Pressure on governments for more effective crime control is, however, becoming stronger; even tacit government tolerance of criminal activity causes scandal in public opinion in the highly industrialized democracies.

In this chapter four assumptions are made about the current state of international police co-operation: first, it is going through a period of rapid and significant change; second, these changes are symptomatic of important developments in the international system and the states which make up that system; third, forms of international co-operation raise fundamental questions about the nature of policing; fourth, although police functions have become highly controversial within the highly industrialized democracies, there is now more agreement about the issues involved in international police co-operation than at any time in the recent past.

This chapter deals in turn with the context of police cooperation, with special reference to the doctrine of sovereignty, the historical development of police forces, and how theories of the state may contribute to the understanding of current changes; the characteristics of contemporary police co-operation, relating, in particular, to different types of crime, to frontier controls, and to relations between the police and judicial authorities; the changing pattern of international crime, and the evolution of public and official attitudes; and, finally, the limits, both practical and desirable, of international police co-operation. These are large and complex subjects which deserve more extensive treatment than is possible here. They form, however, an essential background to the difficulties which police co-operation encounters and which limit its further development.

The Historical and Theoretical Context

The assertion that something is changing immediately raises the question of exactly what is changing. The answer may be expressed simply: contact between police forces of sovereign and independent states has been intensifying to the point where there is a qualitative shift in its nature. It has become routinized, and some senior policemen are participating in an international professional community on a regular and systematic basis.

The contact provokes sensitivities and suspicions precisely because it touches the core of state sovereignty; foreign police intrusion or direct influence on state territory are usually regarded as blatant infringements of sovereignty. There is a reluctance to use the word sovereignty in contemporary political analysis because any definition includes the notion that the state is the final and absolute authority within a given territory.[2] The nineteenth-century claim, never fully realized, of the state as 'the sole, exclusive fount of all powers and prerogatives of rule'[3] is no longer an axiom of political life. Since 1945 military, political, and economic changes have ensured that all major policy decisions made within states must take very careful account of the external environment. However, the principle of sovereignty still has relevance in policing and criminal justice because all agencies with authority to investigate criminal offences are state agencies and all criminal laws applied to individuals are national laws.

In police matters, the degree of sensitivity about sovereignty depends on the kind of international co-operation which takes place. The issues are different if it is between police responsible for state security, criminal investigation, frontier control, or customs law enforcement. The very diversity of police functions, as well as the sensitivities associated with international co-operation, raise the fundamental question: what are the police for?

In the advanced industrial democracies, the police are widely accepted as an essential arm of the state to protect the constitutionally established public authorities and as necessary for the protection of the liberties, rights, and property of individuals and associations. These roles are, in the absence of revolutionary change, unlikely to alter fundamentally.[4] Although the police function is very old, the origins of the police forces of the advanced industrialized democracies are relatively recent: the professional police forces covering the whole of the state territory had their beginnings in eighteenth- and early nineteenth-century Europe. These police forces were often used to further personal and domestic ambitions, but justifications for establishing them were to enforce the law, to protect citizens against criminals, calamities, and public disturbances, and to secure the institutions of the state. Behind these justifications lay the belief that the legitimacy of state authority rested in part on the ability of the state to protect the life and property of its citizens.

The fear felt in most countries of an over-mighty police institution, especially in centralized state systems in the Napoleonic tradition, usually ensured that these tasks were divided between several authorities and a bewildering variety of forms of police organization came into being. Some forms of policing were claimed to be completely different from others. The most remarkable of these was the British tradition of regarding the police as the servants and protectors of society, politically independent, because deriving their powers from the common law and not statute, and therefore not subject to government control in the performance of their professional duties. Another was the American pattern, where law enforcement commenced as a state and local responsibility, with the federal authorities slowly setting up a large number of independent agencies with powers of enforcing specifically federal laws. The police systems which developed in continental European countries were regarded in Britain and the United States as being the harbingers of tyranny. In the European countries, scepticism has often been expressed as to the possibility that police activities can be properly co-ordinated and controlled in systems with a large number of police authorities. These attitudes have by no means disappeared, and there is little prospect that the fragmented and decentralized law-enforcement agencies of the United States and the United Kingdom will be replaced by unified national police forces on the lines of the national police of France, Spain, or Italy, despite recent trends in the United Kingdom towards increased centralization.

Because the police, in normal circumstances, have the monopoly of the use of force[5] in the highly industrialized democracies, police functions cannot be defined without reference to the most fundamental political questions concerning the purpose of public authority and the ends of the state. These questions are the perennial topics of political philosophy: the nature and justification of the state, the meaning of sovereignty, the notion of an international society, and, for individuals, the problem of the nature of our duties beyond the boundaries of the states of which we are citizens. In these areas there are no certainties except in the minds of uncritical ideologues. Marxist scholars have helped to revive an interest in the theory of the state in recent years. Scholars influenced by Marxism have also written on the police, both in the tradition of radical pamphleteering, splendidly exemplified by Edward Thompson, and in the sober academic work of Tony Bunyan and of Michael Brogden.[6] Representing the police as an instrument of class oppression may serve some political interests in certain circumstances, and, indeed, in some countries at some times, it is almost certainly true. But Marx and his followers have been consistently criticized for what Anthony Giddens calls 'class reductionism', in other words, seeking to explain too many of the characteristics of modern societies in terms of class domination and class struggle. This seriously undermines the usefulness of Marxist theory in analysing the police. A similar criticism can be made of structuralist interpretations of penal policy, advanced in recent years by Michel Foucault and Michael Ignatieff. Both these authors have interpreted the establishment of modern prisons and police forces as the structural necessity of industrializing societies to discipline the working class. This approach to the changing forms of policing is altogether too deterministic.[7]

Other contending theories of the state – pluralist, élitist, corporatist, statistic, social democratic, new right – although frequently admitting the importance of the police, have little specific to say about policing.[8] Different analyses of police roles and functions and, by extension, the nature of international police co-operation can be based on these theories. Some modern sociological accounts, developing the thought of Max Weber, greatly assist the study of the professionalization and bureaucratization of the police in the nineteenth and twentieth centuries. A contemporary political sociologist, Pierre Birnbaum, has, in an incisive way which could be further developed, shown the link between the organization of the police and the forms of state which emerged in Europe in the late Middle Ages.[9] The contribution of other scholars to the debate on the state and the links between theories of the state and the police cannot be examined here, but the starting-point of any examination of policing must be clearly set out.

This study is based firmly in a sceptical liberal tradition. States are assumed to be the result of a process of historical development in which economic structures played a role, but not always the decisive role, in the crucial political and military struggles which formed these states. Marxist and some modern conservative views about the overriding importance of economic forces or of the market are rejected. States in which representative institutions and an independent judiciary have developed were based or have come to be based on a large measure of consent among their citizens. This consent may in some cases be based on ignorance of alternatives, but it plays a significant part in determining the form and the nature of policing in these states. Privilege and exploitation exist in liberal democracies, but the social organization within them cannot simply be reduced to conflict between antagonistic social classes; class consciousness plays a varying, but never a dominant, role. The relations between states and their citizens, and states with one another, is in a constant process of change; critical reflection on problems and political action are necessary to adapt to change. This process of adaptation, essentially the political process, is necessary to secure the legitimacy of state authority.

The police can be regarded as the most basic and essential of government institutions because, apart from the occasions (exceptional in the highly industrialized democracies) when the army is used to maintain order, the police have the monopoly of the legitimate use of force against citizens within the territory of the state. Governments, therefore, have powerful instruments, in the form of police forces, at their disposal with which to enforce their will, but, for technical and political reasons, governments are seldom in complete control of them. Many government agencies may, indeed, be granted limited legal autonomy to perform certain tasks and this is frequently the case of the police. However, police organizations cannot be understood only in terms of legal authority or the functions they are required to fulfil; the professional and individual interests of policemen play a role in moulding police institutions and in directing their activities.

The police have a symbolic role as the representatives of authority, stability, and order as well as a functional role of performing certain essential tasks and duties. This combination makes them feared and suspected by dissident groups, by those concerned about the rights of individuals, and by members of governments. It has been relatively easy to create anti-police feeling by representing the police as instruments of oppression. These representations, whether Marxist or not, are at best gross simplifications. The way in which the police are involved in society and in the governmental structure varies a great deal because in all societies the police are only one of several forms of social control.

It follows from this very general starting-point that the position and significance of the police vary according to time and place. Police functions and operations are not, for example, the same in the less developed countries as they are in the highly industrialized democracies. Events occur in the one category of countries which are inconceivable in the other. Incidents in Senegal in April 1987, for example, could have no parallel in the highly industrialized democracies. Following the sentence of two policemen to terms of two years' imprisonment for torturing to death a suspect whom they had arrested, there were serious police riots – whereupon the government suspended, and then sacked, the whole national police force. Senegal had, of course, adopted the model of an advanced country – France – and therefore had a substitute for the police in the form of the *gendarmerie*. Without the *gendarmerie* this action would have been impossible, but such an action would not be feasible in France unless the French state itself was on the brink of disintegration.

There is a dearth of comparative studies of the police: as a distinguished contributor to this field writes, 'By and large, the police have not been subjected to comparative analysis. Until very recently neither historians nor social scientists appeared to recognise that police existed, let alone that they played an important part in social life.'[10] This situation is changing, although it is still the case that most in-depth studies concern police within individual states. More research is necessary to analyse developments in highly industrialized democracies, such as the professionalization of the police, the creation of specialized police forces, and the acquisition by the police of some autonomy and independence from governmental control, as well as the growth of discretionary police practices which are to a degree outside the law. Similarities have become much more marked in recent years because in the police, as in virtually all other domains, a process of learning from the experience of others has got under way.

Changes in police institutions are frequently influenced by the practices and by the experience of other countries. When police reforms are envisaged, foreign examples are examined. Some convergences have even taken place in legal systems, still remarkable for their diversity. International harmonization of criminal law is of fundamental importance because police practices are greatly influenced, where they are not directly controlled, by the judicial authorities. The examining magistrate (the *juge d'instruction*) and the public prosecutor, or the absence of one or both, can have a profound effect on police organization and behaviour. Equally important, the police, whatever claims British police constables make to complete independence, are *in the last resort* always subject to governmental supervision and control. Police autonomy in areas where professional judgement is required depends, even in the United Kingdom, on the restraint of the government and the legislature. It is not part of a natural or necessary order.

These simple propositions about the subordination of the police to the courts and to the government have to be elaborated in great detail to convey a true impression of how this subordination is manifest in different contexts. Also, examples can be readily found in every major country of the police apparently escaping the control of either the government or the courts or both. Having final authority over the police and actually exercising it as a matter of routine are two very different things. But these propositions illustrate the limits of international police co-operation. The extent of this co-operation is severely limited by political and legal constraints. On the other hand, the degree of autonomy over professional matters, which all police forces enjoy, has assisted international co-operation. As in domestic policing, the rigidities of legal constraints are made more tolerable by the existence of informal arrangements which, although not authoritatively sanctioned, gain acceptance. Allowing the growth of informal practices is more congenial to some national traditions than to others; it has advantages and drawbacks.

Characteristics of Contemporary Police Co-operation

Particular attention is paid in this study to international criminal investigation co-operation – the communication of information on request and the co-ordination of police operations on criminal matters – because interesting developments have taken place in this area and because it goes to the very heart of the difficulties posed by co-operation. The factors generating this co-operation have been present since the nineteenth century: urbanization, the development of rapid transportation systems, large numbers of people crossing international boundaries, almost instantaneous communications after the development of the telegraph, great increases in the volume of financial and commercial transactions, and the development of large international markets. Virtually all those factors which have contributed to the increasing wealth of the highly industrialized countries have facilitated the growth of international criminality. In addition, certain factors – tastes in the rich countries for narcotic and psychotropic drugs, and the necessity of exporting the profits of crime to escape legal and fiscal controls – have drawn groups in less developed societies into international criminal networks.

Multilateral police co-operation through Interpol has some similarities with a modern military alliance. Both are based on an understanding of mutual interests and of the nature of the enemy to be combated. They are characterized by permanent secretariats, systems of communication, and some pooling of resources. Within a multilateral alliance, and in police co-operation, close bilateral arrangements may exist between certain members. Leading members of an alliance and an international police organization may enjoy somewhat greater freedom of action than the smaller and weaker states, but it is difficult to modify the basic understandings of the alliance without provoking major upheaval. However, international police co-operation is a much more untidy system of relationships than a military alliance. NATO, the Warsaw Pact, and other military alliances are based on a specific security threat and an agreement, both in military and political terms, about how that threat should be countered. A single treaty covers most forms of military collaboration among the allies, although important practical matters such as arms procurement may be left out.

In the field of crime, there is no specific enemy, since criminals can only be identified after crimes have been committed. There are also a large number of specialized international agreements intended to contribute to the suppression of specific forms of crime – narcotics, prostitution, counterfeiting, fraud, traffic in stolen goods – but very few have any provision for operational co-operation in policing. The UN single convention on narcotic and psychotropic drugs which is currently being negotiated has such provisions, but these are highly controversial. In bilateral agreements, discussed in Chapter 7, arrangements are sometimes envisaged which come near to operational collaboration, but in multilateral understandings the closest approach to this collaboration is the regular exchange of information and co-ordination of some police strategies. Treaty obligations usually commence after legal processes have started, not at the stage of criminal investigation by the police. Even in those regions where bilateral police agreements between states are the rule, as between West Germany and its non-Communist neighbours, the treaties usually envisage voluntary co-operation. They legitimize direct police-to-police contacts but, like the 1960 German–Belgian agreement and the 1977 German–French agreement, they do not impose obligations on states to co-operate. These agreements often seem designed to limit rather than extend police contacts. In practice, however, there are often close, informal bilateral relations based on direct personal contact.

Some important police functions – public order, welfare, and environmental policing – involve little international co-operation because it is not thought to be either practical or desirable or necessary. Nevertheless, some police co-ordination takes place in these fields. The transfrontier demonstrations against the siting of power stations along the German, French, and Swiss frontiers in the 1970s and 1980s stimulated some co-ordination of policing the demonstrators. Similarly, the movement of football supporters from one country to another has resulted in contact between police forces for public-order purposes. In September 1987 representatives of the relevant ministries and police authorities of the European Community countries met in London to co-ordinate the strategy on football hooliganism and appointed contact officers in each country who would be directly in touch with one another to deal with transfrontier problems. Police officers in the host country of a major international match sometimes travel to the guest country for briefing. In 1988 the Spanish government requested the sending of UK police officers to Spain to assist in controlling rowdy UK holiday-makers. But public-order problems are posed overwhelmingly within the borders of states and, when political groups have on the odd occasion 'invaded' a foreign country, such as Northern Ireland Democratic Unionists in 1986 led by Mr Peter Robinson into the Republic of Ireland, they are easily contained by the local police force.

Similarly, the functions of promoting social welfare and protecting vulnerable groups within society – the young, the old, the mentally ill, and religious and racial minorities – generally have few international policing implications, although they may be a complicating factor in the problems posed by international migrations. The one very important exception to this is traffic in women. Early in the twentieth century there was American pressure to establish international co-operation on this issue,[11] in the inter-war period it was a matter taken very seriously by the ICPC. It remains a problem, even in Europe, and international rings have recently been exposed by joint police action.[12] However, as a result of changing public attitudes towards prostitution and widespread decriminalization of prostitution, it has become increasingly difficult to take effective police action against the traffic. Consequently, Interpol is less used as a facility to combat the traffic in women than it was in the past.[13]

Despite the growing number of international agreements in environmental protection, co-ordination of enforcement of environmental rules is still in its infancy except in the rare examples of transfrontier natural parks. Economic and political interests continue to prevent this form of police co-ordination coming on to the agenda, even though it is widely recognized that some of the most troublesome pollution problems, such as poisonous effluent in the Rhine and the Mediterranean, and atmospheric pollution, are international in character. Interpol itself has tried to make police opinion more sensitive to environmental issues by publishing a number of reports.[14]

A though welfare and environmental policing are still regarded as local matters, there is much international discussion, and several international treaties and conventions on these matters have been negotiated. Police officers are sometimes involved in these discussions, although they are always a small minority of the participants, and they are occasionally consulted when international conventions are being negotiated. The United Nations has regular meetings on traffic in persons, on combating drugs, and on crime prevention. Similar meetings take place under the aegis of the Council of Europe and a small number of police officers participate in most of them. Interpol has held seminars on crime prevention and circulates information about crime prevention. Police officers responsible for airport security, such as the North West European Association of Air and Seaport Police, have international meetings, and study how incidents have been handled in other countries; the international contact officers (appointed in every major airport, after the Montreal Convention 1972) who can be telephoned or telexed whenever necessary, participate in such meetings. In one area in civil policing, traffic control, foreign systems are frequently studied and international seminars held. This is also true of the most prominent kind of public-order policing, crowd control. International contacts and meetings therefore abound.

A relatively free flow of information about police matters is channelled either through forum organizations or via nationally or internationally sponsored training programmes. Police training services such as the UK Police College at Bramshill, the French Service Technique de Coopération Internationale de Police (STCIP), the French National Police College at Sens, and the FBI College at Quantico receive visits of foreign police personnel and have students from other countries on courses. This activity results in the dissemination of information about all aspects of policing. In Trevi 2, there is an exchange of information about the technical aspects of policing – police methods, training, and equipment. Developments of this kind have contributed to the widening of police horizons.

Regular police contacts on operational matters are intensifying quickly. Frontier police and customs services must routinely co-operate with their counterparts on the other side of land frontiers and in certain regions very high levels of co-operation are achieved, exemplified by the joint controls at the Franco-German border. This co-operation is to be further enhanced by the Schengen agreement of 14 June 1985, which, in three stages, will establish a common police and frontier control at ports of entry to Benelux, France, and Germany: at the internal frontiers of this geographical bloc individuals and goods will not be regularly controlled, and this has important police implications.

Immigration and customs co-operation, to a greater extent than mutual assistance in criminal matters, is a trade in services and based on considerations of mutual advantage. The nature of customs business falls into three categories and the forms of international co-operation are somewhat different in each. The first is preventing tax evasion and fraud; the second is repression of the traffic in prohibited goods such as narcotics and child pornography; the third is serving national strategic or foreign-policy objectives such as preventing the export of so-called 'critical' technology to the Soviet bloc countries.

In the first area there is a high degree of co-operation through customs agreements, in multilateral discussion and exchange of information through the Customs Co-operation Council (CCC; established in 1953), and informal co-operation between customs officers, sometimes of an unorthodox kind. But no country yet accepts the responsibility of enforcing the fiscal legislation of another state. In the second, customs officers are often acting in concert with other police agencies and intelligence sources outside the customs services. The drugs problem gave a considerable impetus to customs co-operation, as to police co-operation, and was the most important factor leading to the 1977 negotiation of an ambitious international agreement, the Nairobi Convention.[15] The CCC has been adopting a more activist role in recent years with the establishment in 1984 of its enforcement committee, an enforcement division within the secretariat, and the regular circulation of information through its enforcement bulletin.[16] In terms of seizures of prohibited goods, customs services apparently have a good record compared with other police agencies, but real effectiveness could only be measured by comparing seizures with an unknown quantity – the volume of smuggled goods. In combating drugs traffic, joint police–customs co-operation is now regarded as essential both nationally, as in the Organized Crime Drug Enforcement Program in the United States, and internationally, in the growing links between Interpol and the CCC.

In the case of the third type of activity the *sine qua non* of success is the co-operation of the non-Communist advanced countries. Without this, the re-export of 'critical' technology would be very easy. A committee composed mainly of NATO countries and Japan, the Co-ordinating Committee for Export Controls (COCOM), established in 1949 with a headquarters in Paris, is charged with drawing up a list of goods which should not be exported to the eastern bloc and with co-ordinating customs cooperation to enforce this prohibition. The Japanese firm Toshiba, and the Norwegian firm Konigsberg Vaapenfabrikk, have breached COCOM rules and, in 1987, have suffered serious penalties.[17] In all these categories the same basic methods are used: a professional knowledge of ingenious systems of evading customs controls, intelligence work, well-informed sources, and random checks. Customs and immigration administrations both face enormous problems posed by huge movements of persons: even a relatively small country like Yugoslavia has over 100 million entries per year; the United States has 300 million; West Germany a staggering 900 million. These massive movements of population have completely changed the basic issues of frontier control and have implications for all kinds of policing.

Co-operation between customs and immigration authorities is often defined as mutual administrative assistance and this presents fewer difficulties than mutual assistance in criminal matters. When criminal offences and courts of law are involved, the transaction of business becomes more complicated for reasons related to sovereignty, discussed earlier in this chapter. Co-operation between court systems in different countries has been established through treaties of mutual legal assistance, but arrangements are often slow and unsatisfactory. This has particularly been true of extradition where states jealously guarded their prerogatives. The United Kingdom and the Republic of Ireland have not yet ratified the European Conventions on Extradition (1957) and Mutual Assistance in Criminal Matters (1962), although the United Kingdom has declared an intention to sign in 1989. Even the commitment in the European Convention on Terrorism either to extradite or to try persons accused of terrorist offences has met with reservations by certain states: France did not ratify until 1987 because of fears of infringing rights to political asylum. Moreover, this Convention, although important because it seeks to criminalize terrorist offences, does not touch the procedural difficulties of extraditing from one jurisdiction to another.

An additional complication for international relations is the constant tension in certain states between the courts and the police over international relations – in some jurisdictions virtually all matters concerned with criminal charges are controlled by either the courts or other legal authorities such as public prosecutors. This leaves virtually no autonomy for the police criminal investigation departments and therefore no space for international police co-operation as an activity with some independence from the legal authorities. Once the legal process has commenced, international co-operation usually proceeds via Ministries of Justice and diplomatic channels and these are very slow. Occasionally, however, a French *juge d'instruction*, holding out against this tendency, will order an enquiry to be made via Interpol.

All police officers agree with the proposition that effective criminal law enforcement requires rapid action and therefore international circulation of information by the police. This circulation has developed informally through the ICPC from 1923 and then through ICPO–Interpol: attempts to stop it by legal action have failed. In the absence of a treaty basis (supported by enabling legislation making treaty obligations binding on domestic courts) for the communication of police information, there will doubtless be further attempts at legal action in those countries where it is still possible. The present informal system, with no international treaty and a low level of direct government involvement, has certain clear advantages but legal and political difficulties could call it into question. The low juridical, governmental, and public profile of Interpol has been a strength but it is also an Achilles heel.

The Changing Pattern of International Crime

International crime is something of a misnomer. Except for 'crimes against humanity' and war crimes, which are not the objects of international police co-operation, there are no international crimes. The states define crimes through the criminal law; state officials are responsible for prosecuting criminals and for the administration of justice. International co-operation is therefore directed towards mutual aid in enforcing the laws of sovereign states. Despite the highly specific nature of each state's criminal law and the very wide range of acts defined as crimes, there is very broad agreement across the world about what constitutes serious crime – murder, kidnapping, traffic in human beings, traffic in drugs, theft, and fraud. This agreement depends, to a large degree, on the dominance of western liberal values: as William Seagle has noted, 'while heresy and treason are the great crimes of theocratic and absolute societies, murder and theft are the great crimes of democratic, secular and individualistic societies'.[18] However, a consequence of this agreement has been a large number of international conventions and treaties for mutual aid in the suppression of these crimes.

Serious crime is the main subject of international police co-operation and when such crime has transfrontier implications it is often called international crime. However, the areas of criminal activity which are the subject of international co-operation change over time and with the state of public opinion.

Petty crime is usually a very minor element in police co-operation, but there are exceptions. In the inter-war period the public anxiety about the petty criminality of itinerant gypsies caused the old ICPC to take notice of it. In the 1970s international gangs of shoplifters operating in London and other major European cities attracted similar attention. Car theft, even on the massive scale experienced in the United States, is regarded as a local problem, but this is not the case in West Germany, where a high proportion of luxury cars stolen are exported. In all such instances, crime ceases to be treated as petty when it becomes both widespread and organized.

Changes in government policy can affect the pattern of international crime. The abolition of exchange controls facilitates the transfer from one country to another of ill-gotten gains as well as certain forms of international fraud. Tightening up regulations for the registration of credit transfers and of tax laws can, as American experience has shown, make organized crime more difficult. Since the early 1970s two forms of crime – armed political violence, usually called terrorism, and drug trafficking – have brought the problems of international police co-operation to the attention of governments. Terrorism came as a direct challenge to state authority which found the advanced industrialized democracies almost totally unprepared. The drugs traffic, on the other hand, is a profit-seeking operation based on a market created by the criminalization of the non-medical use of narcotic and psychotropic drugs. There are some tenuous similarities between the two – both have an important international dimension and both are deeply rooted in some societies. Connections between the two, mainly in the less developed countries, have been found in so-called 'narco-terrorism' (the financing of terrorism by drug trafficking) and in the use of drugs as an alternative currency for the illegal purchase of weapons. Both pose intractable problems of public policy and of policing. Political action as well as police action is necessary to make an impact on them.

There are historical precedents for the wave of terrorism which has affected many countries in the last two decades. The anarchist bomb outrages and the assassinations of the last two decades of the nineteenth century made a similar impact on European governments and public opinion. In 1897, on the initiative of the Italian government, a secret conference was convened in Rome, at which Ministries of the Interior and police were represented, with the object of co-ordinating anti-anarchist measures and circulating information about anarchists. Similar initiatives took place in the 1970s with the establishment of the Club of Berne and the Club of Vienna to co-ordinate anti-terrorist measures among adjacent countries. The Trevi Group is significant because it is a more systematic form of co-operation. It established a secure communications network for anti-terrorist intelligence messages and has attempted to extend its scope into other forms of police co-operation. Interpol was not directly used for terrorist crimes until the 1980s because of a restrictive interpretation of its statutes which forbid involvement in political, religious, or racial cases. At the Luxemburg General Assembly of 1984 this interpretation was modified and the Interpol network has been extensively used since that time for crimes connected with terrorism offences.

The problem posed by narcotic and psychotropic drugs has created pressures for even more sustained and routinized police co-operation than the problem of terrorism. In the early 1960s drug abuse was still regarded as a mainly American problem, but this attitude rapidly disappeared, especially after 1970, when drugs became an obvious problem for all highly industrialized democracies and some developing countries. The nature of the trade in drugs makes international co-operation among police and customs authorities essential if any impact is to be made on it. The objective sought, first by the Americans and now by most European countries, is a common strategy by producer, transit, and consumer countries to repress the traffic. Political, economic, and technical difficulties stand in the way of achieving this. There are sharp differences of view between producer and consumer countries about where the major responsibility lies. The producer countries in the third world, which face intractable problems, often naturally take the view that the root cause is the insatiable market for drugs in the rich countries. Part of the huge profits derived from these markets is used to corrupt officials in poor countries which are sometimes heavily dependent on revenues from drug cultivation. Even when the governments of these countries are resolved to co-operate in drug law enforcement, their police forces are not sufficiently well trained and equipped to be a match for the drug traffickers. The Americans, in particular, have sometimes taken the view that, if supplies could be cut off, the drugs problem would be solved.

Drug trafficking is the one area in which there has been significant operational activity by police agencies outside national territories. All major European countries now have drug liaison officers posted abroad, but the United States leads the way with over sixty overseas offices of the DEA in forty-three countries. DEA action has reached the level of military operations in Columbia and Bolivia. The successes claimed for these operations raise the question of whether extraterritorial operational activity, with the consent and collaboration of the relevant governments, is a pattern for future activity or whether, for technical, legal, and political reasons, it is likely to be confined to special situations in the drugs field. One of the main reasons why special bilateral arrangements have proliferated in the drugs field is that the co-operation provided through Interpol channels was too slow and joint operations could not be organized through them. The two forms of co-operation – bilateral and multilateral – are now widely seen as complementary.

Terrorism and narcotics are two pressing issues which have compelled a greater degree of governmental attention to the issues of international police co-operation in the highly industrialized democracies. But a third reason why this co-operation is on the agenda is probably even more compelling in the long run. It is posed with considerable urgency in western Europe. Within the European Community, a target of a single market has been set for 1992. This means a common external frontier for Europe and the virtual abolition of all frontier controls between the states of the Community. Frontier controls have, in the past, been a crucially important barrier to the movement of suspect persons and goods. During the German Presidency of the European Community in 1988, Chancellor Kohl proposed at a summit meeting of heads of government a European bureau of investigation along the lines of the FBI. This proposal encountered scepticism, particularly from Prime Minister Thatcher, but increased police co-operation is necessary if frontier controls are dismantled. Outside the Community, frontier controls have to be simplified and streamlined in order to cope with ever-increasing volumes of traffic, so similar problems are faced. The ever closer integration of the highly industrialized economies and the main financial markets will further break down the barriers represented by international frontiers. Police surveillance and control will have to be adapted to prevent international criminals taking advantage of the new situation. The development of a strengthened system of police co-operation, in Europe or elsewhere, must be carefully scrutinized in order to prevent the emergence of a 'secret society' of international police officers and to protect individual liberties.

The Limits of International Police Co-operation

The difficulties posed by co-operation in criminal matters across different systems of law have already been mentioned. The current practical problems are extradition, rules of evidence, data protection, differences in police powers, misunderstandings of law-enforcement problems in other countries, and communications difficulties. The problem of extradition is a very old one and remains an obstacle to the administration of justice. Despite the proliferation of extradition treaties, these have to respect the procedural rules of natural legal systems. The Interpol 'red notice' is a request for arrest of a suspect with the assurance that an extradition request will follow. For some countries in the English common-law tradition, this assurance has been regarded as insufficient and evidence against a suspect must be presented, although US courts now issue arrest warrants almost automatically on request of an Interpol red notice. All western European countries, except the United Kingdom and the Republic of Ireland until they sign the European Convention on Extradition, regard the red notice as an international arrest warrant. The evidence required by British courts, and by the Irish courts where practice in this derives from the doctrines of English common law, to allow extradition is more stringent; this may involve the physical presence of witnesses to establish whether there is a case to answer. Again, rogatory commissions to establish evidence for foreign courts are not a traditional part of British judicial procedure and they have been accepted only with reluctance by American courts in criminal cases.

There is no universally accepted definition of letters rogatory and rogatory commissions. Letters rogatory are usually regarded as a form of introduction from a competent legal authority to an investigator seeking assistance in gathering evidence in a foreign jurisdiction. A rogatory commission is a vehicle by which the results of a foreign enquiry can be brought home by the requesting state and used as evidence in its courts. A rogatory commission facilitates the presentation of the evidence of witnesses unable or unwilling to attend the court in the requesting country. Until recently, in the British legal practice, the first were not needed and the second were not recognized. The US courts were also unwilling to use these instruments until the 1960s.[19] In general, until the relatively recent past, the US courts have shown a marked reluctance to grant judicial assistance in criminal matters. Change was stimulated in the United States as well as in Europe by the 1962 European Convention of Mutual Assistance in Criminal Matters. A number of mutual assistance treaties between the United States and other countries were negotiated and the US courts came to recognize, as a matter of routine, the letters rogatory issued by foreign courts in criminal cases. There is now an evident desire in the United States, as in the other highly industrialized democracies, to press forward with mutual assistance whilst preserving due process guarantees and ensuring that rights recognized in domestic law are not undermined by the execution of treaties. However, what the courts recognize as evidence is an important constraint on police work.

What happens when criminal charges are brought and cases come before the courts is beyond the scope of this book. But the nature of legal systems must always be kept in mind when considering the practice of international police co-operation. One illustration is that, in most highly industrialized democracies, the request for information or the circulation of information must have a legal basis. This requirement has frequently become much more stringent in recent years with the passage of data protection legislation. The problem is scarcely posed in Britain, where police information is excluded from data protection legislation and where the courts have been reluctant to intervene in the procedures of criminal investigation. Until recently the police in England and Wales (but not in Scotland) were allowed to collect and disseminate information at their discretion. The international circulation of police information can be made secure against national data protection legislation and the intervention of national courts by two methods. Either legal immunity can be granted to the authority which engages in this activity – the *de facto* situation in the United Kingdom and the formal situation in the United States after the presidential order of 1983 giving legal immunity to Interpol; or treaties or treaty-like agreements (either ratified by parliaments or enabling legislation enacted) can be reached with agencies to whom the information is circulated, which is the solution favoured in West Germany. There is a third possibility but this was available in a unique situation. During the negotiation, discussed in Chapter 3, for the second

Headquarters Agreement with Interpol, the organization accepted data protection rules close enough to French practice to avoid any legal challenge in French courts.

There may be broad international agreement on what constitutes serious crime, but the criminal law which police forces enforce varies from country to country. There are also variations in the penalties for serious crimes, as well as the rigour with which the law is enforced. These differences are sometimes dealt with in relatively straightforward ways: countries where the death penalty has been abolished refuse to extradite if a suspect runs the risk of the death penalty or extradite only on the condition that the death penalty is not imposed. But, at the level of police co-operation, the issues are more complex and are often blurred. The law on drugs and proxenetism may vary between two neighbouring countries and the rigour with which the law is enforced may also vary. Both may make the police unwilling to pass on information. In the latter case, if there is any suspicion that the police are corrupt, the reluctance may become total. In all cases, mutual trust and a common approach to problems form the effective basis for co-operation. Whether or not the trust and common approach exist depends to a degree on the nature and the operation of the legal system. There is, for example, a better police understanding between those European countries with a codified law tradition, on the one hand, and between those European and non-European countries with a common law tradition, on the other. This relates also to cultural and linguistic factors, but the legal tradition is, none the less, important.

In the long run, there will be pressures to harmonize criminal justice systems and serious proposals to do so go back to the series of international conferences, held between the two world wars, on the unification of criminal law. The idea of an 'espace judiciaire européen' was first floated by President Giscard d'Estaing as a way of combating terrorism, and it has been enthusiastically taken up by others, such as Prime Minister Felipe Gonzales of Spain. The proposal is that a uniform law should be administered throughout the European Community on a particular type of crime and that there could be a European prison for those convicted of the crime. If harmonization takes place, it is likely to be a very slow process, even in Europe. Without harmonization of criminal law and judicial procedures there are strict limits to police co-operation in criminal matters. Many would argue that, in principle, these strict limits are desirable, because legislative power in the area of criminal law should be kept as close to local communities as possible. Legal sanctions may become less effective the more remote the sanctioning authority becomes. Police accountability should similarly be kept close to the people. The authority of the rules of criminal law and public co-operation with the police in criminal investigation are better preserved if there is clear public support for them. International courts and international police have their place, but it remains a limited one until the cultural and political bonds created by the nation-state have been loosened and replaced by a greater sense of international community.

At the present time, police co-operation occupies a relatively small space both in the huge volume of official exchanges between states and in the collaborative activity of states in international organizations. It is a rather untidy mix of global, regional, and bilateral arrangements, established without a great deal of thought given to the overall pattern. Some serious consideration of the pattern has started in policy-making circles, because of the growing volume of business; and, if present trends continue, this business will expand rapidly. An overall review is necessary, although it will not necessarily happen, because there are potential conflicts between the forms of co-operation which already exist. Unless some general understandings are reached, the proliferation of special *ad hoc* arrangements could cause considerable confusion.

Notes

1. See A. W. McCoy, *The Politics of Heroin in Southeast Asia* (New York, 1972). In 1988 the CIA has been linked with drug trafficking in Central America, particularly through close association with General Noriega of Panama; there are also allegations that China and Warsaw Pact countries have promoted drug trafficking; see J. Ranelagh, *The Agency: The Rise and Decline of the CIA* (London, 1986), 691 n.
2. For a recent discussion, see S. D. Krasner, 'Sovereignty: An Institutional Perspective', *Comparative Political Studies*, 21/1 (1988), 66–94.
3. G. Poggi, *The Development of the Modern State* (Stanford, 1978), 92.
4. For a discussion of this point, see D. H. Bayley, *Patterns of Policing: A Comparative International Analysis* (New Brunswick, 1985), ch. 9, 'The Future of Policing'.
5. This view is sometimes contested by feminists who argue that men use violence against women and this is regarded as legitimate by large sections of society.
6. E. P. Thompson, *Writing by Candlelight* (London, 1980), 91–256; T. Bunyan, *The History and Practice of the Political Police in Britain* (London, 1976); M. Brogden, *The Police: Autonomy and Consent* (London, 1982).
7. A. Giddens, *The Nation State and Violence* (Cambridge, 1985), 143. M. Foucault, *Discipline and Punish* (London, 1977); M. Ignatieff, *A Just Measure of Pain* (London, 1979); both authors sought to escape the charge of determinism; for a criticism of their position, see C. Emsley, *Policing in its Context, 1750–1870* (London, 1983).
8. For a recent review, see P. Dunleavy and B. O'Leary, *Theories of the State* (London, 1987); R. R. Alford and R. Friedland, *Powers of Theory: Capitalism, the State and Democracy* (Cambridge, 1985); M. Carnoy, *The State and Political Theory* (Princeton, 1984).
9. P. Birnbaum, *La Logique de l'État* (Paris, 1982), 134 ff. The contemporary writing which can be classed as neo-Weberian (see G. Poggi, *Development*, and T. R. Gurr and D. S. King, *The State and the City* (London, 1987)) is closest to the general view presented in this chapter.
10. Bayley, *Patterns of Policing*, 3.
11. The international conventions on traffic in women and children of 18 May 1904, 4 May 1920, and 30 September 1920 were negotiated largely as a result of American pressure.
12. In March 1987 the Police Judiciaire of Metz uncovered, with the help of the Portuguese, Luxemburg, and Dutch police, a ring which forced young Portuguese women into prostitution in northern Europe.

13. Information supplied by the General Secretariat of Interpol.

14. 'Police Intervention and Co-operation in the Traffic in Wild Animals', Report to the General Assembly, Accra, 1976; 'Role of the Police in the Protection of the Environment', Report to the General Assembly, Nairobi, 1979; 'Role of the Police in the Protection of the Environment', Report to the General Assembly, Manila, 1980.

15. CCC, *Introducing the Nairobi Convention on Mutual Administrative Assistance for the Prevention, Investigation and Repression of Customs Offences* (Brussels, n.d.); G. D. Gotschlick 'Action by the Customs Cooperation Council to Combat Illicit Drug-Trafficking', *Bulletin on Narcotics*, 35 (Oct.–Dec. 1983, 77–81.

16. G. R. Dickerson, 'The Customs Cooperation Council and International Customs Enforcement', *Police Chief* (Feb. 1985), 16–18. CCC, *The Customs Cooperation Council: Its Role in International Customs Enforcement* (Brussels, n.d.).

17. *Financial Times*, 27 Oct. 1987.

18. W. Seagle, *The History of Law* (New York, 1946).

19. L. Paikin, 'Problems of Obtaining Evidence in Foreign States for use in Federal Criminal Prosecutions', *Columbia Journal of Transnational Law*, 3/2 (1984), 233–71; A, Ellis and R. L. Pisani, 'The United States Treaties on Mutual Assistance in Criminal Matters: A Comparative Analysis', *International Lawyer*, 19/1 (1985), 189–223; 'Transnational Aspects of Criminal Procedure', *Michigan Yearbook of International Legal Studies 1983* (New York, 1983).

2

Introduction from *Cops Across Borders*
Ethan Nadelmann

The Internationalization of U.S. Criminal Law Enforcement

The internationalization of U.S. law enforcement cannot be explained entirely or even primarily in terms of the need to respond to a proliferation of transnational criminal activities. Rather, the principal impetuses underlying many of the more significant developments in the history of U.S. international criminal law enforcement were provided by federal statutes criminalizing activities that had not previously been regarded as criminal. Most contemporary efforts, for instance, are concerned with the enforcement of criminal laws that did not exist a century or even a few decades ago – not just drug prohibition laws, but also criminal laws directed at insider trading, money laundering, computer fraud, and the smuggling of sophisticated weaponry and other technology to blacklisted countries. The United States' imposition of immigration controls on Chinese migrants in the late nineteenth century and most other foreigners a few decades later similarly created a need for a substantial law enforcement effort. And the proliferation of federal statutes during the 1980s explicitly extending U.S. jurisdiction to terrorist and other violent acts against U.S. citizens abroad provided the legal basis for a substantial internationalization of the FBI's investigations. Conversely, the rendition of fugitive slaves constituted a central concern of U.S. international law enforcement efforts before the Civil War, and efforts to suppress the illicit traffic in alcoholic beverages preoccupied U.S. officials involved in international law enforcement matters between 1920 and 1933. Both ended with the abolition of the laws they were intended to enforce.

Source: *Cops Across Borders: The Internationalization of U.S. Criminal Law Enforcement* (Pennsylvania: Pennsylvania State University Press, 1993), pp. 1–14.

   Given the initial impulses provided by Congressional and other legislative criminalizations, subsequent developments can be explained by a variety of factors. The United States' assumption of global economic and security responsibilities following World War II brought with it a host of international criminal law enforcement responsibilities ranging from the policing of hundreds of thousands of U.S. military personnel abroad to the creation of police training programs in dozens of less developed nations. Many increases in international law enforcement activity were motivated by perceived increases, both real and unreal, in particular types of transnational criminal activity. The explosion in transnational drug trafficking beginning in the 1960s, for instance, generated an international law enforcement response of unprecedented dimensions. The increase in transnational violations of U.S. securities laws that inevitably accompanied the dramatic internationalization of the securities markets during the 1980s similarly invited a response by the Justice Department and the Securities and Exchange Commission. Other international criminal law enforcement initiatives were motivated principally by domestic political considerations, such as when the Nixon administration extended its "war on drugs" to foreign countries during the early 1970s, and when the Reagan and Bush administrations did likewise during the 1980s. Additional incentives were provided by the proliferation of Congressional hearings addressing transnational drug trafficking and other criminal activities. The expansion of international criminal law enforcement capabilities in and of itself generated increasing activity and invited new laws. And in many cases, the principal motivations for developing a law enforcement agency's international capabilities could be traced to interagency rivalries and the desires of agency chiefs to claim more jurisdiction and responsibilities for their agencies.
   The internationalization of U.S. law enforcement has involved an increasing number of federal agencies, activities, and resources. The Office of International Affairs (OIA) in the Justice Department's Criminal Division, and the Office of Law Enforcement and Intelligence (L/LEI) in the State Department's Legal Adviser's Office, both created in 1979, have assumed leading roles in coordinating extradition and other mutual legal assistance relations with foreign governments. In 1985, the Securities and Exchange Commission created its own special office devoted to handling international enforcement matters. And in 1987, the Justice Department initiated a policy of stationing its own attorneys abroad. Growing numbers of U.S. prosecutors now communicate with their foreign counterparts and travel abroad seeking cooperation and evidence in criminal cases. American judges confront an increasing number of cases in which evidence and witnesses must be obtained from abroad. And U.S. law enforcement agencies – most notably the Drug Enforcement Administration (DEA) but also the Federal Bureau of Investigation (FBI), the Internal Revenue Service (IRS), the Immigration and Naturalization Service (INS), the Secret Service, the U.S. Customs

Service, the U.S. Marshals Service, the criminal investigative branches of the military services, and even state and city police departments – have dramatically increased their international responsibilities and activities. Some of these activities have been assisted by the U.S. military and the intelligence agencies, and backed by the diplomatic efforts of the State Department, high-level Justice Department officials, and the White House. They also have come under increasingly frequent and intensive Congressional scrutiny as federal legislators have stepped up dramatically their legislative and rhetorical responses to transnational drug trafficking and other transnational criminal activity.

A few indications of the pace of the expansion can be found in the personnel statistics. Between 1967 and 1991, the number of U.S. drug enforcement agents stationed abroad rose from about 12 in eight foreign cities to about 300 in more than seventy foreign locations. Between 1979 and 1990, the number of attorneys in the Criminal Division's Office of International Affairs rose from 4 to 40. During the same period, the U.S. national central bureau of Interpol, based in the Justice Department, increased its staff from 6 to 110, its budget from $125,000 to $6,000,000, and the number of law enforcement agencies represented from 1 to 16. The number of foreign police agencies with representatives in the United States also increased during this time, from no more than two or three to more than a dozen, and growing numbers of foreign law enforcement officials could be found in the United States on police business.

Other indications can be found in the caseload statistics. Between the early 1970s and 1990, for instance, the number of extradition requests to and from the United States each year increased from approximately 50 to 500. The number of requests for evidence and other forms of judicial assistance similarly increased, from less than 100 a year to well over 1,000. And the number of warrants for fugitives believed to be abroad rose from a few hundred to many thousands. Between 1976 and 1986, the annual caseload of the U.S. Interpol office rose from about 4,000 to 43,863, and the volume of message traffic from 14,365 to 101,859. These dramatic increases, I must stress, reflected a burgeoning of *both* transnational criminal activity *and* the capacity and desire of U.S. government agencies to handle international criminal law enforcement matters.

The Challenges of International Enforcement

The principal objective of most criminal law enforcement efforts, both domestic and international, is to "immobilize" criminals. Immobilization involves identifying individuals who engage in criminal activity, finding and arresting them, gathering the evidence necessary to indict and convict them, and finally imprisoning them; it also can, and increasingly does, include the identification, seizure, and forfeiture of the criminal's assets. For certain types of crimes, immobilization also requires seizing the criminal's contraband, be it stolen goods, drugs, weapons, counterfeit currency, computers, or anything else a criminal seeks to sell or buy illegally. As one DEA agent put it: "The bottom line is to get the dope off the street and put the cat in jail." Presumably, the more effective governments are at immobilizing criminals, the more successful they will be at deterring crime, disrupting criminal organizations, and diminishing the total level of criminal activity.

To successfully immobilize criminals, criminal justice systems typically require three things: information, evidence, and the body (i.e., the criminal). It is generally true that the more dispersed these things are, and the less they are to be found within the physical jurisdiction of the investigating government, the greater are the obstacles to successful law enforcement efforts. Law enforcement efforts within a single jurisdiction must contend with bureaucratic frictions, such as those within and among criminal justice agencies, and with legal frictions, such as those between citizens' civil liberties and the investigatory requirements of law enforcement agents. Additional frictions can arise among different jurisdictions even within one country; one need only consider the turf squabbles and other frictions that occasionally color the interactions of the FBI and other federal law enforcement agencies with local police agencies and with one another, or those that impede close cooperation between criminal justice officers of different states.

International law enforcement efforts must contend not just with the types of domestic frictions described above but also with those that stem from the need for sovereign states to interact. Whether one takes the perspective of the police officer, the prosecutor, the diplomat, or the theoretician of international politics, the fundamental "problem" of international law enforcement is the sovereign – that is, exclusive – power of governments within their own borders and virtually nowhere else. Stated otherwise, the effective jurisdiction of a state's law enforcement agents extends no further than the territory of that state (and the vessels and embassies that fly its flag). In practice, this means that although U.S. law may authorize American police to arrest and question people abroad, foreign laws do not bolster this authority; indeed, they often forbid any law enforcement activities by foreign agents. The same is true of the American prosecutor, whose subpoenas and other demands, if delivered abroad, are not backed by the police power of the state in which they are delivered. A state can claim extraterritorial effect for its criminal laws, but it is hard-pressed to directly enforce those laws beyond its borders. The sovereign power of states generally forecloses unilateral police action by one state in the territory of another. It requires that most international law enforcement efforts be in some sense bilateral, cooperative ventures. And it means that the popular image of the Interpol agent as a police officer with international arrest powers is entirely fictional.

The basic fact of state sovereignty is not the only obstacle to international law enforcement efforts. Sovereign states are distinguished not only by the territories they occupy but also by distinctive political, social, economic, and legal systems and cultures. No two are identical; the differences generate both opportunities for transnational criminals and frictions for international law enforcers. For the former, foreign territories and alien systems offer safe havens, lucrative smuggling opportunities, and legal shields and thickets to disguise their criminal enterprises. The latter, by contrast, typically find their police powers strictly circumscribed and their international efforts complicated by alien political and legal systems and inadequate transnational infrastructures. The challenge they confront is to nullify the advantages that criminals derive from operating across borders and to reduce, circumvent, or transcend the frictions that hamper international law enforcement.

The political frictions that complicate international law enforcement efforts are not substantially different in kind from the frictions that hamper other domains of international relations. Governments that are politically hostile tend to provide only the most limited forms of assistance in criminal justice matters, and may even applaud and abet criminal acts committed abroad, particularly if the act is in some respect political. Among closely allied states, conflicting political interests and viewpoints, often involving powerful domestic constituencies, may impede cooperation in law enforcement matters. And even in the absence of significant bilateral frictions, a state's pursuit of particular international law enforcement objectives is often constrained by the fact that criminal justice objectives are rarely alone, much less predominant, on its foreign policy agenda. No government has unlimited political capital available to seek all its objectives. Often the pursuit of one undermines the furtherance of another. Objectives tend to be rank-ordered, and different components of a government vie to give precedence to accomplishment of their specific objectives. This bureaucratic jockeying is a familiar dynamic of the foreign-policy-making process in most governments – one in which high-level criminal justice officials in the United States and other nations are increasingly involved and influential but hardly triumphant.

The frictions that do differ in kind from other domains of international relations are largely a consequence of asymmetries among criminal justice systems. The most basic of these involve differences in what states choose to criminalize. Most governments are reluctant to assist others in the enforcement of criminal laws that are not reciprocal. U.S. officials today, for instance, are handicapped in their efforts to investigate the extraterritorial dimensions of tax and securities law violations by the fact that many of these violations are not regarded as criminal by other states. The same was true of international drug enforcement efforts in decades past, of efforts by the United States and a few other states to enforce their prohibitions on the traffic in alcoholic beverages during the 1920s, and of Great Britain's efforts to suppress the international traffic in African slaves during the early decades of the nineteenth century. In a similar vein, authoritarian states are typically frustrated in their efforts to obtain assistance from nonauthoritarian regimes in enforcing criminal laws against nonviolent political activity; and law enforcement officials in theocratic states bemoan the lack of foreign assistance when it comes to the prosecution of heretical activities that are criminalized within their own nations but not elsewhere. Frictions result when states seek assistance but are rebuffed, when states employ unilateral law enforcement measures that infringe upon the sovereign prerogatives of other states, and when powerful states pressure weaker ones to conform.

Far more common, and often just as frustrating as the criminal law asymmetries, are the procedural, cultural, and institutional asymmetries that hamper law enforcement cooperation even among governments that share the same criminal laws and sincerely want to assist one another. U.S. law enforcement agents trying to operate abroad, for instance, are continually confounded by different methods of criminal investigation, alien bureaucracies, and unfamiliar cultural norms. Many drug enforcement techniques regarded as essential in the United States – including undercover operations, electronic surveillance by means other than telephone taps, and various methods of recruiting informants – have been forbidden or severely circumscribed elsewhere. Plea bargaining may be proscribed, police-prosecutor relations may differ markedly, interrogation practices may seem alien, and standards of propriety may not compare. U.S. prosecutors seeking evidence and fugitives from abroad must contend with unfamiliar procedures and different laws, some reflecting basic differences between the common law system of the United States and the civil law systems that dominate in much of the non-Anglophone world, others reflecting little more than national idiosyncrasies. The frictions generated by these asymmetries create a drag on international law enforcement efforts; at the same time, efforts to circumvent and overcome these frictions, such as by acting unilaterally and by pressuring foreign states to accommodate their procedures and institutions to U.S. law enforcement needs, create frictions in their own right.

The Nature of International Enforcement

Governments and their law enforcement agencies have responded to these obstacles in a variety of ways, depending upon the degree to which their domestic societies are open or closed, the extent of the powers and resources accorded the police, the nature of the laws they are obliged to enforce, and the power of the criminals they confront. Most rely to some extent on unilateral measures both internally and externally. Governments keep track of foreigners within their borders; they mount police operations against those involved in the sale and purchase of goods exported and imported illegally; and they compile records of domestic transactions with an eye toward identifying those that are illicit. A few states, notably the United States, have also devised means of enforcing their laws extraterritorially by means of domestic legal processes, such as subpoenas issued to local branches and personnel of multinational corporations, and backed by court-ordered sanctions, requiring them to provide documents located abroad. Beyond a state's borders, its law enforcement agents retain some capacity for action on the high seas, where no nation is sovereign. Law enforcement officials working near their nations' borders have been known to cross into neighboring territories in "hot pursuit" of transnational bandits. Those based abroad may undertake unilateral law enforcement tasks in the context of joint investigations conducted in tandem with local police officials; or they may conduct their own investigations unilaterally, employing whatever discretion is required and operating in much the same fashion, and with just as few police powers, as private detectives. More dramatic measures, such as the unilateral abduction or murder of fugitives abroad, are not unknown; they are, however, relatively rare, more often conducted by agents of intelligence and security agencies than by criminal justice officials, and not always readily characterized as international law enforcement measures.

Abundant obstacles deter states from employing unilateral law enforcement measures beyond their borders. Most significant are the lack of sovereign powers and the illegality of such actions under both international law and the laws of the affected state. Also significant are the logistical difficulties, the desire to avoid generating tensions in foreign relations, the fear that one's unilateral actions will invite comparable initiatives by foreign agencies within one's own borders, and the general preference of most governments for cooperative measures over those likely to require or generate conflict. Unilateral extraterritorial measures are typically resorted to out of frustration with the inability or unwillingness of a foreign state to provide assistance, and with two objectives in mind: to obtain the information, evidence, or people required in a specific investigation; and, if the demanding state is sufficiently powerful, to pressure the uncooperative foreign state to be more forthcoming in the future.

It is not surprising that, given the severe limits on unilateral extraterritorial law enforcement activities, international law enforcement arrangements tend to be bilateral and generally cooperative. These are often episodic in nature, particularly where two states share relatively few law enforcement problems in common, or when police agencies with relatively little experience in international law enforcement matters become involved in an investigation requiring them to look beyond their borders. More frequent interactions, however, lead to patterns of relations that may point out recurring sources of conflict arising from political differences as well as tensions between different law enforcement systems, which in turn create pressures for more formal accommodations and the establishment of guidelines for future interactions. The results may include the stationing of police liaisons in one another's embassies, the creation of bilateral working groups of law enforcement officials, the negotiation of extradition and other legal assistance treaties, and the enactment and revision of domestic legislation to facilitate international cooperation against transnational crime. The net intention and effect of these arrangements, apart from the symbolic purposes occasionally served by them, is to facilitate the work of the police and prosecutors who pursue the routine law enforcement tasks involved in immobilizing transnational criminals.

Some areas of international law enforcement have invited not just bilateral but multilateral, and even global, arrangements, prompted in good part by the inadequacy of unilateral and bilateral law enforcement measures in the face of certain types of transnational criminal activity. These cannot compare with bilateral approaches in accommodating the mutual preferences and peculiarities of two different law enforcement systems; they are obliged instead to settle for the typically low level of accommodation required to win the adherence of a diversity of states. As a result, the symbolic incentives and functions of multilateral arrangements are generally greater than those of bilateral treaties. But multilateral arrangements also offer numerous advantages, not the least of which is that they may obviate the need to negotiate individual bilateral arrangements with large numbers of foreign governments. They can prove especially useful in facilitating law enforcement interactions between governments that are politically hostile, or that share relatively few law enforcement concerns in common; the communications facilities of Interpol, for instance, have proven of particular value in facilitating correspondence among police agencies in the less-developed world as well as among them and the police agencies in Europe and the United States with which they have relatively little contact. Some multilateral arrangements are designed to meet the particular law enforcement needs of multinational political alliances, such as CoCom, the postwar regime established by members of NATO and Japan to restrict the flow of sophisticated technology to Warsaw Pact countries. Others may reflect the common legal systems of countries linked by geographical proximity, similar political systems, and/or political alliances: the members of the Council of Europe, for instance, or the Soviet bloc states from the 1950s to 1989, or the majority of Latin American countries.

All multilateral law enforcement arrangements – be they regional police conferences, international police organizations such as Interpol, or the dozens of multilateral law enforcement conventions addressing either particular types of transnational activity or cooperative mechanisms such as extradition – are intended to help law enforcement agencies reduce, transcend, or circumvent the frictions generated by conflicting sovereignties, political tensions, and differences among law enforcement systems. They seek to attain consensus on the substance of each nation's criminal laws, to create commitments to cooperate, and to establish the guidelines and frameworks required to regularize and facilitate international cooperation among law enforcement systems. On a more fundamental level, these arrangements are motivated by the desire to make law enforcement systems more like one another, the guiding assumption being that like systems are better able to communicate and collaborate than unlike systems. The entire evolutionary process can well be described as one of *harmonization*, in which the notion incorporates three sorts of processes: that of *regularization* of relations among law enforcement officials of different states, that of *accommodation* among systems that retain their essential differences, and that of *homogenization* of systems toward a common norm.

Success and Failure

Why do some international law enforcement efforts succeed and others fail? The answers are many, but in the chapters that follow I advance two general propositions: that success or failure in particularly difficult cases is strongly influenced by the willingness of U.S. law enforcement officials to challenge the sovereign prerogatives of foreign states; and that success or failure over the long term depends upon the capacity of U.S. law enforcement officials to overcome the political and criminal justice obstacles to effective cooperation between the United States and foreign states. In other words, I contend that success in the first instance depends upon the willingness of U.S. officials to create, or risk generating, frictions with other states, and that success in the latter instance depends upon the capacity to reduce frictions by harmonizing criminal justice systems.

The principal criteria of success or failure in both instances are neither rates of transnational criminal activity committed or deterred nor proportions of smuggled goods seized, but rather whether transnational criminals are immobilized. The former criteria are both notoriously difficult to evaluate as well as influenced by many factors other than the quality and quantity of U.S. international criminal law enforcement efforts. One need only consider the dramatic range of estimates regarding the amount of heroin or the number of illegal immigrants that enter the United States each year; or the way in which law enforcement officials annually recite, without any evidence whatsoever, the mantra of seizing 10 percent of all drugs smuggled into the United States; or the varied factors that influence the type and amount of illicit drugs exported to the United States, and consumed therein, from one year to the next; or the sheer impossibility of establishing the number and magnitude of violations of U.S. securities, tax, and money laundering laws each year. Defining success or failure in terms of whether or not criminals are immobilized may seem a relatively trite indicator – not unlike "body counts" in counterinsurgency warfare – but it does represent both the actual objective of most international criminal law enforcement efforts and the most clearly defined and measurable one.

The Americanization of Foreign Systems

The internationalization of U.S. law enforcement during the twentieth century has shaped the evolution of criminal justice systems in dozens of other countries. No other government has pursued its international law enforcement agenda in as aggressive and penetrative a manner or devoted so much effort to promoting its own criminal justice norms to others. Foreign states have responded to the U.S. initiatives by signing extradition and other law enforcement treaties, by hosting U.S. law enforcement agents within their borders, and most significant, by adopting U.S. approaches to criminal law and policing. Beginning with the adoption of the United States' prohibitionist approach to drug control during the first decades of the twentieth century, foreign governments have followed in U.S. footsteps, adopting U.S.-style investigative techniques, creating specialized drug enforcement agencies, stationing law enforcement representatives abroad, and enacting conspiracy statutes, asset forfeiture laws, and checks and bans on drug-related money laundering. Since the 1970s, pressures to cooperate in U.S. drug trafficking investigations were largely responsible for instigating changes in the laws of Switzerland, the Bahamas, and other financial secrecy jurisdictions to authorize greater assistance to U.S. and other law enforcement authorities. And even apart from the area of drug control, the influence of the United States was readily apparent during the first decades of the twentieth century in shaping foreign and international approaches to white slavery, during the Cold War era with respect to export controls on weapons and sophisticated technology, and since the mid-1980s with respect to the regulation of securities markets, in particular the criminalization of insider trading. The result has been something of an "Americanization" of criminal justice systems throughout much of the world.

This argument obviously limits the extent to which generalizations about the nature of international criminal law enforcement can be derived from an examination of U.S. behavior. The ability and willingness of the United States to pursue its international criminal law enforcement agenda as aggressively as it has is relatively unique in the annals of international criminal law enforcement. Great Britain's global campaign against the slave traffic during the nineteenth century represents perhaps the only clear precedent. Similarly, the fact that the United States has dealt with the frictions between its own criminal justice norms and those of other states principally by inducing other states to change their norms and accommodate their systems to U.S. requirements, rather than vice versa, presents something of a special case. Nonetheless, there is much about the challenges U.S. officials have encountered in trying to immobilize transnational criminals, and the ways they have responded, that is typical of most states. The fact that U.S. law enforcement officials have on occasion acted more aggressively and unilaterally than officials of other states in obtaining information, evidence, and criminals from abroad does not mean U.S. officials have not struggled with the same types of issues and frictions encountered by others.

Objectives and Structure of This Book

The chapters that follow seek to elaborate on these themes in developing further the main objectives of this book. My principal objectives, pursued in each of the chapters, are to describe and explain the activities and issues that lie at the intersection of U.S. criminal justice and foreign policy. Chapters Two and Three examine the internationalization of U.S. policing, and particularly criminal investigation, from the origins of the nation's history until the early 1990s. The history of U.S. international criminal law enforcement efforts is one in which themes of both change and continuity are readily apparent. On the one hand, the complexity and scale of contemporary international criminal investigations have little in common with the ad hoc international police endeavors of a century ago. And one need only compare the concerns of nineteenth-century law enforcers with transnational bandits, filibusters, runaway slaves, and illegal slavers to the twentieth-century concerns with illicit drug smugglers, high-tech bandits, insider traders, and money launderers to understand how dramatically the substantive focus of U.S. international criminal law enforcement efforts have changed. On the other hand, the basic concerns with controlling the nation's borders, suppressing smuggling, and renditing criminal fugitives have remained constant. And the basic challenges presented by the need to deal with foreign sovereigns, conflicting political interests, and alien criminal law enforcement systems have persisted.

Chapters Four and Five analyze the efforts of the DEA to immobilize drug traffickers in Europe and Latin America. Chapter Four examines how DEA agents have dealt with the frictions generated by Europe's civil law traditions and general resistance to DEA-style investigative methods, and how European approaches to drug enforcement have gradually become "Americanized." Chapter Five examines the nature of drug-related corruption in Latin America and the efforts of DEA agents to immobilize drug traffickers notwithstanding that corruption. The next two chapters examine the efforts of U.S. officials, particularly those in the Justice Department and the State Department's Legal Adviser's Office, to obtain evidence and fugitives from abroad. Chapter Six focuses on the negotiation of mutual legal assistance treaties to facilitate the collection of evidence from foreign jurisdictions in a form admissable in U.S. courts. Chapter Seven analyzes both the evolution of U.S. extradition treaties and practice as well as the evolution of less formal means of recovering criminal fugitives from foreign territories.

Chapters Four and Five, the two DEA chapters, provide a link between the two chapters that precede them and the two that follow. Like Chapters Two and Three, the DEA chapters focus on the international activities of U.S.

police officials and the nature of transgovernmental police work. But like Chapters Six and Seven, they examine in some detail how U.S. law enforcement officials have dealt with the challenges that arise in trying to extract information, evidence, and people from foreign jurisdictions. The latter four chapters contribute to my subsidiary objectives, which are to explain why some international law enforcement efforts prove more successful than others, to argue that the U.S. "war on drugs" has provided the crucial impetuses for many of the most substantial developments in the internationalization of U.S. criminal law enforcement since the late 1960s, and to provide evidence in support of the thesis that criminal justice systems throughout much of the world are evolving toward a more harmonious network of relationships strongly influenced by U.S. pressures, models, and examples.

3

Transnational Policing and the Makings of a Postmodern State

James Sheptycki

The category of the 'postmodern' is an abstraction and is, perhaps, not one that comes easily to criminologists. John Rajchman has conveniently located the genesis of the term within the 'hybrid field of social theory, literary criticism, cultural studies and philosophy that helped turn the term into a self-evident journalistic label' (Rajchman 1991: 119). According to him, the term began its life as a reaction to the 'modernist' conventions of art and architecture – the data of conception: *circa* 1975–6. And yet, he tells us, it was several years before its efflorescence was evident beyond the élite coterie of the avant-garde. However, and as one might expect with an abstraction such as 'the postmodern', its genealogy is not as tidy as Rajchman's analysis suggests. Significantly, for the criminologist of sociological bent, the term was used more than a decade previously by C. Wright Mills. In his estimation we 'are at the ending of what is called the Modern Age', which 'is being succeeded by a post modern period'. 'Perhaps', Mills tells us, 'we may call it: The Fourth Epoch' (Mills 1959: 166).

What characterized this postmodern period for Mills was the problem that

> too many of our standard categories of thought and of feeling as often disorient us as help to explain what is happening around us; that too many of our explanations are derived from the great historical transition from the Medieval to the Modern Age; and that when they are generalized for use today, they become unwieldy, irrelevant, not convincing ...

Source: *The British Journal of Criminology*, 35(4) (1995): 613–635.

> our major orientations ... have virtually collapsed as adequate explana-
> tions of the world. (p. 166)

In trying to write the present as history we continually come up against
the sense that social life is undergoing some kind of transformation but, as
David Garland (1995) has warned, the character and scope of the changes
involved, especially at the empirical level, are very much at issue. To use the
category of the 'postmodern' is to accept that we have entered into something beyond mere refinement, reformation, and re-articulation of what has
gone before. It is also to accept that, in such a time, intellectual labour cannot be expected to uncover what can be held up as 'objective truths'. As Rorty
(1989) argues, there is no standpoint outside the particular historically conditioned vocabularies we are using and, if we live in an age where our major
orientations ('final vocabularies', in Rorty's terms) have collapsed, then all
we can perceive is fragmentation – all explanations appear arbitrary.

The term as Rajchman knows it is especially imbued with this sense of
deep fissure in the fabric of history. Once it escaped from the lexicon of art
criticism into broader discourses about the nature of contemporary experience it rapidly became the catch-all adjective into which all the forebodings
(or proclamations) of great social change – and consequent epistemological
flux – could be loaded. To paraphrase Garland (1995), a decade and a half
after its incendiary evanescence has rendered it less than *recherché* to the
cultural élite, it has 'at last reached the distant shores of criminology where
its precise implications have yet to be worked out'. Within the locus of criminology the term might be seen as yet another 'fashion accessory' adopted
by those 'who hope to impress by their taste in terminology'. On the other
hand, the essential contestability of the term might also create the analytic
space for new entrants to the field to carve out a distinctive discourse and
research enterprise.

Robert Reiner (1992, 1994) has begun the attempt to situate criminological analysis of the police and policing within the rubric of the postmodern. According to him, commonplace conceptions of policing have become
anachronistic in an era characterized by a dynamic of fragmentation, dis-
organization, pluralism and decentring. At the edge of the Fourth Epoch
we can no longer conceive of the police as a single body with an omnibus
mandate. More than two decades ago Egon Bittner (1974) noted that the
modern police were the last of the basic building blocks to be put in place
in the structure of modern executive government. The surest expression of
governmentality (Pasquino 1991), the modern police were a product of the
nineteenth century wherein the state system was imposed on Europe.[1]

The pattern varied across Europe, but generally speaking the concept
'police' began as a broad form of governmentality which included activities
as diverse as the regulation of markets and the securing of food supply and
distribution, responsibility for street cleaning, lighting and paving, and

the licensing of single sheet newspapers and manufacturing enterprises (Pasquino 1991). Gradually these functions were hived off to specialist agencies, although 'policing' still maintained something of this sense.[2] Concomitant with this hiving-off process was the rise in the crime control function, especially the management of 'folk-devils' (Cohen 1972) and responsibility for the control of civil disorder (Thompson 1963; Vogler 1991). The image of the folk-devil is, of course, a long-standing one – one can think of Pearson's (1983) characterization of the 'hooligan' in the late nineteenth century: 'a hulking lad full of the devil' (p. 32) – and the classification and containment of the folk-devil in all his guises remains a central police task.[3]

In the language of Weber, the state system imposed an administrative monopoly over territory with demarcated boundaries (Giddens 1987: 171). This power was turned inward, enabling the state 'to define and enforce collectively binding decisions on the members of a society in the name of the common interest or general will' (Jessop 1990: 340). It was the police agency which came to embody this administrative mandate via a diffuse notion of order maintenance: what Egon Bittner calls 'a solution to an unknown problem arrived at by unknown means'. As he put it: 'The policeman and the policeman alone, is equipped, entitled and required to deal with every exigency in which force may have to be used' (Bittner 1974: 35). Thus, this standard history of police and policing has led us to understand the notion in terms of a diffuse range of activities intended to secure the order and prosperity of nationally bounded states. Policing is intimately bound up with the imposition of the nation-state system and the state is thus 'the most powerful reference point for our present understanding of the wider political relevance of policing institutions' (Walker 1994: 21). Reiner has suggested, however, that this conception of the police is 'threatened fundamentally by the advent of those social changes labelled as "postmodernity"' (1994: 756).

Transnationalization – A Postulate of Postmodern Policing

So the general claim is that policing has entered upon a significant historical transformation that fundamentally changes its institutional framework. Ethan Nadelmann, of the Woodrow Wilson School of Public and International Affairs at Princeton University, has commented on an important aspect of this shift from an American perspective. He is worth quoting at length:

> Until recently, few would ever mention criminal justice and foreign policy in the same breath. Coordination between the State and Justice Departments, for instance, was rarely necessary, especially in matters of criminal law enforcement. This dichotomy no longer exists. Law enforcement, traditionally a domestic function of government, has become more internationalized. Police and prosecutors who rarely dealt with their foreign counterparts now do so with increasing frequency. Diplomats who seldom addressed transnational criminal matters now find them high among

their assigned priorities. And politicians who typically identified crime as a local concern now focus much of their rhetoric and law-making on criminals beyond United States borders. These developments do not mark a passing phenomenon but rather the emergence of new and important dimensions to criminal justice, United States foreign policy and international politics (Nadelmann 1990: 37).

Given the apparent shift currently underway in policing, it might be that we can say that it is becoming in some sense 'postmodern'. This historic shift, the claim might go, forms part of the broad shift in contemporary society towards transnational social practices and the 'globalization of the social system' (Sklair 1991). These changes in our conception and expectations of policing are part and parcel of a broader shift, a shift in discourses about folk-devils. Criminologists are beginning to talk about 'multinational systemic crime' (Martin and Romano 1992) a concept which is typically focused on terrorism, espionage, drugs, and arms trafficking (Gilmore 1990*a*, *b*; Malcher 1991; Robertson 1991). Yet, there are other areas of concern: crimes against the environment (Block 1993; Hemmings 1993; Tysoe 1993), the crimes of 'big capital' (Pearce and Tombs 1993), transnational fraud (Commonwealth Secretariat 1991, 1992, 1993; Clarke 1993; van Duyne 1993), art and antiques theft (Esterow 1967; Gregory and Collier 1992), trade in endangered species (Nowikowski 1992), internationally co-ordinated racist violence (Jensen 1993; Witte 1993) and perhaps others.[4] These transnational folk devils require a transnational police effort, but this removes policing from its nesting site in the state and situates it in the realm of transnational practices. This transnationalization and the corresponding erosion and diminution of the state system, that most pre-eminent of modernist institutions, represents the harbinger of the postmodern. We are at the edge of the Fourth Epoch.

That, at any rate, is the hypothesis. But how are we to understand and apprehend this shift to transnational policing? We could begin by noting that concerns with transnational criminality are by no means a recent phenomenon. The idea for the International Criminal Police Commission (Interpol) was first mooted in 1914 although, due to the outbreak of the First World War, Interpol was not constituted as an organization until 1923 (Anderson 1989; Fooner 1989; Bresler 1992). Interpol, the first forum for international police co-operation, took as its brief a wide range of folk-devils including traffickers in stolen art and drugs and 'white slavers', as well as the more commonplace fraudsters, thieves, and murderers who sought to dodge the long arm of the law by fleeing across national boundaries. We could note especially that the international 'war on drugs', the most active area for transnational police co-operation, was also given its first organizational framework early in this century, following conferences at Shanghai and the Hague in 1909 and 1912. Here we can note that, while the original framework set down at the Hague in 1912 kept virtually all of the responsibility for policing drugs trafficking at the strictly national level, with some scope for bilateral arrangements, by 1943 the League of Nations had become the focus of efforts to create a truly transnational effort (Renborg 1943).[5]

That there are historical antecedents does not necessarily refute the hypothesis. What is required is a more detailed analysis of recent developments in order to assess the claim that transnational policing has reached a certain mass which makes it qualitatively different from what has gone before. Current developments in police co-operation in Europe offer a perfect test of this hypothesis for, if the underlying institutional and conceptual grid which shapes policing has been embedded in the structures and ideologies of the nation-state system, then the developing patchwork of the European Union provides an outstanding exception (Walker 1994: 20). In short, the practices which comprise police co-operation in Europe may provide a new surface of emergence for discourses about the maintenance of social order.

Before proceeding to test this hypothesis, however, there are some related issues which need to be addressed. These concern the fact that most crime is local in character; that is, most police work is grounded in relatively small geographical locales. One can think of domestic violence, for example, which accounts for approximately 20 per cent of all homicides and perhaps a quarter of a million assaults annually in the UK (Edwards 1989; Sheptycki 1991a). Criminologists know that the vast bulk of other types of recorded crime is equally local in character, but what criminologists also know is that the transnational trade in criminological knowledge is contributing to a quickened pace of change within disparate police organizations. Again, to take the example of domestic violence, it has been a transnational trade in knowledge about this type of violence and methods of policing it that has contributed to a growing global awareness of the issue and, hence, a transnational confluence of policing practice (Sheptycki 1991b, c, 1993). The transnationalization of policing has also developed in other ways. Community policing is a policing mode which has attained something of a global reach (Bayley 1989; Graham 1990; Mantila 1987; Razdan 1986; Scharf 1989; Skolnick and Bayley 1988) and yet, as a policing technique, it is still connected with low level surveillance, which can be conceptualized as 'governmental technology' (Stenson 1993). So the transnationalization of the community policing paradigm could also offer an interesting test of the hypothesis stated above, in so far as it impinges upon the boundaries between the local and the global. One might ask: what does it mean for a phenomenon like 'community policing' to become transnational? Although this is a pertinent question, and one which requires an answer, I wish to bracket this off from this discussion as the community policing paradigm warrants analysis in its own right.

A second way in which this issue can be raised relates to another contemporary transformation in policing. The 'rebirth of private policing' (Johnston 1992), where order maintenance functions shift from state agencies to the free market supplied by security firms, can also be conceptualized as a significant historical break. This shift has been characterized as a 'quiet revolution'

(Stenning and Shearing 1980) that has fundamentally altered conceptions of policing as state-centred activity (Shearing 1993). This problematic runs entirely counter to the definition put forth in the first section of this paper and provides another sense in which discourses about police and policing are in flux. Here again, private policing is normally connected with the maintenance of security over relatively small fixed geographical locales and yet it too is a transnational enterprise with private companies bidding for contracts across national jurisdictions (Johnston 1992: 204–24). This shift provides another excellent test of our hypothesis but, again, it warrants its own separate treatment.

This paper is intended to focus attention on developments in transnational police co-operation in Europe, a field which gives ample room to test the postmodern thesis. The following section reviews some of the most important literature on this topic in order to ground the analysis pursued in subsequent sections in a concrete way. It provides a guided tour of the myriad organizational forms that have been put in place in Europe to facilitate the transnational police enterprise. Following that, there is a sociological analysis of these fragmented institutional forms, which focuses on the technological infrastructure for police co-operation. This, in turn, will allow the discussion to return back to the postmodern thesis in the conclusion.

Pieces of the Machinery of Order

Sociologists and others who theorize about the nature of police and policing often remark on the problematic nature of these terms (Klockars and Mastrofski 1991). In discussing developments in transnational European policing, problems of terminological inexactitude must be stressed at the outset. One common use for the term 'police' in the transnational context refers to the use of military forces for the purposes of intervention in conflict situations (Pugh 1988). Such proposals were put forward at the League of Nations and the United Nations has also become immersed in such efforts – the conflict in Korea was referred to, at the time, as a 'police action'. Some argue that the fusing together of counter-terrorist policing, intelligence activity, and military operations in the context of Northern Ireland gives this type of 'policing' a very active sense today (Tomlinson 1993); others only imply it (Malcher 1991). There is yet further variation in types of policing activity in Europe. In addition to the various measures for policing terrorism and other 'political' crimes, there are police involved in special 'cross-border initiatives' dealing with illegal immigration, drugs and arms trafficking, and a range of other criminal activity. These units are concerned with policing ports, airports, rail and road links (including the Channel Tunnel) – such units work closely with another policing-type institution: customs and excise. And yet there are still more: tax and revenue policing initiatives to deal with money laundering, various forms of fraud and corruption, for example (Common-wealth Secretariat 1991, 1992, 1993; Punch 1993). Then too, there are the various forestry and fisheries police. One study identified 105 separate police agencies – but this did not count many in the above mentioned categories (Benyon *et al.* 1993). It is commonly held that the USA has the most differentiated policing system in the world (Walker 1977) with literally thousands of different police agencies, from the federal to the local level. The overlapping jurisdictions created by the American patchwork has been held to lead to 'linkage blindness' (Egger 1990). Linkage blindness can be understood as a lack of information networking between law enforcement agencies leading to the overlap and duplication of functions and expertise. According to Egger, this overlap may lead to competition between law enforcement agencies or, at very least a 'systemic myopia'. Europe's wide variety of law enforcement agencies might be expected to have led to an analogous situation, compounded by the problems of working in a multi-linguistic environment with a multiplicity of legal frameworks.

Assessing transnational policing in Europe is a murky business. The most up-to-date effort at mapping this enterprise available in English has been attempted by the Centre for the Study of Public Order at the University of Leicester (Benyon *et al.* 1993). This study tried to put order to the field by reference to a three-tiered typology which defined policing enterprises at the macro, meso and micro levels. While this typology produced an admirable schema, setting down virtually all of the existing frameworks for transnational police co-operation in Europe in an economical fashion, it did so at the expense of portraying the character of the system as a system. Be that as it may, in order to familiarize readers with the current state of play it is at least necessary to lay out the primary structures which are said to lie at the macro level.

Most descriptions of transnational policing initiatives in Europe begin with a discussion of Interpol – *l'Organisation Internationale de Police Criminale*, probably because it is the oldest framework for police co-operation (see Sheptycki 1994 for a brief summary of the history of this organization). Its primary purpose is to promote mutual assistance between police organizations in separate countries and it does so by functioning as a communications network. Contrary to popular images, Interpol does not have its own operational officers who deal with criminal matters – the man from Interpol never arrested anyone. Primarily, Interpol works by facilitating information sharing and message switching between the member police agencies. Police personnel from the various member countries are placed on secondment in Interpol offices at the national level (National Central Bureaux (NCBs)) or in the central bureau at Lyon, France, to help facilitate intelligence gathering and exchange between police agencies in the various member countries. In 1992 this network handled just over one million messages, 80 per cent of which were generated within European countries and 40 per cent of which emanated from European Union countries. The size and importance of the Interpol operation prompted the British government to recommend that decision makers in the European Community avoid 're-inventing the wheel for the sake of political innovation' and that 'any future agreement on a European Information System should be closely linked to the Interpol network' (Secretary of State for the Home Department, 1991, Recommendation 18).

However, Interpol is a unique policing organization in that it was not constituted through any international treaty, nor any convention or similar legal instrument (Fooner 1989: 45). Rather, it was founded upon a constitution that was written by a random group of police officers who did not submit the draft to their respective governments for approval or authorization. No diplomatic signatures were ever placed on the draft, nor was there a submission of the constitution to governments for ratification. One commentator referred to the organization as a 'policeman's club' (Bresler 1992). Conscious of the sensitive nature of such an organizational mandate to issues of national sovereignty, a basic principle, that such sovereignty should always prevail, was written into Article 3 of its 1956 convention. Thus, Interpol's mission was defined as the 'efficient repression of common law crimes and offences to the strict exclusion of all matters having a political, religious or racial character' (quoted in Fooner 1989: 80). While Interpol did intervene in some of these types of situations on an *ad hoc* basis, high profile terrorism was considered problematic for the simple reason that conflicting definitions of terrorism might have prompted large numbers of members to leave the organization (Bresler 1992: 162–3).

The uncertain legal basis of the organization probably contributed to inaction in crimes of terrorism; it was only in 1972, with the signing of the Headquarters Agreement in France, that the organization attained formal legal status in that country (this despite the fact that its headquarters had been housed there since the end of World War Two). One year previously the organization negotiated a special arrangement with the United Nations and with this recognition came formal arrangements with a number of other agencies including the Council of Europe, the Customs Co-operation Council, and the International Civil Aviation Organization.[6] Yet still, Interpol remained reluctant to involve itself with anything other than 'ordinary law crimes'. It was not until 1983 when President Ronald Reagan clarified the USA's position, signing an executive order designating Interpol a Public International Organization entitled to the privileges, exemptions, and immunities conferred by standing US legislation on such organizations, that things began to change in earnest. At this time expenditure by the American government on the Interpol NCB in Washington DC went from an annual $125,000 to $6m over a ten-year period (Bresler 1992: 177).[7] It was also during this period that US law enforcement personnel stepped into key positions in the Interpol organization and the 'doctrine of the conflict area' was articulated, allowing the organization to take a more proactive role in policing terrorism.[8]

It was Interpol's writing out of 'political' crime from its operational brief that prompted a 'reinvention of the wheel' during the 1970s. Following the massacre perpetrated by Black September on 5 September 1972 at the Munich Olympic Games and other similar terrorist attacks during the late 1960s and early 1970s, the European Council of Ministers established their own intergovernmental framework for dealing with this type of crime – TREVI. This constitutes the second major macro level network for police co-operation in Europe. TREVI is a high level ministerial group which also includes senior police officers; currently the 12 members of the European Union form the core, but there are also seven 'friends of TREVI' who attend meetings as observers. They are: Austria, Canada, Morocco, Norway, Sweden, Switzerland, and the USA. This organization's original brief was 'terrorism', but it has since been widened out to include drugs trafficking, serious organized crime, police training and technology, communications and information technology, public order, disaster prevention, and the abolition of internal borders. This organization, together with what Benyon describes as meso level structures – such as the Police Working Group on Terrorism (PWGOT) and the Mutual Assistance Group (MAG, which deals with customs related issues) and the *Comité Européen pour la Lutte Anti-Drogue* (CELAD, which deals with drugs trafficking), provide formal channels for liaison officers from the various police agencies in Europe to move between and within these agencies in tackling various specific crimes.

Liaison officer programmes enable police officers from the various national police agencies to work together on special projects. An excellent example of this mode of co-operation can be found in the efforts to control 'football hooliganism' during the 1990 World Cup finals in Italy. Liaison officers from a wide number of police agencies cooperated in this effort. This involved forward intelligence gathering in order to identify 'key' actors in an effort to prevent serious incidents before they happened. It also involved small teams of police officers from various national agencies who escorted their own nationals to matches to give aid and assistance, again in pinpointing key individuals, to Italian police (House of Commons 1991).[9] However, the most prominent example of this type of activity that the TREVI group has produced is the development of a system of Drug Liaison Officers (DLOs).[10] This system includes postings between police in the various European states and some outwith the EU. As can be seen, liaison officer programmes give an operational capacity to this transnational policing structure, albeit one which is mediated through other formal arrangements. The complexity of these arrangements lends the TREVI system an opacity beyond that of Interpol.

The TREVI system consists of an elaborate multi-tier structure including a ministerial level, a senior officer level, and a working group level staffed by officials and law enforcement personnel (Walker 1993*b*). Currently there is no permanent Secretariat and this has prompted some discussion of a 'democratic deficit' (McLauglin 1992). In the terms of political science,

TREVI has an intergovernmental structure, that is, it is mandated by formal relations between sovereign governments. As such, its decisions remain outside the competence of the European Parliament. It has no headquarters or budget, making monitoring and evaluation of its initiatives all but impossible. Despite, or perhaps because of, the relative secrecy of its decisions, TREVI's success in acting as a stimulus for European police co-operation, not just in the key areas of terrorism and drugs, but also over a wide variety of issues, cannot be underestimated. However, despite its success, the progress of the European Union may also have sown the seeds of its eventual demise (den Boer and Walker 1993). Before discussing this possibility, the nascent Europol and the effects of Article K of the Maastricht Treaty, however, it is necessary to look first at the Schengen agreement which provides the frame for the third macro level transnational policing effort in Europe.

The Schengen Agreement provides one of the key inter-governmental fora for police co-operation in Europe and constitutes the third macro level structure to be discussed here. The primary objective of the Schengen agreement has been to 'harden' the external borders of the European Community (now Union) and thus make it possible to dissolve the internal ones. The Schengen Agreement of 1985 consolidated and widened an earlier achievement of the Benelux countries (Belgium, the Netherlands, and Luxembourg) which effectively removed border controls between those countries. While progress along these lines has encountered some political stumbling blocks, issues about visa and asylum policy in particular, it seems evident that there is a broad degree of consensus among policy makers in Europe regarding the way forward, and this extends to the usual range of subjects, including surveillance of external borders, co-operation between police forces, and legal authorities in matters regarding criminal law, extradition policy, the sharing of criminal information (including information on individuals), and the delegation of the enforcement of criminal judgments, as well as drugs, firearms, and telecommunications policies. This consensus for co-operation may have arisen because, as one well-placed commentator stated:

> Such co-operation, I would stress, is a worthwhile objective in its own right. This is true for the Schengen countries as it is for the Community as a whole, and it is true whether or not internal frontiers come down. In a Community with internal frontiers, such co-operation has been desirable but optional – and very little progress has been achieved in these fields over the years. In a Community without internal frontiers the work is both urgent and necessary. That is why the list of subjects covered in the Schengen Supplementary Convention is precisely the agenda on which the Community as a whole is now working. (Brittan 1991)

The organizational structure of Schengen, as might be expected, is exceedingly complex. At its apex is an Executive Committee (provided for in

Title VII of the Convention) which consists of Ministers and Secretaries of State of the member countries. However, most of the actual work carried out is supervised by the Central Negotiating Group (CNG) which consists of about 120 senior officials and police officers. The Central Group supervises the operations of all sub-working groups and presents decisions to the European Council of Ministers. Underneath the CNG are four principal working groups with a further 11 subaltern working groups, again related to a whole gambit of issues from telecommunications to firearms, drugs, agricultural products, the environment, and much more besides. This structure represents the most ambitious attempt to promote practical police co-operation within Europe. As with the TREVI arrangements, there is something of a democratic deficit, with no parliamentary and very little judicial control of the organization (O'Keefe 1993). Although there may be potential to attribute some jurisdictional competence to the European Court of Justice under Article K3 of the Maastricht Treaty, the accountability of the Executive Committee to the national parliaments is severely limited. Article 132 of the Schengen Convention provides that the Committee may decide its own rules of procedure and set up any working groups it wishes. The lack of control of the actions of the Executive Committee has prompted the conclusion that there is a fundamental flaw in the descriptions of the Schengen Convention as a prototype for future co-operative arrangements (Benyon *et al.* 1993).

The fourth macro level structure to be considered here is a relatively new kid on the block: Europol. This is an, as yet, untested law enforcement structure. The idea for such an organization was first put forward by German Chancellor Helmut Kohl at a meeting of the European Council of Ministers in June 1991 and was subsequently taken forward by the TREVI ministers. The original intent was to establish a framework for a fully operational Euro-police, akin to the Federal Bureau of Investigation in the USA. This, however, is still a long way off. As Lode van Outrive, the rapporteur on Europol for the Committee on Civil Liberties and Internal Affairs, stated in the European Parliament: 'we do not have the political, legal and procedural structures we would need for an operational European federal police force' (Debates in the European Parliament, 21 January 1993, 3–426/281).[11] The structure of accountability was explained in the British House of Lords by Earl Ferrers. It will

> ... operate under the authority of a ministerial agreement. Under the terms of the agreement the unit will be accountable to TREVI Ministers of the European Community member states. In this country that is my right honourable friend the Home Secretary. In practice though Ministers will delegate the responsibility for the day-to-day running of the unit to officials. That is likely to require the creation of an executive committee with representatives from each member state which will monitor the activities and the management ... the precise arrangements about the frequency of

the committee's meetings and its detailed functions have yet to be worked out, but the coordinator ... will report via the committee to TREVI Ministers. (Hansard, vol. 541, no. 85, 27 January 1993).[12]

So, the nascent Europol emerged from the womb of TREVI. The original motion tabled by Chancellor Kohl called for the creation of a single European Police Office which would combat international and European crime, an idea which approximated the federal structure of the German *Bundeskriminalampt* (BKA). Although this was accepted by the majority of ministers involved, the UK being a notable exception, this plan was too ambitious, at least in the short term. What has emerged instead came from the successes of TREVI Working Group III on drugs and organized crime; this was a European Drugs Unit (EDU), which was given a mandate to co-ordinate intelligence exchange relating to drug trafficking and the exchange of drugs liaison officers. These ideas were nurtured by the inclusion of Title VI and the Declaration on Police Co-operation in the Maastricht Treaty on European Union. Article K1(9) of the Treaty states that police co-operation is a matter 'of common interest' and calls for 'the organization of a union-wide system for exchanging information within a European Police Office (Europol)'. While Europol is limited to a drugs intelligence unit at the moment, it is clear from a report to the European Council by the TREVI Ministers that this is but a first step and that 'the scope of Europol can be progressively widened so that the experience gained in establishing the drugs capability can be applied to other relevant types of crime which pose a threat to Member States ... Without wishing to prejudge the outcome of future work, it is likely that money laundering and aspects of organized crime linked to drug trafficking would be included at an early stage in the responsibilities of Europol'.[13] There is every reason to expect that, in the long run, TREVI and Europol will merge back into one another (Fijnaut 1993).

Under Article K6 of the Maastricht Treaty these activities may be questioned by the European Parliament, which has the right to be informed by the Presidency and the European Commission. Further, under the provisions of this Article, the European Parliament will hold an annual debate on these issues. However, the control that the European Parliament has over transnational policing co-operation under the terms of the Treaty is weak; there is a procedure set out whereby the Community may acquire legislative competence in some areas of justice and home affairs, but this is not the case for police co-operation or, indeed, even for judicial co-operation in criminal matters or customs co-operation. It is the Co-ordinating Committee created under Article K4, which consists of senior civil servants from the member countries (it is, as yet, unclear how they will be appointed), who will exert day-to-day control. This control will, again, be asserted through a system of subaltern working groups. As such, any control the European Parliament has will be insulated from the workings of this apparatus by several layers of bureaucracy, but there is a second avenue of accountability, as Earl Ferrers stated in the House of Lords:

> The Government are fully aware of the need to ensure that Europol and the Europol Drugs Unit are fully and properly accountable to the parliaments of all the member states, including the Parliament of the United Kingdom (Hansard vol. 541, no. 85, 27 January 1993).[14]

Nevertheless, questions about the democratic deficit with regard to this last of the macro-level institutions to be examined here have been raised. It has been noted elsewhere that as an adjunct to the TREVI group, which has no procedures for democratic accountability, Europol can be open to similar criticism. Some concern has already been expressed in the European Parliament over the lack of control and the paucity of mechanisms for assessing the effectiveness of its operations.[15] The respective parliaments of the countries that make up the European Union are no less insulated from this apparatus. Indeed, they may be more so and, hence, may be seen as less likely to offer an avenue for democratic accountability.

Thus we have a catalogue of major structures for transnational police co-operation in Europe. As Lord Morris of Castle Morris put it, not without some apparent sense of exasperation, 'there are no fewer than four major [police] organizations trying to secure *business*. They are TREVI, Interpol, Schengen and Europol' (Hansard, vol. 541, no. 85, emphasis mine). Perhaps not surprisingly, given the high-level ministerial negotiations that have produced these mechanisms (that is, with the exception of Interpol) most of the analysis that has been produced of these 'macro-level structures' has been carried out by political scientists. What this discussion makes apparent is that much of what has transpired in terms of transnational policing initiatives in Europe remains firmly grounded in intergovernmental agreements, that is: the individual states that comprise Europe remain key actors. Over and between these sovereign units has been thrown a thick web of relations which constitute a multiplicity of transnational social control networks. It appears that this web anchors these sovereign states to each other and bolsters their solidity, rendering them a collective conglomerate.

However, a descriptive overview of these structures, while a useful and necessary aid to understanding, does not amount to an analysis of the actual workings of the transnational policing enterprise. A more sociological approach is necessary if we are to evaluate and understand the nature of the changes that are transpiring. Some of the above-mentioned commentators have tried to ask similar questions by reference to the emergence of a 'post-Hobbesian state' (Walker 1994; Streeck and Schmitter 1991), wherein the emerging supranational European state is expected to lie somewhere between the 'sovereign units' that comprise it. The post-Hobbesian state, so this theory goes, will be based on diffuse networks constituted by multiple voluntary exchange between such units who will maintain an unambiguous monopoly of the legitimate use of coercive force (Walker 1994: 34). The hypothesis established in this paper, predicated on the postmodern problematic, seeks to penetrate beyond this in order better to comprehend the nature of the fluctuating accomplishments of these institutional mirages.

Fragmentation, Pattern, and Order?

Anthony Bottoms and Paul Wiles have argued, persuasively, that the transnational exchange of capital has unfettered it from the state. Capital, so this argument goes, has become so transportable within global financial communications networks that it is no longer really possible for governments to control and direct its flows. This has led states to seek new forms of co-operation, including the creation of supranational institutions like the European Union. According to Bottoms and Wiles, 'this is one of the processes which has led to what is sometimes called the "hollowing out" of the state'. This hollowing-out process is said to have 'removed the power of decision making to a macro level beyond the control of the state' (Bottoms and Wiles 1994: 15). In terms of this discussion about transnational police co-operation, the 'hollowing out thesis' seems at odds with the observations made so far. The four macro-level institutions discussed in the previous section seem to exhibit a *thickening* of state controls over coercive apparatuses, although it is arguable whether this thickening is conditioned by the liberal democratic ideals associated with Western states (McLaughlin 1992). While there is an acknowledged tendency for the emergent structures of transnational policing to compete with one another (van Reenen 1989: 49–50; Johnston 1992: 202), this competition seems at least partly to do with the fact that the transnational structure itself reifies national state apparatuses. That these structures for police co-operation function at all might seem remarkable. However, while 'there is no immediate prospect of criminal law harmonization in the EC, there is nevertheless a remarkable similarity between European states in their specification of the main categories of crime' (Walker 1994: 32). Thus it seems entirely possible that these transnational arrangements can continue to function within a state system characterized by heterogeneity (as evidenced by a lack of harmonization of criminal law), purely on the basis of a consensus on the main categories of criminality. Transnational police co-operation, it appears, can proceed on the basis of what has historically been a central tenet of the modern state, its monopoly of formal social control: the folk devils are dealt with regardless.

However, this apparent thickening turns out to be illusory when we examine the technical apparatus upon which transnational law enforcement depends. A key indicator of the growth and change of transnational law-enforcement capacity is improvement in telecommunications and information management systems. Technological change signifies a great deal; as

Shoshana Zuboff (1988) argues, a 'fundamental change in an organization's technological infrastructure wields the power of the hand at the turning rim. Technological change defines the horizon of our material worlds as it shapes the limiting conditions of what is possible and what is barely imaginable' (p. 387). There is no doubt that there has been a technological revolution of sorts in transnational policing. Looking briefly at the law-enforcement situation in the Western hemisphere, in May 1986 Interpol 'induced the United Nations, through its drug fund for Drug Abuse Control, to finance a telecommunications network in the Caribbean region' (Fooner 1989: 150). The first stage of this programme was reached by 1989 with a fully operational network covering 26 countries based at the regional Interpol NCB in Puerto Rico. Interpol upgraded its entire global network during the 1980s; some NCBs went from using Morse code to fax machines almost overnight (PRSU 1992). By the early 1990s the Interpol central station transmitted some one million messages annually (Interpol 1989).[16]

In the European context, the special focus of this paper, this technological leap has been just as marked and the Interpol network offers a prime example. Estimates range from 400,000 to 800,000 text-messages handled by the Interpol network in Europe annually – depending on where the boundaries of Europe are said to lie. TREVI's principal communications technology is a secure facsimile network (TSFN), which facilitates a high-level ministerial trade in information. One of the central preoccupations of TREVI has been to make suggestions on practical frameworks for the introduction of information technology (Walker 1993a). The Schengen Agreement acknowledged the need to abolish obstacles to the free movement of goods and persons, that is: 'internal' border controls, and it authorized the detailed discussion of a number of issues concerned with police and criminal justice co-operation, especially criminological data transfer. The Schengen Agreement offers yet another excellent example of transnational policing, since it has its own separate European criminal intelligence system, known as the Schengen Information System (SIS). The SIS was conceived to facilitate information exchange between the national police forces of the nine signatories to the Schengen Treaty through a central data processing unit based in Strasbourg. This system was scheduled to come on line for six of the Schengen member states (Belgium, France, Germany, Luxembourg, the Netherlands, and Spain) in February 1994, with Portugal, Greece, and Italy delaying until some future date.[17] It is expected that in the near future it will be possible to exchange fingerprints and pictures via the SIS: the system has a current theoretical maximum of eight million personal records and a further seven million records on objects. Current estimates are that it will be dealing with two-and-a-half million enquiries annually before the end of the decade. The fourth information management system in the offing in Europe is attached to Europol's European Drugs Unit (EDU). After some delays Europol headquarters have been established at the Hague with plans for compiling a database of personal information related to drug traffickers. It is early days for this new effort and questions remain as to its relationship with the SIS and Interpol. Europol was suggested in order to create a law enforcement apparatus that has operational capacity within the whole of the European Union and hence represents another significant prototype for what transnational policing might eventually look like. However, this organization is, as yet, only embryonic. In the interim, the information processing systems that currently exist, or are planned for, call for consequent developments of national criminal intelligence systems in order to link trans-European policing efforts with operational (that is: national) police units.

The great concentration of databases on criminals and criminal activity has come about out of a perceived need to build in economies of scale and to facilitate transnational communication.[18] In the UK the Secretary of State recommended to Parliament that 'a National Criminal Intelligence Service be established, with an operational arm operating through a revamped regional crime squad structure and incorporating the existing national intelligence units' (Secretary of State for the Home Department, 1991, Recommendation 32). He also recommended that the Interpol NCB for the UK should be part of the National Criminal Intelligence Unit (later designated the National Criminal Intelligence Service (NCIS)) and that 'European Liaison Officers in police forces should also be designated Interpol Liaison Officers' (Recommendation 10).[19]

Looking at the growth of information technology in the sphere of policing and crime control in Europe offers a confusing vista. Zuboff argues that:

> Information technology is a label that reflects the convergence of several streams of technical developments including microelectronics, computer science, telecommunications, software engineering and system analysis. It is a technology that dramatically increases the ability to record, store, analyze and transmit information in ways that permit flexibility, accuracy, immediacy, geographic independence, volume and complexity. Information technology has a unique capability to restructure operations that depend upon information for the purposes of transaction, record keeping, analysis, control or communication. (Zuboff 1988: 415)

Advance in the criminological application of information technology, in this broadest sense, is well underway in Europe. The Interpol Criminal Information System, housed in Lyon, France, is equipped with Automated Search Facility (ASF) software which allows Interpol NCBs, as well as other official services having a 'police mission', direct access. The ASF currently contains particulars of some 130,000 persons, about 80,000 of which are drug offenders.[20] At the same time there are significant legal and political barriers to comprehensive networking between the numerous workstations in the various organizations. The Ministerial Agreement on the establishment of the Europol Drug Unit, for example, states that 'the transmission of personal information to non-Member States or to international organizations [i.e. Interpol] by the liaison officers will not take place', prompting one commentator to conclude that 'the prospect of an integrated international criminal intelligence system is ... far from immediate' (Cameron-Waller 1993).

In looking for evidence of the hollowing out of the state, the vast growth of 'cyberspace' in police and crime control efforts gives interesting results. On the one hand, the increase in 'informated space' yields a potential for an organizational revolution. However, these technological improvements are being laid down within pre-existing political and legal foundations.[21] As Lord Morris of Castle Morris noted, there is a sense in which these various organizations compete for business (Hansard, vol. 541, no. 85). There is a great deal of cross-over of responsibility within these organizations. Frequently one person will be given several roles to play, for example, Interpol liaison officer and European liaison officer as well as an operational role, say on a stolen car squad. Still, the degree of fit between organizations is not seamless. The technological space that is being created in the crime control apparatus remains underpinned by older institutional structures (national and subnational) which prevent the establishment of a unified informated space. The political and legal agreements that have been struck in order to constitute these umbrella organizations are piecemeal and disjointed, reflective of the highly differentiated nature of police organizations operating in Europe. The picture is further complicated when the large number of bilateral arrangements for cross-border policing are taken into account. These arrangements constitute unique organizational arrangements that stand between national police forces mediating cross-border police co-operation, which, themselves, operate in their own 'informated space' (Gallagher 1992).

The resultant picture is a patchwork quilt. According to Benyon

> [i]n addition to the Trevi Group, Interpol, the Schengen Agreement and the nascent Europol, there is a wide array of less formal arrangements for promoting police co-operation in Europe. The number of these law enforcement networks, groups and agreements is large and together they form a complicated, interconnecting, mesh of formal structures and informal arrangements, serviced by a range of information systems (which are often incompatible). (1992: 32)

In short, while technological refitting in the numerous policing enterprises which constitute European policing to date has been dramatic, it has not brought about a single unified cyberspace. Benyon characterizes this state of affairs as 'incremental drift'. The extent to which this verifies or refutes the 'hollowing out of the state' thesis depends on how we interpret the nature of this shift. As Zuboff says

> only rarely is there a grand design ... instead, there is a concentration of forces and consequences, which in turn develop their own momentum.

> Sometimes the lines of force run in predictable straight paths. At other times, they twist and spiral, turn corners, and flow to their opposite. Activities that seem to represent choices are often inert reproductions of accepted practice. In many cases, they are convenient responses to the press of local exigencies. (Zuboff 1988, p. 389)

Put another way, looking to information technology to provide a simple unified frame for transnational policing is misguided. Some criminologists argue that institutional responses to crime should properly be seen as fragmented (Ericson and Carriere 1994). They label criminological approaches which are principally concerned with the rational deployment of personnel and technology and the use of strategies and tactics calculated to secure a territory against those who threaten its people and things 'General Schwarzkopf Criminology'. What is argued for in contrast is an 'institutional approach' (Gladstone *et al.* 1991) which views a myriad of groups and organizations (including criminologists and Schwarzkopfs) using crime and its regulation in order to constitute themselves.[22] In painting these sociological observations about the apparatus of crime control on to a transnational canvas, a fragmented picture would indeed be the expected result. But to what extent have these changes constituted a hollowing out of the state? On the one hand, it is apparent that older practices and discourses and the nation state remain alive in these new arrangements – and this has led to an apparent fragmentation. On the other, when we prioritize our perception of these older forms we subsume the real weight of history within our own estimation of a diversity of interests that pervade collective behaviour. Zuboff warns that 'to narrow all discussion of technological change to the play of these interests overlooks the essential power of technology to reorder the rules of the game' (Zuboff 1988: 389). This would seem to suggest that this vast and ungovernable patchwork of informated spaces, existing in the transnational interstices of state power, might indeed be a significant diminution of the nation state's near monopoly of policing.

The Paradox of the Postmodern State

In terms of testing the postmodern hypothesis then, our examination of technological and intergovernmental advance is revealing. What seems to be happening is a new unfolding dialectic in discourses on crime and its control (the technical management of folk devils). This dialectic is situated in a metaphorical transnational space that has opened up in the state system. Where once borderlines on maps held an abstract solidity seemingly more firm than the border guards that policed them, our current discourses reveal a concern about interstitial spaces *between* governed territories. In the European context, some commentators have put forward the notion of 'harmonization', a process by which Europe as a whole can be constituted as a *governable* territory

(Barry 1993). The idea of the dissolution of Europe's 'internal borders' and its corollary the (as yet ill-defined) 'external frontier', has raised questions about 'security' (Ramsbotham 1991) and conclusions that 'better policing and intelligence work are more important than physical border controls' (Philip 1989). Harmonization, something akin to Habermas's notion of 'the scientization of polities' – whereby issues become a technical problem examined and managed by restricted groups of bureaucrats, experts, and professional lobbyists – can thus be interpreted, in part, as a transnational criminological enterprise equipped with the epistemological underpinnings of governmentality.

The apparent resilience of the will to govern and its attendant vocabulary has led some criminologists to conclude that we are entering upon late or high modernity (Bottoms and Wiles 1994; Garland 1995). Garland has pointed out that while many of the discussions about criminology (and by extension policing, including transnational policing) are infused with the sense of deepening crisis, we can ask if current developments signal a significant historical shift or if this sense of crisis has led us to overdraw the changes underway. For example, he argues that, while Foucault singled out the prison as a modern institution perpetually in crisis and undergoing reform, 'he might more accurately have noted that all modern institutions share this characteristic, be they schools, or hospitals or even government itself' (Garland 1995, ms., p. 20). Crisis, then, is not enough evidence on which to base any claims about the depth of current historical shifts. What would be required is evidence of a deeper social restructuring.

The analysis undertaken here leans towards a vision of the current historical conjuncture that depicts social order (social control) as 'split into a multitude of contexts of action and forms of authority ... [wherein] the nation state declines in importance and the cohesive totality is replaced by a multiplicity of sites of reproduction' (Giddens 1992, as quoted in Reiner 1994). Like the modernist institutions which are but sub-units of the state (the prison, police organizations, and the like) the authority and self-identity of the nation state is not a stable, circumscribed conception but a boundary of separation which must be constantly policed and this holds doubly true for the nascent European suprastate. The tension emerging in Europe is that two principles of organization currently vie for the right to define that which must be separated out. Until very recently state-centred modes of order policed and managed technically the usual suspects: terrorists, drug dealers, *mafiosi*, and other 'folk devils'. In the current conjuncture new – transnational – organizations also claim the right to manage these outsiders. This management is a costly enterprise, more so because of its fragmented nature. Ironically, it is an expression of governmentality that seems free floating (i.e. ungoverned), in so far as it is not beholden to an identifiable source of legitimized political power. Yet it must be stressed, in spite of the fragmentary nature of this policing enterprise, it has a coherence; the pattern of the patchwork quilt emerges from the folk-devilry it seeks to order.

The history is too short to make predictions as to what or, indeed, if a coherent and unified institutional framework will emerge from these processes; we know not what the Fourth Epoch may bring. In the interim we are left with a fragmented vision. We can see both a thickening and a hollowing out of the nation state, we can see both the emergence of transnational policing and its firm anchorage in sovereign units, we see both fragmentation and unity in the technical capacity to manage deviance and disorder. Order maintenance itself is subject to contingency, the chaos of ruthless fate and fumbling chance. In effect, police, criminologists, and other experts on social control are no longer really modernists but they have yet to assume a new coherence and identity. If we assume that there is a new distinctive identity which *may* emerge in the Fourth Epoch we could say that, at present, we are merely postmodern.

Notes

1. The history of policing in Europe can be understood as part and parcel of the imposition of the state system as evidenced by the relatively late arrival of the Carabinieri, the national police agency in Italy, which can be explained by the fact that the peninsula was not a unified state until 1870. See Bayley (1979) for a more detailed account of this police history.

2. As an interesting aside, I have observed in Scottish police stations that police have been involved in the fight against the Colorado beetle. One might think that insects are an unlikely illegal alien to be on police wanted lists but, in Scotland, police and Ministry of Agriculture officials are actively co-operating in efforts to control the possible importation of this pest. The hiving-off process has resulted in specialist 'police' agencies, but it seems that the police organization still clings to vestiges of a role first prescribed for them almost 200 years ago. This too has taken on a transnational dimension.

3. The designation 'folk devil' is in no way intended to deride the victims of crime or to suggest that the object of crime control is based on a mythology, rather it is intended to signal the place that such elements of disorder have in the drama of crime control, transnational or otherwise. That place is as an object for the crime control apparatus, to be classified, contained, controlled, and otherwise set apart from the 'normal'.

4. For example, child abduction in custody disputes is commonplace enough and this too can take on an transnational dimension. The Interpol communications system has been used in a number of these circumstances. As yet, there is no commentary on this form of international criminality in the scholarly literature.

5. Following a certain normative reasoning, the large-scale market demand for recreational drugs was seen as having an 'inevitable consequence': 'that drugs must be controlled in all countries and territories'. The logic was that '[A] single weak spot constitutes a grave danger, for other countries or for the entire world'. Further, 'this could be done only by co-operation among all governments, by the elaboration of satisfactory rules for control, by asking governments to accept international obligations to apply at least such rules (by becoming parties to international instruments) and by providing international supervision of governments, to guarantee that they effectively apply the rules' (Renborg 1943: 3).

6. It is generally accepted as fact among informed commentators that Interpol was given full status as an intergovernmental organization in 1971. Bresler states that 'the United Nations accorded Interpol full legal status as an intergovernmental international

organization' (1993: 131). However, Interpol itself merely lays claim to having a 'special relationship' with the Economic and Social Council of the UN. The terms of the resolution passed appear to fudge the issue, stating that the relationship accords to Interpol 'the same conditions and procedures as are applicable to ... organizations having consultative status ... with the Council'. That is to say, UN Resolution 1579(L) pertaining to the Special Arrangement for Co-operation between the United Nations and the International Criminal Police Organization (Interpol) does not say that Interpol is an organization having IGO status but merely states that it is to be treated *as if* it were. By implication, this means that Interpol actually retains a less exalted status as a non-governmental organization. I am grateful to Inspector Paul Swallow of the Metropolitan Police International Unit for pointing this narrow although important distinction out to me.

7. The American government put money into international policing in a more direct way. The Drugs Enforcement Administration (DEA) has over 60 offices world-wide staffed by over 200 operational agents (Nadelmann 1990: 39). Nadelmann argues that there is an overwhelming American predominance in transnational policing activity, 'the DEA's capacity to pursue its objectives world-wide is certainly greater than that of any other law enforcement agency' (p. 48). In 1993 it was estimated that the DEA had 2,800 agents assigned to drug enforcement at home and abroad and its budget was estimated to be US$718m (*Law Enforcement News*, vol. XIX, no. 385 15 September 1993). That is up from some 2,117 agents operating at a cost of $200m in 1976 (Nadelmann 1993: 149).

8. The Secretary General of Interpol, Raymond Kendal, explained the doctrine of the conflict area thus: 'We make a distinction between what happens within what we would call the conflict area and what happens outside the conflict area. So, let's suppose we were dealing with Israel and Jordan: what goes on in that particular conflict area would not be of interest to us for international police co-operation while it remains in that conflict area. On the other hand, if a Jordanian comes to Paris and shoots the Israeli Ambassador, then it does become our concern because it is outside the strict conflict area and in answer to supporters of the PLO who say to me publicly at conferences: 'We are freedom fighters and everything else,' I say, 'While you are fighting for freedom in your own country, fair enough! But if you use that argument to permit terrorist acts outside the context of what is in the internal freedom struggle, then that takes away from you the protection of being a freedom fighter ...' (Bresler 1992: 183–4).

9. While police co-operation is well advanced, juridical co-operation is not. Thus, when 'trouble' occurs host countries have usually opted not to pursue criminal charges and 'hooligans', under escort by police, have simply been 'herded' into compounds and, in turn, on to air transport back to their own country of origin. Thus the management of one of the most visible folk devils in Europe can be seen as a purely technical exercise which has very little to do with the criminal law.

10. Of course there are others. For example, in the wake of widely publicized outbreaks of racist violence in Germany and France in the spring of 1993 the TREVI ministerial meeting at Copenhagen in June of that year initiated an investigation into the possibility of transnational orchestration of racist violence (*The Guardian*, 2 June 1993).

11. Mr van Outrive, Member of the European Parliament representing the Netherlands, is an outspoken critic of aggressive law enforcement tactics in the 'fight against drugs' (NB: 'the war on ...' metaphor is frequently watered down in a European context). In particular, he has expressed his extreme doubts regarding costs and benefits of the fight against drugs. Further, he has expressed doubts 'concerning the efficiency, reasonableness and harmlessness of a repressive military demeanour' and noted that it is 'generally known that drugs trafficking is the first and foremost cause of police corruption'. Finally, his argument against the criminalization of recreational drugs rests

on questions about the motives of those who campaign for the continuation of the war on drugs: 'we do not know whether those who advocate the repressive approach, and also the illegal nature of everything to do with drugs, are genuinely concerned about public health and the connections between politics and the large-scale economics of drugs trafficking, or whether they tolerate that – precisely through its totally illegal character – the interests of mafias and organized criminals are served, because they obtain extremely high incomes which in turn enable them to fund all kinds of economic and political activity.' (*Debates in the European Parliament*, 15 May 1992, No. 3–418).

12. According to the Ministerial Agreement on the establishment of the Europol Drugs Unit (November 1992, unpublished document) 'without prejudice to the responsibility of individual Ministers for the control of their national liaison officers, the Ministers will collectively exert a general oversight of the activities of the Unit ... the Coordinator will submit a six-monthly written report of his management and the activities of the Unit. The Coordinator will also provide any other report or other information which is asked for by the Ministers.'

13. Quotation taken from a document entitled: The Development of Europol. Report from TREVI Ministers to the European Council in Maastricht (undated and unpublished).

14. Indeed, Article K2(2) specifically guarantees the retention by member states of their existing responsibilities for law and order and internal (read national) security.

15. 'Drug Squad to be Part of "Fortress Europe" Strategy', *The Independent*, 3 June 1993.

16. The USA example offers a measure of the extent of increase in telecommunications traffic. The Washington DC NCB processed 4,000 requests for information in 1976, this increased to 48,000 by 1987 (Nadelmann 1990: 47).

17. As of the time of writing (February, 1995) the SIS has yet to come on line for message transfer, due to technical difficulties.

18. The recent trend towards centralization in British policing 'is partly due to the British police discovering economies of scale ... [and that] the regional structure of the police makes it difficult to co-operate abroad' (*The Economist*, 'Policing the Police', 26 February 1994).

19. The Interpol NCB was duly incorporated into the NCIS network on 1 April 1992. It processed a total of 102,346 messages that year relating to some 15,633 cases (National Criminal Intelligence Service Annual Report 1992/93).

20. Currently Interpol is the only transnational policing enterprise with an online capability of this sort. I asked one officer in the International Bureau of the UK National Criminal Intelligence Service (NCIS) what would be the theoretical maximum number of records that the system could house. His answer was that 'as regards the cocaine side, which is the area that I know about, we know that there are in excess of 70,000 Columbians in London alone ... we know that approximately 60 per cent of these are involved in the cocaine trade'. When I asked him to clarify if that meant that there were records on some 42,000 Columbians in London alone his reply was 'Yes' (from taped interview).

21. In addition to the barriers that older national organizational frameworks place in the way of a unified 'cyberspace', there are also the legal barriers of the data protection legislation. For an overview of these issues see den Boer and Walker (1993). There is, however, an offsetting tendency, as Didier Bigo (1994) argues, which is the trend towards an 'internal security field'. The ideology of internal security, a domain of practices and ideas which subsumes all of the folk devils from illegal immigrants and asylum seekers to organized criminals, terrorists, drugs and arms dealers, encourages the future development of a security service to police the enforcement of the new security regime.

22. In Mary Douglas's terms, organizations create themselves by 'harnessing all informational processes to the task of establishing themselves' (Douglas 1987: 102).

References

Anderson, M. (1989), *Policing the World*. Oxford: Clarendon Press.

Barry, A. (1993), 'The European Community and European Government', *Economy and Society*, 22/3: 314–27.

Bayley, D. H. (1979), 'Police Function, Structure and Control in Western Europe and North America: Comparative and Historical Studies', in N. Morris and M. Tonry, eds., *Crime and Justice I.* Chicago: Chicago University Press.

—— (1989), *A Model of Community Policing: The Singapore Story*. Washington, DC: US National Institute of Justice.

Benyon, J. (1992), 'Issues in European Police Co-operation', *Leicester University Discussion Papers in Politics*, No. P92/11.

Benyon, J., Turnbull, L., Willis, A., Woodward, R., and Beck, A. (1993), *Police Co-operation in Europe: An Investigation*. Centre for the Study of Public Order, University of Leicester.

Bigo, D. (1994), 'The European Internal Security Field: Stakes and Rivalries in a Newly Developing Area of Police', in M. Anderson and M. den Boer, eds., *Policing Across National Boundaries*. London: Pinter.

Bittner, E. (1974), 'Florence Nightingale in Pursuit of Willie Sutton: A Theory of Police', in H. Jacob, ed., *The Potential for Reform of Criminal Justice*. Beverley Hills, CA: Sage.

—— (1980), *The Functions of the Police in Modern Society*. Chevy Chase, MD: National Institute of Education.

Block, A. A. (1993), 'Defending the Mountaintop; A Campaign against Environmental Crime', in F. Pearce and M. Woodiwiss, eds., *Global Crime Connections; Dynamics and Control*. London: Macmillian.

Bottoms, A. E., and Wiles, P. (1994), 'Crime and Insecurity in the City'. Paper presented at the International Society of Criminology International Course on 'Changes in Society, Crime and Criminal Justice in Europe', Leuven, Belgium, May, 1994.

Bresler, F. (1992), *Interpol, A History and Examination of 70 Years of Crime Solving*. London: Sinclair-Stevenson.

Brittan, Sir Leon (1991), The Newsam Memorial Lecture, The European Single Market; Implications for Policing. Bramshill Staff College November 1991, unpublished document.

Cameron-Waller, S. (1993), 'The Role of Interpol in the Modern World: Global Developments of Interest', *Commonwealth Law Bulletin*, 19/4: 1955–60.

Clarke, M. (1993), 'EEC Fraud: A Suitable Case for Treatment', in F. Pearce and M. Woodiwiss, eds., *Global Crime Connections; Dynamics and Control*. London: Macmillian.

Cohen, S. (1972), *Folk Devils and Moral Panics; The Creation of Mods and Rockers*. Basil Blackwell: Oxford.

Commonwealth Secretariat (1991), Action Against Transnational Criminality. Papers from the 1991 Oxford Conference on International and White Collar Crime.

—— (1992), Action Against Transnational Criminality, Vol. 2. Papers from the 1992 Oxford Conference on International and White Collar Crime.

—— (1993), Action Against Transnational Criminality, Vol. 3. Papers from the 1993 Oxford Conference on International and White Collar Crime.

den Boer, M., and Walker, N. (1993), 'European Policing after 1992', *Journal of Common Market Studies*, 321/1.

Douglas, M. (1987), *How Institutions Think*. London: Routledge and Kegan Paul.

Edwards, S. S. M. (1989), *Policing 'Domestic' Violence*. London: Sage.

Egger, S. (1990), *Serial Murder; An Illusive Phenomenon*. New York: Praeger.

Ericson, R. V., and Carriere, K. D. (1994), 'The Fragmentation of Criminology', in D. Nelken, ed., *The Futures of Criminology*. London: Sage.

Esterow, M. (1967), *The Art Stealers*. London: Weidenfeld and Nicolson.

Fijnaut, Cyrille, ed., (1993), *The Internationalization of Police Co-operation in Western Europe*. Deventer: Kluwer Law and Taxation Publishers.

Fooner, M. (1989), *Interpol; Issues in World Crime and International Criminal Justice*. New York: Plenum Press.

Gallagher, F. (1992), 'Kent County Constabulary – Its European Perspective', *Police Requirements Support Unit, Bulletin* 42.

Garland, D. (1995 forthcoming), 'Penal Modernism and Postmodernism', in T. Blomberg and S. Cohen, eds., *Law Punishment and Social Control*. New York: Aldine de Gruyter.

Giddens, A. (1987), *Social Theory and Modern Sociology*. Cambridge: Polity Press.

Gilmore, W. (1990*a*), *Combating International Drugs Trafficking: The 1988 United Nations Convention Against Illicit Traffic in Narcotic Drugs and Psychotropic Substances* (Explanatory documentation). Commonwealth Secretariat, London.

——— (1990*b*), 'International Action Against Drug Trafficking: Trends in United Kingdom Law and Practice', *The International Lawyer*, 24/2: 365–92.

Gladstone, J., Ericson, R. V., and Shearing, C., eds., (1991), *Criminology: A Readers Guide*. Toronto: Centre for Criminology, University of Toronto.

Graham, J. (1990), *Crime Prevention Strategies in Europe and North America*. Helsinki Institute for Crime Prevention and Control (HEUNI).

Gregory, F., and Collier, A. (1992), 'Frontier Crime and International Crime, Problems, Achievements and Prospects with Reference to European Police Co-operation', in M. Anderson and M. den Boer, eds., *European Police Co-operation; Proceedings of a Seminar*. Department of Politics, University of Edinburgh.

Hemmings, N. (1993), 'The New South Wales Experiment: The Relative Merits of Seeking to Protect the Environment through the Criminal Law by Alternative Means', in *Action Against Transnational Criminality*, Vol. 3. The 1993 Oxford Conference on International and White Collar Crime, Commonwealth Secretariat and the International Bar Association.

House of Commons (1991), 'Session 1990–91 Policing Football Hooliganism', Second Report, vol. I. Report together with the Proceedings of the Committee, London: HMSO.

Interpol (1989), *International Criminal Police Review*, 421, November–December, pp. 25–30.

Jensen, E. (1993), 'International Nazi Cooperation; A Terrorist Oriented Network', in T. Björrgo and R. Witte, eds., *Racist Violence in Europe*. New York: St. Martin's Press.

Jessop, B. (1990), *State Theory: Putting Capitalist States in Their Place*. Cambridge: Polity Press.

Johnston, L. (1992), *The Rebirth of Private Policing*. London: Routledge.

Klockars, C. B., and Mastrofski, S. D. (1991), *Thinking About Police*, 2nd edn. New York: McGraw-Hill.

Malcher, A. (1991), 'The 1990s – The Decade of International Unrest', *Police Journal*, 64/3.

Mantila, A. (1987), *Community Policing – The Opinions of Neighbourhood and District Policemen of their Work*. Helsinki Institute for Crime Prevention and Control (HEUNI).

Martin, J. M., and Romano, A. T. (1992), *Multinational Crime: Terrorism, Espionage, Drug and Arms Trafficking*. Newbury Park, CA: Sage.

McLaughlin, E. (1992), 'The Democratic Deficit: European Union and the Accountability of the British Police', *British Journal of Criminology*, 32/4: 473–88.

Mills, C. W. (1959), *The Sociological Imagination*. New York: Oxford University Press.

Nadelmann, E. (1990), 'The Role of the United States in the International Enforcement of Criminal Law', *Harvard International Law Journal*, 31/1.

——— (1993), 'US Police Activities in Europe', in C. Fijnaut, ed., *The Internationalization of Police Co-operation in Western Europe*, Deventer: Kluwer Law and Taxation Publishers.

Nowikowski, F. (1992), 'Argentina's Lone Animal Protectionist', *Police Journal*, 65/2: 165–70.

O'Keefe, D. (1993), The Schengen Agreements and Community Law. Unpublished paper presented at the European Institute of Public Administration Colloquium, Schengen. A First Assessment After the Opening of the Frontiers, Luxembourg, 14–15 October.

Pasquino, P. (1991), 'Theatrum Politicum: the Genealogy of Capital – Police and the State of Prosperity' in G. Burchell, C. Gordon, and P. Miller, eds., *The Foucault Effect: Studies in Governmentality.* London: Harvester Wheatsheaf.

Pearce, F., and Tombs, S. (1993), 'US Capital versus the Third World: Union Carbide and Bhopal', in F. Pearce and M. Woodiwiss, eds., *Global Crime Connections; Dynamics and Control.* London: MacMillan.

Pearson, G. (1983), *Hooligan: A History of Respectable Fears.* London: MacMillan.

Philip, A. B. (1989), *European Border Controls: Who Needs Them?* London: The Royal Institute of International Affairs.

Police Requirements Support Unit (PRSU) (1992), 'From Morse to Email in a Decade: Communications at Interpol London', *PRSU Bulletin*, 42: 5 – 60.

Pugh, M. (1988), 'The Concept of an International Police Force; Lord Davies and the British Debate in the 1930s', *International Relations*, 9/4: 335–52.

Punch, M., ed. (1993), *Coping with Corruption in a Borderless World.* Deventer: Kluwer Law and Taxation Publishers.

Rajchman, J. (1991), *Philosophical Events; Essays of the 1980s.* New York: Columbia University Press.

Ramsbotham, O. (1991), *Britain, Germany and the New European Security Debate*, Paper No. 1. London: Institute for Public Policy Research Defence and Security.

Razdan, U. (1986), 'Community Participation in Crime Prevention', *Indian Journal of Criminology*, 14/1: 22–8.

Reiner, R. (1985), *The Politics of the Police.* Brighton, Sussex: Harvester Wheatsheaf.

—— (1988), 'British Criminology and the State' in P. Rock, ed., *A History of British Criminology.* Oxford: Clarendon Press.

—— (1992), 'Policing a Postmodern Society', *Modern Law Review*, 55/6: 761–81.

—— (1994), 'Policing and the Police', *The Oxford Handbook of Criminology.* Oxford: OUP.

Renborg, B. A. (1943), *International Drug Control: A Study of International Administration by and through the League of Nations.* Washington, DC: Carnegie Endowment for International Peace.

Robertson, K. (1991), 'Terrorism: Europe Without Borders', *Terrorism*, 14: 105–10.

Rorty, R. (1989), *Contingency, Irony and Solidarity.* Cambridge: CUP.

Scharf, W. (1989), 'Community Policing in South Africa', in T. W. Bennett, ed., *Policing and the Law.* Cape Town: Juta and Co. Ltd.

Shearing, C. D. (1993), 'Policing: Relationships Between Public and Private Forms', in M. Findlay and U. Zvekic, eds., *Alternative Policing Styles.* Deventer: Kluwer Law and Taxation Publishers.

Sheptycki, J. W. E. (1991a), An Investigation into Policing Policy in Relation to Domestic Violence in London England. Unpublished Ph.D. dissertation.

—— (1991b), 'Innovations in the Policing of Domestic Violence', *Policing and Society*, 2: 117–37.

—— (1991c), 'Using the State to Change Society; The Example of Domestic Violence', *Journal of Human Justice*, 3/1: 44–66.

—— (1993), *Innovations in Policing Domestic Violence; Evidence from Metropolitan London.* Aldershot: Avebury.

—— (1994), Review article of F. Bresler's 'Interpol', *British Journal of Criminology*, 34/2: 244–6.

Sklair, L. (1991), *Sociology of the Global System.* London: Harvester Wheatsheaf.

Skolnick, J., and Bayley, D. H. (1988), *Community Policing: Issues and Practices Around the World.* Cambridge, MA: ABT Associates Inc.

Stenning, P. C., and Shearing, C. D. (1980), 'The Quiet Revolution: The Nature, Development and General Legal Implications of Private Policing in Canada', *Criminal Law Quarterly*, 22: 220–48.

Stenson, K. (1993), 'Community Policing as Governmental Technology', *Economy and Society*, 22/3: 373–89.

Streeck, W., and Schmitter, P. C. (1991), 'From National Corporatism to Transnational Pluralism: Organized Interests in the Single European Market', *Politics and Society*, 19: 133–64.

Thompson, E. P. (1963), *The Making of the English Working Class*. Harmondsworth: Penguin.

Tomlinson, M. (1993), 'The Northern Ireland Factor', in T. Bunyan, ed., *Statewatching the New Europe*. London: Statewatch.

Tysoe, S. (1993), 'Corporate Liability for Water Pollution Offences in England and Wales', in *Action Against Transnational Criminality*, Vol. 3. Oxford Conference on International and White Collar Crime, Commonwealth Secretariat and the International Bar Association.

van Duyne, P. C. (1993), Money Laundering in Europe; Estimates in a Fog. RDC Ministry of Justice. Unpublished paper.

van Reenan, P. (1989), 'Policing Europe After 1992: Co-operation and Competition', *European Affairs*, 3/2: 45–53.

Vogler, R. (1991), *Reading the Riot Act; the Magistracy, the Police and the Army in Civil Disorder*. Milton Keynes: Open University Press.

Walker, N. (1993a), 'Accountable Policing; the International Dimension', in R. Reiner and S. Spencer, eds., *Accountable Policing: Effectiveness, Empowerment and Equity*. London: Institute of Public Policy Research.

—— (1993b), 'Calling European Policing to Account', *Edinburgh University Working Paper Series – A System of European Police Co-operation after 1992*. Edinburgh University Department of Politics.

—— (1994), 'European Integration and European Policing: A Complex Relationship', in M. Anderson and M. den Boer, eds., *Policing Across Transnational Boundaries*. London: Pinter.

Walker, S. (1977), *A Critical History of Police Reform*, Lexington, MA: D.C. Heath.

Witte, R. (1993), 'Racist Violence: An Issue on the Political Agenda?', in T. Björrgo and R. Witte, eds., *Racist Violence in Europe*. New York: St. Martin's Press.

Zuboff, S. (1988), *In the Age of the Smart Machine: The Future of Work and Power*. Oxford: Heinemann.

4

The Role of Enforcement of Law in the Establishment of a New International Order: A Proposal for a Transnational Police Force

Robert C. Johansen and Saul H. Mendlovitz

Introduction

The central problem of international relations is the willingness of governments to threaten or use violence to settle disputes. This willingness is unlikely to diminish until nonmilitary means for defending and advancing group interests become more reliable and common. To achieve this requires strengthening nonmilitary norms governing decision-makers' behavior. The strength of such norms depends on internal moral checks, of which there are few in international conduct, and external punishments and rewards. The most familiar and effective external incentive for influencing behavior in all human societies is the enforcement of law or quasi-legal norms. It follows, therefore, that nurturing the development and enforcement of international legal norms – this most maligned subject (often with good reason) among academic analysts and practitioners of international relations – is potentially the most fundamentally transforming element of foreign policy.

Many diplomats, scholars, and social activists remain pessimistic about efforts gradually to replace militarily-backed national self-help with enforcement[1] of international law by officers acting on behalf of a wider world community. At the same time, some useful experience with incipient

---

Source: *Alternatives: Global, Local, Political*, VI(2) (1980): 307–337.

enforcement mechanisms occurs, for example, with international peacekeeping forces, which have occasionally functioned with success,[2] and with the monitoring activities of the International Atomic Energy Agency.

Although skepticism is justifiable about enlarging the functions of a peacekeeping or law-implementing UN force, excessive pessimism diverts attention from exploring how such a force could help rectify functional inadequacies in the global political system. This pessimism about change infects policy-making processes with a negative self-fulfilling quality. Government officials usually recognize this only *after* they have turned the reins of political power over to someone else. As Cyrus Vance warned after resigning as the U.S. Secretary of State, "We must have in our minds a conception of the world we want a decade hence. The 1990 we seek must shape our actions in 1980, or the decisions of 1980 will give us a 1990 we will regret."[3] To help avoid at least some future regrets, a reappraisal of the potential usefulness of global enforcement is essential.

This essay seeks to avoid both the irrelevant legalism symbolized by treaties such as the Kellogg-Briand pact to outlaw war, and the do-nothing "realism" of those who reject the need to offer specific policies aimed at fundamentally altering the practices of international relations. Our purpose is to examine the need for means to supplement national self-help in law enforcement, to explore their possible nature, to explain the contribution of a transnational enforcement agency to the creation of a more just world polity, and to discuss the transition process for creating such an agency. The process of change that we are examining is more political than legal. If successful, this process domesticates international politics and transnationalizes national politics. By reinforcing norms through more effective enforcement of them, the goal is to increase the governability of world society, as well as to increase the governing ability of global organizations.

To consider how to increase security in the 1980's is a much broader task than to consider how to prevent war. An equally important and even more encompassing goal of human security is to eliminate the degradation and oppression which hundreds of millions of people suffer whether they live during periods of war or peace. The discouraging diplomatic record of the past three decades demonstrates that new, more serious efforts to increase security and end the degradation of life for one-third of humanity demands more than politics as usual. The basic structure and functioning of the present international system bears re-examination, because that system cannot adequately prevent collective violence, promote economic equity, assure worldwide justice and human rights, and secure the environment. To put it bluntly, the present system of international relations has built into it a significant probability of irretrievable disaster for the human race. Yet the impediments to realizing preferred values are political rather than technological or material. They can be changed.

Thus one of the most urgent imperatives is to develop a strategy for moving toward a preferred system of world order in which norms defining the human interest[4] become guides to policymaking. The most critical norms are well-known and rhetorically embraced, if not practiced. By increasing the human capacity to enforce specific norms aimed at realizing preferred world order values of peace, economic well-being, social justice, and environmental balance, we can increase the seriousness with which decision-makers will take these values.

With these considerations in mind, the time has come to reconsider the utility of a standing transnational constabulary or police force that can transcend narrowly defined national interests and respond more effectively to the global human interest. To be sure, the word "police" often carries deep negative connotations because in numerous contexts police have enforced an unjust political order. Nonetheless, there is no better term available to describe a person who acts on behalf of public authority to uphold community-established legal norms. The terms "peacekeeping force" describe well an interpositional patrol along an armistice line, but they do not encompass law enforcement where war poses no threat.[5] It is essential in this examination to remind ourselves that a police force can help to establish justice as well as to keep peace.

1. The Need for a Transnational Police Force

A. General Considerations

While a transnational police force would not usher in a golden age, it could, to a significant degree, help meet the need for enhancing the obligatory quality of international norms in each of the four value areas noted above. Nowhere is this need more apparent than in the field of war prevention where a subtle but profound growth of the acceptability of violence is under way.[6]

The Carter and Reagan administrations' overt decision to develop further nuclear capabilities for fighting war with "limited nuclear strikes" will lead to an enormous increase in destructive capability and an erosion of the fragile existing code of conduct against the use of nuclear weapons. The arms race also has been exacerbated by the Soviet willingness to use military force in Afghanistan and the U.S. decision to establish rapid deployment forces. In addition, the past two years have witnessed armed conflict among several socialist societies in Asia and a series of declared and undeclared wars on the African continent. The trend toward violence is further illustrated by the vast increase over the past five years in the sale of arms by the industrialized societies (with roughly 70 percent sold by NATO countries and 27 percent by members of the Warsaw Treaty Organization) and the substantial growth in the number of arms producers.[7]

Although it is true that revolutionaries often use arms in the course of social reform, in the long run it is likely that the sale of sophisticated armaments will aid the repressive, *status quo* forces of the world as much as, if not more than, the bearers of a more just social order. To be sure, dispossessed people in every continent are rightly questioning the legitimacy of past political orders that have not met their needs. As authority erodes, the potential for violence often increases. On the one hand, dissatisfied groups often genuinely feel they have no alternative to using overt violence to combat structural violence to which they have been subjected. On the other hand, repressive governmental tendencies flourish to combat what a dominant group of people see as a threat to their established order. The growth of civil strife provides fertile ground for authoritarian "solutions," whether growing from the right or left, whether from the holders or seekers of political authority. Recurring repression raises the limits for what is acceptable violence and lowers the expectations for what can be done to curtail it.

A transnational police force for these situations as well as others that have occurred in the past could have contributed greatly to alleviating human suffering. For example, the killing and injuring of many innocent people could doubtless have been prevented in the Lebanese civil war in 1976 if a highly trained transnational force could have established a humanitarian corridor in Beirut from which all belligerency was excluded. Similar actions could also have been useful during the Nigerian civil war (1967–70); the conflict, which involved West Pakistan, East Pakistan, and India, leading to the creation of Bangladesh (1971); the chronic violence in Northern Ireland; and the migration of thousands of Kampucheans and their subsequent habitation in areas along the border with Thailand, while under constant threat to their lives (1979–80).

Moreover, a halt to nuclear proliferation and substantial progress in arms reductions cannot be achieved without International Atomic Energy Agency (IAEA) inspection that eventually includes all military as well as civilian nuclear plants and compulsory compliance to universal rules by all states. This can hardly be guaranteed without global enforcement officers.

A transnational police force could also help realize other preferred values of justice, economic well-being, and ecological balance. For example, in the effort to eliminate racist or colonial governments, a UN force to intervene on behalf of racial equality in Namibia or South Africa would be preferable to national intervention. Moreover, in desperate situations, even a humanitarian mission such as food distribution often requires security forces to prevent hoarding by some and inaccessibility by others. Acting on their own behalf, national elites often use grain as a political or military tool against their opponents, as has been alleged by all parties in the Vietnamese-Kampuchean conflict. Among recipients, ethnic quarrels often break out during efforts to alleviate food shortages. Up to now such activities have not required transnational monitoring because assistance has been largely bilateral. But politically divisive uses of world food reserves would be better resisted by multilateral administrative bodies. Transnational inspection and enforcement could provide the monitoring to make major steps toward equity more possible.

Finally, to protect the oceans from ecological decay, tankers flying flags of convenience and multinational consortia of corporations mining deep sea nodules, for example, eventually must be monitored by persons who represent authoritative international decisions.

Advancing toward a preferred world requires moving away from undependable norms, unilaterally interpreted, and enforced only through national self-help. Whether people live in peasant villages or urban skyscrapers, the achievement of a substantially more just life for this planet's people requires movement toward the enforcement of preferred norms on individuals, including heads of governments. The consequences of such a development would produce no permanent state of justice, nor even unmixed social benefits. Nonetheless, the functional and ecological unity of life on Earth means either that some rules will be globally enforced or that human suffering will multiply. The risks of a rationally designed alternative world order, however problematic, are more acceptable than the emerging order shaped by diplomatic drift, official timidity, and reluctance to contemplate fundamental change.

Creating a transnational police force and generating political and moral support for it will nourish the taproot of system change. Such a force would provide an opportunity to begin living a part of the future in the present. When a global police force eventually will be able to monitor national military conduct and enforce laws – whether to guard against clandestine movements of military forces across a border, direct armed attack, racial discrimination, or deployment of weapons of mass destruction – the transformation of human civilization may be comparable in its far-reaching significance to the social metamorphosis that attended the shift from hunting to farming 10,000 years ago.

Even though such a complete transformation obviously is not imminent, focusing on its importance enhances one's understanding of challenges that now press upon us. What proposed innovations could become focal points around which to mobilize support to enhance the reliability of just, global norms? Critical problems, planetary in scope, are now evident in relating population humanely and equitably to the use of food, energy, and non-renewable resources; in handling disposal of persistent, toxic substances; and in decreasing acts of human brutality and collective violence. This essay will focus only on the last of these areas of concern, but the utility of the global enforcement function is present in the other areas as well.

B. Demand for Four Types of Enforcement

Within the limited scope of this essay, the world's population needs transnational enforcement in four different areas. In the first, enforcement can serve (1) to prevent border clashes from breaking into fullscale war, and (2) to discourage third parties from supplying military equipment to the initial belligerents or from participating in competing military coalitions. This most familiar kind of enforcement activity, which will be labeled here Type A enforcement, has in the past been performed by various UN *ad hoc* peacekeeping forces and observation groups. Along the Lebanese-Syrian border in 1958, for example, UN personnel performed unarmed observation where infiltration of arms was suspected, while along the Israeli-Egyptian border from 1956 to 1957, the UN forces carried arms to prevent violations of the armistice lines.

In recent years the likelihood of border incidents turning into open violence has increased. Examples with ominous portents include: Ethiopia-Somalia, Iran-Iraq, China-Soviet Union, Soviet Union-Afghanistan-Pakistan, North Korea-South Korea, Vietnam-Kampuchea, China-Vietnam, Greece-Turkey, Angola-South Africa, Morocco-Algeria, Lebanon-Syria, and Israel and its neighbors.

Humanitarian intervention represents a second category of activity (Type B), the purpose of which is to use transnational enforcement as an opportunity to aid innocent victims caught in the crossfire of war. This type includes providing sanctuary for non-combatants who seek shelter during civil war, and attempting to quell internal conflicts that have genocidal tendencies.

The growth of political repression and brutalization in the treatment of some ethnic minorities, the poor, and political dissidents suggests that the need for Type B action will be quite high within the next decade. Class conflicts, tribal diversity within many African states, and linguistic-cultural diversity in India, Ireland, Lebanon, Iran, Ethiopia, Sudan, and elsewhere illustrate the potential for future civil strife that might involve heavy human costs and foreign participation.

A third need is to restrain officials who resist internal implementation of norms enjoying nearly universal support in the world community (Type C enforcement). Evidence of chronic brutality, torture, or structural violence might be the basis for this kind of enforcement. It could involve sending a force to Namibia to neutralize officials trying to implement apartheid. Systematic torturing of political prisoners can also be considered a crime against humanity and in violation of the Nuremburg precedent. A global enforcement agency eventually could be empowered to gather authoritative evidence of any alleged violations of that precedent to deter local officials from further violations. Enforcement of the Nuremburg principle could be considered in contexts such as the period after the Chilean military junta seized power from Salvador Allende's administration in 1973. Type C action might well emphasize the positive side of law enforcement, the "do's" as well as the "don'ts" in upholding international law.

In the longer run, transnational monitoring and enforcement will also be necessary to implement arms reductions (Type D).[8] Impartially gathered information about all nations' military deployments and transnational patrol of disputed borders are probably prerequisites to reversing the arms buildup.

A readily available transnational police force could enhance many nations' security, especially along disputed or tense borders. Such a force could also raise expectations for nonviolent conflict resolution so that arms, even though present, would become increasingly superfluous for conflict resolution. Eventually, universal prohibitions of some weapons and armed forces could be enforced by police acting on behalf of all countries.

As Table I indicates, a wide range of activities, with substantial impact on the international system, are possible even with the kind of police enforcement that is feasible to carry out in the present and immediate future.

C. National Enforcement, International *ad hoc* Peacekeeping Force, or Permanent Transnational Police Force?

1. National Enforcement. In any of the four areas, national enforcement carries the obvious and crucial drawback of encouraging either counter national intervention or else "one-sided" enforcement. The latter places the weaker side under duress and promotes partisan conflict resolution without recourse to any community procedure for the weaker side to air its grievances against the enforcing agent. National enforcement neither satisfies elemental requirements for just procedures nor stimulates systemic change.

There are some cases in which the need for third party enforcement is so obvious that, in the absence of transnational police, national enforcement action fulfills a similar – although not equivalent – function. The use of national military forces usually lacks the effectiveness and impartiality that a transnational force should possess. Examples of national action include the Syrian army's occupation of Lebanon to enforce a truce on warring Lebanese factions. In addition, Tanzanian military forces ousted an almost universally criticized Uganda dictatorship in 1979, Tanzania received almost no protest over its action against President Idi Amin because he had become an embarrassment to most African governments and Tanzania seemed free of imperial ambitions. Vietnamese efforts to replace the widely criticized Pol Pot government of Cambodia have not met with similar approval, perhaps because of ambiguity about Vietnamese political designs on their weaker neighbor. These national efforts, which are rationalized as attempts to enforce global peacekeeping norms, further illustrate the need for a transnational force.

2. Ad hoc forces. International peacekeeping forces of an *ad hoc* nature obviously can and have carried out some Type A and B enforcement action. Small or non-aligned nations no doubt will continue to perform a valuable function in providing special training in riot control, peace observation, and border patrol for contingents they earmark for UN duty, to be available when requested. Indeed, for additional countries to provide the necessary training, personnel, and equipment for UN peacekeeping forces would be a genuine service to world peace.

Table 1

World order value	Goal of enforcement	Concrete objective	Real or hypothetical illustrative activity	
			With host consent	Without host consent
Peace	Type A: to restrain violence across international borders	1. to prevent border incidents from becoming international war	UNEF in 1956	armed patrol of Israeli–Egyptian border in 1967 even after host consent was withdrawn*
		2. to avert intervention by third-party, national forces	UNOGIL in 1958	armed patrol of Angolan–South African border in 1976*
Peace, human rights	Type B: to conduct humanitarian intervention	1. to provide sanctuary for non-combatants during civil war	ONUC 1960–64	Lebanon 1976*
		2. to curtail civil strife with genocidal tendencies	ONUC	Bangladesh 1971* Thai-Kampuchean border 1978–80* Lebanon 1976–80*
Peace, human rights, ecological balance	Type C: to restrain officials who resist the domestic application of global norms	1. to decrease structural violence in domestic arenas	N.A.	restrain officials implementing apartheid*
		2. to protect victims of political repression or torture	N.A.	prevent torture of political prisoners in Chile in 1974;* restrain Ugandan President Idi Amin's treatment of political opponents and prisoners*
Peace	Type D: to limit national capability for committing collective violence	1. to monitor arms control agreements	the SALT I treaty;* Nuclear Non-Proliferation treaty; Treaty of Tlatelolco*	monitor all borders where infiltration of armed forces is suspected;* monitor missile test firings through an international satellite observation agency*
		2. to enforce arms reduction agreements by: (a) preventing unilateral escalation of the arms race (b) discouraging preemptive war or foreign intervention by one state aimed at stopping a rival from continuing a suspected violation of a process of arms reduction		confiscate equipment or fissionable materials in violation of disarming process*

* Hypothetical examples
N.A. = not applicable

Yet there are ways in which *ad hoc* forces are inadequate for even Type A enforcement. When the second United Nations Emergency Force (UNEF II) was created in 1973, for example, the Security Council required *immediate* placement of the forces in the field. Only because the Secretary-General could transfer some troops from the United Nations Force in Cyprus (UNFICYP) could a force be on the scene within twenty-four hours. Such a procedure could not be depended upon in the future, as there are seldom surplus UN forces available for immediate relocation.

3. Transnational police force. It is even more important for Type B than for Type A action that the peacekeeping forces be seen as agents of the global community rather than as bearers of an alien nationality, simply deputized into international service. Here the force is likely to have substantial involvement with the indigenous population of the host nation. Particularly if the force remains in place without enjoying the continued consent of the host, merely wearing blue arm bands over foreign national uniforms would be a handicap.

A host nation that later terminates its consent for allowing an *ad hoc* UN force to remain in its territory may use bilateral diplomatic channels to persuade the donor states to withdraw their earmarked contingents from the UN force, rendering the latter's continuing operation impossible. Such a chain of events occurred when Egypt requested that UNEF leave Egyptian soil in 1967. Israel had never consented to UN forces being on its territory, and while the Secretary-General groped for a solution, the Indian and Yugoslavian governments informed the UN that their forces could not remain in UN service without Egyptian consent. U Thant withdrew the force. The result was war. This experience with *ad hoc* forces provided two lessons: first, the UN force may need to remain in place without host consent; second, *individuals* directly recruited into a permanent force would be potentially far more reliable than an *ad hoc* group dependent on contributed battalions from member states.

Guidelines for UNEF II suggest that once in place the force cannot be withdrawn without Security Council consent, but whether the force could be relied upon to remain, given the possibility of withdrawal action similar to the Indian-Yugoslavian precedent, is far from certain. In short, although some Type A and B enforcement can be carried out by *ad hoc* forces, such enforcement is severely limited, especially when consent of the host is not present or the force is needed quickly. In addition, for political and psychological reasons, as well as more narrowly military considerations, a permanent, directly recruited police force could handle this type of enforcement more reliably and effectively.

4. Creative diplomacy. The purpose of UN peacekeeping to this point has been not only to prevent or decrease violence between two antagonists, such as Israel and Egypt, but also to isolate the conflict from intervention by outside powers, such as the United States and the Soviet Union. The late Dag Hammarskjold used the terms "preventive diplomacy" to describe the use of an international force to prevent national intervention and counter-intervention in conflicts where the major powers preferred a UN peacekeeping role to intervention by a powerful rival. These forces carried out a primarily prophylactic role. In contrast, Type C and D activities might more aptly be termed "creative diplomacy." In particular, they have a positive aim to create new attitudes, procedures, and structures in order to implement justice and arms reduction, rather than pour water on hot spots. To be sure. Type C and D actions also perform a prophylactic function insofar as they avert future violence, say, between antagonistic ethnic groups within a country (Type C), or discourage aggressive war because of internationally enforced arms reductions (Type D).

Creative diplomacy upholds the positive law; preventive diplomacy puts out brushfire wars. Creative diplomacy seeks to create conditions conducive to justice and peace, and in that regard it may take sides in order to arrest a violator of community-established norms; preventive diplomacy seeks to restore the *status quo ante* or simply to stop the fighting, and in that regard it is no-fault enforcement, paying heed primarily to only one norm – the prohibition against use of armed force across national boundaries. Creative diplomacy recognizes the need to take action against structural violence; preventive diplomacy is concerned only with overt violence.

The need for a permanent police force is even more evident in Type C enforcement than in Type A or B. Type C action can be most successful when it is absolutely clear that the enforcing agents are acting not for a foreign nationality but instead for the world community. The more the police carry the prestige of the world community with them and the less they carry a vestige of an opposing national interest, the greater will be the likelihood for their success. A small force can often have a dramatic impact upon local authorities if it clearly represents a higher, more embracive, rather than merely an equal and opposing authority. This impact was witnessed in the United States when President Eisenhower sent the national guard to integrate the public schools in Little Rock, Arkansas, and again when Attorney-General Robert Kennedy sent a Federal marshal to ask the Governor of Alabama to stand aside and let a young black woman enroll in the state university. Similarly, the mere presence of unarmed UN observers seemed to interrupt the infiltration of arms across the Lebanese border during the UNOGIL operation. The power of moral principle also expresses itself when its agent is a private actor, as Mohandas Gandhi demonstrated with satyagraha against the British. No officer of the world community can, of course, miraculously overturn existing injustices. Many attempts would no doubt fail, at least at first. The U.S. and Indian examples are not fully analogous because they occurred in centralized legal systems. The point is that officials who represent a wider community and act upon prevailing ideas of what is right often wield an authority far in excess of their mere physical strength.

For Type D enforcement a permanent, transnational force seems essential. Arms issues are so sensitive and the arms reduction process likely to be so fraught with obstacles and fears that only inspection and dependable enforcement by genuinely transnational agencies could implement this goal. Indeed, one of the strongest arguments for establishing a police force now is that the process of disarmament in the more distant future will be enhanced by a transnational enforcement agency whose experience and reliability are widely known. Procedures could be well established before the more delicate phases of arms reductions would begin. Transnational enforcement is so vital to this long range process that it is sensible to begin using transnational monitors for *verification* (even without enforcement) of existing arms control agreements. A permanent police force could have been charged with the responsibility for developing means to inspect the SALT I agreement between the United States and Soviet Union and the Treaty of Tlatelolco for a nuclear free zone in Latin America. It could also be asked to monitor a new, equitable non-proliferation regime[9] and the existing ban on atmospheric testing of nuclear weapons.

Finally, the most important argument for creating a permanent, transnational, individually recruited, constabulary force is that in modest yet significant ways, it would encourage a humane transition toward a preferred system of world order. This point will be explored in greater detail following a description of the force itself.

The Nature of a Proposed Transnational Police Force

Concrete discussions of international organizations that do not yet exist usually convey an atmosphere of unreality because of understandable skepticism about governments' willingness to create such organizations. Yet a brief sketch of a global police force is necessary to suggest here the direction that concerned officials and pressure groups may want to move governments.[10] As the negotiations for the law of the sea make clear, it is occasionally true that what seemed irrelevant theorizing and impractical advocacy a decade ago, now has been written into the text of a treaty – compulsory judicial settlement of all disputes arising out of the exploitation of the sea's hard minerals.

A. Size

An initial force of 5,000 persons would provide sufficient personnel to carry out most small missions and provide the immediate forces needed to respond to sudden crises. If additional forces are needed in emergency situations before the police force can be adequately enlarged, the original group could serve as the nucleus and officer core for earmarked contingents contributed by various UN members.

B. Recruitment and Training

The members of the police force should be directly recruited by the UN from among individuals who volunteer. Wide geographic and linguistic representation are essential. No more than 5 percent of any battalion should come from a single national society. Those persons accepted will need to be well-educated, sympathetic to preferred world order values, emotionally mature, and able to speak at least two of the five UN languages. Some would also be fluent in additional, widely-spoken languages such as Arabic, Hindi, and Swahili. The force should be well-paid, with adequate provision for medical care, retirement benefits, and recreational opportunities. Guidelines for all these matters as well as for training should build upon the experience of UNEF and ONUC. Because of its training, discipline, and unique planetary mandate, the proposed transnational force should earn a trustworthy and prestigious reputation.

C. Location

The force could be located in perhaps three or more base camps, so that at least one part of it could be moved quickly to a troublespot anywhere in the world. Such geographic separation would also enable the force to prepare better for action in different climatic, cultural, linguistic, and social contexts. A force located near Latin America, for example, should include many Spanish officers. In Africa, the force would need appropriate equipment for operations in both jungle and desert terrain. Unless performing disaster relief or development functions when not needed for police action, the forces should be located in sparsely populated areas where they would be least likely to interfere with the lives of local inhabitants and least subject to any national interference with their operations. There could be no local restriction of their freedom to move from their base camps to troublespots.

D. Financing

Providing appropriate salaries and fringe benefits, modern equipment, careful training, efficient transportation, and necessary logistical support would be expensive.[11] To establish bases and possibly create an international satellite monitoring agency would raise the cost, as would the use of the force in the field. Nonetheless, the amount required would be less than one percent of present world military expenditures.

Perhaps financing could be obtained through conventional UN budgetary procedures and allotments. A new formula might also be considered. When total costs for the force are determined, they could merely be divided among all the members of the UN on a scale proportional to each national government's portion of total global military expenditures. Each country's quota could be figured over the preceding five-year period to avoid wide fluctuations. This idea has the merit of also encouraging decreases in military expenditures because the "tax" for the transnational force would be directly linked to a national government's expenditures on its own forces. Insofar as such expenditures often exacerbate international tension and violence, it is appropriate that the biggest military spenders should pay the largest share of the cost of a transnational force. In most cases, they also happen to be the most able to pay.

In addition to this financing procedure, an endowment fund could be established to pay for unanticipated costs when the peace force would go into action. Private individuals and organizations could be allowed to contribute to such a fund. Enlightened legislators in some states might pass legislation enabling individuals to divert a portion of their national income tax from national military expenditures to endowment for transnational police enforcement.

E. Control

The proposed procedures for controlling the permanent police force are rooted in but move beyond UN experience with *ad hoc* forces. Of course, nothing in the proposals here would take away any existing UN authority to engage in enforcement action. The Security Council may, under Chapter VII, legally require members to take coercive action against a threat to or breach of the peace. In addition, the Security Council may request less than obligatory enforcement, by merely asking members to volunteer their forces, as was the case for Operations des Nations Unies au Congo (ONUC). Finally, the General Assembly, under the Uniting for Peace Resolution, may recommend that peacekeeping forces be sent into action in cases where the Security Council is unable to discharge its primary responsibility for peacekeeping due to disagreement among the permanent members. All of these possibilities for enforcement would remain, and the standing police force could easily be put at the disposal of either the Council or Assembly under these time-honored procedures.

In addition, the police force should be allowed to go into action under the somewhat more flexible guidelines indicated in Table 2.

A simple idea underlies these suggestions: the more consensus among nations, the more coercive the enforcement may be.[12] The main proposed departure from existing procedure is to allow enforcement action, without host consent, in the absence of unanimity among the permanent members of the Council.[13]

An alternative approach would be to place responsibility for use of the transnational police in the hands of a semi-autonomous, carefully selected body of respected persons, able to commit the force to action and to preside over its command in the field. The group could be selected and guided by policy lines laid down by the Security Council. It is doubtful that the

Table 2

Purpose	Host consent	Decision required
1. Unarmed on-site observation	Yes	request of UN Secretary-General alone
2. Unarmed satellite surveillance	No	2/3 GA vote
3. Type A armed patrol or observation	Yes	2/3 GA vote
4. Type A armed patrol or observation	No	2/3 GA vote, including at least 3/5 of the permanent Members of SC
5. Type B humanitarian intervention	Yes	2/3 GA vote, including at least 3/5 of the Permanent Members of SC
6. Type B humanitarian intervention	No	4/5 GA vote, including at least 4/5 of the Permanent Members of SC
7. Type C enforcement	No	4/5 GA vote, including at least 4/5 of the permanent Members of SC
8. Type D enforcement	No	4/5 GA vote, including at least 4/5 of the Permanent Members of SC

GA = General Assembly
SC = Security Council

Council would be willing to create such a body at the present time, but it could provide a procedural change in which the permanent members might unanimously agree to delegate some of their authority to an agency they create. The latter could then act without being subject to the veto principle. Its least controversial actions could be taken by majority vote; the most controversial ones should doubtless require unanimity.

The creation now of a police force that would build up a tradition of trustworthiness and impartiality could gradually enhance the governability of world society by decreasing nations' presently felt need for a veto power. The permanent members would then more accurately weigh the risks of giving up the veto against the risks of letting the arms buildup and nuclear proliferation continue in the absence of a vetoless, enforceable strategy for disarmament.

Regardless of the precise voting formula adopted for using the police, it seems wise to vest day-to-day command and control in the Secretary-General and a staff committee and officers he or she designates, in consultation with the Military Staff Committee or similar body representing members of the UN.

F. Operations

As the preceding description reveals, the proposed force operates more as police than as an army. Wherever possible, violators of law would be treated as individual persons rather than as states, in order to make enforcement more feasible and to avoid a direct attack on the prestige of an entire national society. The transnational force normally would not seek to conquer or hold territory, nor to overwhelm an entire population. No image of an enemy should guide their actions. Only in establishing humanitarian corridors might territory be held, and then it would be of limited size and for a short duration.

Unlike armies, the police would aim to uphold the law, rather than implement the political objectives of a belligerent. Thus the skills and weapons of policemen are required. In addition, the force should receive preparation, similar to a well-trained national guard, for dealing with riots and disorders such as those resulting from natural disaster or opposition to racial desegregation. Members should be trained to isolate violent individuals or groups, to restore order, to patrol borders, and to protect innocent victims of illegal behavior. This approach seems more realistic in the nuclear age than the UN Charter's emphasis in Chapter 7 on military coercion.

Weaponry should be strictly limited because the purpose is to prevent violence, not escalate it. The police would have at their disposal no weapons of mass destruction. They would no doubt carry small arms and equipment similar to that possessed by many conventional police, civilian militia, and national guard forces, but the goal should be to use the least lethal means possible in upholding the law. Relatively humane pacifying agents, such as rubber bullets, tranquilizers or temporary incapacitators, and tear gas should be relied upon wherever possible. Border monitors presumably would use non-intrusive advanced technology, such as electronic surveillance and satellite observation, to carry out their mandate. They would also require aircraft for transportation and logistical support.

III. The Impact of a Transnational Police Force

A. On the Operations of Enforcement Agencies

A standing police force has several advantages over the *ad hoc* forces that are currently used by the United Nations. A transnational police force can respond to a crisis more quickly because it is always ready to go into action. It can function more effectively because it has an integrated force and command structure. It is more reliable because its members are loyal to the UN rather than to national seats of authority. It would have a helpful tradition of common experience and impartiality that *ad hoc* forces cannot achieve to a similar degree. It could more easily continue operating in the field without host consent. In addition to performing the preventive diplomacy functions associated with past *ad hoc* forces, the proposed police force in some instances could also carry out humanitarian intervention and safeguard the right of self-determination. An impartial use of police during civil strife in Santo Domingo in 1965, for example, could have established a humanitarian corridor for protection of noncombatants, thus removing the justification professed by U.S. officials in sending U.S. marines. Ostensibly sent to protect U.S. civilians in the Dominican Republic, marines in fact were used to influence a local political outcome.

An expanded role for a transnational force raises the question of whether the new enforcement would be fair. The impact of a police force would admittedly not be equal upon all societies. Those with border conflicts might receive the services of the police in a way that those without them would not. Racist regimes would feel more threatened than groups pressing for racial equality. Even more troublesome, the great military powers would seem immune to some kinds of enforcement. However, because the transnational force is designed to function as police rather than as soldiers, different levels of military power among states would not produce the differential in enforcement that would attend the deployment of a transnational conventional military force. The police could not function against a determined, aggressive army, whether fielded by a great or a medium power. In the limited areas in which the police force would operate, it would be more likely to help protect those victimized by regionally or globally dominant states which abuse their power than to benefit the great powers who presently need no transnational police to protect their dubious privileges. In addition, the proposed border patrols and aerial monitoring would actually help redress some present inequities favoring the superpowers. The latter now conduct regular satellite photography of much of the rest of the world, but their collected data is denied to all other countries. A global agency would provide unbiased information to the world as a whole. Moreover, if transnational police observation of borders would have any political impact at all, it almost always would serve to deter the strong from tempting military adventures and thereby to give some additional protection to the weak. Such a force could help establish a principle that great powers have no justification for sending their military forces into any nonaligned country, even if seemingly invited, as claimed by the United States and Soviet Union respectively, in Vietnam and Afghanistan.

At worst the transnational force would be inactive in its early years, and therefore would not affect the events that would have occurred in its absence. At best it would help protect the militarily weak against the militarily strong in areas outside the latter's vital interests. No less important, the presence of transnational police would also enable the world community to narrow the scope of the "vital interests" that officials of great powers traditionally used to justify military intervention. If global police officers made most societies more resistant to infiltration of arms and covert action by a regional or superpower rival, then there would be less perceived "need" and virtually no believable rationale for any great power to mount counter-interventionary activity.

Moreover, small powers would not need to overarm to resist regional rivals, for regionally hegemonic states would be less capable of military expansion. In case of aggression, the international foundation would have been laid to take multilateral sanctions against the aggressor if previously present transnational monitors provided accurate information about military attack.

In the early years of the police's experience, it is at least conceivable that Type C enforcement to protect the rights, say, of political dissidents might be as effective against a superpower as against a small state because the power of enforcement would come largely from the public embarrassment that would accompany transnational monitors' reports about repression, indigenous dissidents' requests for global police protection, and national governmental resistance to allowing the presence of transnational police officers.

An equally serious problem of selective enforcement would be the differential that might arise between enforcement in societies, on the one hand, that have freedom of the press and ease of movement into and within them, and those societies, on the other hand, that have strictly controlled journalism and restrictive travel policies for potential visitors and their own citizens. Regardless of cause, enforcement admittedly would penetrate some national sovereignties more than others. Yet it remains true that uneven enforcement – except for Type D where it could not be allowed – is preferable to no enforcement.

The highest good is not to treat all national *governments* equally, but to help realize preferred values for the *people* of the world. More people will benefit with transnational enforcement, even if unevenly carried out, than will benefit from the continued absence of such enforcement – an absence that would be dictated by the idea that enforcement should not begin until all states support the idea of global police on equivalent terms. The greater a government official's intention to adhere strictly to globally established norms, the stronger will be his or her endorsement of a transnational police force.

B. On Attitudes and Behavior

The creation of a universal force would offer a new focal point for developing transnational legitimacy and attract new patterns of human loyalty. As the members of the police force transcend their strict national identities, the legitimizing process will proceed. This in turn would lead to changed behavior in national societies. Diplomats arranging peace settlements would start depending more on the availability of the global police, as has already occurred to some extent with *ad hoc* forces in the Middle East. What would have been the effect of transnational police in Vietnam between 1954–65, in place of the International Control Commission? Might elections have been held as prescribed in the Geneva Accords of 1954?

The existence of a transnational police force would have a profound impact on peoples' consciousness. The type of change this force could promote is similar in its fundamental consequences to the historical attitudinal shift which occurred when people stopped asking "Who should be the king?" and instead began asking "Should we have a king?" A transnational police force will encourage more people to begin asking, "What should be the function of military power in international affairs?" "Should we have national military forces?" Students of attitudinal change report that patterns of loyalty are transferred when new agencies start delivering services one needs or wants. Some day youth may feel that to be a transnational police officer is a calling at least as noble as to become a pilot in a national air force.

C. On the Global Political System

A standing police force would gain experience to facilitate a gradual expansion of its functions in the global political system. The idea would grow among governments and the general public that the transnational officers perform duties that sovereign states should support and respect.

Existing elitist regimes would begin – even if reluctantly – to be more responsive to their citizens' grievances because such regimes could no longer easily justify repression for security reasons and because Type C enforcement might otherwise come into play. Also, because of a general decline in the role of military organizations, there would be less capacity for political repression and more likelihood of popular governments. If humanitarian corridors protected civilians, they might become bolder. Some domestic conflicts might be pressed more vigorously, in order to get international attention. But such pressures will come from those who believe that they enjoy the support of the international community and that nonviolent, police enforcement will advance their cause. This is more likely to advance justice in the long run than the present configuration of military power. Of course, the prospect exists now of dissidents using violence to get the UN's attention, but without much prospect for international enforcement to minimize violence during radical change. Other, potentially lethal conflicts occasionally will remain non-lethal because one actor may wish to avoid the possibility of intervention by transnational police. Creative diplomacy, which requires transnational police, holds some promise for the dispossessed because it would begin dealing with forms of structural violence which now victimize the weak and poor.

If only the less industrialized nations would benefit from creative diplomacy, its political feasibility would be low indeed. There also would be some benefits for the industrial countries as well. To be sure, they will suffer some short-range costs, primarily economic in nature, during the movement toward a more just world polity, but a short-run compensation would be to have a transnational law enforcement agency presiding over the process of even painful change rather than to face interventions by competing industrialized powers. A second compensation would be the knowledge that a potentially useful force was being established in conjunction with the growth of transnational law. Both would help stabilize and regularize the processes of world politics in the future.

If a transnational force were used to monitor existing military deployments and eventually to enforce arms agreements – activities which now usually involve only the superpowers – it would enhance the influence and participation of the rest of the world in reversing the arms buildup. This would advance equitable political participation and stimulate arms reductions.

In addition to monitoring existing arms agreements, a standing force could police nuclear free zones that would be gradually expanded to encompass ever larger segments of the globe. There would be uniform inspection around the world, so states could be assured that there were no nuclear forces in rival territories.

Once the proposed police force was established and proven to be somewhat effective, it would produce far-reaching ramifications throughout the global political system. For example, the governments that are leaders of military coalitions would gradually lose influence over subordinates in the coalition as security began to depend less on alliance structures. Concomitantly, internal military elites would be weakened as security depended less on national military power. The politically weak states would be relatively empowered because of decreased dependency on equipment-producing states and alliance leaders.

The diminished importance of weapons would probably produce smaller military budgets and decreased political influence by military and military-dependent corporate officials within domestic political processes. As transnational monitoring increased, the perceived need for secret intelligence gathering and covert operations would decline. Governments could not so easily claim that rivals were upsetting other governments through military means. Middle-range powers would require fewer weapons because they could call quickly for transnational patrols on their borders if a rival mobilized. The arms trade would thus decrease, which would dampen arms buildups in many regional contexts.

IV. The Transition Process

A strategy for establishing a transnational police force should consider issues of general constituency mobilization, UN enforcement operations, control procedures, and the relevant norms for enforcement. It is useful for analytic purposes to consider the roles of three different sets of people and organizations.

The first group consists of national policymakers, their domestic supporters, and the nation-state system as a whole. The second group includes the United Nations, inter-governmental organizations associated with it, and regional international organizations. The third group is made up of common people acting as individuals and through private organizations. Each group can be viewed as a system or subsystem operating within the overall context of world politics.[14]

The strategy most likely to be effective is for people in the third system to take initiatives to create institutions of the second system to increase the obligatory quality of norms applicable to the first system. The reason that progress has been slow is that the third system has difficulty influencing the second system except by acting through the first system. The latters' dominant members (the great powers) seldom support measures for positive transformation of the international system. Moreover, the third system also is often not enthusiastic about nurturing authority and power in the second system. Progress may now be somewhat more likely because people recognize the first system can no longer provide security, regulate the world economy, protect the environment, insure a dependable supply of resources, or guard against national denials of human rights. In the 1980's there will be more pressures against first system inertia than ever before.

A transnational enforcement agency can be established only if it enjoys at least limited support among all three systems. The strategy proposed here is to increase the leverage of people in the third system by using institutions within the second system to encourage powerful actors in the first system to give greater weight in decision-making to *long-range* self-interest. This orientation is more compatible with creating a life of dignity than present short-range interests defined in terms of accumulating national wealth and power. In some cases a natural alliance of political forces may spring up between third system people who live in the First World and first system actors in progressive Third World governments. Both groups have serious grievances against maintaining existing first-system dominance in global decision-making.

A. Mobilization

The key to political success will be to involve change agents from throughout the globe. Supporters might range from student associations to trade unions, from liberation movements and counter-elites to sympathizers within existing elites, from women's groups to civil rights organizations. The first focus could be upon national policy-making elites, scientists and intellectuals, and people drawn from churches and other religious communities, but many others must be involved as soon as possible. The following suggestions are not intended as a blueprint for action but as illustrations to stimulate others to think about a variety of possible efforts for mobilization.

Year 1. Establish a global committee of moral, intellectual, and spiritual leaders, chosen from among all of the world's religious faiths, to promote the idea of transnational police enforcement as one vehicle for moving closer to a social order inspired by universal compassion for all human beings.

- Establish similar transnational committees of scientists, writers, lawyers, students and groups presently involved in social change.
- Encourage teachers to conduct research and teaching with a central focus on transnational enforcement of law.

Year 2. Publish a list of states formally committed to establishing a transnational police force. Leadership groups formed earlier could mobilize local support around the effort to press their respective national governments to join the list of supporters.

- Create a transnational group designed to offer moral and material support to individuals who attempt to transfer a portion of their personal income taxes from use for national military purposes to an endowment for a transnational force. Such tax transferring would, in most instances, be acts of civil disobedience. Local chapters of tax transfer groups would also lobby national governments to legalize the transfer of tax from national military use to transnational police work.
- Encourage tourists to refrain from travel to any countries not endorsing the proposed police. Consumers could boycott the goods exported from non-signatories of a call for a global enforcement agency.

Year 3. Convene a UN Special Session on world security and enforcement of just law to consider establishing a standing police force. This would provide an arena in which all major issues could be debated and a focal point around which the groups created earlier could mobilize support. Non-governmental groups with an interest in transnational police enforcement should be encouraged to play an active role in the session. Certainly experienced police officers from national societies should be at least as well represented as officials of national armed forces.

B. UN Enforcement Operations

Selected examples from past UN experience illustrate some progressive development in the effort to provide international – as distinct from national or transnational – enforcement.

> 1947 – Establishment of a UN peace observation team in the Balkans (UNSCOB).
> 1949 – Establishment of a UN force for cease-fire supervision in Indonesia.
> 1956 – Establishment of a UN force for cease-fire supervision and interposition between the belligerents, with the force remaining in place only for the duration of host consent (UNEF).
> 1960 – Establishment of a UN force for enforcement of internal law and order, as well as interposition between antagonists in civil war (ONUC).
> 1973 – Establishment of a UN force for cease-fire supervision and interposition functions, with the force remaining in place until the Security Council agrees to its withdrawal (UNEF II).

The following sketch of hypothetical developments illustrates how an effectively functioning police force could develop:

- The Security Council might approve the principle that the presence of *any* UN force cannot be terminated without Security Council consent, as is apparently now true in the single case of UNEF II. The Council might also endorse the principle that a decision to withdraw a UN force once in place should not be subject to a veto, thus establishing a precedent for some vetoless voting procedures. This could be done by agreeing in advance that such a vote would be considered a procedural matter, requiring a simple majority, or that certain actions could be taken by a two-thirds Council vote including, say, three-fifths of the permanent Members. If such a procedure could be agreed upon, it later could be extended to the decision to place the police in the field. This more flexible voting procedure would be helpful but not at first required, as Table 2 indicates.

- Sympathetic governments could carry out intense diplomatic and educational activity to gain official support for the proposed police force. These Political initiatives doubtless will come from the smaller powers who have been most supportive of UN *ad hoc* peacekeeping forces.
- After several years of successful educational and diplomatic efforts, recruitment and training of the force could begin.
- Some personnel in UNFICYP and UNEF could be gradually replaced with members of the new police force.
- The Security Council or General Assembly could begin to establish guidelines for Type B enforcement without host consent.
- A humanitarian corridor might be maintained with the consent of the host state, during a civil war (Type B enforcement).
- Guidelines could next be established for Type C enforcement, perhaps later to be carried out in Namibia, if independence from South Africa had not already been achieved.
- After about five years of successful operation, the Council might approve the police taking custody of the Holy Places in Jerusalem, making at least portions of the city immune to control by the police or military forces of any national government.
- Type C enforcement might be considered to prevent architects of apartheid from impeding the movement toward majority government in South Africa.
- A humanitarian corridor might next be established during a civil war, even in the absence of consent from the host state.
- Later on, the UN might request police officers to enforce arms control agreements voluntarily ratified, but from which no state may withdraw without Security Council approval. Still later the transnational force might help implement arms reduction agreements on one or several states which have not adhered to an arms agreement that all other states of the world have ratified.
- The police also could enforce restrictions on the transfer of conventional arms. In the more distant future, the police force would enforce a multilaterally-negotiated, universally-applicable, compulsory procedure for dismantling national armed forces.

C. Authoritative Control Procedures

A crude picture of the desirable changes in control has already been out-lined in Table 2. At first, very little enforcement would occur without nearly unanimous consent. Later, as the police force gained experience and political support, its functions could move from Type A and B action to Type C and D.

D. Norms

The content of a new code of conduct for nations, which can enhance the prospects for peace and justice, is inspired by the values of people in what we have called the third system, and, to a much lesser extent, of the ideals underlying the second system. The old principles of international law, of course, are derived from the traditional preferences of the dominant actors of the first system. The basis for synthesis is to emphasize the convergence, in the long run, between what is ethically desirable and what is politically prudent, between the global human interest and the long-range interest of national societies.

Any effort at enforcement, even in domestic contexts, encounters fre-quent disputes about which legal norms should be enforced and how they should be interpreted. Third party interpretation and application of rules is almost always preferable to one party's – the stronger party's – enforcement of norms on the other party to a dispute. The latter condition, of course, illustrates both the central problem of international relations today and the virtue of a transnational enforcement agency. Such an agency discourages parties to a dispute from judging their own case by providing third party observation and regulation of deviant behavior.

At the beginning, the police could uphold only those laws enjoying nearly universal support in a relatively uncontroversial context. As new rules even-tually are developed to avert nuclear proliferation, to prevent reckless dis-posal of radioactive wastes or oil tanker ballast, to establish compulsory taxing authority to increase economic equity, to curtail covert intelligence operations, to restrict the transfer of conventional arms, and to enforce a uni-versal disarming process, the role of global police officers will increase. Their utility will be more obvious, and their previous experience will make the world community more willing to rely on global enforcement to apprehend those persons violating the new code of conduct that must eventually be practiced to protect the world's ecosystem and people from the instruments of violence and exploitation.

E. Synergistic Effects

Each of the above dimensions of the transition process is intertwined with the others. As educational and diplomatic efforts proceed, the small, proposed force can be created and undertake its first operations. Once it has proven its usefulness, and support widens, more flexible procedures can authorize its use. At the same time, the pressure of activists and the growing functional unity of the planet will bring new legal norms into being.

One additional impetus to the development of a public transnational police force could be the organization of a *private* transnational peacemaking force. Such a force might exert a substantial influence on the global political process. Its potential is explored in Appendix A.

F. Conclusion

Despite the lack of enthusiasm for the idea by many governments in the past, the creation of a modest transnational police force could become feasible in the near future if medium and small powers initiated a campaign toward that end. Certainly the inadequacies of enforcement through national self-help or *ad hoc* international forces will become increasingly clear and damaging to the interests of many states, including the superpowers, in the future.

The use of a world police force presents many difficulties, but even occasional uses of it in the 1980s will help create a more humane 1990s. A police force can provide rewards and punishments to increase – to a modest yet promising degree – compliance with international laws aimed at enhancing justice and peace. It can help reduce the use of military power and dampen the fires upon which arms buildups feed. Perhaps more important a global police force can increase justice by strengthening the weak and discouraging the strong from yielding to the temptation to intervene outside their territories and to ignore callously the norms of justice and fair play.

Global norms will increasingly affect our lives whether we like them or not, whether we plan for their impact or not. For example, pollution of the atmosphere or oceans by one state eventually affects all. Inflation in any large national economy damages the economic health of an entire region and, possibly, of the world economy. The use of nuclear weapons by one or two combatants increases radiation for people everywhere. Simply the manufacture of nuclear bombs, because of environmental side effects, affects even future generations. The question is not whether global norms will have growing impact on our lives, but whether the future practices of nations will be based on preferred values instead of ugly outgrowths of the most powerful and selfish political and economic forces of our day. The question is: will the norms of an emerging global civilization be defined and enforced by what the strongest governments and corporations and the most ruthless and desperate political factions can get away with, or will the code of conduct be implemented by officers acting on the basis of community–established procedures developed in pursuit of the global human interest?

At a time when there are so few initiatives that seem both feasible and likely to promote the transformation of a functionally deficient international system, a carefully established transnational police force looks like an attractive political goal for which to strive.

Appendix: The Need for a Private Enforcement Agency

A predecessor and later a supplement to a public transnational police force could be a somewhat similar group, but one that would be privately financed, recruited, and trained. Such a private group could be created by establishing a board of perhaps twenty persons, each with a reputation for fairness, compassion, and world-mindedness. This board of directors should include women and men from diverse races, systems of beliefs, and locales. They could establish the guidelines for recruiting and training persons in the force. In addition, they would decide how and where to use it.

Once again, the principle should be followed that the greater the consensus on the board, the more firmly the peacemaking force might act. For example, by majority vote an unarmed observation group could be sent to South Africa during a strike or political protest, whereas at least a three-fourths vote of the directors should be required to send a large number of persons to South Africa to engage in civil disobedience as a way of bringing pressure to bear upon the white government to end apartheid.

A private group would have the obvious virtue of being able to establish itself and to begin operations without waiting for national governments to support it. Within a few years, if people of goodwill around the world would pool their resources, there could be created a small force of well-educated, multilingual, disciplined people skilled at mediation, peace observation, and nonviolent direct action for the purpose of upholding international norms already enjoying wide consensus. In addition to action taken as a result of its own initiatives, the force might also be used for disaster relief, for helping carry out projects of groups such as Church World Service, or for responding quickly to crises upon special request by the UN. These activities might help pay some of the force's expenses, prevent the boredom of idleness, and provide experience that would build the *esprit de corps* necessary for effective functioning in the field.

In addition to carrying out functions that would have genuine humanitarian value in themselves, the creation of a private agency would encourage global system change. Even if this force engaged in only a few operations each year, its very presence would doubtless exert a small but nonetheless significant humanizing influence upon national behavior, an influence responsive to the expression of the human interest in peace and justice. Insofar as some governments might fear the attention such a force would bring to normatively deficient governmental behavior (such as apartheid or torture of political prisoners), those governments might modify their policies. Moreover, the presence of such a *private* force might make some governments more likely to support a *public* police force – which would be under government control through the United Nations – in order to render action by a privately administered force unnecessary. In any case, if such a force were created and proved to be effective, it would doubtless be imitated by the UN.

Perhaps the most, important contribution of the private constabulary function to the transition process toward a transformed international system would be determined by the reputation and selection of directors of the peacemaking force. In the long run, the private enforcement agency should, through accretion, take on more and more elements of legitimacy so that it would become a quasi-public agency and eventually carry the authority of a genuinely public group serving the commonweal. To bring about this transformation, it is imperative that the private group limit its actions to enforcing norms that clearly enjoy widespread community support. In addition, the public figures that govern the force should enjoy some popular following, but without the indebtedness to the vested interests of the *status quo* so often reflected in the actions of legislative and executive officials in present political structures. In countries of the world where democratic processes and the press may function freely, the members might be elected. In other areas, the board may select its own members. Groups such as the Gandhi Peace Foundation, the World Council of Churches, the Papacy, and similar organizations might nominate people of moral authority. Part of the board might be drawn from among former members of the International Court of Justice. At least in the beginning, no directors should simultaneously hold positions in the executive or legislative branches of national governments or the boards of directors of large corporations. Such institutions represent concentrations of power too closely associated with existing geo-political structures.

A further legitimizing feature of the private peacemaking force would be its strict adherence to nonviolence. What the force lacked in authority because it was not a public institution, it would gain by openly approaching tasks without any means to inflict physical violence upon others. Its deliberate vulnerability would communicate the principle that it would rather postpone success in its immediate mission than inflict violence upon others. Similarly, it would in action be acknowledging that it could succeed in accomplishing its objective only if it enjoyed widespread support for its goals. Moral authority would have to take the place of more conventional public authority that grows from a monopoly on the right to use force.

Another important consequence of such a private peacemaking force would be to focus increased public attention upon global human interests and less upon national interests. In a world where competing national interests dominate most people's consciousness, it should not be surprising that a *private* group, inspired by universal values, could express the common interest of all humanity better than most existing *public* institutions, motivated by partisan desires to accumulate power and wealth.

If the force were well trained, highly motivated, strictly nonviolent, and limited to relatively unambiguous acts in defense of human rights, it could speed the process of mobilizing support for a public, transnational police force.

Notes

1. In this essay we follow conventional usage of the term "enforcement." It means carefully prescribed action by public officers to prevent illegal behavior and uphold law. This use departs from the technical use of enforcement in Chapter VII of the UN Charter. There the term is reserved for a Security Council decision that legally binds members to take sanctions against a designated state.
2. The utility of several different *ad hoc* peacekeeping forces is beyond dispute. It is fairly clear, for example, that the partial withdrawal of Israeli troops from the banks of the Suez Canal in 1973 was made possible because U.N. peacekeeping forces were available.
3. Excerpt from his Harvard Commencement address, quoted in the *New York Times*, June 8, 1980.

4. The concept of the human interest is elaborated in Robert C. Johansen, *The National Interest and the Human Interest: An Analysis of U.S. Foreign Policy* (Princeton: Princeton University Press, 1980), pp. 19–34, 391–93.

5. "Constabulary force" seems more acceptable but is also more antiquated and cumbersome.

6. This trend and violence-prone structures of dominance are described in Yoshikazu Sakamoto and Richard A. Falk, "World Demilitarized: A Basic Human Need," *Alternatives VI*, 1, pp. 1–16.

7. See, for example, Stockholm International Peace Research Institute, *Armaments or Disarmament? The Crucial Choice* (Stockholm: SIPR1, 1979), p. 9.

8. For a comprehensive discussion of the need for an alternative security system to reverse the arms buildup and enhance human security, see Robert C. Johansen, *Toward a Dependable Peace: A Proposal for An Appropriate Security System* (New York: Institute for World Order, 1978).

9. The present Non-Proliferation Treaty is inequitable in seeking to place responsibility for the most serious nuclear dangers on those states who do not have weapons rather than those who Possess them. It seeks to prevent horizontal proliferation of weapons to additional countries without halting vertical proliferation of weapons in continuously growing stockpiles of nuclear weapon countries. For elaboration of these arguments see *Denuclearization for a Just World: The Failure of Non-Proliferation*, Declaration prepared by a group of concerned scholars at the Lisbon Conference of the World Order Models Project, 13–20 July 1980, *Alternatives VI*, 3, 1980. See also Robert C. Johansen, "The Proliferation of Nuclear Weapons and the Non-Proliferation Treaty," Position Paper for the World Order Models Project, Lisbon Conference, 1980, mimeographed (20 pages); and "Non-Progress in Non-Proliferation," *Sojourners*, September 1980, pp. 3–5.

10. Persons interested in more detailed discussions of the possible nature of transnational forces should see Lincoln Bloomfield, *International Military Forces* (New York: Little, Brown, 1964); Derek Bowett, *United Nations Forces* (New York: Praeger, 1964): Grenville Clark and Louis Sohn, *World Peace Through World Law* (Cambridge, MA: Harvard University Press, 1962); William R. Frye, *A United Nations Peace Force* (New York: Oceana Publications, 1957); Arthur Waskow, *Quis Custodiet? Controlling the Police in a Disarmed World* (Washington, D.C.: Peace Research Institute, 1963); Arthur I. Waskow, *Toward a Peacemakers Academy* (The Hague: Dr. W. Junk Publishers, 1967).

11. In 1957, William R. Frye (fn. 10) estimated that the annual operating cost of a 7,000 person force would be $ 25 million when it was not in action.

12. Arthur I. Waskow discusses this principle in *Toward A Peacemakers Academy* (fn. 10) and in *Quis Custodiet?* (fn. 10).

13. These proposals do not discuss the possibility that the category of permanent members may at some point include Japan, India, Brazil, Nigeria or others. Such changes would not affect the suggestions made here for control.

14. This analytic framework is taken from Richard Falk, "Normative Initiatives and Demilitarization: A Third System Perspective" (pp. 339–356 of this issue).

5

Transnational Policing: The Globalization Thesis, a Typology and a Research Agenda

Ben Bowling

Introduction

The idea that contemporary policing requires collaboration across international boundaries has become accepted as a fact. Transnational policing is most frequently cited as a solution to organized crime. For example, in the pages of this journal last year, Block (2008, p. 74) argued that 'contrary to a few decades ago', today's organized crime involves activity in more than one country and therefore, to tackle it successfully, 'police need to seek cooperation partners across borders to share intelligence, coordinate operations, secure evidence, and track down suspects' (2008, p. 74). A similar argument has been made about the changing character of terrorism: it has become more transnational in scope, involves complex global conspiracies and therefore, the answer lies in transnational police cooperation.

Seeing the growth of transnational policing simply as a functional solution to transnational organized crime and terrorism is flawed on two grounds. First, neither organized crime nor terrorism was ever constrained by national boundaries. The prohibition of alcohol in 1920s' USA, for example, was very much a transnational matter with the authorities contending with smuggling from Canada, Mexico, Europe and the Caribbean. Human trafficking – known then as the 'white slave' trade – and other forms of transnational organized crime were the key issues that stimulated the creation of Interpol in 1923,

Source: *Policing: A Journal of Policy and Practice,* 3(2) (2009): 149–160.

and have concerned police officials ever since. Political violence has also been transnational in character historically. Public concern about 'international anarchist terrorism' in the late 19th century provided a great stimulus for international police cooperation (Bach Jensen, 2001). Second, and more importantly for the purposes of this paper, fusing transnational police cooperation with organized crime limits our understanding of the ways in which globalization is affecting the form and function of contemporary policing.

Research in this area has developed gradually over the past two decades. Malcolm Anderson's *Policing the World* (1989) and *Policing the European Union* (1995) described the formal structures and politics of international law enforcement cooperation and prised open the 'Pandora's box of issues and problems' created by cross-border criminal investigations (Anderson *et al.*, 1995, p. 2). Anderson concluded that 'a gradual transfer of internal and external security control is taking place from the nation state to international institutions' (1995, p. 179). In the USA, Ethan Nadelmann examined international police organizations, cooperative mechanisms, regional police conferences and dozens of multi-lateral law enforcement arrangements 'intended to help law enforcement agencies reduce, transcend or circumvent frictions generated by conflicting sovereignties, political tensions and differences among law enforcement systems' (Nadelmann, 1993, p. 10). He noted that the USA was uniquely aggressive in promoting its own criminal justice norms in the transnational arena, expanding the scope of criminal law, methods of enforcement (e.g. electronic surveillance, informers, undercover policing and 'controlled deliveries'), the scope of criminal procedure (e.g. asset forfeiture, extradition and maritime law enforcement) and leading the way in extra-territorial policing practices.[1]

Following these pioneers, there have been numerous studies of various aspects of transnational policing including Gregory (1996) on United Nations' policing, Sheptycki (1995, 1998a, 2002a) on police cooperation in the English Channel region, Bigo (2000) on European liaison officers and Bowling (2005) on policing the Caribbean. A number of recent edited collections have contributed to opening up the field still further (Sheptycki, 2000; Goldsmith and Sheptycki, 2007; Brown, 2008). Nonetheless, the pace of change has been so rapid that practice on the ground is running way ahead of the research, law and policy that might guide it. The aim of this paper is to delineate the dimensions of transnational policing practices and sketch out an agenda for descriptive, explanatory and normative research.

The Globalization Thesis: Implications for Policing

Although police researchers have focused extensively on international police cooperation as a response to organized crime and terrorism, the 'great globalization debate' (Held and McGrew, 2003, pp. 1–50) suggests the need to think much more broadly about the impact of globalization on policing practice. For Held and McGrew, globalization embodies a transformation in the spatial organization of social relations and transactions in ways in which distant localities are linked. Local happenings are shaped by events occurring many miles away and vice versa. Because transnational networks have become more extensive, intensive and faster flowing, global forces are having a greater local impact. Globalization researchers have noted the emergence of an integrated world economy, leaps forward in transport and telecommunications technologies and numerous other dimensions of global interconnectedness. These have led to the globalization of insecurity in its broadest sense prompting many other changes relevant to understanding contemporary policing.

Driven by technological innovation, political change and economic policy choices, product, capital and labour markets are integrating and world trade is increasing.[2] The total volume of merchandize traded around the world increased four-fold between 1995 and 2007 and the global market in commercial services increased six-fold in the same period.[3] It is impossible to estimate accurately the effect that these changes have had on crime, but we need only assume that the *proportion* of world trade in illicit merchandize and services has remained constant to conclude that transnational crime has grown. On that assumption, increases in legal markets will be accompanied by increased global flows of illicit agricultural and manufactured products (e.g. counterfeit medicines, narcotics and psychotropic drugs), professional and commercial services (e.g. sex work and money laundering) and of the people buying and selling them. Neoliberal policies such as market deregulation and the removal of border controls seem likely to increase the illicit flows in a globally connected marketplace.

The people of the world are increasingly on the move. The number of British residents travelling overseas increased from under 30 million in 1987 to over 70 million in 2007 and the number of visitor arrivals from 15 to 30 million.[4] This reflects a worldwide growth of 60% in worldwide air travel between 1995 and 2007.[5] The increase in world travel for business, the growth in tourism and the emergence of expatriate and diaspora communities create new issues for policing, not all of which are concerned with transnational organized crime. It is probable that the number of 'ordinary crimes' involving foreign nationals in countries around the world has grown simply because the number of foreign residents and visitors has increased and because of the growing ease, speed and frequency of international travel. We can also anticipate a growth in the 'service' role of the police in investigating reports of people missing overseas and repatriating the remains of nationals dying abroad. One of the most significant examples of transnational police cooperation so far in this century had nothing to do with organized crime or terrorism. Responding to the Tsunami of December 2004 involved cooperation among 3,000 officers drawn from police forces across the affected region and beyond.[6] The British police service alone sent more than 700 staff from 40 police forces to assist with the relief effort and to help identify the bodies of those killed in the disaster.

The capacity to communicate around the world has radically increased through personal computers and mobile telephony. The number of Internet users rose four-fold between 2000 and 2008 to 6.7 billion.[7] There were four billion mobile phones in use worldwide in 2008, up from 2.7 billion in 2006.[8] Again, it seems obvious that growing global interconnectedness through telecommunications creates new opportunities for illegality and facilitates criminal collaborations. But it also opens up new possibilities for 'horizontal' communication and collaboration among police officers in the field. This has the effect of reducing bureaucratic drag and political control.

It is almost impossible to verify the claim that transnational organized crime is a growing threat, but it is beyond doubt that policing is transnationalizing. The natural assumption is that the former is causing the latter: increasingly global criminal activity leads organically to a growth in transnational policing (Sheptycki, 1995, 2007a). However, it is also evident that police and governments are actively *driving* the globalization of policing. Although the manifest justification for this development is the problem of transnational organized crime and terrorism, there are other less conspicuous drivers. Globalization theorists contend that interconnectedness is causing a reconfiguration of the state as governments attempt to manage the contradictions emerging when national boundaries no longer constrain the human activity within its borders. Faced with the realization that many of the issues facing national governments – economic restructuring, climate change, population growth, global migration – are not within their power to control, structures and processes of governance are changing in ways unrelated to changing patterns of crime.

National governments are adapting their organisational configuration and working practices in response to the emergence of supranational governance structures. The World Trade Organisation, World Bank and International Monetary Fund are shaping the future of global economic governance including in such fields as money laundering and corruption. Political structures 'above government' (such as the European Union or United Nations) are playing a significant role in shaping the environment within which policing takes place (Sheptycki, 1998b,c, 2000; Loader, 2000). While the 'third pillar' of justice and home affairs is the Johnny-come-lately of supranational governance, bodies such as the United Nations Office of Drugs and Crime (UNODC) and the International Criminal Court (ICC) are shaping ideas and practice in criminal law enforcement. Each sphere of governance above the nation state is creating an impetus for the (trans)formation of policing structures.

The Dimensions of Transnational Policing

It is tempting to overstate the pace and impact of globalization. For example, Tony Blair declared, 'in 1997 the challenges we faced were essentially British. Today [in 2006] they are essentially global.'[9] Hyperbole aside, the earlier

Table 1: Transnational policing: A socio-spatial typology

Locus	Network	Examples
Local	Local law enforcement agencies linked with overseas counterparts	Drug squad, Special Branch, Counter-terrorism police Criminal Investigation Departments, Interpol's National Central Bureau, Operation Trident (MPS)
National	National security structures created to be able to coordinate a national response and to work with international partners	UK Serious Organised Crime Agency (SOCA), MI5, MI6, GCHQ, US national agencies such as FBI, DEA, Homeland Security, National Joint Intelligence Headquarters linking police, customs, immigration and airport security
Regional	Regional security structures and associations	EUROPOL, SIS; Frontex; SECI, SEPCA, ASEANPOL, SARPOL, Baltic Sea Task Force, BCOC, ACCP, RSS, CCLEC, CARICC, SAARC PICP
International	Liaison officers posted in overseas diplomatic missions	UK SOCA liaison officers, FBI, DEA, US Treasury Department, US State Department Security Service, Australia Federal Police, Royal Canadian Mounted Police
Global	Policing entities that have a global reach	Interpol HQ, UN Police Division, UN Office of Drugs and Crime (UNODC); World Customs Organisation (WCO); International Criminal Court (Investigation Division); Egmont Group/Financial Action Task Force (FATF)

SIS: Schengen Information System; Frontex: European Agency for the Management of Operational Coopera-tion at External Borders; SECI: Southeast European Cooperation Initiative, Regional Centre for Combating Trans-border Crime (Bucharest, Romania); SEPCA: Southeast Europe Police Chiefs Association; ASEANPOL: Association of Southeast Asian Nations' Police Association; SARPOL: South African Police Association; BCOC: Bureau for the Co-ordination of Combating Organised Crime, for the Commonwealth of Independent States (Moscow, Russia); ACCP: Association of Caribbean Commissioners of Police; RSS: Regional Security System of the Eastern Caribbean; CCLEC: Caribbean Customs Law Enforcement Council; CARICC: Central Asian Regional Information and Coordination Centre; SAARC: South Asian Association for Regional Cooperation; PICP: Pacific Islands Chiefs of Police (PICP).

discussion nevertheless generates the hypothesis that *all aspects of policing will undergo transformation* as the world becomes more economically, politically, technologically and socially interconnected. The globalization thesis requires us to examine the changes likely to occur in the working lives of police officers – from the local community constables to the liaison officers posted around the world. The typology set out in Table 1 is an attempt to delineate the dimensions of transnational policing at different socio-spatial levels.

The premise of this table is that the word *transnational* refers to activ-ity that transcends national boundaries, passing through them without nec-essarily being affected by them (Mann, 1997). Ulrich Beck (1992) argues that interaction across national frontiers in networks with a high degree of mutual dependence and obligation has led to a *self-perception of transna-tionality* among a growing number of actors, institutions and agreements. The most important distinction in Table 1, therefore, is between the interna-tional – which refers to relationships among nationally constituted bodies – and the transnational that refers to all the types of policing in the table.[10]

Global Policing Networks

An obvious starting point for an examination of *global policing* is the devel-opment of Interpol, the International Criminal Police Organisation.[11] Formed in 1923, Interpol was intended to be a communication network designed to promote mutual assistance between police organizations. Each member country has a National Central Bureau (NCB) located on its own territory and staffed by officers from its own police forces. These NCBs cannot be forced to comply with any directive issued centrally by Interpol. They remain bound by the operational context of the policing establishment in the host country and operate within limits set by its own laws (Anderson *et al.*, 1995; Sheptycki, 2004).

Interpol provides four core functions (Cameron-Waller, 2008). First, it provides a secure global communication system enabling police forces from 187 countries around the world to speak with each one another. The current communication system, known as I24–7, is an email facility that can move information such as fingerprints, photographs, etc., and can be used to provide police forces with the capacity to share information. Second, it provides databases on suspected people, stolen property and identity documents, etc. that can be accessed through the global communication system. It is designed to discover whether a person is the subject of an arrest warrant in a country where a prosecutor has said that if the person is found abroad, he or she will be extradited, the basic requirement for the issue of an Interpol Red Notice. Third, Interpol offers operational support round the clock through a command and coordination centre. This is a contact point for member countries faced with a crisis linking the General Secretariat, NCBs and regional offices. Support can involve strategic assistance with major sporting events or the deployment of incident response teams to the sites of terrorist attacks or natural disasters. The fourth function is training national police forces to develop responses to serious transnational crime and terrorism.

Interpol has grown in size and scope and in the complexity of its activity. It now provides analytical support, intelligence and liaison facilities in difficult cases and a range of other similar activities. Although it remains principally a mechanism for sharing information, it is increasingly involved in operational activity, including investigative support. For example, Interpol provided operational assistance to a murder investigation in Jamaica, the investigation of credit card fraud in Trinidad and Tobago, in identifying plane-crash victims in Cameroon and fugitive investigation in Austria.[12]

Developing Regional Policing

In many regions of the world, the creation of regional governance structures (such as the European Union) has been mirrored by the development of regional policing entities (such as Europol). These range from professional associations with an annual conference to those with much greater operational ambitions. Europol, for example, was intended to improve the operational effectiveness of police cooperation among European member states starting with a drugs unit (Anderson *et al.*, 1995; Williams and Vlassis, 2001,

p. 266). The Europol Convention signalled 'a silent revolution in the history of international police cooperation in Europe. Never before have so many forms of cross-border police cooperation been regulated in such detail by convention' (Fijnaut, 2001, p. 288). Its mandate rapidly expanded beyond drug trafficking to include financial crime, people trafficking, terrorism and organized immigration crime and now provides legal, strategic and technical advice and training to top-level officials of national law enforcement agencies. Although Europol does not have executive powers, it does serve as a central intelligence and support unit enabling it to identify and links among targets in different countries (Marotta, 2001, p. 313). While Green (1998) sees Europol changing from non-operational to explicitly operational, Sheptycki (1998a) argues that the organization simply adds another administrative level to an increasingly complex patchwork of policing.

Strengthening National Security Capacity

Resistance to the creation of national police forces among local police chiefs has gradually given way to the force of the argument that some kind of organization is required to coordinate national functions and to provide a single point of coordination with multi-national law enforcement efforts. In Britain, for example, the Serious Organised Crime Agency (SOCA) brought together functions previously carried out by the National Crime Intelligence Service[13] and National Crime Squad[14] with Customs and Immigration enforcement and leadership from the Intelligence and Security Services (Bowling and Ross, 2006; Harfield, 2006). Many European countries have created similar bodies (Sheptycki, 2007b).

Creation of a national security policing capacity has also very consciously involved establishing links among the 'wider police family' (Bowling and Newburn, 2006). Although 'blue uniformed' public police remain central to the policing enterprise, other organizations play a growing role. In many parts of the world, defence forces, established to provide military force against foreign invasion and to provide aid to the civil power in times of unrest or civil emergency, are now working largely to a law enforcement agenda. In the Caribbean, for example, the army and hybrid military/policing agencies support the police on land, while the coastguard has extensive involvement in armed policing of territorial waters (Bowling, 2010). Border protection agencies including Customs, Immigration and Airport Security, and private security firms also play a role in national policing infrastructure, as do security and intelligence agencies such as MI5, MI6 and GCHQ in the UK. Although these agencies work independently, there are increasingly strenuous efforts to create systems and structures for sharing information to bring their work together through the creation of a national joint intelligence committee or headquarters convened either for strategic planning or to coordinate specific operations.

Overseas Liaison Officers

The overseas liaison officer is a relative newcomer to the policing scene (Goldsmith and Sheptycki, 2007, p. 11). While military and trade attachés have long been a feature of diplomatic life, the permanent presence of a police officer in a foreign embassy or high commission is a recent phenomenon (Bailey, 2008; Sheptycki, 1998a; Bigo, 2000). The liaison officer, posted overseas for four years or more, is the first point of contact for visiting police officers and those requesting information or assistance. The heart of the job involves investigating criminal collaborations based on intelligence gathered from various sources and communicated between local policing agencies around the world. Bigo (2000) describes them as marginal to their own organizations but integral to a profound change in the architecture of global security. The people working in this field play a key role in the management of information and are initiating new policing practices across a web of local, national and transnational security institutions.

The world leader in this area, the US Federal Bureau of Investigation (FBI), has around 340 employees, agents and support staff, assigned to permanent overseas positions, little more than 1% of its total strength (Fowler, 2008, p. 111). This is likely to grow in the future with an FBI representative stating that 'the US would like to base an FBI office in very country of the world, eventually' (Fowler, 2008, p. 122). In the view of the Bureau's director,

> the globalization of crime – whether terrorism, international trafficking of drugs, contraband, and people, or cyber crime – absolutely requires us to integrate law enforcement efforts around the world. And that means having our agents working directly with their counterparts overseas on cases of mutual interest – not only to solve crimes that have been committed, but to prevent crimes and acts of terror by sharing information in real time. (Fowler, 2008, p. 110)

The US Drug Enforcement Agency also has an extensive transnational policing capacity (with 78 offices in 58 countries), as does the US Treasury Department, State Department Diplomatic Security Service, Bureau of Alcohol, Tobacco and Firearms and the Federal Marshals Service. Other nations' police forces with a commitment to overseas include the Royal Canadian Mounted Police that observes that 80% of the Federal investigations that they undertake extend beyond national borders justifying the posting of 35 Mounties in 25 locations around the world. The Australian Federal Police (AFP) has 80 liaison officers in 27 countries. The UK Serious Organised Crime Agency (SOCA) has a small force of 140 overseas liaison officers in countries around the world who play a role in providing advice and capacity building, training and mentoring and coordinating joint operations. Although the rich world has developed furthest in this field, many other countries are deploying liaison officers overseas; for example, there are at least 100 officers from all over the world resident in London.

The Globalization of Local Policing

Although the discussion of transnational policing is inevitably focused on new institutions and the novelty of police officers travelling abroad to work, the most significant impact of global interconnectedness may be happening much closer to home. It seems likely that neighbourhood policing is undergoing 'interactive globalization' in which indigenous practitioners have become globally aware (Cain, 2000). In a global age, borough commanders must police their local communities while remaining conscious of the impact of global forces on the locality. They are naturally concerned with illegal drug markets on their patch, but cannot ignore their links to the transnational supply and distribution networks that feed them. In the Caribbean, local policing involves extensive collaboration with neighbouring islands, with the Americas and Europe (Bowling, 2010). Drug squad commanders in particular are involved in almost continuous transnational collaborations. The CID less so, but still involves working with locally based officers in pursuit of travelling criminals. Innovations in British policing – such as Metropolitan Police *Operation Trident*, targeting gun crime within London's black community – has involved collaboration with police in various Caribbean islands (most extensively in Jamaica) as part of a *local* crime reduction strategy (Fuller, 2001). This involves intelligence sharing, dispatching detectives to the Caribbean to interview witnesses and attend the funerals of homicide victims, as well as hosting Jamaican officers in London. The fact that US big city police forces, such as the NYPD and Miami Dade, have posted liaison officers in various cities around the world points in the same direction. Again, the point extends far beyond crime to have relevance to the service and public order functions of the police. Policing major sporting events – the 2012 Olympic Games in London being just one example – is a major transnational policing operation even while it is focused on specific localities.

The globalization of local policing is a necessary corollary of the creation of international systems and structures and the posting of liaison officers overseas. International cooperation can be done by email, telephone or travelling overseas to gather evidence or interview witnesses. Local police officers are required to respond by sending or receiving *Commissions Rogatoire,* as required by Mutual Legal Assistance Treaties. When a detective travels overseas, a local officer must accompany him or her as minder and guide. If police powers to arrest are required, the local man or woman is needed to provide lawful authority. A similar point can be made about the operation of Interpol. Although it is headquartered in Lyon, its institutional capacity relies on the functions of the NCBs and local police constables linking local detectives through a global network. Despite its obvious importance, little research has yet explored the impact of global forces on ordinary local policing.

Towards a Research Agenda on Transnational Policing

Transnational policing is developing in a variety of different socio-geographical spheres to the extent that it is possible to say that global policing exists as an empirical reality (Bowling and Murphy, 2009). It is emerging within local police forces, national agencies, and regional and other transnational bodies. The current state of play is well expressed by Andreas and Nadelmann (2007):

> The international orientation of policing priorities and international extension of policing practices have reached unprecedented levels. Though still far from forming a globetrotting international police force with sovereign authority, states now agree and collaborate on more cross-border policing matters than ever before. Substantially driven by the interest and moralizing impulses of major Western powers, a loosely institutionalised and coordinated international crime control system based on the homogenization of criminal law norms and regularization of law enforcement relations is emerging and promises to be an increasingly prominent dimension of global governance in the twenty-first century.

It is important to distinguish the existence of global policing from the idea of a *global police force* (Bowling and Murphy, 2009). The idea of a contingent of globally mobile officers with a universal power of arrest has featured in fiction and mooted as an option by some commentators (e.g. Brown, 2008). The case for a World Police Force is relatively straightforward: crime transcends national boundaries, it is beyond the capacity of any individual police force to respond to it and the problems involved in the sharing of information and practical cooperation across national boundaries prevents the world's police from providing an effective response. The solution therefore is to create a body unfettered by the constraints of national borders to respond to these problems. The main obstacle is national sovereignty. As Nadelmann (1993, p. 5) puts it:

> the fundamental 'problem' of international law enforcement is the sovereign – that is, exclusive – power of governments within their own borders and virtually nowhere else ... The sovereign power of states generally forecloses unilateral police action by one state in the territory of another. It requires that most international law enforcement efforts be in some sense bilateral, cooperative ventures. And it means that the popular image of the Interpol agent as a police officer with international arrest powers is entirely fictional.

It may be that the idea of a global *police force* is a non-starter (Bowling and Murphy, 2009), but the existence of *global policing* requires that we embark urgently on a programme of research to address some important questions emerging from this field.

The first order of business is to understand exactly what is the nature of the problem to which transnational policing is the solution. As far as it can be known, what is the extent and nature of 'international crime' and insecurity and what is its impact on police and communities? What forms of social harm and insecurity have become priorities, how are these priorities set, by whom and in whose interests? Is the current focus on transnational organized crime and terrorism justified as the greatest threats to human security (Cabinet Office, 2008, Abbott *et al.*, 2007)? This raises still further questions such as how and by whom, should transnational policing structures and processes be resourced; after all, 'he who pays the piper calls the tune'.

There is a clear need for some description of the nature and extent of the transnational activity emerging within local, national, regional, international and global socio-spatial networks. How far and how fast is local policing, in fact, changing in response to increased global interconnectedness? What is the nature and extent of cooperation between police forces in each sphere? Much of our thinking in this area has focused on the idea that networks are forming largely between police officers who somehow represent the nation state, and therefore that policing is *international*. However, this is idea is clearly contradicted by the fact that much transnational cooperation is occurring between sub-national units (Sheptycki, 2007b). There remains insufficient systematic research simply describing the work of regional organizations and their products and of emerging global organizations such as Interpol or the United Nations Police Division. It would be interesting to know the degree to which cooperation at these different levels tends to be short-term, reactive and *ad hoc* and how far it is long-term strategic or preventative in focus. It is extraordinary that after nearly 90 years of Interpol's existence, there exists no empirical work on the operation of the NCBs (Cameron-Waller, 2008).

The transnationalization of policing demands an exploration of theoretical debates in the fields of governance, citizenship, social stability and inclusion. The police have been controversial historically because they are charged with guarding the human right to security of the person (which is itself no easy task), but they also have the power to remove fundamental rights to life and liberty (Kleinig, 1996). How to maintain safe communities while controlling state power to interfere arbitrarily with personal freedom lies at the centre of debates about the future of democratic governance.

Anderson *et al.* (1995, pp. 287–289) argue that effective police cooperation requires a robust supranational system of accountability to ensure long-term public support and popular legitimacy. However, it is far from clear where transnational policing should draw its legitimacy and authority and to whom it should be accountable. Should the Interpol constitution be radically overhauled and made democratically accountable so that it could

authorize a more extensive operational capacity? Should the detective function of the International Criminal Court be extended so that it could investigate a broader range of serious crimes more intensively? Should the United
Nations Police division expand its capacity beyond the provision of security
to failed states to a broader mandate? Is there scope for the creation of a
new global policing body or one that could provide authorization of and
accountability for policing that transcends national boundaries (Bowling
and Murphy, 2010)?

Whatever the solution, it is clear that the present legal framework for
cross-border police accountability is inadequate (Sheptycki, 2002b; Loader,
2000, 2002), the result of which are troubling gaps in jurisdiction through
which human beings can fall (Bowling and Murphy, 2009). We need empirical and normative research that examines the ways in which the activities
of emerging systems of global police cooperation are regulated by national
and international law. For example, to whom are the commanders of transnational policing operations accountable? What is their legal/constitutional
position? What mechanisms exist for ensuring fiscal, political and managerial accountability? Who is responsible when things go wrong – who might
investigate complaints across international boundaries? What happens – as
in the unfortunate case of Mr Derek Bond, the British pensioner detained
for three weeks in South Africa at the request of the FBI – when cases fall
between gaps in jurisdiction (Bowling and Murphy, 2009)?

Together with a general lack of transparency, we are forced to take on
trust the expertise, efficiency and effectiveness of transnational policing operations and their legality, integrity and proportionality. Research and public
inquiries around the world have raised questions about discrimination, corruption, incompetence and ineffectiveness in domestic policing and there is
no reason to believe that policing 'above government' will be immune from
these problems. Transnational policing raises ethical questions about policing
because it often involves intrusive techniques and repressive styles of policing (McLaughlin, 1992, p. 483). These have the potential to undermine civil
liberties, especially for those seen as an 'unwanted presence' and where the
social order is insular, xenophobic and exclusionary. Recent laws in Britain
and the USA introduced on terrorism, security and migration focus on undesirable aliens, widen policing powers and intensify 'immigration policing'
(Weber and Bowling, 2004, 2008).

If global policing is to claim professional status, we need to know what
research and practical knowledge informs and drives strategic development
and operational practice. What is its foundational ethical framework? Is it
guided by an espionage, military or constabulary ethos (Sheptycki, 2007a;
Bowling 2006)? How are 'transnational police officers' selected, educated
and trained? What mechanisms ensure integrity, legality and adherence to
international human rights norms? Finally, we should know much more than
we do today about how transnational activity impacts on 'local' policing and

ultimately how it impacts on the human experience of public order, safety and liberty in the villages, cities and towns in which we live.

Conclusion

Despite the current global economic downturn and fears of protectionism, it seems likely that transnational policing in its various forms will continue to expand in coming decades. The impact of linkages emerging from expanding telecommunications networks, ease of international travel, joint training institutions, conferences and other forums within which police officers from different countries are encountering one another is being consolidated by supranational governance institutions and justified politically by persistent anxieties about transnational organized crime and terrorism. The effects of these changes will be felt by local police constables who will find themselves increasingly communicating with counterparts from other countries. Police officers who might have expected to spend their entire career working within the same police force, or perhaps in one or two shire or big city police forces, can now expect to work in one of the national agencies that have only just been created.

A growing number of police officers can anticipate travelling abroad to work during their career, some on a shuttle basis, others spending years overseas as 'police diplomats' akin to trade and military attachés. In order for the enormous challenges presented by the shifting nature of policing to be based on a solid normative and legal framework and an evidence base to guide practice, a major programme of research is needed. This will require advanced scholarship in the fields of criminology and criminal justice, police studies, criminal law, legal philosophy and public international law to get to grips with the difficult questions of law, governance and regulation in the transnational sphere. It will require empirical researchers to pursue funding to describe and explain the new transnational policing practices. It will need the cooperation of the police and other security sector agencies themselves to facilitate access, promote the research endeavour and engage constructively in the urgent debate about what constitutes good policing in an age of globalization.

Notes

1. In *Cops across Borders*, Nadelmann points out that this three-fold process of *regularization, accommodation* and *homogenization* has been neither reciprocal nor equal in its application. Essentially, foreign governments have accommodated US models of international law enforcement. Nadelmann, taking a broad overview, argues that the process of transnationalization is, in fact, *Americanization* (1993, p. 470).
2. World Trade Organisation – *World Trade Report 2008: Trade in a Globalising World.*
3. *World Trade Report 2008*, chart 13, p. 102.
4. Office of National Statistics.
5. World Travel Monitor, IPK International.

6. BBC News, 28 February 2006. http://news.bbc.co.uk/1/hi/uk/4758010.stm (accessed 25 February 2009).
7. Internet World Stats, Usage and Population Statistics. http://www.internetworld-stats.com/stats.htm.
8. *The Wall Street Journal*, Monday, 16 February 2009, citing Informa Telecoms & Media, a London-based research company.
9. Tony Blair's valedictory speech to Labour Party Conference, Tuesday, 26 September 2006.
10. There is a tension at the boundaries between the national, regional and international since it could be argued that the 'regional' is a specific form of international and that what is defined here as 'international' is in fact an extension of national actors into the transnational realm. For the purposes of the analysis that follows, it is the description of the network set out in column 2 of the table, rather than the label, that is most important.
11. Space prevents me from exploring the work of the other global policing entities referred to in Table 1 such as the UN Police Division, World Customs Organisation and the Investigation Division of the International Criminal Court.
12. Interpol, *Annual Report* 2007.
13. The National Crime Intelligence Service (NCIS) was created in 1992 and placed on a statutory footing by the 1997 Police Act.
14. Created by the 1997 Police Act and operational from 1998, the National Crime Squad (NCS) was formed from six regional crime squads.

References

Abbott, C., Rogers, P., and Sloboda, J. (2007). *Beyond Terror: The Truth about the Real Threats to Our World*. London: Rider.
Anderson, M. (1989). *Policing the World*. Oxford: Oxford University Press.
Anderson, M., Den Boer, M., Cullen, P., Willmore, W., Raab, C., and Walker, N. (1995). *Policing the European Union: Theory, Law and Practice*. Oxford: Oxford University Press.
Andreas, P. and Nadelmann, E. (2007). *Policing the Globe: Criminalization and Crime Control in International Relations*. Oxford: Oxford University Press.
Bach Jensen, R. (2001). "The United States, International Policing and the War against Anarchist Terrorism 1900–1914." *Terrorism and Political Violence* **13**(1): 15–46.
Bailey, N. (2008). "Overseas Liaison Officers." In Brown, S. D. (ed.), *Combating International Crime: the Longer Arm of the Law*. London: Routledge-Cavendish.
Beck, U. (1992). *Risk Society: Towards a New Modernity*. London: Sage.
Bigo, D. (2000). "Liaison Officers in Europe." In Sheptycki, J. (ed.), *Issues in Transnational Policing*. London: Routledge.
Block, L. (2008). "Combating Organized Crime in Europe: Practicalities of Police Cooperation." *Policing* **2**: 74–81.
Bowling, B. (2005). "Sovereignty vs. Security: Transnational Policing in the Contemporary Caribbean." *Caribbean Journal of Criminology and Social Psychology* **10**: 1–2.
Bowling, B. (2006). "Bobby, Bond or Babylon?" *Safer Society* **28**(Spring): 11–13.
Bowling, B. (2010). *Policing the Caribbean*. Oxford: Oxford University Press.
Bowling, B. and Murphy, C. (2009). "Global Policing: Transnational Law Enforcement in Theory and Practice." Paper presented to the Institute of Advanced Legal Studies, London, 23 February.
Bowling, B. and Murphy, C. (2010). *Global Policing*. London: Sage.
Bowling, B. and Newburn, T. (2006). "Policing and National Security." Paper presented to the London-Columbia Workshop on Police, Community and the Rule of Law, Institute of Advanced Legal Studies, London, March 2006.

Bowling, B. and Ross, J. (2006). "The Serious Organised Crime Agency: Should We Be Afraid?" *Criminal Law Review* (December): 1019–1034.

Brown, S. (ed.). (2008). *Combating International Crime: The Longer Arm of the Law.* London: Routledge-Cavendish.

Cabinet Office. (2008). *The National Security Strategy of the United Kingdom: Security in a Interdependent World.* Cm 7291. London: Cabinet Office.

Cain, M. (2000). "Orientalism, Occidentalism and the Sociology of Crime." *British Journal of Criminology* **40**(2): 239–260.

Cameron-Waller, S. (2008). "Interpol: a global service provider." In S. David, Brown *Combating International Crime: The Longer Arm of the Law.* London: Routledge Cavendish.

Fijnaut, C. (2001). "Transnational Organised Crime and Institutional Reform in the European Union: The Case of Judicial Cooperation." In Williams, P. and Vlassis, D. (eds), *Combating Transnational Crime: Concepts, Activities and Responses.* London: Frank Cass.

Fowler, S. (2008). "Legal Attachés and Liaison: The FBI." In Brown, S. (ed.), *Combating International Crime: The Longer Arm of the Law.* London: Routledge-Cavendish.

Fuller, M (2001). "Operation Trident Targets London's Rising Gun Crime." *Policing Today* 7(Summer): 22–25.

Goldsmith, A. and Sheptycki, J. (eds). (2007). *Crafting Transnational Policing: State-Building and Police Reform across Borders.* Oxford: Hart.

Green, P. (1998). *Drugs, Trafficking and Criminal Policy – The Scapegoat Strategy.* Winchester: Waterside Press.

Gregory, F. (1996). "The United Nations Provision of Policing Services (CIVPOL) within the Framework on 'Peacekeeping' Operations: An Analysis of the Issues." *Policing and Society* **6:** 145–161.

Harfield, C. (2006). "SOCA: A Paradigm Shift in British Policing." *British Journal of Criminology* **46**(4): 743–761.

Held, D. and McGrew, A. (eds). (2003). *The Global Transformations Reader: An Introduction to the Globalization Debate.* Cambridge: Polity.

Kleinig, J. (1996). *The Ethics of Policing.* Cambridge: Cambridge University Press.

Loader, I. (2000). "Plural Policing and Democratic Governance." *Social & Legal Studies* **9**(3): 323–345.

Loader, I. (2002). "Governing European Policing: Some Problems and Prospects." *Policing and Society* **12**(4): 291–305.

Mann, M. (1997). "Has Globalization Ended the Rise and Rise of the Nation-State?" *Review of International Political Economy* **4**(2): 472–496.

Marotta, E. (2001). "Responding to Transnational Crime – the Role of Europol." In Williams, P. and Vlassis, D. (eds), *Combating Transnational Crime: Concepts, Activities and Responses.* London: Frank Cass.

McLaughlin, E. (1992). "The Democratic Deficit: European Unity and the Accountability of the British Police." *British Journal of Criminology* **32**(4): 473–487.

Nadelmann, E. (1993). *Cops across Borders: The Internationalization of U.S. Criminal Law Enforcement.* University Park, PA: Pennsylvania State University Press.

Sheptycki, J. (1995). "Transnational Policing and the Makings of a Postmodern State." *British Journal of Criminology* **35**(4): 613–635.

Sheptycki, J. (1998a). "Police Co-operation in the English Channel Region, 1968–1996." *European Journal of Crime, Criminal Law and Criminal Justice* **7**(3): 216–236.

Sheptycki, J. (1998b). "Policing, Post-modernism and Transnationalisation." *British Journal of Criminology* **38**(3): 485–503.

Sheptycki, J. (1998c). "The Global Cops Cometh." *British Journal of Sociology* **49**(1): 57–74.

Sheptycki, J. (ed.). (2000). *Issues in Transnational Policing.* London: Routledge.

Sheptycki, J. (2002a). *In Search of Transnational Policing.* Aldershot: Avebury.

Sheptycki, J. (2002b). "Accountability across the Policing Field: Towards a General Cartography of Accountability for Post-modern Policing." *Policing and Society* **12**(4): 323–338.

Sheptycki, J. (2004). "The Accountability of Transnational Policing Institutions: The Strange Case of Interpol." *Canadian Journal of Law and Society* **19**(1): 107–134.

Sheptycki, J. (2007a). "Transnational Crime and Transnational Policing." *Sociology Compass* **1**(2): 485–498.

Sheptycki, J. (2007b). "Police Ethnography in the House of Serious Organized Crime." In Henry, A. and Smith, D. J. (eds), *Transformations of Policing*. Aldershot: Ashgate, pp. 51–79.

Weber, L. and Bowling, B. (2004). "Policing Migration: A Framework for Investigating the Regulation of Mobility." *Policing and Society* **14**(3): 195–212.

Weber, L. and Bowling, B. (2008). "Valiant Beggars and Global Vagabonds: Select, Eject, Immobilize." *Theoretical Criminology* **12**(3): 355–375.

Williams, P. and Vlassis, D. (eds). (2001). *Combating Transnational Crime: Concepts, Activities and Responses*. London: Frank Cass.

History

6

The International Campaign against Anarchist Terrorism, 1880–1930s

Richard Bach Jensen

D avid C. Rapoport has chosen to label the first era of modern terrorism as the "anarchist wave," a persuasive designation.[1] This article will examine the specifically anarchist qualities of the first wave, presenting a short overview of its archetypical era between 1880 and World War I, concentrate on analyzing the little-known efforts to control anarchist terrorism during that period, and conclude with both a sketch of anarchist terrorism after 1914 and a brief comparison between present-day terrorism and its nineteenth-century predecessor. Although the Irish Fenians, the Italian nationalists, and the Russian populists, particularly the Nihilists, all made their contributions to the creation of modern terrorism, it is only after 1880 with the widespread appearance of anarchist terrorism, or "propaganda by the deed," that terrorism became a European-wide, and then an international, phenomenon. The powerful and frightening symbolism inherent in the idea of anarchy and anarchism, and in the reality of the anarchist bomb thrower and assassin, proved so powerful that it tended to dominate all perceptions of terrorism, at least until the Bolshevik revolution of 1917. Anyone who threw a bomb or assassinated a prominent person tended to be labelled an "anarchist" whether or not he or she subscribed to anarchist ideology.

The period from 1880 to 1914 might be termed the canonical, and certainly the most famous, era of anarchist terrorism.[2] It was a worldwide phenomenon spread and connected by emigration (principally from Europe) and immigration, and by worldwide webs of shipping lines, communications networks, and not least, by cheap publications – above all, the mass market

Source: *Terrorism and Political Violence*, 21(1) (2009): 89–109.

newspaper. Countries on every continent, except Antarctica, experienced acts of terrorism committed by real and alleged anarchists; even those lands free of anarchist violence became seriously concerned about such deeds. Anarchist assassinations and bomb-throwings occurred in sixteen countries on three continents: in Europe, Australia, and North and South America.[3] Among other places, important anarchist groups developed in Egypt, China, and Japan. In 1898 Kaiser Wilhelm did not visit Egypt precisely because he feared an attack by resident Italian anarchists. In 1910, before their arrest and trial, Japanese anarchists were apparently plotting to murder the Emperor.[4] For Australia, one can point to a single act of propaganda by the deed, and that is, the July 27, 1893, bombing of the ship *Aramac* by an Australian anarchist named Larry Petrie (or De Petrie) during a labour dispute.

Multiple acts of violence in India demonstrated both the global reach of the "anarchist wave" and the way in which the anarchist label was applied (and misapplied) to non-anarchist terrorism. Anarchism, which normally viewed the nation-state and religion as oppressive forces, exercised relatively little influence on the development of Indian terrorism.[5] Nonetheless, before the first World War the British press and the British government tended to label all Indian nationalists carrying out violent anti-British deeds as "anarchists," and linked them directly to anarchist *attentats* in Europe. Following an April 1908 bomb explosion killing two Britons in Bengal, the London *Times* quoted a "high police official" in India as attributing "the Anarchist tendency now to be observed in India to the influence upon a certain section of the population to the doings of Anarchists in Europe and America."[6]

The death toll caused by anarchist terrorism, at least outside of Russia, was relatively small compared to today's horrifying standards. According to my calculations, during the period 1880–1914 and leaving the Tsar's empire apart, at least 160 people died and about 500 were injured due to anarchist bombs, guns, or daggers.

Anarchist terrorism in Russia deserves a separate discussion both because of its peculiar features and its late development. It did not exist before the 1905 revolution. In that revolution's conditions of insurrection, quasi-civil war, and the temporary collapse of central state authority, however, terrorist acts by both Socialist Revolutionaries and anarchists mushroomed astronomically. Four thousand people were murdered in 1906–1907 for political ends, and if Anna Geifman's estimates are correct, *at least* half of these were killed by anarchists. She claims that the majority of the 17,000 wounded and killed between 1901 and 1916 by terrorists suffered their fate at the hand of the anarchists.[7]

If, outside of Russia, anarchist terrorism before World War I killed relatively few people, it is significant for a number of other reasons. "Anarchists began the use of letter-bombs and automobiles for terrorist purposes." In Russia, some became suicide bombers.[8] They also initiated the mass and random slaughter of innocent civilians.[9] This feature of anarchist terrorism, although it had begun in Spain, reached its height in Russia with its limit-less, "motiveless," and purely criminal terror. In Spain, besides the terrorist bloodbath, the special contribution made to terrorism's murderous history (and often attributed, perhaps falsely, to the anarchists) was the anonymous bombing campaign in which explosions went on for years at a time, but with-out a clearly identified author or motivation. Anarchist "deeds exercised an enormous impact due to the powerful symbolism of the targets chosen and the advent of a mass journalism eager to publicize terrorist acts." For exam-ple, seven European, Russian, and American monarchs and heads of state or government were assassinated by anarchists (or former anarchists) in the fourteen years between 1894 and 1912. No other terrorist group in history murdered so many rulers. Several other assassinations during this period, e.g., of Prime Minister Petkov of Bulgaria in 1907, and of the King and Crown Prince of Portugal in 1908, were often attributed to the anarchists, although probably falsely. "Anarchist ideology had less to do with unleashing this wave of terrorism than local and national traditions of violence and conditions of socio-economic and political malaise" in individual nations.[10]

International Efforts to Control Anarchist Terrorism, 1880–1914

Anarchist terrorism was both a reality and an illusion. While the anarchists perpetrated some astonishing acts of violence, with one or two important exceptions, these were never linked to conspiracies of any size nor were they connected to a grand plan to destroy Western civilization and obliterate all the monarchs and ruling heads of state and government in Europe and the Americas (if not the entire globe). Yet the authorities often feared and the media frequently suggested that this was the case. By connecting together a disparate series of events, many having nothing to do with anarchism, newspapers helped create the "myth" of anarchist terrorism as a fearsomely powerful phenomenon sweeping through the world. Many governments, frightened publics, and vengeful anarchists (as well as those who aspired to the name of anarchist) came to believe in this myth.

Between 1880 and 1914, fear of anarchist violence, or better, fear of the anarchist myth and a cataclysmic subversion of society, was the essen-tial reason behind repeated efforts at both the national and international level to contain or defeat anarchist terrorism.[11] Many nations passed anti-anarchist legislation. During the mid 1880s, and in response to the Fenians and Nihilists as well as the anarchists, several countries in northern and central Europe passed laws against the criminal use of explosives: Britain (10 April 1883); Germany (9 June 1884), Austria (27 May 1885), and Belgium (22 May 1886); Switzerland passed a comparable law in April 1894. During the far more violent nineties and the first decade of the twentieth, at least thirteen countries passed laws specifically designed to curb propaganda by the deed. These countries included France (laws of April 1892, December 1893, and July 1894), Spain (July 1894 and September 1896), Italy (July 1894), Denmark (April 1894), Sweden (June 1906), Bulgaria (March 1907), and Argentina (June 1910). These laws included heavy penalties for the abusive and lethal use of explosives, public support for and incitement to commit anarchist crimes, trying to subvert the military, and belonging to an anarchist association. France and Portugal placed restrictions on publishing the proceedings of anarchist trials. The United States passed two laws (3 March 1903 and February 1907) excluding the immigration of anarchists and providing for their deportation. The states of New York and New Jersey (April 1902), and Wisconsin (May 1903) passed laws punishing advocacy of "criminal anarchy."[12]

International Police Cooperation

International cooperation against the anarchists was usually more successful bilaterally, and especially between police forces, since it could be developed out of a common police culture based on shared expertise, rather than international diplomatic cooperation between nation-states, particularly at the multilateral level. In an era of intense nationalism, political divisions between rival governments made it very difficult to organize comprehensive multilateral policing, which only fully emerged with the founding of Interpol's predecessor in the 1920s.

As far as the anarchist terrorists were concerned, substantial international attempts to combat them (as well as the Nihilists and revolutionary socialists with whom they were often confused) can be traced back at least to the 1870s. These efforts developed in the context of growing discontent among the working classes, increasing efforts to organize labour (efforts often led by radicals), and a rash of assassination attempts culminating in the killing of Tsar Alexander II in March 1881. Attempts made in the 1870s and 1880s to create multi-national cooperation against Nihilists and members of the socialist International failed. Therefore countries such as Italy, Russia, and Britain resorted to the unilateral creation of international policing networks.

In the 1880s, Britain had little to fear from anarchists or socialist revolutionaries, but it did experience major difficulties with the activities of the "Fenians," Irish nationalists based in the United States who hoped to provoke a rebellion in Ireland through carrying out terrorist actions in Britain. The Fenians, probably the originators of history's first modern terrorist campaign, had no connection with the anarchists. Nonetheless, the British response to the Fenians, their passage of anti-explosive laws and creation of the Special Branch (a secret political or investigative police which also guarded persons in high office) inside London's Metropolitan Police Department, helped them in the 1890s to deal successfully with the anarchist threat.

In the 1890s more intensive, systematic, and widespread bilateral, police, and diplomatic collaboration against the anarchists replaced the sporadic police and diplomatic cooperation against them (and other terrorist groups) of the previous decade. France, Spain, Italy, Austria, and Germany placed or hired police and/or informers in other countries and worked to promote international police cooperation through the exchange of information about the anarchists both at border crossings and between central police organizations. The mid-1890s, following anarchist bombings in France, Belgium, Spain, Portugal, and Italy, witnessed a pinnacle of activity as France, Italy, Austria-Hungary, and the federal states of the German Empire concluded bilateral agreements to monitor and exchange information on the anarchists. Germany and Austria worked from behind the scenes to promote much of this cooperation. To some extent Austria resumed the role that Metternich, the famous Hapsburg foreign minister, had played in the first half of the century in creating an anti-subversive policing system, although Austria's actions were on a smaller scale and proved less successful. The headstrong Kaiser Wilhelm II pushed Germany to take an active role against the anarchists, but his government, for a variety of reasons, including fear that a leading German position might expose the emperor to increased risk of assassination, preferred a lower profile. In December 1893 Spain, scene of the bloodiest anarchist bombings of the nineties, sought to take the lead in forging a European, multilateral anti-anarchist accord, but failed due to the opposition of France and Britain.

In the 1890s and later, controversies raged over the extradition and expulsion of anarchists. Countries of asylum for the anarchists, pre-eminently Switzerland and Britain because of their long-standing traditions of liberalism and giving sanctuary to political refugees, usually, but not always, fended off pressures placed on them to crack down more firmly on their resident subversives. Policies of expulsion and extradition became increasingly important in combating anarchism as countries sought to get rid of both domestic and foreign anarchists by ejecting them (or getting countries of asylum to expel or extradite them). Spain was a sharp thorn in the side of many European countries, since it was prone to empty its prisons of scores of often destitute anarchists, whom it then pushed across foreign borders or dumped into leaky vessels bound for England.

As an example of how anarchist terrorism was metamorphosing into a global, and not simply a European, problem, in 1897 Argentina, fearful of becoming an anarchist haven, concluded an accord with Italy to provide mutual notification of the departure for each others' shores of known anarchists. Vast European, particularly Italian, immigration had carried some of the anarchists to prosperous Argentina, as well as to many other countries. Anarchist terrorism did not erupt in Argentina during the 1890s, however, although it did about fifteen years later, in 1909–10.

During the 1890s, Britain became the envy of all Europe by largely avoiding anarchist terrorism. In part this was due to the greater stability of its institutions and popularity of its political leaders (e.g., Gladstone and Queen Victoria) than those on the Continent. Britain was more democratic than Spain or Italy (although not France). Even more importantly, by 1900 Britain had developed the largest organized labour movement in the world with more than double the number of union members of Germany and four times that of France. French anarchists, such as Emile Pouget, who in 1894 had been forced to flee to England by government repression, observed this amazing development and became increasingly involved in anarcho-syndicalism, the anarchist version of unionism.

British policing and intelligence were also better than in the rest of Europe. During the 1890s the British detective (epitomized in literature by Sherlock Holmes, who in 1887 made his appearance in a Conan Doyle story, although the British sleuth became popular only a few years later) supplanted the French as the gold standard for investigative excellence. The Special Branch now prevented several anarchist bombings. Protected by the Special Branch and other English police, no British or foreign monarch or statesman suffered anarchist assassination or even assault while on British soil. In the 1890s, both the British and the French also created facilities for the safe (or mostly safe!) disposal of recovered bombs.

The 1898 International Anti-Anarchist Conference of Rome

In November and December 1898 occurred the only European-wide anti-anarchist congress ever held and history's first international gathering convened to combat terrorism. In September 1898 the assassination of the Empress Elizabeth of Austria, reputedly benevolent and once considered Europe's most beautiful woman, shocked contemporaries more than many earlier terrorist deeds. Moreover the murder of an Austrian Empress by an Italian anarchist on Swiss soil was truly an international crime. These factors, together with all the anarchist *attentats* of the previous years, led to the calling of the conference.

Some contemporary diplomats and later historians have dismissed this little known and secret conference as "not worth the paper [its final protocol] was written on," to quote the French ambassador who attended the meeting. In fact one of Rome's most important accomplishments remained unwritten and off the record, i.e. the agreement for more cooperation and information exchange concluded by police representatives and officials in two secret meetings held during the conference. Sir Howard Vincent, perhaps the most colourful character at the meeting, founder of Scotland Yard's Criminal Investigation Division and of the Special Branch, and the British delegate who initiated the secret police meetings, asserted that the Rome gathering prevented "anarchist outrages" for a year and a half.

A balanced overall assessment of the Rome Conference would conclude that some of its recommendations for legislative and administrative measures, as well as rules governing extradition and expulsion procedures, proved to be dead letters, while others did not. The Rome anti-anarchist accord was in fact quite influential in promoting the "Belgian [or *attentat*] clause," which exempted assassins of heads of state from the usual protection provided in extradition treaties for those who committed political crimes.

It also led to wider use of *portrait parlé*, an offshoot of the famous French criminologist Alphonse Bertillon's complex method of identification termed anthropometry or Bertillonage. This was the world's first precise, and apparently "scientific," system of describing the human body and identifying criminals. As Jean Viguié, head of the French *Sûreté* and a delegate to the conference, explained it, *portrait parlé*, by focusing on the dozen or so fixed qualities of the human face (such as the shape of the ear and the forehead) and describing them in a systematic and precise fashion, would enable an observer to pick out a suspect "in any place, at any hour."

> If the police of every country definitely adopt it, it will be like a universal eye staring at noted criminals as they pass by and infallibly unmasking them despite the perfection of their most well executed disguises.

The acquisition of this "universal" unmasking "eye" required, according to Viguié, "only" thirty lessons of two hours each.[13]

The Rome Conference's promotion of *portrait parlé* was important because one of the reasons that anarchists were able to find safe haven in so many places is that they were invisible to the authorities. After an Italian immigrant resident of Paterson, New Jersey, crossed the Atlantic to assassinate King Umberto I, the police chief of Paterson told journalists that there were no anarchists in the town (although it was one of the biggest anarchist centres in the United States due to the abundant work it provided anarchists and others in its huge silk factories).[14] The police chief's ignorance was due to the fact that he spoke no Italian and knew little of the large immigrant community of Italians, Spanish, and other Europeans who were living in his town. Anarchists were also invisible because, besides the relatively little known *portrait parlé* and the cumbersome system of Bertillonage, no scientific means of identifying people existed. Finger printing was developed by the British in India during the mid-1890s, but was not universally adopted elsewhere for over a decade. The French waited until the 1930s to abandon the use of Bertillonage. Besides the disguising screens provided by language barriers and identification difficulties, most countries in the world, Russia being an important exception, did not require passports before World War I. People could move from one country to another with relatively little effort (other than by the police) to keep track of them.

A fourth way in which anarchists could find safe haven was journeying to territories where central authority, particularly police authority, was weak or divided. This included the United States, which before 1910 had no centralized bureau of investigation, such as the FBI, and before the 1920s, no centralized criminal identification system or record depository. Policing was divided between the various states and cities; communication between these police authorities was sporadic at best. Egypt was also a country of divided authority to which anarchists flocked. Each European state, through capitular agreements, policed its own nationals residing in Egyptian territory. Tangier in Northern Morocco became a magnet for anarchists (it was sometimes referred to as another "Paterson") since Morocco, under its Sultan, was "a disordered mosaic composed of minute particles." Increasing French and Spanish influence on and control over Morocco, and particularly over Tangier (which eventually became a free port and international city), prolonged the confusing internal situation.[15]

An even more important result of the Rome Conference than promoting *portrait parlé* was its facilitating European police cooperation and providing a point of departure for subsequent anti-anarchist accords, such as the St. Petersburg Protocol of 1904. As Mathieu Deflem has pointed out in *Policing World Society*, a common police culture based on shared expertise and crossing international boundaries was able to implement procedures that politicians acting publicly could not.[16] Contemporary fears, particularly from those on the Left and sometimes echoed in later historical writing, that the Rome Conference was a resurrection of the early nineteenth-century Holy Alliance, aimed at crushing all revolutionary, socialist, or even reformist impulses in Europe, proved to be largely unfounded (although the governments of Russia, Germany, and some other countries might have welcomed such a development).

Two assassinations on either side of the Atlantic, that of King Umberto of Italy (July 1900), and of President McKinley (September 1901) exercised an enormous impact on anti-terrorist policing. They highlighted the inadequacy of protection provided for Italian and American heads of state. One can make the case for a significant change around the turn of the century, amounting to a virtual revolution, in the way leaders were guarded. As a result of the anarchist threat, at least four major countries carried out police reforms that made protection of leaders bureaucratic, systematic, and official, rather than, as in the past, ad hoc and personal. Just as "scientific policing" was the goal toward which much of late nineteenth-century police reform aimed, so now for the first time in history the protection of high officials became a kind of science. In 1883 the British Special Branch was formed to guard monarchs as well as fight terrorists, in the 1890s the Berlin police began a systematic, bureaucratized guardianship of the Kaiser, in the fall of 1900 a special police unit was created in Italy to protect the king, and in 1902 the U.S. Secret Service assumed full-time responsibility for the protection of the president. Based in part on the Italian system, in January 1914 Greece created a special public security service for sovereigns and high-ranking personages.

The assassinations of Umberto and McKinley also led to a second important development, the dispatch of police detective forces to regions all over the world that harboured large groups of anarchists. Germany, Austria-Hungary, and France had already developed small anti-subversive police networks and, except for France, slowly expanded them in the twentieth century. From its centre in Paris, Russia's enormous police agency abroad continued its aggressive monitoring of anarchists and other so-called subversives. After the June 1910 bombing of the Teatro Colon in Buenos Aires, one of the world's great opera houses, Argentina sent agents to the major European ports to carry out surveillance of emigrants leaving for Argentina who might possibly be dangerous anarchists.

Especially significant was Italy's creation of a network of police and informers in the United States, South America, Spain, France, Switzerland, and England to monitor the activities of anarchists living in far-flung communities of Italian emigrants. Italy had had some informers and police abroad before, but never on this scale and never across the Atlantic. Prior to 1900, the Italian government had given only sporadic and limited importance to building a permanent international intelligence network to monitor Italian anarchists (and revolutionary socialists of all sorts) who might be potential assassins and bomb-throwers. In the nineteenth century, Italian consulates in cities known to harbour subversives might hire informers, but there was only one Italian policeman posted abroad to coordinate spying efforts. This was Ettore Sernicoli, who took up his position in Paris in May 1882. After the shock caused by the assassination of King Umberto, however, Italy created an international police system probably second only to Russia's in terms of its size and scope. Beginning in October 1900, Italy sent policemen to hire informers and monitor anarchists in New York City (and throughout America), and in Buenos Aires (and across Argentina). In June 1901 a policeman was posted to Brazil, and in July 1901, to London. In February 1902, at the request of the Egyptian Khedival Government, which acted under the supervision of the British, Italy sent six police officers to Egypt to serve in the country's anti-anarchist surveillance unit attached to its ministry of the interior. By 1907 police commissioners had been dispatched to Zurich, Switzerland, Lyon, France, and Montpellier, Vermont (in the latter case, with the intention of monitoring the militant anarchist editor Luigi Galleani and the Italian anarchist stonecutters who were working in the quarries of Barre, Vermont). By 1908, police were posted permanently to Nice and Marseilles in France and on a frequent, perhaps permanent, basis in Barcelona (where they cooperated with French and German police agents who were also there monitoring the anarchists); by 1913 to Berne and Geneva in Switzerland. In September 1912, after the end of the Turkish-Italian war over Libya, a police office was even set up in Constantinople.

Good intelligence effectively acted upon is one of the keys to preventing terrorist outrages, as the American experience of 9/11 should indicate. After a few misadventures, such as that with police commissioner Prina in London, Italian police intelligence, both national and international, improved and probably deserves some credit for the virtual disappearance of anarchist terrorism as an important issue in Italian life and politics between 1900 and World War I (by contrast, the same cannot be said for Spain, where bombs and assassinations continued to cause serious disruptions to society). Forewarned by confidential informers, the Italian police under Prime Minister Giolitti's expert overall control seem to have prevented a number of assassination attempts. In early June 1906 the police discovered several bombs at the shop of an anarchist barber in Ancona, and two weeks later, they discovered three bombs secreted near the railway track over which the king was scheduled to journey for his visit to the Adriatic port, one of Italy's most important anarchist centres.[17] In 1911, with the assistance of the Italian consuls in Geneva and New York City (and presumably with the help of the Italian police official residing in New York), three anarchists, apparently intending to strike at the king as he visited the Turinese Exposition celebrating Italy's unification, were arrested at Genoa and Turin. Notario and Costelli, the anarchists arriving in Genoa from New York, were in the possession of arms, explosives, and publications glorifying the assassin Bresci.[18] In her detailed history of public security under Giolitti, Fiorenza Fiorentino also notes various additional anarchist plots originating from abroad that were possibly prevented by police intelligence work (although Italian agent provocateurs were partially responsible for some of these plots).[19] This record of successful intelligence work stands in stark contrast with what happened in Italy in the 1890s, when those who planted the bombs that killed people outside the Italian parliament and damaged the ministries of Justice and War (as well as other buildings) were never discovered. At the time, Prime Minister Crispi lamented that the detective service of the Italian police was virtually non-existent.[20]

On the other hand, in its first years the newly expanded Italian anti-anarchist intelligence system also committed a few glaring plunders. Ettore Prina, the Italian police officer assigned to anti-anarchist work in London, had an abrasive and tactless personality unsuitable for the delicate task of handling informers. In September 1902 a recently dismissed anarchist informer earlier recruited by Prina travelled to Brussels and fired three shots at King Leopold of Belgium. Rubino, the ex-anarchist informer, had used money obtained from police officer Prina to purchase his revolver and ammunition and to pay his way over to Brussels.

The Prina-Rubino scandal highlights what was a persistent problem in anti-anarchist policing, i.e., that, on a number of occasions, the police itself either instigated terrorism or through inept handling of informers provoked and facilitated terrorist acts. The worst instances of this occurred in Spain and Russia. For example, in 1903 a captain of the civil guard, the Spanish gendarmes, organized a bomb conspiracy in Tarragona, near Barcelona, in order to impress his superiors by later foiling the plot.[21] The most spectacular case of Spanish police-instigated terrorism was that of Joan (or Juan) Rull, a former anarchist who for money turned police informer and for a time became the confidant of the governor of Barcelona. In July 1907 he was arrested (and later tried and executed) for planting, and in several cases setting off, the very bombs he was supposed to be helping discover and defuse.[22] In September 1911, Dmitrii Bogrov, a double agent whose former anarchist comrades had discovered his police connections and threatened to execute him unless he killed a high official, murdered Russian Prime Minister Stolypin at a performance of the Kiev Opera. The Russian police, who should have been more alert to signs of Bogrov's unreliability, provided him with a ticket for the gala occasion.[23]

Besides creating or enlarging international networks of police and informers, the two transatlantic murders of heads of state stimulated a renewed effort to achieve a multi-national anti-anarchist accord. Germany and Russia spearheaded this effort, which resulted in the conclusion of the secret St. Petersburg Anti-Anarchist Protocol specifying procedures for expulsion, calling for the creation of central anti-anarchist offices in each country, and in general, regularizing inter-police communication regarding anarchists. Ten eastern, south-eastern, central, and northern European nations (Russia, Rumania, Serbia, Bulgaria, the Ottoman Empire, Austria-Hungary, Germany, Denmark, and Sweden-Norway) signed the Protocol on 14 March 1904. Spain and Portugal soon adhered (June 15 and 25, 1904), Switzerland became a de facto participant (31 March 1904), and Luxembourg concluded a trilateral accord with Germany and Russia alone (May 1904).

Interestingly, Italy and the United States, the two most aggrieved parties, as well as France and Britain, did not sign the anti-anarchist protocol. Besides America's long-standing reluctance to become involved in European entanglements, Secretary of State Hays's dislike of the Germans and Russians, and the difficulty of signing a secret treaty that could not be ratified by the Senate in public session, America's refusal was due to the lack of a national policing system that could cooperate effectively with the Europeans. Italy voiced concerns about provisions in the protocol providing for anarchist expulsion back to their home countries, which might become a form of disguised extradition (and contrary to Italian law) and the possibility that thousands of Italian anarchists might be forced back to Italy with no legal means of preventing their unwelcome return.[24] In November 1913 Spain requested that Germany once more invite Italy and the United States, as well as the Latin American countries of Argentina, Brazil, Cuba, and Panama to join the anti-anarchist league, because significant numbers of anarchists resided in all these states.[25] Spain also asked for more effective exchanges of information about the anarchists, the use of a single language when communicating, and the establishment of the requirement that, at the request of consular officials, captains assist in keeping track of anarchists on board their vessels. Little seems to have come of the Spanish proposals, and none of the states listed by Spain subsequently adhered to the Protocol. Another failed initiative involved Japan. Perhaps in response to fears of its small native anarchist movement, in February 1909 Tokyo inquired about adhering to the Protocol, but, for unknown reasons, soon dropped its request (October 1909).

Before World War I, some signs appeared that anti-anarchist cooperation between the European states was decreasing. In the fall of 1913 Switzerland refused to transport Italian anarchists being expelled from Germany directly to the police in Italy, as they had done in the past; henceforth the Swiss insisted that diplomatic channels be used. The Germans thought that this change of policy resulted from internal Swiss politics and concern for the viewpoint of the socialist party.[26] At the beginning of the next year, Sweden, Norway (which had now broken away from Sweden and become a fully independent state), and Portugal (which in 1910 had become a republic) informed Berlin that they also would no longer permit direct police to police communications regarding the expulsions of anarchists (as the St. Petersburg Protocol provided) but instead that such communications would have to go through diplomatic channels.

Eventually political and ideological divisions between rival governments, culminating in World War I, undermined and destroyed the St. Petersburg Protocol's attempt to create a formal anti-anarchist alliance (although it operated among the Central Powers to the end of the war). How should one assess the overall impact of the St. Petersburg Protocol? Historians of the Russian secret police do not see it as having played a big part in the Tsar's efforts to thwart anarchists and violent revolutionaries. Diplomatic and bilateral police ties appear to have been the normal channels for interaction between the Russian secret police abroad and foreign authorities. This made all the more sense because the Russian political police abroad was centred in France, a country that had not signed the Protocol. Spain clearly appreciated it (as well as the help and information provided by foreign governments through other channels), only wanting to expand the Protocol's sphere and effectiveness.

Perhaps the best way to assess the protocol, as well as the Final Act of the Rome Conference, is to look at them in a larger context. Both diplomatic agreements encouraged more effective police cooperation and information exchange, and they operated in conjunction with a web of bilateral accords that had been signed in the mid 1890s among a large number of European states who never adhered to the Protocol. While the state of research does not allow one to point to specific cases where these formal agreements stopped terrorists, they are part of general trends toward better European intelligence, which at least in the Italian case, can plausibly be shown to have prevented some acts of terrorism.

Political and Social Policies to Curb Terrorism, 1880–1914

One can point to the various examples showing that better police cooperation and intelligence forestalled assassinations and bombings, as best exemplified by the efforts of Britain's anti-terrorist Special Branch set up in the

1880s and by the Italians after 1900, but still conclude that anarchist terrorism did not decline in most of Europe after 1900 primarily because of police measures alone. Heavy handed repression during the 1890s frequently led to anarchist acts of revenge, setting off chain reactions of violence that had often seemed impervious to police repression. Since the mystique of the powerful anarchist terrorist had such a strong grip on the imagination of the age, the allure of "propaganda by the deed," i.e., violent anarchist acts, could only be countered by undermining and devaluing this image and by opening up alternate outlets for the energies of discontented proletarians and middle class idealists who became terrorists and assassins. These developments took place most strikingly in France and Italy, but, disastrously, not in Spain.

Examining the situation in Italy during this period, it is clear that during the 1890s excessive Italian policies of repression had politicized anarchist violence, creating martyrs and a thirst for revenge that culminated in the assassination of King Umberto in 1900. After 1900, however, the policies of the Italian government worked in a significant fashion to diminish, downplay, and redefine the role of anarchist terrorism. The Italian government was able to break the chain reaction of violence, repression, and revenge that had characterized the relationship between the anarchists and the authorities during the nineties. Labour union and strike activity became available as a safety valve for proletarian energies due to the progressive social policies of Giolitti, the dominant political figure first as Interior Minister and then as Premier. The growing socialist party, together with mushrooming strikes and labour organizations, including syndicalist groups, all served to absorb and domesticate anarchist and proletarian energies, diverting them away from individualistic acts of propaganda by the deed and toward more organized and non-violent efforts to alter society.

Moreover, Giolitti worked consistently, and relatively effectively since the public proved receptive to his messages and policies, to shape, limit, or deny publicity for anarchism and anarchist violence. This was very important since, as many scholars, e.g., Walter Laqueur and Bruce Hoffman, have observed, publicity and media coverage are a key factor in nurturing and sustaining terrorism.[27] One way Giolitti downplayed anarchism was to refuse it special treatment. Giolitti refused to pass anti-anarchist laws or to sign on to new anti-anarchist diplomatic accords (although he adhered to those already agreed to, such as the bilateral treaties between Italy and neighbouring states signed during the 1890s and the Rome Final Act of 1898). He refused to mention the word "anarchist" in connection with, for example, the 1912 attempted regicide, Antonio D'Alba, and for the most part was able to prevent D'Alba's picture from appearing in the newspapers. Giolitti, whose efforts coincided with evolving attitudes in Italian society, largely succeeded in changing the frame of reference for understanding and dealing with anarchist acts of violence from that of deeds of political and social protest to crimes committed by juvenile delinquents and psychopaths. These were best dealt with by the courts and the psychiatrists, rather than by the government and the legislature.

Of further help in creating a new mindset congenial to Giolitti's approach to terrorism, was the increasing permeation throughout Italian society of the ideas of Cesare Lombroso and other criminal anthropologists. In 1894 Lombroso had argued in a famous, although very controversial, book that anarchists, and in particular anarchist assassins and bomb-throwers, were epileptic, insane, the victims of congenital disease of various sort, degenerate, hysterical, and often suicidal. While later on Lombroso's ideas became increasingly discredited, at the time Italians accepted them as mostly legitimate.[28]

In France, where anarcho-syndicalism was born in 1895, policies and socio-economic developments comparable to those in Italy also defused the anarchist menace (although early on the French rejected Lombrosianism).

The situation in Spain differed from that in France and Italy, since in the Iberian Peninsula anarchist violence remained an important phenomenon even after the turn of the century. Anarchists made serious attempts on King Alfonso's life in 1905, 1906, and 1913 resulting in the death of scores, and assassinated Prime Minister Canalejas in 1912 after he had cracked down on the anarchist press and labour movement. Spain's worst outbreak of violence before World War I occurred in Barcelona in 1909. A general strike called to protest the drafting of men for combat service in Morocco led to five days of street fighting involving the anarchists and others. After the police and army had crushed the rebellion, killing at least 200 people, they subjected the prisoners to torture and executed five, including Francisco Ferrer, the well-known anarchist educator. The Ferrer case became a *cause celebre* throughout Europe, and his execution, far from dealing a deathblow to the movement he symbolized, only created a martyr and sympathy for the anarchists.

In Spain the passage of special anti-anarchist laws and the creation of anti-anarchist police squads exacerbated rather than ameliorated the problem of anarchist violence since these measures were frequently followed by cases of police cruelty and arbitrariness, and by examples of judicial injustice. Madrid signed the Rome and St. Petersburg Protocols, but since neighbouring France and nearby Italy refused to participate in the 1904 agreement, Spain was denied many of the benefits of international police cooperation and intelligence exchange.

Spain's labour movement also served it badly, since it failed to function, or functioned only sporadically, as a safety valve for worker and anarchist discontent. Before World War I, the Spanish proletariat remained poorly organized and prone to bursts of intense, but short-lived, activity rather than to sustained efforts. The Spanish Socialist Party and its affiliated labour union grew very slowly, and continuous, large-scale anarchist involvement with the organized labour movement did not commence until 1910–11, with the founding of the *Confederacion Nacional del Trabajo*. For the first few years, however, the CNT was weak, its membership only 15–30,000, and not until

1917–18, when it reorganized along strictly syndicalist lines, did it begin to become a really effective organization representing hundreds of thousands of workers. Intransigent employers and hostile government policies also hindered the evolution of the Spanish labour movement.

Spain's slow rate of economic and social development, which was much behind that of France and Italy, combined with the Spanish government's policy of brutally and arbitrarily repressing dissent and strike activity and its failure to develop an effective policing apparatus, explain the continued incidence in the Iberian peninsula of extreme forms of political violence. The Spanish government's failure to remould the public image of the anarchist, which remained more that of a persecuted martyr than of a common criminal, exacerbated the problem of anarchist violence in Spanish society.

A combination of economic, social, and political factors, linked with a systematic government effort to redefine and downplay the nature and importance of anarchist terrorism, provides the best explanation for why this form of violence declined in certain countries but not in others. Careful police intelligence work and international police cooperation, together with a more rigorously professional system of protection for monarchs and heads of state, could aid in reducing the problem of anarchist terrorism, but heavy-handed repression only worsened it.

Anarchist Terrorism after 1914

The phenomenon of anarchist terrorism after 1914 has been much less studied than the pre-war variety. Although the single most lethal act of anarchist terrorism in its entire history took place during this period, i.e., the Wall Street bombing of September 1920, on the whole anarchist terrorism was a much less salient feature of international life. In effect anarchism lost its publicity, or at least much of it, displaced in the newspapers and in popular imagination by the notoriety, above all, of the Bolshevik Revolution, but also by other events, such as the Irish struggle for independence, which unleashed its own formidable terrorist campaign. Based on a cursory analysis of newspaper accounts and on various other sources, one can conclude that at least seven countries in the Americas and Europe witnessed acts of anarchist violence. These were, by degree of importance, Spain, the United States, Italy, France, Argentina, Brazil, and Portugal. Anarchist terrorism in these countries led to the death, excluding those killed in Spain during 1919–21 and the 1930s and in Russia during its revolution and civil war, of at least 93 people and to the injury of some 375.

For this period Spain must be examined separately, as Russia was earlier, because of the extraordinary conditions of quasi-civil war that prevailed there, or to be more precise, in Catalonia in the years 1919–1921. In Barcelona virtual civil war raged between the labour movement and intransigent employers supported by the Spanish authorities, particularly by the army.

Rival groups of gunmen, *pistoleros*, some affiliated with the government and the employer associations and others with the anarchists and the CNT carried out tit for tat assassinations and bombings. According to one source, between January 1919 and December 1923, over 700 people were murdered by the rival gangs and, presumably, roughly half of these victims were due to the anarchists.[29] At the height of the violence an average of sixteen people in Barcelona were being assassinated weekly. The government and employer-affiliated forces threw bombs into a workman's music hall and murdered dozens of syndicalist leaders, including many moderates who opposed violence, while in revenge anarchist "action groups" assassinated employers, the editor of a newspaper, the former Civil Governor of Barcelona (Count Salvatierra), Prime Minister Eduardo Dato (8 March 1921), and the Cardinal Archbishop of Saragossa (4 April 1923). This is the period of the "First Wave" of terrorism that most closely approximates the social strife, civil war, and terrorism in present-day Iraq, since in both cases we have a weak central government, and government authorities and government opponents deeply implicated in terrorist activities.[30]

After Spain, the United States experienced the bloodiest wave of anarchist terrorism post-1914. Between July 1914 and September 1920, anarchist explosives killed 52 to 62 people in the United States, including 8 anarchists whose bombs blew up prematurely.[31] Among the more famous events of the post-war "Red Scare," at the end of April 1919, was the mailing of thirty bombs to various high ranking officials, from the Attorney General and a Supreme Court justice to mayors, congressmen, and a Bureau of Investigation agent. On June 2, 1919, explosions at the homes of various officials took place almost simultaneously in seven American cities. "The culminating event of this wave of anarchist violence was the terrible Wall Street explosion of 16 September 1920, the deadliest act of terrorism in American history before the Oklahoma City bombing of April 1995."[32] The large dynamite bomb filled with heavy cast-iron slugs killed 33 people and injured over 200. Several historians believe the bomber was Mario Buda, a follower of Luigi Galleani, who was an Italian immigrant, anarchist, and advocate of terrorism.[33]

After Spain and the United States, Italy experienced the worst terrorist incidents after World War I. Bombings, apparently by anarchists, killed a few people in Milan (Hotel Cavour, 14 October 1920) and Turin (11 May 1921). Then on March 23, 1923 an anarchist bomb exploded at the Diana Theatre in Milan, killing 21 and injuring 172 people. While Italians had acquired the reputation of being the foremost assassins in Europe, slaughtering people uninvolved in politics in horrible bloodbaths was without precedent in the Italian peninsula. In the mid 1920s to early thirties, Italian anarchists made one or two (depending on how the youthful Anteo Zamboni's beliefs should be characterized) *attentats* on the life of Mussolini and were involved in various conspiracies against *il Duce*.

In France anarchists shot Prime Minister Clemenceau in the shoulder on 19 February 1919 and murdered an editor of the rightwing *Action Française* newspaper on 22 January 1923. Some bombings also occurred in Portugal (9 March 1921).

In Brazil and Argentina, a handful of bombings and one anarchist assassination took place between 1917 and 1925. Among the anarchist targets were the Palace of Justice in Buenos Aires (15 August 1920) and the Stock Exchange and Foreign Minister buildings in Rio De Janeiro (19 February 1920). In 1923, Argentine Colonel Varela was assassinated in Buenos Aires for ruthlessly repressing ranch labourers in Patagonia.[34] Between 1926 and 1928, Miguel Arcangel Roscigna, leader of the Argentinean "anarchist expropriators," who on one occasion collaborated in crime with Durutti, the famous Spanish anarchist, robbed several banks, leading to the death of a policeman.[35] Having fled to Uruguay, the expropriators were captured and tortured by Luis Pardeiro, Montevideo's police chief. In February 1932, anarchists seeking revenge gunned down Pardeiro and his chauffeur. This colourful, if gruesome, banditry, sometimes described as a mutant offshoot of the anarchist movement, in retrospect appears as a robust strand in anarchist history. Vienna suffered cruel anarchist robberies and murders in the 1880s, the Pini-Parmeggiani gang robbed in France and Italy in the 1890s, Marius Jacob and his band of *illegalistes* in the early 1900s, and in 1910–11 the Bonnot gang terrorized France and Belgium. The anarchists were not alone in their politically motivated (or at least partially politically motivated) robbing, since before World War I the Bolsheviks and other left-wing extremists had frequently robbed Russian banks.

The post-World War I surge of anarchist violence, which often took place in the context of severe social and economic dislocation, petered out in most of the world after the mid-1920s as prosperity and political stability, sometimes under dictatorial regimes, returned to Europe and the world. Powerful dictatorships led by more or less charismatic leaders ruthlessly repressed the anarchists in Russia (after the Bolshevik revolution of 1917), Italy (after the 1922 fascist takeover), and Spain (following military coups by General Primo De Rivera, 1923–30, and General Franco, 1939–75). These were three countries that had earlier been key centres of anarchism and anarchist terrorism. Anarchist violence only revived briefly in Spain in the mid-thirties at the onset of the Spanish Civil War. The Bolsheviks were now in the limelight as the greatest threat to Western, capitalist civilization, not the anarchists. Some anarchists had initially tried to co-opt the attractive power of the Bolshevik image by styling themselves "Anarcho-Bolsheviks" (as in Spain), but soon came to realize that Soviet Communism championed a ruthless dictatorial state that was the opposite of what the anarchists desired.[36] With the rise of fascist dictatorships in Italy and Germany, anarchists found an enemy, along with the Soviet Union, more to be reviled than the former targets of their wrath (but yet, the anarchists were often impotent to strike with terrorist acts against those powerful police states).

Symbolic of the end of the age of anarchist terrorism were changes in international legal thinking (which also reflected a fundamental shift in the climate of opinion). Ever since a resolution passed in 1892 by the Institute of International Law, anarchist, or "social," crimes had been defined as "criminal acts directed against the bases of the entire social order [*toute organisation sociale*], and not against only a certain State or a certain form of government."[37] In 1934 the International Conference for the Unification of Penal Law, held in Madrid, replicated this definition almost exactly when it wished to devise a legal formulation punishing terrorism:

> He, who with the aim of destroying every social organization [or 'the entire social order', '*toute organization sociale*'] employs any means whatsoever to terrorize the population, will be punished.[38]

After three Croatian nationalists (with Mussolini's support) assassinated Yugoslav King Alexander and French Prime Minister Barthou while they were being driven through the streets of Marseille in April 1934, it was no longer possible to view terrorist deeds as primarily the acts of anarchists. In the uproar over the assassinations, the League of Nations convened an international conference to draw up a convention for the prevention and punishment of terrorism. Completed in November 1937, although never fully ratified, this accord made no mention of anarchist or social crimes.[39] Subsequently, the menacing advances of Nazi Germany, and even more, the horrors of World War II and the holocaust, made most people forget that anarchist violence had once been considered the greatest single threat to civilization.

Epilogue: Nineteenth Century Anarchist Violence and the Recent Wave of Religious Terrorism

Several authors have emphasized the similarities between the terrorism of the anarchists and the more recent wave of terrorism inspired by religious zealots.[40] At least some resemblances are evident not only between the two groups of terrorists but also between government responses to these menaces. Both sorts of terrorists had (or were feared to have) "weapons of mass destruction," dynamite for the anarchists and nuclear and biological weapons for the current crop of terrorists. Contemporary writers referred to the explosive power of dynamite in apocalyptic terms comparable to those used by Oppenheimer to describe the first atomic bomb.[41] Ironically, more primitive weapons often proved more practical and lethal: box cutters and airplanes for the al-Qaedists, the dagger and the pistol for the anarchists.[42]

By the early twentieth century, anarchist terrorism appeared to be a universal threat, like al-Qaeda today, with real or alleged anarchist assassinations and bombings occurring on nearly every continent. A plausible argument can also be made that the periods at the end of the nineteenth century and more recently are similar since both have been eras of especially intense economic "globalization" leading to severe disruptions of traditional society. These dislocations have led to socio-economic and political malaise congenial to the germination of terrorism. In the case of the anarchists, but probably much less so with the Jihadists, unemployment, economic depression, the prohibition of legitimate labour organization and strike activity, corrupt political systems and governments insensitive to popular demands, provided fertile grounds for producing terrorists.

In a number of instances, immigrant populations, people forced to leave their homelands for economic or political reasons, proved to be the source of terrorists, be they anarchists, e.g., Italians living in Paterson, New Jersey, or Jihadists, e.g., Saudis residing in Germany. The role of diasporas in fomenting terrorism, however, should not be exaggerated. Only about half of the Italian anarchists involved in violent deeds, 1889–1914, can be linked to an emigrant experience and apparently only two (or fewer) out of two dozen terrorists became anarchists after leaving Italy.[43] The other half stayed and committed their assassinations and bombings inside the peninsula. Before 1914, 20 percent or less of the French and Spanish (and none of the German) anarchists involved in propaganda by the deed were émigrés.[44]

The socio-economic causes of terrorism seem much more important for the anarchist terrorists than for the Jihadists. The seminal event in generating al-Qaeda's terrorism was the Soviets' invasion of Afghanistan and Osama Bin-Laden and other Arabs' role in expelling them. Unlike anarchism, Jihadism's fundamental complaint is not the product, or primarily the product, of socio-economic distress. Rather it is a protest against what al-Qaeda perceives to be Western, "crusader" imperialism. Therefore, al-Qaeda's major discontent appears to resemble more that of the Irish, Algerian, and other anti-imperialist and anti-colonialist terrorists of the period from the 1920s to the 1960s, what David C. Rapoport has called the second wave of terrorism, than that of the propagandists by the deed.[45]

James Gelvin has noted that both al-Qaeda and the anarchists have (or had) a predilection for attacking symbolic targets (the World Trade Center, the Pentagon, parliament buildings, stock exchanges, opera houses et cetera). While this is certainly true, every terrorist movement has chosen to hit symbols of their enemies' power in order to garner publicity and achieve maximum shock value. One wonders if the anarchists and al-Qaedaists are significantly more prone than other terrorists to choose such targets. It also needs to be pointed out that many of the people who were the subjects of anarchist attack were selected in revenge for specific abuses for which they held some responsibility, such as torturing innocent anarchists or shooting down unarmed men, women, and children. The anarchists' victims were not simply abstract symbols of repression.

Gelvin's most interesting claim is his contention that al-Qaeda and the anarchists are similar since both wish to destroy the modern nation-state, either because they see it as a Western, colonialist imposition (al-Qaeda) or as a universal cause of human oppression (anarchism). But Gelvin fails to note that once the evil State is destroyed, the anarchists and the Jihadists dramatically part company. While Bin Laden envisions the birth of a massive Islamic empire or caliphate strictly ruled by religious law or sharia, the anarchists looked toward liberation from the bonds of all hierarchical authority, religious structures, and both secular and religious law.

Islamic terrorism's increasing resort to suicide bombings as a tactic finds a precedent among the Russian Nihilists (who introduced the practice in 1881) and the anarchists, although only sporadically and on a much reduced scale.[46] A fatalistic resignation to being captured and possibly martyred was a more common anarchist attitude than consciously planning to self-destruct during the terrorist deed. Suicide bombings by anarchists occurred only in Russia and were not that frequent.[47]

The decentralized and loosely organized quality of al-Qaeda has also been cited as paralleling anarchist terrorism. In both cases the myths of powerful anarchist and Islamist terrorist movements have served to attract followers throughout the world who act or acted in the name of groups and ideologies with which they often had minimal connections. Before World War I, the salient impulse behind anarchist violence was spontaneous individual action. As anarchism itself evolved and became more organized (after the mid 1890s, syndicalist organizations emerged as increasingly important outlets for anarchist energies), so too did anarchist terrorism. Between 1914 and 1920 the Italian Galleanists organized an impressive terrorist campaign culminating in 1919 in nearly simultaneous bombings across the United States.[48] But this was rather exceptional and the anarchists, despite the fears of the authorities, never organized international terrorist campaigns comparable to al-Qaeda's East Africa bombings of 1998 or the 9/11 attacks (although it *seemed* that the anarchists had achieved this during 1892–94 when, in rapid succession, their bombs exploded in France, Spain, and Italy). The anarchists never foreshadowed al-Qaeda by creating terrorist training camps or central command posts.

If the apparent similarities between the anarchists and al-Qaeda often break down when subjected to close scrutiny, intriguing comparisons can be made between public fears and government responses during the two eras. To the seemingly cataclysmic and universal threat posed by the terrorists, governments, in the 1890s–early 1900s as well as today, have responded with unprecedented efforts at international cooperation. As for the United States, while the anti-terrorist rhetoric of Theodore Roosevelt matched that of George W. Bush in its apocalyptic intensity, the former's concrete actions did not. The leadership of the coalition against the anarchists fell to the more conservative (in fact reactionary) Germans, Russians, and for much shorter periods, the Austrians and the Italians, not to the Americans. In both cases, the coalition of the Western world against the terrorists fell apart after an initial unity (e.g., all of Europe attended the 1898 Rome Conference; the world stood solidly behind the United States immediately after 9/11). The dissolution of the anti-terrorist alliance was due to the differing ideological bents and national interests of the various states (e.g., Western Europe, except for Iberia and Scandinavia, refused to adhere to the 1904 St. Petersburg Protocol backed by the conservative eastern empires; in 2003 only Britain and Spain joined the United States in supporting an attack on Iraq).

In the nineteenth century, as today, a strong temptation existed (and exists) for governments to exploit and exaggerate the danger of terrorism in order to attain political goals distinct from simply repressing terrorism. For example, German Chancellor Bismarck in the 1880s and Italian Prime Minister Francesco Crispi in the 1890s used the fear of anarchist terrorism to pass laws later employed to suppress their countries' respective socialist parties. This was despite the fact that the socialists did not support terrorism.

As I pointed out above, the present civil war *cum* terrorism in Iraq finds its precedent in Barcelona's 1919–21 period of terrorism and civil war between the anarchist-dominated labour movement and intransigent employers supported by the Spanish authorities. In both situations we find a weak central government, and government authorities and government opponents deeply implicated in terrorist activities. War and civil war unleash the bloodiest terrorist campaigns, as the reign of terror that followed the Russian Revolution of 1905 and the experience of Italy and America after World War I demonstrate.

In its use of torture and military tribunals Spain provides another point of comparison with contemporary governmental responses to terrorism. Lacking good intelligence about terrorist activities, both Spain and the United States resorted to torture to ferret out information. In both cases, whether it be at Montjuich prison in 1897 or Abu Ghraib in 2004, this strategy backfired, failed to end terrorism, and blackened the reputations of the governments involved. As governments and police forces have improved their intelligence gathering capacities, they have tended to become less heavy-handed and brutal in their reaction to real or potential terrorist acts. Evidence for this can be found in Italy, where after 1900 the Italian government reformed, improved, and greatly expanded its police and created a secret international force to monitor the activities of the anarchists. This significantly increased the level of its knowledge about and understanding of the Italian anarchists. Previously the situation had often been comparable to shadow boxing, with the authorities and the anarchists ignorantly striking out at symbols of each other, rather than at concrete realities. For instance, the Italian government long remained obsessed with the threat posed by Errico Malatesta, the famous anarchist leader, although he had publicly disavowed propaganda by the deed in the early 1890s, and cannot be directly linked to any violent anarchist deed after the 1870s.

In the early twentieth century the government in Rome also abandoned the use of military tribunals and arbitrary detention (*domicilio coatto*) for holding anarchists unconvicted of any crime. In the 1890s at least one anarchist was beaten to death while in police custody. But after 1900 we have no verified proof of the Italian police torturing anarchists (at least prior to Mussolini). Even after Italy stopped the practice, Spain continued to use military tribunals to try alleged anarchist terrorists and others, but this institution served it no better than Guantanamo and its deeply flawed system of military tribunals have served the United States. The strong suspicion that these military tribunals convict or have convicted innocent people led, for example, to an international outcry against Spain, accused of creating a new Inquisition. In Spain, it produced famous martyrs, like Francisco Ferrer, out of the very anarchists the military tribunals were supposed to crush and discredit.

In both the nineteenth century and today, it is clear that, at least in an initial phase, the terrorists and their official opponents came, and have come, to resemble one another. The terrorists' criminality and brutality, their methods of conspiracy and secrecy have influenced and corrupted governments and police desperately trying to thwart their violent deeds. Because of this, the "cure" for terrorism has sometimes appeared as bad or worse than the problem itself.

Certainly any overall analysis that compares the terrorism of the anarchists and the Islamists should not stop with the terrorists themselves, since their actions and reactions are closely intertwined with those of the authorities, the media, and the public. Martin Miller has suggestively designated this societal-terrorist embrace a *"danse macabre."*[49] Another general conclusion must be that, although some precedents can be found in anarchist terrorism for the later violence of al-Qaeda, the differences between the two phenomena are equally striking. Perhaps closer parallels can be cited between the reactions in the two eras of the affected governments and publics. In both situations, at least in much of Western Europe and the United States, the initial overreaction of the authorities, themselves under pressure from a panic-stricken public, gave way to more measured and sophisticated responses, in part because brutal repression has so often backfired.

Notes

1. David C. Rapoport, "The Four Waves of Modern Terrorism," in *Attacking Terrorism: Elements of a Grand Strategy*, ed. Audrey Kurth Cronin and James M. Ludes (Washington D.C.: Georgetown University Press, 2004), 47, 50–52.
2. For a more detailed discussion of the development of anarchist terrorism see Richard Bach Jensen, "Daggers, Rifles and Dynamite: Anarchism Terrorism in 19th Century Europe," *Terrorism and Political Violence* 16, no. 1 (Spring 2004), 116–153, and "The Evolution of Anarchist Terrorism in Europe and the United States from the Nineteenth Century to World War I," in *Terror: From Tyrannicide to Terrorism*, ed. Brett Bowden and Michael T. Davis, with a Preface by Geoffrey Robertson (St Lucia, Queensland: The University of Queensland Press, 2008), 134–160.

3. Acts of anarchist violence occurred in Italy, France, Belgium, Spain, Portugal, Switzerland, Britain, Germany, Austria-Hungary, Russia, the United States, Sweden, Denmark, Argentina, Australia, and perhaps Turkey.

4. Ira Plotkin, *Anarchism in Japan: A Study of the Great Treason Affair 1910–1911* (Lewiston/Queenston/Lampeter: Edwin Mellen, 1990).

5. See Peter Heehs, "Foreign Influences on Bengali Revolutionary Terrorism 1902–1908," *Modern Asian Studies* 28, no. 3 (1994) and *The Bomb in Bengal: The Rise of Revolutionary Terrorism in India 1900–1910* (Delhi: Oxford UP, 1993). Heehs emphasizes the indigenous sources of Bengali terrorism. While the Indian terrorists were not interested in anarchist ideology, they may have picked up some bomb-making techniques from them. More influential were the organizational models of the non-anarchist Russian revolutionaries. See Michael Silvestri, "'The Sinn Féin of India': Irish Nationalism and the Policing of Revolutionary Terrorism in Bengal," *Journal of British Studies* 39 (October 2000), 465.

6. *Times* (London), 4 May 1908; a sample of other articles falsely linking Indian terrorism to European-style anarchism include "Indian Anarchism," *Times* (12 February 1909), "The Methods of Indian Anarchism," *Times* (16 February 1909), "The Attempted Assassination of Lord Hardinge," *Times* (24 December 1912); "Kipling on the Manufacture of Indian Anarchists," *Spectator* (London), 19 March 1910, 459–460, and many others.

7. Anna Geifman, *Thou Shalt Kill: Revolutionary Terrorism in Russia, 1894–1917* (Princeton: Princeton University Press, 1995), 125.

8. Geifman (see note 7 above), 131. The Russian anarchists, however, were not the first suicide bombers. In 1881, the members of the People's Will who volunteered to try to assassinate Tsar Alexander II were aware that they might very well not survive the explosion: "the bombs' effectiveness could be guaranteed within a radius of about a metre. It was essential, therefore, that they should be thrown very carefully and from a very close range. The assassin had not the slightest chance of escaping death or capture." Franco Venturi, *Roots of Revolution*, trans. Francis Haskell (New York: Universal Library, 1960), 711–12.

9. Felice Orsini's deadly attack on Napoleon III in January 1858, which killed eight people and injured 142, might seem to be an exception to this generalization. But Orsini's aim was to assassinate Napoleon III, not kill the bystanders.

10. All the quotations in this paragraph are from Jensen, "The Evolution of Anarchist Terrorism" (see note 2 above), 160.

11. See my forthcoming book, *The International Campaign against Anarchist Terrorism*, where the documentation for much of this essay will be elaborated more fully.

12. Eugenio Florian, *Trattato di Diritto Penale. 2: Introduzione ai delitti in ispecie delitti contro la sicurezza dello Stato* (Milan, 1915), 2nd ed., 138–161; William Loubat, "*De la legislation contre les anarchists au point de vue international*," *Journal de droit international prive*, 22 (1895), 1–22, and 23 (1896), 294–320.

   Criminal anarchy was defined as: "the doctrine that organized government should be overthrown by force or violence, or by assassination of the executive head or any of the executive officials of government, or by any unlawful means." Sidney Fine, "Anarchism and the Assassination of McKinley," *American Historical Review* 40, no. 4 (July 1955), 793–94.

13. Report of the administrative committee, secret official records of the Rome Conference (Rome: Imprimerie du ministère des affaires etrangères, 1899), 122–23.

14. "Searching among Paterson Anarchists," *New York Times* (1 August 1900), 1.

15. Katherine Cabates, "The Diplomatic Relations of the Major Powers in the International Zone of Tangier" (Master's Dissertation, Georgetown University, 1954), 42, 46.

16. *Policing World Society: Historical Foundations of International Police Cooperation* (Oxford: University Press, 2002).

17. *Corriere della Sera*, 3–7, 25–26; 28 June 1906. The bombs found ca. 23 June 1906 were in a castle wall at Castelferretti, near Falconara.
18. Fiorenza Fiorentino, *Ordine pubblico nell'Italia giolittiana* (Rome: Carecas, 1978), 81–2.
19. Ibid. 92–3, 110–11, 118–19. Fiorentino (92–3) cites the 1911 case of Lelio Luzi, who may have been an agent provocateur, urging on a certain Umberto Adami, a fanatical admirer of Bresci, living in Zurich.
20. Domenico Farini, *Diario di fine secolo*, ed. Emilia Morelli (Rome: Bardi, 1961–62) 1:455.
21. Joaquin Romero Maura, "Terrorism in Barcelona and its Impact on Spanish Politics 1904–1909," *Past and Present* 41(December 1968), 172.
22. Ibid., 156–7.
23. Geifman (see note 7 above), 237–40; Jonathan Daly, *The Watchful State: Security Police and Opposition in Russia 1906–1917* (Dekalb: Northern Illinois Press, 2004), 124–8.
24. Memorandum from Interior Minister (and beginning in 1903, Prime Minister) Giolitti to the Italian foreign minister, 12 May 1902. Series P: politica, 1891–1916. B.47; Italian Foreign Ministry [hereafter, IFM]; Giolitti to foreign minister, most confidential, Rome, 30 May 1904, Polizia internazionale, B. 35, IFM.
25. Marques de Lema (Madrid) to Spanish Ambassador (Berlin), 22 November 1913. Archivo Historico, Spanish Ministry of Foreign Affairs, *Orden Publico, legajo* 2753.
26. Department IIIb, Foreign Ministry, Berlin, 13 November 1913, German Central Archive, Berlin (Formerly Potsdam). Foreign Ministry, Band 3, n. 19, 35515.
27. Laqueur, *The Age of Terrorism* (Boston: Little, Brown, 1987), 121–7; Hoffman, *Inside Terrorism* (New York: Columbia University Press, 1999), 176–8.
28. See Jensen, "Criminal Anthropology and the Problem of Anarchist Terrorism in Spain and Italy," *Mediterranean Historical Review* (December 2001), 31–44, and Mary Gibson, *Born to Crime: Cesare Lombroso and the Origins of Biological Criminology* (New York: Praeger, 2002).
29. Robert Kern, *Red Yearsz/Black Years. A Political History of Spanish Anarchism, 1911–1937* (Philadelphia: Institute for the Study of Human Issues, 1978), 74; Gerald Brennan, *The Spanish Labyrinth* (Cambridge: University Press, 1971), 73–4; George Woodcock, *Anarchism* (New York: New American Library, 1962), 379.
30. A few symbolic anarchist attacks, which might be qualified as terrorism, also occurred during the Primo de Rivera dictatorship, i.e., the November 6–7, 1924, attacks on the Atarazanas prison in Barcelona and the Vera de Bidasoa frontier station. Kern (see note 29 above), 66; Murray Bookchin, *The Spanish Anarchists: The Heroic Years 1868–1936* (Oakland, CA: AK Press, 1997), 191.
31. For the details of the anarchist deeds, see Paul Avrich, *Sacco and Vanzetti: The Anarchist Background* (Princeton: Princeton University Press, 1991), 99–103, 137–162.
32. Jensen, "The Evolution of Anarchist Terrorism," (see note 2 above), 157.
33. Ibid., 205–205; Nunzio Pernicone, "Luigi Galleani and Italian Anarchist Terrorism in the United States," *Studi Emigrazione* 30 (September 1993), 469.
34. *New York Times* (26 January 1923), 19.
35. Osvaldo Bayer, *Los anarquistas expropriadores* (Buenos Aires: Planeta, 2003), 11–88.
36. For the anarcho-bolsheviks, see Kern (note 29 above), 54, 56.
37. *Annuaire de l'Institut de Droit International*, 12 (1892–94), 167.
38. Unfortunately Bogdan Zlataric, "History of International Terrorism and its Legal Control," in *International Terrorism and Political Crimes*, ed. M. Cherif Bassiouni (Springfield: Charles Thomas, 1975), 480, omits "*toute*" in his translation of "*toute organization sociale.*" Cf. *V*ᵉ *Conference Internationale pour l'unification du droit penal* (Madrid, 14–20 October 1933). *Actes de la conference* (Paris: A. Pedone, 1935), 335.
39. Zlataric (see note 38 above), 483.

40. In a speech given last November and in an article, Professor James Gelvin of the University of California at Los Angeles has produced the most detailed comparison to date. He also cites eight other authors, from a writer in *The Economist* to Niall Ferguson, who briefly allude to these alleged similarities. www.international.ucla. edu/cms/files/JamesGelvin.pdf: and "Al-Qaeda and Anarchism: A Historian's Reply to Terrorology," *Terrorism and Political Violence*, 20, no. 4 (2008), 563–581.

41. Jensen, "Daggers" (see note 2 above), 116–117.

42. Daggers and pistols were more effective tools of assassination than bombs, although the latter proved more lethal for the innocent bystanders, as in the case of the 1906 attack on Spanish King Alfonso XIII.

43. Francesco Polti, an eighteen-year-old shop assistant who was involved in a plan to blow up the Royal Exchange in London and Luigi Lucheni. It seems likely that Lucheni, who had loyally served in the Italian army and subsequently worked as a servant for his aristocratic officer, became an anarchist after he emigrated to Switzerland where he mixed with anarchists and radicals. After his arrest in 1898, however, Lucheni claimed that he had been an anarchist at heart from an early age.

44. This analysis is based on my own compilation. For one of the most complete listings of anarchist *attentats*, see: http://artic.ac-besancon.fr/histoire_geographie//HGFTP/ Autres/Utopies/anarterr.doc or http://artic.ac-besancon.fr/histoire_geographie// HGFTP/Autres/Utopies/anitadat.doc.

45. Rapoport, "The Four Waves of Modern Terrorism," in Audrey Kurth Cronin and James M. Ludes, editors, *Attacking Terrorism: Elements of a Grand Strategy* (Washington, D.C.: Georgetown University Press, 2004), 46–73. Richard Bach Jensen, "Nineteenth Century Anarchist Terrorism: How Comparable to the Terrorism of al-Qaeda?" *Terrorism and Political Violence*, 20, no. 4 (2008), 589–596.

46. For details, see ibid.

47. Geifman (see note 7 above), 132.

48. For the details of the anarchist deeds, see Pernicone (note 33 above), 482–487, and Avrich (note 31 above), 99–103, 137–162.

49. '"Dance Macabre': Problems in the History of Terrorism," presented at a conference on "What Can and Cannot Be Learned From History about Terrorism: A Dialogue between Historians and Social Scientists," the Human Factors Division, Science and Technology Directorate, Department of Homeland Security, Arlington, Virginia, June 15–16, 2007. This paper was published as "Ordinary Terrorism in Historical Perspective," *Journal for the Study of Radicalism* 2, no. 1 (2008), 125–154.

7

Bureaucratization and Social Control: Historical Foundations of International Police Cooperation

Mathieu Deflem

Ours is not a political but a cultural goal.... It only concerns the fight against the common enemy of humankind: the ordinary criminal.

> – *Vienna Police President Hans Schober, 1923*

They don't know what we are doing.... We do the work.

> – *New York City Police Commissioner Richard Enright, 1923*

A steady road leads ... to the current position of the policeman as the "representative of God on earth."

> – *Max Weber*

Introduction

In this article, a study in the sociology of social control, I use a theoretical model based on the work of Max Weber to account for the development of international police organizations from the middle of the 19th until the early 20th century. Although much sociological research has been devoted to the study of police (e.g., Bittner 1970; Black 1980; Marx 1988; Skolnick 1966), it remains a truism, as Jacobs and O'Brien (1998) argue, that many dimensions of police and policing remain conspicuously understudied by

Source: *Law & Society Review: Journal of the Law and Society Association*, 34(3) (2000): 739–778.

sociologists. It is remarkable that political sociologists have, for the most part, neglected to study police institutions, especially when we consider that Max Weber related his famous conception of the state explicitly to the institution-alized means of force. Recall that Weber defined the state as "that human community which within a certain territory ... claims for itself (with success) a monopoly of legitimate physical coercion" ([1919]:506; see also Weber [1922]:514–40, 566–67, 815–68). And when Weber specified the functions of the modern state, he explicitly included "the protection of personal security and public order (police)" ([1922]:516).

Yet, despite Weber's reference to the institution of police, sociologists have mostly been interested in the state as the center of power over a ter-ritory, rather than in the bureaucratic apparatuses of legitimate force the state has at its disposal. I demonstrate that it makes sound sociological sense to study police as a force in and of itself, even though it is not unrelated to other dimensions of society.[1] Specifically, I investigate dimensions of the internationalization of police, defined as that institution formally charged to lawfully execute the state's monopoly over the means of coercion (Bittner 1970; Manning 1977:105). Hence, this analysis is not about the police (in the plural) as a force of law-enforcement officials, but about police (in the singular) as an institution sanctioned by states. Specifically, I undertake a historical study of several international organizations of police that were formed since the middle of the 19th century.

International dimensions of police have been of growing concern in recent years (e.g., Deflem 1996a; Huggins 1998; Marx 1997; McDonald 1997; Nadelmann 1993; Sheptycki 1995). From a sociological viewpoint, the inter-nationalization of the police function is particularly puzzling because pub-lic police agencies are central organs of national states that claim and are willing to protect at large costs their jurisdictional sovereignty. Cooperation among public police institutions at an international level, therefore, seems to be inherently paradoxical to their nation-bound function, acutely posing the question of why police nonetheless cooperate across national boundaries.

The centerpiece of my analysis is the International Criminal Police Com-mission (ICPC), the forerunner of Interpol, which, founded in Vienna in 1923, is among the most enduring, and in this sense successful, interna-tional police organizations. The origins of the ICPC provide a useful case that can be comparatively examined in relation to other international police initiatives that for various reasons were not successful. Of these, I discuss the Police Union of German States, formed in 1851; the First Congress of International Criminal Police, organized in Monaco in 1914; and the Inter-national Police Conference, held in New York in 1922.

On the basis of Max Weber's theories of bureaucracy, the central argu-ment of my analysis is that international police organizations with broad international representation could only be formed when police institutions were sufficiently autonomous from the political centers of their respective national states to function as relatively independent bureaucracies. When this structural condition of institutional autonomy was fulfilled, I further maintain, police institutions would collaborate across the borders of their respective national jurisdictions on the basis of a shared system of knowledge concerning the development and enforcement of international crime. In the discussion, I focus on the theoretical implications of this analysis and bring out the merits of a Weberian perspective of social control.

International Police and Bureaucratization

Weber's theories of bureaucracy have not been very influential in the sociology of social control. Studies of police bureaucracies mostly focus on only one organization or aspect of policing (e.g., Ethington 1987; Ng-Quinn 1990; Theoharis 1992), while other studies criticize the Weberian preoccupation with formal rationality (e.g., Herbert 1998; Heyman 1995). Relatedly, studies of social control that use a bureaucracy perspective tend to emphasize the dangers involved when state agencies operate without sufficient democratic control (e.g., Benson, Rasmussen & Sollars 1995; O'Reilly 1987; Gamson & Yuchtman 1977; Useem 1997). The relevance of these studies cannot be denied, but based on the notion that critique cannot be constitutive of analysis, I follow a different route and develop a Weberian framework to empirically uncover historical developments of police. Let me first briefly repeat the key elements of Weber's perspective of bureaucracy.[2]

Bureaucracy and the State of Police

Corresponding to Weber's suggestion that societal rationalization has gone in the direction of an increasing reliance on principles of efficiency in terms of a calculation of means ([1922]:514–16), he considered the modern state bureaucracy to be the quintessential expression of formally rationalized societies (551–79). In fact, Weber went as far as to equate bureaucracy with modern power: "domination (*Herrschaft*) is in everyday life primarily administration (*Verwaltung*)" (126). As institutions in charge of implementing policies decided upon in the polity, state bureaucracies operate on the basis of an organizational design that includes that they are: subject to a principle of jurisdiction; hierarchically ordered; operating on the basis of files; separated from private households; relying on specialized training; employing a full-time staff; and guided by general rules (551–54). Most critically, Weber observed, the modern bureaucracy operates on the basis of a "formalistic impersonality" oriented at employing the most efficient, and only the most efficient, means, given certain goals (128). Efficiency and specialization also enhance bureaucratic knowledge, including technical know-how (expertise) and information (accumulated in the exercise of official business) (Weber [1918]:352–54).

Among the social consequences of bureaucratization, Weber found most significant the trend toward bureaucratic autonomy; that is, the gradual formation of a bureaucratic machinery that is relatively autonomous from political and popular control. Weber discussed the societal conditions under which bureaucracies were formed ([1922]:556–66), but he argued that such external influences were "not indispensable" preconditions and that they could not account for bureaucratic activity (558). Instead, it was the technical superiority of the bureaucracy "without regard for the person" that Weber regarded as "the decisive factor" for the spread of bureaucracy as the most dominant form of organization (562, 561). The sole regard for a purposive-rational execution in the modern bureaucracy is what Weber argued to account for the drift of bureaucracy toward independence beyond and possibly even against political control (Weber [1919]:541–42).

Rationalization processes have historically influenced a bureaucratization of the modern police function across Western societies (Bayley 1985:23–52; Manning 1977:41–71).[3] Notwithstanding national variations, police development has gone in the direction of the creation of a specialized bureaucratic apparatus, in both functional and organizational respects (Bayley 1985:12–14; Manning 1977:109–11; Skolnick 1966:235–39). Functionally, public police institutions have gradually come to be responsible for order maintenance and crime control, tasks for which police can legitimately resort to force. Organizationally, police bureaucratization is reflected in characteristics that closely follow Weber's typology: police bureaucracies are hierarchically ordered, with a clear chain of command (discipline); agents are formally trained experts who, as full-time appointed officials (professionalization), perform specialized duties (division of labor); and policework follows set rules and procedures (professionalism) and is driven toward the use of technically efficient means, such as secrecy and force (purposive rationality).

Before I elaborate a bureaucratization model of international police on the basis of Weber, I wish to acknowledge that a similar perspective is founded in Michel Foucault's theories of discipline and governmentality ([1975], [1978]). These studies conceive of social control as the management of a depoliticized society of living subjects (e.g., Simon 1988; Stenson 1993). Such a Foucauldian model can usefully bring out aspects of a technology of policing and its internal dynamics, but it has also been criticized because it cannot satisfactorily deal with the ambivalent developments of law and social control in terms of justice as well as coercion (Habermas 1985:279–343) and because it neglects the embeddedness of punishment and control in a broader societal context (Lacombe 1996). Although there may be debate on the validity of these criticisms against Foucault (Deflem 1997; Garland 1990, 1997), these concerns were of key significance to Weber, for his perspective took into account the external conditions that favored the bureaucratization process without neglecting its internal logic (Albrow 1970:45–49;

Page 1985:162–71). Thus, although a Foucauldian perspective can surely be complementary to a Weberian analysis, the hypotheses I advance in this article take advantage of Weber's theory to focus attention on the dynamics that work toward bureaucratic autonomy without neglecting the external contexts in which bureaucratization takes place.

A Weberian Model of International Police Cooperation

Applying Weber's perspective of bureaucracy, I outline a two-layer model of international policing that differentiates between structural conditions and operational motives. Structural conditions ensure that national police agencies are in a position to move beyond the confines of their respective national jurisdictions. These conditions are necessary but insufficient for police agencies to engage in international cooperation. When structural conditions are met, international police organizations need an additional motivational basis to become operational. Relying on Weber, I specify the structural conditions and operational motives of international policework in terms of two aspects of bureaucratic autonomy: (1) As a structural condition for cooperation across national jurisdictions, police institutions must have gained a sufficient degree of independence as specialized bureaucracies from their respective governments; and (2) International policework can be actualized when police institutions share a system of knowledge and expertise on international crime.

My first hypothesis relates to the necessary conditions that need to be fulfilled to create a structural opportunity for international policework. Sociologist Peter Blau ([1964]:64–68) has specified conditions for exchange among collectivities by suggesting that interorganizational exchange can occur when organizations are interdependent in terms of tasks or objectives. Absent supranational enforcement duties, police bureaucracies cannot be interdependent in terms of a functional division of labor. However, given similarity in the institutional position of police bureaucracies across nations, formal congruence in positions can be considered a condition for interorganizational cooperation across national jurisdictions. In other words, police institutions can engage in cooperation with similarly bureaucratic police agencies from other nation-states, because of their comparable autonomy relative to the political centers of their respective states. If such autonomy is not achieved, police cooperation will remain limited in scope of international participation and cannot extend beyond the confines of politically akin states, i.e., national states that resemble one another in ideological respects and/or entertain close ties in international relations.

The introduced notion of autonomy does not imply an absolute independence or detachment of police from the state. On the contrary, public police institutions are always agents of state control, and as public police institutions they can derive their legitimacy only from states. Autonomy of police, therefore, remains a matter of degree relative to the (historically variable) control from national governments. Yet, with these qualifications in mind, the conditions of police autonomy from the political powerholders of the state relate to the fact that police bureaucracies rely on a means-ends rationality to employ what are held to be the technically most efficient – not necessarily the politically most opportune – means, given set goals. The irony is that police institutions can then perform state-sanctioned enforcement duties in a manner that is no longer bound to the state. My first hypothesis, then, can be stated as follows:

> Hypothesis 1: *The greater the extent to which national police institutions have successfully gained a position of institutional independence from their respective political centers, the greater is the chance that those institutions are in a position to engage in international cooperation.*

An alternative way of formulating this hypothesis is that police institutions are in a position to cooperate internationally when they have gained bureaucratic independence from the political centers of their respective states (formal bureaucratic autonomy). Or, conversely, a lack of institutional autonomy will impede the formation of international police structures. Police institutions that remain tied to the political centers of their states will either insulate themselves from international duties to stay within the boundaries of their national jurisdictions, or will engage in transnational activities that are intimately related to national tasks. International activities under these circumstances will not go beyond unilaterally conducted policework abroad, temporary bilateral cooperation for specific duties, or limited multilateral forms among police of politically like-minded states.

Beyond favorable structural conditions, police agencies must also develop certain operational motives to form a new field of activities that transcends the borders of national jurisdictions. In this respect, I rely on Meyer and Rowan's (1977) suggestion that the operational rules of bureaucratic organizations function as "myths" that define problems and specify solutions in terms framed by and for the bureaucracy. It is useful to call these cultural systems of knowledge myths, not to convey the notion that they are empirically false but that it is not primarily relevant whether they are. Together with the level of organizational efficiency, these myths influence the organization's legitimacy, activities, and resources, while minimizing external inspection and control.[4] The organizationally defined myth that motivates international police collaboration is provided by a professional conception and interest in the control of international crime. The reason police can lay claim to, define, and offer solutions to the international crime problem relates to the fact that police institutions, as Weber ([1918]: 352–54) argued about bureaucracies in general, can accumulate specialized knowledge, including official information about the extent of, and expertise to deal with, international crime. Such systems of knowledge have operational consequences across national jurisdictions to the extent that they are shared among national police institutions.

Hypothesis 2: *The greater the extent to which national police institutions can rely on a common organizational interest in the fight against international crime, the greater is the chance that those institutions will collaborate in international policework.*

Alternatively formulated, this hypothesis states that international cooperation of police can be achieved when police institutions have established specialized systems of expert knowledge related to the fight against international crime (operational bureaucratic autonomy). Or, conversely, international police cooperation is unlikely to succeed – even despite favorable structural conditions – when participating agencies do not share an agenda on international crime.

In the next sections, I analyze selected cases in the history of international police cooperation on the basis of the suggested hypotheses. The centerpiece of my investigations is the International Criminal Police Commission, but I expand the case of the ICPC with cross-sectional data on three relatively unsuccessful attempts to formalize international policework from the middle of the 19th century onward to show how conditions and outcomes combined under varying historical circumstances. Since the history of international policing is relatively unknown, I first present a brief descriptive sketch of the development of international policework from the 19th century onward.

The Internationalization of the Police Function and the Origins of Interpol (1851–1923)

The formation of the International Criminal Police Commission in 1923 is historically rooted in a long series of efforts aimed at fostering police cooperation across the jurisdictions of national states. Among the antecedents of international police cooperation are various forms of international policework throughout the 19th century, particularly in Europe, that were designed to protect established autocratic political regimes (Bayley 1975; Busch 1995:255–64; Fijnaut 1979:107–45). These international forms, indeed, primarily concerned political police activities, as the targets of such initiatives were typically the presumed opponents of conservative governments, such as anarchists, social democrats, and the growing labor movements. Most of these cooperation efforts were not formally structured in a permanent international organization but occurred on the basis of specific needs and would be terminated once those needs were met. Yet, at times, steps were taken to create more organized and permanent organizational structures of international police. The Police Union of German States, formed in 1851, was such an organization, bringing together police from various German-speaking states to control political activities. Similar plans of a political nature would still be taken during the latter half of the 19th century. As late as 1898, for instance, Italian authorities organized the "Anti-Anarchist Conference of Rome," which was attended by representatives of 21 European countries, in an attempt to formally structure the international policing of the anarchist movement (Jensen 1981; Fijnaut 1979:930–33). Although a follow-up meeting was held in St. Petersburg in 1904, these efforts yielded few practical results.

In the early decades of the 20th century, the number of international police initiatives sharply increased. Most of the these plans were not successful, but the remarkable increase in attempts to structure international policework clearly manifests a more general globalization in cultural and organizational respects that took place in various institutional domains (Boli & Thomas 1997; Meyer et al. 1997). At this time, also, international police cooperation gradually depoliticized in terms of goals and became more formalized in organizational respects. The first 20th-century initiative to organize international enforcement against crimes of a non-political nature was taken at the First Congress of International Criminal Police in Monaco in 1914. Such attempts to formalize multilateral police organizations were dominated by police from Europe and rarely extended beyond the Continent.

The main counterpart to European police cooperation in the early 20th century originated in Latin America, where (unsuccessful) plans to establish international police cooperation were voiced at international police conferences in Buenos Aires in 1905, in São Paolo in 1912, and in Buenos Aires in 1920 (Marabuto 1935:26–27). U.S. police agencies were at this time more concerned with the federalization of police in matters of interstate commerce. In the United States no international police cooperation plans were initiated until the International Police Conference in New York in 1922. Clearly, then, when the International Criminal Police Commission was founded in Vienna in 1923, it represented the culmination of an internationalization of police that had been set in motion since at least the 19th-century consolidation of national states. Unlike many of its predecessors, moreover, the ICPC was successful in establishing an enduring structure with wide international representation, the conditions of which I analyze in the following sections.

Institutional Autonomy and the Structural Conditions of International Police Cooperation

The Police Union of German States (1851–1866) and the Failure of an International Political Police in 19th-Century Europe

My first hypothesis states that police agencies must be in a sufficiently autonomous position from the political centers of their states for there to be a structural condition under which police cooperation across national jurisdictions becomes possible beyond the confines of politically akin national states. The negative case of this hypothesis is presented by the failure of 19th-century attempts to forge police cooperation by means of a more or less permanent organization on a European-wide basis. Indeed, most international police efforts in 19th-century Europe were not of a cooperative kind; furthermore, initiated cooperative forms were limited to temporary arrangements and/ or to organizations with relatively restricted participation by police of politically similar or unified national states.

In 1848, various outbursts of popular unrest across Europe aimed to overturn the dictatorial rules of autocratic governments. Established regimes responded harshly and, in consequence, also strengthened their police institutions (Fijnaut 1979:107–45; Liang 1992:18–82). This response led to reforms of various national police powers, which brought about a factual harmonization of police organizations across Europe. Additionally, the revolutionary year 1848 also served as a catalyst for the internationalization of the police function, leading to an increase of international police activities with distinctly political objectives.[5] These international political police activities occurred in the form of intelligence work abroad and/or by means of increased cooperation for shared purposes of political suppression (Fijnaut 1987:33–35). Covert political policework abroad was by its very nature typically unilaterally instigated without the knowledge of police or other authorities of the country in which the activity took place. Unlike this transnational policework, international police cooperation involved bilateral and multilateral efforts to organize information exchange, either through establishing contacts between police officials (the so-called personal correspondence system) or through the distribution of printed information on wanted suspects (published in search bulletins). Whereas the correspondence system was initiated ad hoc by a particular police institution on the basis of a specific need for assistance (e.g., following an assassination attempt on a monarch or statesman), the system of printed bulletins represented a more permanent form of international information exchange (Deflem 1996b). For example, beginning in the 1850s the Viennese police published a biweekly "Central Police Bulletin" (*Central-Polizei-Blatt*), which provided information on wanted suspects (Deflem 1996a:41–42). From the 1860s onward, copies of the Austrian bulletins were regularly sent to police in Prussia, and, by the 1880s, they were distributed throughout Europe (Liang 1992:32).

In the middle of the 19th century, among the most ambitious attempts to formalize international police cooperation was the Police Union of German States, which was founded in 1851 by police of Prussia, Austria, and the German territories of Sachsen, Hanover, Baden, Württemberg, and Bavaria (Deflem 1996b). The Union established various modes of direct information exchange, particularly police meetings and a system of printed magazines. The Union, operative until 1866, was conceived in opposition to individuals and organizations that were thought to threaten the stability of the established political regimes of Europe's national states. Because some political dissenters (especially Communists) were believed to be conspiring from London, Paris, and other capital cities in Europe, the Union particularly devoted efforts to enhance international cooperation among police.

However, despite various efforts to formally structure international police-work throughout the 19th century, these attempts by and large failed and were operative only temporarily or on a restricted international basis. The major-ity of these international police operations remained unilaterally transnational (without foreign cooperation), or of a cooperative kind that was limited in functional respects (initiated for a specific purpose and terminated after it was achieved) and/or limited in international scope (bilaterally or multilaterally among police of politically akin states) (Fijnaut 1979:798–843; Liang 1992:18–19, 33–34). The widespread practice of transnational and limited cooperative policework testifies to the critical concerns over sovereignty in 19th-century Europe and the related antagonism and fragile coalitions that marked the international relationships among states. Such sociopolitical conditions also influenced the fact that efforts to establish international cooperation among police on a broader multilateral basis failed. The Police Union is in this respect no exception, for the organization remained very limited in international appeal, with a restricted membership of police from seven German-language states that were united in the German Confederation, a federal political union that existed from 1815 until 1866. The Union could not count on the support of police from France, Italy, and other European countries, even though they were often as committed to maintaining conservative rule through the policing of politics. And Union agents stationed abroad were mostly involved in secre-tively conducted transnational operations (Deflem 1996b:48–49). National differences in political-ideological respects combined with sovereignty con-cerns to make political police cooperation with broad international representa-tion impossible. Therefore, it is also no surprise that, with the rise of Bismarck and his uncompromising foreign policy, the Police Union's activities gradually began to decline, until the Union was finally disbanded when war broke out between Prussia and Austria (the Seven-Weeks' War of 1866).

In sum, reflecting the dynamics of national and international politi-cal conditions, police institutions during the 19th century were intimately related with the quest of national autocratic governments to consolidate con-servative political rule. As such, it is clear that, although police agencies were institutionally separated from the military, they were closely aligned as the two central organs of state coercion (Fijnaut 1979:127–30). The relevant conclusion is that police institutions during the 19th century remained inti-mately linked to the political dictates of national-state governments and had not yet sufficiently developed as bureaucratic expert institutions that could claim independence from national (and international) political affairs.

The First Congress of International Criminal Police (1914) and the Rise of European Police Culture

Although 19th-century international political police operations were dominated by the dictates of national governments, they contained the origins of a bureaucratic autonomy of police that would characterize later developments of international policing beyond state control. The main reason for this peculiar development is that, although political police objectives were determined by the autocratic governments of national states, police agencies were charged with arranging and executing all necessary measures independently. As a result of this autonomy granted to police at the administrative level, police officials cooperating across national borders would gradually also begin to develop a common culture that would further cement and build international relations among police institutions regardless of the dictates of political governments.

In the second half of the 19th century, strong political antagonism and nationalist sentiments still hindered efforts to organize international police cooperation. Indicative is the failure of the participants of the anti-anarchist conferences of Rome and St. Petersburg to set up a central intelligence bureau and to have appropriate legislation enacted in the various participating countries (Jensen 1981:340). Ideological differences and political antagonism among the countries of Europe, then, not only prevented legislation being passed at the national levels but also posed limits to international police cooperation for political purposes.

Nevertheless, the various efforts taken in international police matters since the middle of the 19th century did lead to the gradual formation of a European police culture that, by the beginning of the 20th century, matured into a non-political system of shared values, oriented at fostering cooperation across national borders.

In the first instance, the administrative autonomy granted to police involved the elaboration of appropriate means of policework. This elaboration involved primarily the institution of various modes of information exchange, such as the bulletin and correspondence systems. These systems, besides transmitting information for investigative purposes, also enabled police to establish and cement relationships on a personal level across national jurisdictions. In fact, as early as 1851, when von Hinckeldey invited police across Europe to form the Police Union, he had already envisioned a conference of "men ... who in their difficult profession know one other as reliable and have learned to appreciate one another" (in Beck & Schmidt 1993:5). Similarly, at the anti-anarchist conference of Rome, a British representative of Scotland Yard acknowledged that the meetings were beneficial "by forming reciprocal friendships leading to greater cooperation" (in Jensen 1981:332). These professional contacts for investigative purposes were further enhanced by courtesy visits among police officials that were conducted for reasons of training and professional diplomacy (Liang 1992:151–55).

During such moments of contact, the professionals of policing began to recognize one another as fellow experts of law enforcement and, in consequence, formed "a fraternity which felt it had a moral purpose, a mission, to perform for the good of society" (Fijnaut 1997:111). From then on, a shared police culture based on professional expertise in matters of the proper means of policing could be extended to also include the appropriate objectives of policing. The development of a depoliticized criminological knowledge was nurtured and found much favor in the modern institutions of police (Deflem 1997).

As one important element of these new sciences of crime, there would also be expressed, time and time again from the mid-19th century onward, the idea that international crime was on the rise as a consequence of a general modernization of social life. For instance, in 1893, the German criminologist Franz von Liszt expressed the idea that criminals specializing in monetary crimes had begun to roam the world and that the police response against them should be internationally coordinated (Marabuto 1935:15). Because of these circumstances of a developing police culture it would become possible for police authorities to independently organize international police cooperation on a multilateral basis.

With the development of a European police culture in mind, it will become clear why the First Congress of International Criminal Police (*Premier Congrès de Police judiciaire internationale*), held in Monaco in 1914, would fail in instituting an international police organization. At the Congress, 300 magistrates, diplomats, academics, and police officials from 24 countries decided to establish and enhance means to improve international police cooperation, including the organization of international police communications by telegraph and telephone (Roux [1914]). A next meeting was to be held in Bucharest in 1916, but the beginning of World War I prevented any practical implementation of the measures discussed at the Monaco Congress.

Despite the fact that the outbreak of World War I effectively meant the failure of the Monaco Congress, I argue that the effort could not have succeeded at any rate because the Congress attendees' conception of the organization of international policework did not take into account developments in police bureaucratization; instead, they still relied on an out-dated model of international policing inherited from the 19th century. Although, as I earlier described, by the early 20th century police experts had already developed a common culture on the means and goals of professional policing, the Monaco Congress was still rooted in principles of national politics and formal systems of law.

From its inception, the Congress was not an undertaking organized by police officials; the initiative to organize it was taken by Albert I, Prince of Monaco. The meeting may have been the Prince's attempt to enhance Monaco's international prestige in world affairs (Bresler 1992:18–20), or it may have been inspired by his awareness of the status of the principality as a resort for the wealthy, posing particular issues of property crimes (Walther 1968:11). Regardless of the Prince's motives, and despite the Congress's explicit focus on criminal and not political police tasks, however, the plan was not instigated by police bureaucrats. And even though the Congress explicitly focused on cooperation among police, most of its attendees were magistrates and government representatives, not police officials. Furthermore, because of the overrepresentation of legal experts and diplomats at the Congress, the discussions largely took place within a legal framework and included debates about the formal arrangements of international law, such as extradition procedures, and proposals of using police measures only for that function. The Congress devoted attention to international measures of policing, but only as one (and the least-discussed) of four conference themes (Roux [1914]:66–198). The Congress thus worked on the basis of a model of formal systems of law that could only mirror the many differences that existed among the various national jurisdictions.

Having recognized existing variations among national legal systems across Europe (and the world), the attendants at the Congress suggested that all participating countries should adopt one national police system, *in casu* that of France, to be used in all international policework. Relatedly, the influential criminalist R. A. Reiss of the Police-Technical Institute at Lausanne suggested the creation of an international police bureau that would not only collect information about international criminals but also have at its disposal an international mobile police force. Although Reiss's suggestion was not approved, other participants at the Congress spoke very favorably about instituting French systems of criminal identification and investigation at the international level. Eventually, the Congress decided, for example, that the Paris criminal identification service would serve as central international bureau and that French was to be used in international police communications (Roux [1914]:200–01). These arrangements evidently placed the French participation in international policework center stage. Not surprisingly, the French delegates at the Congress by far outnumbered the representatives of other nations (Roux [1914]:4–5). Although French-speaking delegates attended the Congress as official government representatives, the governments of other countries, including, most notably, Germany, Austria-Hungary, Great Britain, and the United States, did not send official representatives (delegates from these countries were privately present as observers and did not take part in the discussions).

The negative implications of the international design suggested at the Monaco Congress are particularly manifested in the critical reactions the meeting received from the two German attendants (Finger 1914; Heindl 1914a, b). The German delegates bemoaned the fact that the Congress was primarily an affair of "Latin" countries and, relatedly, that it had decided to adopt the anthropometric system of identification in international policework (Finger 1914:268; Heindl 1914a:649). These criticisms betray deep-seated German-French antagonism of police technique and administration, because the anthropometric Bertillon system of criminal identification (measuring characteristics of the body) was nationally implemented in France, whereas the dactyloscopic system (of fingerprinting) was used in Germany. Therefore, the choice over which identification system would be adopted at the international level was not a mere technical matter, but would necessitate the reorganization of other participating national police systems. At the root of the problem, the German delegates argued, was the intent of the Congress to establish a supranational police instead of instituting a cooperative network among police institutions that would preserve their respective national traits. A decade later, when the ICPC would successfully establish such a cooperative model, one of the German attendants again dismissed the Monaco meeting as "dangerous dreams! Congressional fantasies! Springtime ravings at the Côte d'Azur" (Heindl 1924:20).

In sum, the failure of the Monaco Congress to establish an international police organization can be attributed to the fact that the meeting did not take into account the development of police bureaucracies and their attained level of autonomy from the political centers of national states at the turn of the 20th century. The Congress was still conceived on the basis of a model of formal law and politics that was rooted in 19th-century conceptions of sovereignty and national jurisdiction. It thereby conflicted with police institutions that were already prepared for the 20th century by having developed conceptions of the expert means and goals of policing, nationally as well as internationally. As discussed earlier, evolved European police culture had developed conceptions of the proper means and goals of policing in terms no longer based on legality but on professional expertise and knowledge. This situation also implied a mutual recognition among police officials that the only viable form of international police cooperation with broad participation could not have political objectives and could not aim to institute a supranational police but instead must be designed as a cooperative criminal police organization.

Such a non-political and cooperative structure was precisely what the International Criminal Police Commission (ICPC) successfully introduced in 1923. It was no coincidence, therefore, that the organizers of the meeting that founded the ICPC did not conceive it as a reorganization of the Monaco Congress. And, even though the ICPC would also go through the turmoils of a world war and other periods of international political antagonism, the organization would remain in existence until today.

The ICPC and the Organization of "Purely Technical Matters"

The International Criminal Police Commission was founded in 1923 to provide mutual assistance among national police institutions within the frameworks of the laws of their respective states on matters of ordinary crime, i.e., violations of criminal law (Internationale Kriminalpolizeiliche Kommission [hereafter IKK] 1923). The Commission's headquarters were established in Vienna, and in the years to come, the ICPC gradually expanded its membership and organizational facilities. The membership grew from 22 representatives at the time of the Commission's founding to 58 members by 1934. Almost all European countries were represented, as were police from

Egypt, China, and Japan. The United States became an official member of the Commission in June 1938 when President Roosevelt enacted a bill to that effect.

The ICPC headquarters in Vienna became strategically important for the centralization of information on a variety of police matters, especially notices of wanted criminals received from the participating police institutions. In addition to the establishment of its headquarters, the ICPC used various means to enhance direct police-to-police communication, which constituted its most important achievement in its formative years. These measures included coded telegraphic communications, a radio network, printed publications, and meetings. The Commission's most tangible realizations were the monthly periodical *International Public Safety* (*Internationale Öffentliche Sicherheit*), containing data on international crime and information on wanted suspects, and the international meetings, 14 of which took place in various European capitals before World War II.

In relation to my first hypothesis on the necessary conditions of international police cooperation, a variety of circumstances surrounding the formation of the ICPC indicate that a condition of institutional independence was achieved and explicitly relied upon. First of all, the ICPC was formed at a meeting convened independently by police officials, not as the result of a diplomatic initiative. It was but five years after the end of World War I that the Congress to establish the ICPC was organized by Johannes Schober, the Police President of Vienna, who became the first President of the ICPC in 1923 and remained so until his death in 1932. At the Vienna Congress, Schober stated that he had first developed the plan to establish international police collaboration about a year after the end of the war (IKK 1923:8–10). But, because it was so soon after the fall of the Hungarian-Austrian empire, Schober felt that Vienna would not be suitable for such an important task and that the initiative should be left to Police Captain M. C. van Houten, from the "neutral" Netherlands (IKK 1923:8). Van Houten (1923) of the Dutch criminal police had indeed, as early as December 1919, contacted police across Europe to establish an international police office. But, so soon after the war, van Houten's initiative did not produce the desired results. Four years later, Schober still realized the boldness of the plan but nonetheless hoped that "even in the midst of oppositions between the nations of the earth" the Vienna Congress would unite police "above the political battle," for police cooperation, he argued, was "not a political but a cultural goal" (IKK 1923:1, 9, 2).

The delayed gathering of the Vienna Congress after World War I demonstrates that the degree of institutional independence of police bureaucracies is affected by broader societal developments. Indeed, the immediate political implications of the war were obviously considered too weighty to allow for international police cooperation. But by 1923, circumstances had changed. The period of relative tranquility and pacification in world affairs that had set in after World War I is among the conditions that then favored police institutions to take advantage of their acquired formal bureaucratic autonomy. Of course, as history would dramatically show, this condition of stability was more presumed than real, but it was nonetheless of sufficient reality in perception that it effectively enabled police institutions to expand and take advantage of structural conditions that allowed them to engage in international cooperation.

Importantly, the acquired independence of police institutions partici-pating in the ICPC did not imply a surrender of national sovereignty. On the contrary, the ICPC was explicitly set up (and, as Interpol today, still operates) not as a supranational force but as an international network of national systems of police (Anderson 1989:168–85). As ICPC President Schober emphasized, the Commission would not strive for "something [as] impossible" as "supranationality" and instead would "hold on to the national individuality of all participating states" (in Archiv für Kriminologie 1925:72). Sensitivity about nationality questions was also reflected in the composition of the ICPC executive committee, assembled so that the various posts rotated from one country to another. The only imbalance in terms of nationality was the placement of the ICPC headquarters in Vienna and the appoint-ment of a President of the Commission who was affiliated with the Vien-nese criminal police.

This Austrian advantage was acceptable among the ICPC membership because the Austrian police systems and organization were particularly well advanced, especially in technical respects. As I indicated before, the Austrian police indeed had a long-standing history of collecting files on, and specializing in the fight against, international criminals, particularly in developing systems of information exchange (Liang 1992:18–34). In fact, dating back to the days of the Habsburg dynasty, Austrian authori-ties had initiated several attempts to establish a European police system. Throughout the 1860s, for instance, they attempted to expand the mem-bership of the Police Union and form a European-wide police organization (Liang 1992:151–53). Similarly, after the assassination of Empress Elisabeth of Austria in September 1898, the Austrian Foreign Minister called for the creation of an international police league (Liang 1992:160). Although these plans were unsuccessful, they do indicate Austria's special preoccupation with international policework.

By 1923, then, the acquired expertise, means, and technical prowess of Austrian involvement in international policework could be put to good use, especially for criminal (not political) police matters. The technically domi-nant position of the Viennese police in the ICPC was also accepted because police from the smaller European countries lacked the necessary resources to maintain an international office. Police from Germany and France, though participants in the ICPC, were unacceptable in any leadership position, given their antagonistic positions during and after World War I. Moreover, to secure the sovereignty of the individual nationalities, the Vienna headquarters were designed so that they enabled participation of national police systems without amalgamation. The headquarters only collected information forwarded by participating police institutions and passed on requests from one national police to another. As such, the headquarters did not initiate any investigations but functioned as a mere facilitator of police communications among national systems (Anderson 1989:168–85). International communication technologies by radio and telegraph likewise facilitated interaction among police, as did the meetings, without the formation of a supranational force.

Perhaps most clearly indicating an independence from politics is that the ICPC was established without the signing of an international treaty or legal document. All ICPC activities were planned (mostly at the meetings and through personal correspondence) and executed by and for participating police without input or control from their respective governments. In fact, the Commission had no internationally recognized legal status, and no legal procedure was ever formalized to acquire membership in the ICPC. The Commission did strive for governmental and legal recognition of its established structures, and it appealed for formal sanctioning from the League of Nations, inviting representatives of the League to the ICPC meetings (Palitzsch 1927; Skubl 1937). But, importantly, this appeal for political-legal approval occurred after the Commission had been developed and its structures were already in place, for, as van Houten expressed, the League of Nations was not considered capable of handling "such purely technical matters" (van Houten 1923:46).

As a non-governmental organization, the ICPC was never very successful in having its activities formally sanctioned by the League of Nations, in part because the League independently organized various aspects of police-work, especially in matters of white slavery, narcotics, and falsifications of currencies, themes on which the League held several meetings and passed international resolutions throughout the 1920s and 1930s (Marabuto 1935:113–49). More successful, however, was the ICPC's pursuit of approval from the national governments of the various participating police agencies. This condition was specified in one of the resolutions at the Vienna Congress as a desirable goal of cooperation (IKK 1923:201), and by the 1930s nearly all ICPC members were officially sanctioned by their respective governments and could often rely on additional funds and personnel to set up specialized offices (the so-called National Central Bureaus) needed to maintain international communications with the Vienna headquarters. As such, what we see is an international police network seeking to obtain legal and governmental approval after the organization had already been established and elaborated independently on the basis of professional police conceptions and without regard for political and legal considerations.

The Myth of International Crime and the Motives of International Police Cooperation

The International Police Conference (New York, 1922) and the Limits of International Crime

My second hypothesis states that once structural conditions of institutional independence are fulfilled, international police cooperation can become operational when participating police agencies have successfully developed a common organizational interest in the fight against international crime. The negative case of this hypothesis is presented by the International Police Conference (IPC), the first effort that was taken to formalize international police cooperation after World War I. The International Police Conference was organized at a meeting of police in New York in September 1922 (International Police Conference [hereafter: IPC] 1923; Enright 1925; Welzel 1925). Although the meeting attracted only five foreign delegates, it established the International Police Conference as a permanent organization to promote and facilitate international cooperation among police. However, in terms of membership and operations, the Conference was to be a predominantly American organization. It mostly promoted a coordination of local U.S. law enforcement agencies, with some additional participation from Canadian law enforcement.

The most tangible attempt to make good on the international aspirations of the Conference occurred when a joint meeting was organized with the International Criminal Police Commission in Paris in 1931. There, participants decided to set up an international police bureau in the United States and to discuss, at the next joint meeting, the creation of a "World Organization of Police." But the international bureau was never established and no additional joint meetings were held. In 1932, the IPC was brought under the direction of Barron Collier, a wealthy retired businessman who cultivated a keen interest in international police cooperation (Nadelmann 1993:90–91). Collier tried to put new life in the organization, but apart from meetings in Chicago in 1933 and in Montreal in 1937, the organization eventually ceased to exist.

Although the International Police Conference was not a successful organization, it was created under structural conditions favorable for international cooperation. The Conference was independently organized by police agencies, especially the New York City Police and its commissioner, Richard Enright, which were sufficiently professionalized to operate independently from governmental control. As Enright remarked at the IPC founding meeting, police professionals were in charge of "the work" in law enforcement, whereas the politicians were unknowledgeable (IPC 1923:341). The IPC also sought to establish police cooperation without the signing of a legally binding document, although the Conference did strive for legal-political recognition once formed. The Conference's plan to establish a central bureau, in particular, was to be approved through appropriate federal legislation, and bills to that effect were (unsuccessfully) entered in U.S. Congress in 1922 and 1923 (National Archives, Record Group 165, 2045–739/3).

Structural conditions for international cooperation were, in terms of formal bureaucratic independence, as favorable in 1922 in the United States as they would be a year later in Europe when the ICPC was formed. Yet what the International Police Conference missed was a practical playing field on which to effectively organize the fight against international crime. The self-stated motives of the organizers of the IPC were clear: the organization had to reach beyond national jurisdiction because "the enemies of society, organized or otherwise, are international in their scope" (Enright 1925:89). The internationalization of crime, furthermore, was believed to have been brought about by the rapid social changes after World War I (IPC 1923:14–15; Hart 1925:54). However, an internationalization of crime with sufficient implications for the development of a professional myth that would justify the creation of an international police organization was at this time still missing in the United States.

To be sure, U.S. law enforcement to some extent had been involved in international tasks for many years (Nadelmann 1993:15–102). Early on, since the founding of the Union, for example, a high premium was placed on customs regulations and the revenue that could be derived from their enforcement. Not surprisingly, the U.S. Customs Service was among the first federal U.S. police forces to be created, in 1789, and Treasury agents were among the first to work internationally by cooperating with foreign police or by being stationed abroad (Nadelmann 1993:22–31). Because of the geographical distance between the United States and Europe, and in the absence of a well-developed federal police, law enforcement agencies in the United States remained relatively insulated from the rest of the world. Also, until the mid-20th century, technological means of communication and transportation were not sufficiently developed for there to be any real concern of international criminality between the United States and Europe. Police tasks that related to an increasing mobility in social life (e.g., the policing of immigrant groups) were handled locally or remained mostly restricted to interstate matters (e.g., white slavery). From the late 19th-century onward, these duties were handled by federal U.S. law enforcement agencies, especially the investigative force of the U.S. Justice Department, which, since 1935, has been called the Federal Bureau of Investigation (FBI).

Why then was it that the IPC was nonetheless established with the intent of fostering cooperation across national states? Rather than viewing the formation of the International Police Conference in terms of an organizational myth responding to an internationalization of crime, the IPC should be considered in terms of certain internal police developments in the United States, particularly the police reform movement that sought to fight off political partisanship and corruption and enhance professionalism in policework (Walker 1977). This increasing quest for professionalism also entailed an effort to improve police relations, primarily with the public, but also with police of other nations. Publicly, the IPC presented itself as "the premier police association of the world" (Hart 1925:55) and promoted international cooperation, but not so as to respond to any growing concern over an increase in international crime. In fact, there is no empirical evidence that any international investigation ever originated from the IPC. Striking also is that, between May 1924 and October 1925, the IPC published a monthly periodical, the *Police Magazine* (later renamed *Police Stories*) that covered several articles on foreign police systems but provided no investigative information of any kind. Instead of being oriented toward fighting international crime, the IPC served as an organizational "presentation of self" relative to other professional police forces across the world, especially in Europe. For this reason, it was important for founder Enright to argue that the IPC brought together police from all "civilized nations, states, and municipalities of the world" (IPC 1923:15), even though an overwhelming majority of the organization's membership was from the United States (Deflem 1996a:152). As a professional association, the IPC could not compete with the International Association of Chiefs of Police (IACP), an organization that, since 1893, had contributed to advance professionalism among local U.S. police agencies (Deflem 1996a:68–70; Nadelmann 1993:84–91). There was in fact some competition between the IPC and the IACP, as the result of interagency conflict between the New York City Police, which founded the IPC, and local and federal law enforcement agencies in Washington, D.C., which controlled the IACP. Having positioned itself explicitly as an advocacy group, the IACP could make good on its ambitions of professionalism much more readily than could the IPC on its aspirations to fight international crime. The fate of the IPC was sealed in the absence of any significant concerns over an internationalization of crime that would justify a transatlantic police organization. In terms of concerns over interstate crimes within the United States, as well as with respect to the forms of international crime that at this time occupied U.S. law enforcement, however, the IPC could not compete in any significant way with expanding federal police agencies of the United States, in particular the FBI. Especially during the 1930s, under direction of its famed Director, J. Edgar Hoover, the FBI would indeed successfully gather the means, personnel, and budget to virtually monopolize all international law enforcement duties emanating from the United States (Deflem 1996a:187–89).

The ICPC and the Fight against "The Common Enemy of Human Society"

Whereas the International Police Conference in the United States could not successfully develop a myth of international crime, in this respect the International Criminal Police Commission in Europe was successful. The motivational basis of the ICPC in the first instance was provided by a cross-national rise and internationalization of crime, which police officials argued had taken place after World War I and which they saw as necessitating expanded control across national borders. This operational myth for international cooperation was formed on the basis of a specialized knowledge about the internationalization of crime, as well as the professional means to deal with it. Moreover, knowledge and skills were justified in terms of an expertise that sidestepped legal arrangements and focused not on violations of a political nature but on the ordinary or common criminal (IKK 1923:1).

Regardless of whether the view of a spectacular crime wave at the end of World War I is empirically valid, the notion that it had occurred and that it should serve as a catalyst for international police cooperation corresponds to the self-declared motives of participating police. To some extent, police knowledge on the development of international crime was surely founded in actual developments, but the vigor and intensity with which the notion was defended betrays a reality different from what statistics could support. First, there was the widespread and consequential idea among police authorities that the level of crime had increased dramatically after the war. The Dutchman, Captain van Houten (1923), had already expressed the notion of a spectacular influx of crime in many nations at war's end to justify his initiative in 1919, and Schober had reiterated the theme at the Vienna Congress (IKK 1923:8–10). The reports and statistics that officials from participating nations had provided at the Congress confirmed the necessity of an adequate police response and the commonality of the task among European police. Second, there was also believed to have occurred an epidemic spread of a new class of criminals who abused the modernization of social life and the increase in mobility after the war. They were the money swindlers, the passport, check, and currency forgers, the hotel and railway thieves, the white slave traders, and the drug traffickers (IKK 1934:82–129). With the latest technologies of communication and transportation at their disposal, these criminals had in common a unique capacity to transcend the boundaries of time and space in disregard of the national jurisdictions police institutions were traditionally subject to. The ICPC's preoccupation with these technologically influenced crimes is well demonstrated in that, at its first meeting, it had created a separate division concerned with falsification of currencies; at later meetings, the ICPC continued to have separate discussions on these and other typically modern crimes (Deflem 1996a:120–26).

Thus, police officials organizing the ICPC, to justify collaboration across national borders, argued that a new class of criminals was appearing in all countries that were undergoing rapid social change and technological progress, including, particularly, mobile criminals who were transcending nation-state borders. The adequate police response was conceived as a well-organized international network that would foster cooperation as an efficient means of enforcement. That these conceptions of international crime and their proper enforcement were not just a matter of discourse among police officials is clear from a closer look at the organizational innovations the ICPC introduced.

Primarily, the ICPC was concerned with a coordination of investigative information, as well as of technical know-how, through a variety of newly instituted means of information exchange. The Commission established new systems of technologically advanced means for international communication, specifically, a telegraphic code and a system of wireless (radio) communications (Deflem 1996a:129–30). Additionally, printed publications and annual meetings served to function as efficient means of direct international cooperation, unhindered by legal procedure and diplomatic formalities. The ICPC publications contained information and identifying data on wanted criminals and suspects and various articles on the latest police techniques, written by police professionals in the various participating states. The meetings were likewise planned and attended by police officials and criminalistics experts, rather than by political dignitaries or judicial administrators. The primary concern for an efficiency of means in international policework is also well reflected in the organization of the international headquarters at Vienna. By 1934, the headquarters included specialized divisions on the falsification of passports, checks, and currencies, on fingerprints and photographs, and on fugitives from justice and "Persons Dangerous to Society" (Deflem 1996a:126–31; Marabuto 1935:91–101). The organization of the ICPC headquarters, in other words, was based on expert police knowledge, not on categories of criminal law, and reflected technical know-how on the goals and means of policing, not on procedures of international law or politics.

Perhaps most clearly exemplifying the impact of a professional understanding of international policing beyond politics and legality were the criticisms among ICPC members against existing political-legal controls of international crime, the most prototypical expression of which was extradition. Extradition was indeed by far the most-addressed issue the ICPC dealt with in its formative years. The many formalities involved with, and the slowness of, official extradition procedures were particularly criticized. At the Vienna Congress in 1923, the Commission had already decided that participating police should develop measures to expedite extradition procedures and that, under some circumstances, police could exchange suspects without formal governmental approval (IKK 1923:200–01). At later meetings, the Commission members similarly lamented extradition as an inadequate tool in the fight against international crime (Deflem 1996a:121–25). The procedure was not criticized in terms of jurisdictional sovereignty but because of its inefficiency in fighting international crime, which, as an ICPC resolution of 1928 declared, had been developing "in a manner alarming to mankind as a whole" (IKK 1928). At an ICPC meeting in 1930, the Commission eventually determined to bypass extradition procedures altogether, deciding that ICPC members could make provisional arrests of suspects on the basis of information in the ICPC periodical, even in the absence of an international treaty that sanctioned this provision (Deflem 1996a:136–37). The ICPC, lamenting extradition as an inefficient tool of international police work, in its place suggested various expert police means to efficiently tackle the international crime problem. As the resolutions at the Vienna Congress specified (IKK 1923:197–202), the facilitation of direct police-to-police communications and a swifter exchange of information were the primary tools for cooperation across national borders. Considerations of efficiency dominated in the choice of adequate police techniques, not concerns over legality or justice. Instead of trying to construct an internationally valid legal definition of crime and international crime, the ICPC organized the international headquarters in Vienna on the basis of practical matters of crime detection, international policework, and sophisticated means of police technique and identification, such as fingerprints and photographs. For similar reasons, the ICPC also instituted communication systems through telegraph, radio, and printed documents and organized meetings for police to interact on a person-to-person basis.

In sum, the ICPC membership understood, in expert terms, the increase in international crime and, on the basis of a purposeful-rational efficiency, professionally conceived the means to handle the problem. Technological developments, ironically, were instrumental both in stimulating concerns over international crime and in enhancing the means of the enforcement of law. Even though technological progress brought about increasing opportunities for cross-border criminality, it also led to a growing expertise in the means of policing and criminalistics. Thus, technically sophisticated means of crime detection were important factors that enabled police bureaucracies to effectively develop a myth of international crime that went beyond a mere discourse among experts.

Bureaucratic Autonomy and the Internationalization of Police

I have explained the formation of the International Criminal Police Commission in 1923 and the failure of other attempts to organize international police cooperation since the middle of the 19th century on the basis of a model of bureaucratic autonomy inspired by Max Weber. I argued that police institutions must have attained a degree of separation from their respective governments so that a structural condition of institutional independence was created. Furthermore, an organizational myth of international crime had to be developed among police of different nations to function as a motivational basis around which to crystallize cooperative work. In this discussion I wish to move beyond the historical-empirical evidence on the immediate cases at hand and argue for the sociological relevance and strength of a Weberian perspective of social control.

The Politics of Police

In terms of my first hypothesis, I argued for the relevance of the structural condition of formal bureaucratic autonomy of police institutions participating in international efforts. In the case of the ICPC, formal bureaucratic autonomy is most clearly evinced from the fact that the organization was established independently at the initiative of police officials. Earlier 19th-century efforts to organize police cooperation could not rely on police institutions sufficiently detached from their respective political centers and therefore remained restricted in terms of international scope and participation. The Monaco Congress of 1914 did not take accomplished developments in the bureaucratization of the police function into account and was doomed to fail because the initiative was taken by politicians and magistrates who relied on dated models of legality and international law. Positing the relevance of the structural condition of institutional independence, I did not deny the significance of external factors on the development of police institutions. On the contrary, like Weber suggested with respect to the bureaucratization process in general ([1922]:556–66), certain societal presuppositions had to be met for police institutions to become detached from their political centers. In the case of the ICPC, I mentioned political conditions of pacification that enabled the trend toward bureaucratic autonomy of police in the interbellum decades of the 1920s and 1930s. The model of bureaucratization I developed from Weber as such takes into account the influence from societal conditions that may enable or impede police institutions to acquire independence.

My thesis on formal bureaucratic autonomy underscores the argument that structural differences in independence from politics accounted for the fact that some national police systems could and others could not participate in international police organizations such as the ICPC. This fact suggests that formal bureaucratic autonomy is a determining factor of police internationalization, regardless of the political ideologies of the nations involved and the nature of their relationships in matters of foreign policy. This thesis contradicts perspectives that suggest that the ICPC and other international police organizations are to be explained primarily as efforts to advance the political goals of certain powerful states. Authors defending such perspectives have, in the case of the International Criminal Police Commission, alluded to the ideological persuasion of the police officials who founded and participated in the ICPC and, relatedly, to the political objectives the ICPC was to accomplish under the guise of crime control (Bresler 1992:21–52; Busch 1995:264–74; Greilsamer 1986:21–52).

Political motivations can be most clearly revealed in the case of Johannes Schober, the initiator and first president of the ICPC, who was also Chancellor of Austria on two occasions, in 1921 and 1929, and who served as Austrian Minister of Foreign Affairs from 1930 to 1932 (Hubert 1990). Given Schober's ambitions in matters of international politics, it has been suggested that he founded the ICPC as an instrument of Austrian foreign policy, particularly, as a tool to revive Austria's international prestige, since the country had been left in a state of instability after the war. Relatedly, some argue that the ICPC served as an organizational bastion to fight the spread of communism, the fear of which had taken hold of political elites in Europe (and in the United States) since the Russian Revolution of 1917 (Bresler 1992:21–26). The fact that police from Russia and, later, the Soviet Union did not participate in the ICPC is advanced as the strongest indicator of this perspective.

However, evidence indicates that such political perspectives have serious flaws in accounting for the formation of the International Criminal Police Commission. Specifically, what a state-centered approach cannot explain is that not only did the ICPC explicitly dealt with criminal, not political, activities but also that any preoccupation with political issues at this time actually prevented various efforts to foster police cooperation across national borders. Indeed, during much of the 19th century, police institutions were representative of conservative political regimes and, hence, international police cooperation, especially in Europe, was primarily targeted at the politically suspect opponents of established governments (Bayley 1975; Liang 1992). But, by the early decades of the 20th century, such political ambitions were delegated to separate intelligence forces and no longer guided the international organization of bureaucratic police institutions. It is true that in the years between the two world wars there were still attempts to foster international policework with explicitly political goals – especially with the purpose of controlling Communist movements – and that some of these political ideals were also defended among certain members of the ICPC (Fijnaut 1997). Yet, strikingly, these political policing efforts were never successfully implemented in an international organization. For instance, at a 1920 meeting in Munich, Germany, police from the Netherlands, Switzerland, Germany, and Austria discussed but failed to establish a joint police intelligence network for the suppression of communism (National Archives, Record Group 165, 10058-L-36/1-3). In the late 1930s, other international police meetings with explicit political objectives – including efforts to establish anti-Communist police cooperation organized by police from South America, Nazi Germany, and fascist Italy – were likewise not successful (National Archives, Record Group 242, 21/2525789). The only international police efforts with a political motive that were successful in the first half of the 20th century were instigated unilaterally by national police institutions operating secretively abroad or involved cooperation that remained at a bilateral or restricted multilateral level.

Against state-centered interpretations of international police, therefore, I suggest that certain police institutions, including those of Communist Russia, could not cooperate in the ICPC not because of any political motivations among the membership of the ICPC – no matter how real their political antagonism was at the level of national governments – but because of the structural condition that these non-participating institutions remained too closely linked to their respective political centers. Not the ideological nature of the political regime, but the formal separation of police bureaucracies from their governments (whatever their ideological disposition) enabled police bureaucracies to cooperate in international organizations. This situation suggests that police from Russia did not take part in the ICPC because of their strong attachment to the Communist dictatorship, but also that police from other nations could and did participate in a common structure, although they too were not closely akin in ideological respects and entertained anything but amicable political relationships. The strongest evidence supporting this argument is the cooperation in the ICPC of police from France, England, Italy, and Germany – countries that were also politically hostile during the here-considered years.

Political processes, then, cannot be considered constitutive of international policework, although the structural condition of bureaucratic autonomy is influenced by historically variable circumstances. And, indeed, political conditions are often seen to impede police from attaining or maintaining formal bureaucratic independence. Most clearly, in the case of the ICPC, severe difficulties in upholding professional police relationships mounted by the late 1930s, especially after the Nazi invasion of Poland signaled the prelude to World War II and, even more so, when the United States joined the war effort. Under the extreme condition of warfare, a bureaucratic independence of police cannot be maintained. Hence, international cooperation between police of hostile states was virtually non-existent during the war, although the practical implications of the wartime ICPC – the headquarters of which had fallen under Nazi control – are not entirely clear (Deflem 1996a:248–58).

That police institutions are in a position to cooperate internationally once they have gained formal bureaucratic autonomy implies that cooperation can take place among police of national states that may be very different in political, legal, and other respects. The strength and the survival of the ICPC in this respect is remarkable, considering the great political and cultural heterogeneity that marks the European Continent, dividing the region for hundreds of years. But, putting aside any divisive issues, national police institutions participating in the ICPC could cooperate because of shared professional standards and objectives beyond state politics. This absence of state control only refers to a formal separation of police from the governments of states and is not meant to imply that police institutions are not related to the power and might of states. On the contrary, formally sanctioned with the tasks of order maintenance and crime control, police institutions are arguably the most visible and concrete expression of the state's legitimate monopoly over the (internal) means of coercion (Bittner 1970; see generally, Melossi 1990). In that sense, they are always related to power and force and, as such, are political (Reiner 1985). In fact, the proclaimed reliance of police institutions and other bureaucracies on principles of efficiency and their presentation in strictly professional terms are themselves important strategies of domination (Weber [1922]:122–30).

My point here, therefore, is not to argue that the state and public institutions of social control are not related, nor that formal bureaucracies of social control are not a critical component of state power, but only that the structures and mechanisms of (international) police organizations are not exhausted with reference to the ideological dictates of the political center of states. An alternative perspective could hold that the formation of the ICPC was enabled by agreements among states over the politically recognized utility of an international police organization, but evidence shows that such agreements only came after police experts had already formed such an organization with means and goals they had decided upon without political control.

The thesis of bureaucratic independence harmonizes with Weber's observation that bureaucracies can keep on functioning regardless of whether a society is organized along capitalist or socialist lines and regardless of the nature of the political regime ([1922]:128–30, 560–79). Indeed, as this analysis shows, once a police institution is sufficiently independent from its political center, it can function as an expert apparatus that can engage in collaborative work with other, likewise independent, police bureaucracies. Institutional independence accounts for the fundamental irony of international police cooperation: that police institutions transcend national jurisdictional competence and move beyond the function assigned to them by their respective political centers.

The Laws of International Police

With the structural conditions for police cooperation fulfilled, the motivational basis that operationalized international policework in the case of the ICPC was a professional myth of a cross-national rise and internationalization of crime since the end of World War I. Accompanying the expert conceptions of the goals of international policework, the means to deal with the problem of international crime were likewise subject to professional police judgment. With its emphasis on technically sophisticated means of policing, exemplified by the functionally specialized headquarters and instituted mechanisms of police-to-police communications, the ICPC – unlike the International Police Conference – so accomplished what Weber, with a witty snap at Marx, once called a "concentration of the means of administration" ([1922]:567).

Based on the myth of international crime, the elaboration of the ICPC implies a rationalization as a systematic organization in terms of instrumental efficiency (Smelser 1998:2). However, as there has been some confusion on the issue of efficiency in the reception of Weber's work (Clegg 1994:66–67), as well as the ideal-typical status of Weber's terminology (Albrow 1970:61–66), my analysis implies no conclusions on whether rationalized policework is more efficient or effective. I do not argue that the ICPC was a more efficient instrument in the control of international crime, but instead that it was motivated by, and explicitly designed to accommodate, a professional conception of efficiency. In fact, evidence indicates that the ICPC was not very effective in terms of handling international crime.

Based on the minimal evidence available, the ICPC possessed some 7,000 fingerprints between 1922 and 1927, and the International Bureau in Vienna had, by 1936, reportedly collected information on 3,724 suspects (Bresler 1992:40; Leibig 1936:266). These numbers are not impressive compared to the information collected by most other participating and comparable national police systems at the time. The FBI, for instance, already possessed over 1 million fingerprints as early as 1926 (and about 5 million in 1935). The relative ineffectiveness of the ICPC in investigative respects harmonizes with Weber's insight that the actual power of a bureaucracy in influencing the social structure it acts upon is empirically variable ([1922]:572). Instead of its effectiveness in investigations, the fostering of professional relationships among police officials, especially through the meetings, may well have been among the ICPC's most concrete realizations. These personal contacts, moreover, may also have fueled additional bilateral cooperation among police, complementary to the structures of the ICPC. The notion that the ICPC primarily enhanced cooperation through personal contacts parallels Peter Blau's (1955) famous study of informalism in organizations.

Regardless of its effectiveness, however, it is significant that the organizational structure of the ICPC was developed on the basis of systems of knowledge shared by police professionals. Weber recognized very well the relevance of knowledge for bureaucratic power and ultimately even defined bureaucracy as "domination through knowledge" ([1922]:129). Foucauldian studies of crime control and police, similarly, have indicated the relevance of expert knowledge cultures in terms of a tripartite relationship among theory (criminology), empirical knowledge (criminal statistics), and the instrument of control (police) (Foucault [1978]; see also Deflem 1997). Recent scholarship on police cooperation has also argued for the relevance of knowledge systems for the diffusion of police objectives and police technique in international partnerships (e.g., Deflem 1996b; Nadelmann 1993; Sheptycki 1995). James Sheptycki (1998a, b) has usefully described these shared knowledge systems in terms of a transnational occupational subculture that police across nations have come to develop through information exchange and practical arrangements of cross-border policework. Sheptycki argues that such cross-border arrangements among police defy clear-cut categorization, particularly when one is assessing the rise of transnational policing in terms of a diminishing or strengthening of state power. However, increased complexity in the internationalization of policing need not imply that its historical antecedents cannot be empirically traced and its various components unraveled in terms of a theoretically founded comprehensive approach.

Thus, the bureaucracy perspective reveals that the cultural forces of expert police myths concerning international crime fostered international cooperation practices, demonstrating that bureaucracies are significantly driven by internal dynamics related to organizational strength. Structural conditions of bureaucratic autonomy may furthermore have been strengthened by cultural developments of the expert knowledge systems regarding international crime, dialectically reinforcing developments originally enabled by the condition of institutional independence.

Sociologists of formal organizations have argued in similar terms for the relevance of these developments in the broader context of societal bureaucratization. Comparative sociologist S. N. Eisenstadt ([1956]:69), for instance, explains the drift toward bureaucratic independence from political rulers in terms of the officials' expertise and successful claim to a "professional morale." Wolfgang Mommsen (1989:112) likewise speaks of an "inherent dynamism of bureaucratic institutions" that results in a "self-propelling process," which further accelerates what Henry Jacoby ([1969]:156) calls the bureaucratic "will to do everything." Indeed, it was because of an organizationally developed system of knowledge about the cross-national rise and internationalization of crime that the ICPC could found and expand its organizational structure and facilities, despite the fact even that among the Commission members no clear-cut definition of international crime was ever attained. What did matter and what did operationalize the ICPC was the notion – undisputed among police – that crime was on the rise across the world and that it was more and more of an international nature. This idea entails no functionalist argument that international police cooperation is necessitated by an internationalization of crime, for it is not relevant whether these views on the nature and level of criminality were empirically accurate, but that they were accepted to be valid by police officials and that they therefore effectively motivated international cooperation. In the case of the ICPC, a myth of international crime enabled police institutions to form an international network based on professional expert conceptions, regardless of political and legal concerns and without prior government approval. For as Blau and Meyer (1971:50–59) argue, bureaucratic myths not only mobilize members around organizationally defined causes, they also insulate the organization from control and criticism. This also confirms, as Weber maintained, that state and market do not determine the relative strength of the bureaucracy versus the political rulers ([1922]:128–30, 615). Instead, it is the level of technical expertise attained by the officials that can propel the bureaucracy to take on a course of its own. The functioning of the ICPC on the basis of professional expertise harmonizes with Weber's view of the bureaucratic apparatus as an "almost unbreakable formation" that functions "as a machine" and is "capable of universal application" ([1922]:570, 561, 126). Importantly, this does not mean that international police organizations can totally insulate themselves from concerns over legality and rights. On the contrary, as much as I argued that the development and presentation of international police practices in terms of professional expertise is itself political, so I should note that international policing is subject to criticisms in normative terms, especially with respect to finding new ways to guarantee human rights and democratic accountability in the global age (Deflem 1999).

Expert systems of police knowledge emphasize a particular conception of, and an efficiency to control, international crime in extra-legal terms. In fact, police officials in the International Criminal Police Commission criticized legal conceptions of crime and existing arrangements of international law, because these concepts and systems remained bound to national jurisdictions and were time-consuming and inefficient. The members of the ICPC instead emphasized developments in crime influenced by societal factors (modernization, technological progress), not violations of formal legal systems. In terms of means, also, it was a strong emphasis on efficiency in the Weberian sense of purposive rationality that led to the establishment and elaboration of the ICPC's organizational facilities and accelerated its progression, regardless of legal arrangements and without supervision from political authority. This fact confirms the Weberian viewpoint that, relative to the expertise and know-how of the bureaucrat, the political officeholder is always in the position of "a dilettante" (Weber [1922]:572). Hence, Weber ([1918]:32) argued that "in the modern state real authority ... rests necessarily and unavoidably in the hands of the bureaucracy." The ICPC facilities and activities were indeed planned to be as technologically sophisticated as were the feats of their targets. And only after the structures of international policing were already in place were appeals made to sanction what expert police bureaucracies had already established. The case of the ICPC thus illustrates Weber's ([1922]:128–29) argument that control of a bureaucracy is "only limitedly possible for the non-specialist: the specialist is in the long run frequently superior to the non-specialist in getting his will done."

Conclusion

I have relied on the sociology of Max Weber to defend a perspective of social control that accounts for the formation of international police organizations on the basis of a two-fold model of bureaucratic autonomy. I argued that the fact that national police institutions have acquired institutional independence creates structural conditions favorable for international cooperation, regardless of whether the states of those police institutions approximate one another in political, legal, or other respects. This perspective recognizes the embeddedness of police institutions in broader societal contexts without surrendering to all-too-readily-accepted assumptions about the explanatory powers of state and market. I thus am led to a rejection of such state-centered and/or neo-Marxist arguments, not a priori, but because of their clear short-comings with respect to empirical adequacy requirements. For, although certain societal preconditions were significant in influencing bureaucratic police autonomy, they cannot be considered constitutive of the dynamics of international policework. Instead, expert knowledge systems about a cross-national rise and internationalization of crime provided the motivational basis for an operationalization of international policework.

The paradoxical implication of my theoretical model, then, can be summarized as follows: certain social preconditions favored a trend toward a bureaucratization process, which itself implied increasing police independence on the basis of specialized skills and expertise. As such, in this article I have empirically grounded a Weberian perspective of international policing that is not reductionist in terms of developments of state politics and formal law, for what my analysis has shown is that international police organizations were not reflective of political and legal developments and did not target international criminals as political opponents or legal subjects. On the contrary, the cross-national rise and internationalization of crime as the central motivator of international policing was constructed beyond, even against, national politics and law. Only after police officials had established professional structures and facilities of international policework did they appeal to national and international bodies of government to formally sanction what had already been created under conditions of bureaucratic autonomy.

I have in this study strengthened the empirical foundations of my theoretical arguments by broadening the scope of investigation to research comparatively several instances of international police cooperation, but my perspective needs further corroboration from additional studies. In terms of the internationalization of social control as a broader phenomenon, I have focused on selected historical instances of international collaboration among public police institutions and have not concentrated on the manifold contemporary dimensions of international policing. My conclusions may need to be qualified when one considers other aspects of social control besides those involving public police institutions and late-20th century-developments of international police cooperation that may be qualitatively different from their historical antecedents. Although, elsewhere, I have applied the Weberian model to aspects of current international police institutions (Deflem 1999), other scholars have defended competing theoretical models in their research on punishment (e.g., Goldstone & Useem 1999; Hochstetler & Shover 1997), the police use of force (e.g., Jacobs & O'Brien 1998; Jacobs & Helms 1997), and dimensions of today's international police (e.g., Dunn 1996; Gilboy 1997; Huggins 1998). The intention of my study, however, was to show that, for certain developments of social control, *in casu* the historical origins of international police organizations, a Weberian model of social control may be more valuable. This model would offer support to the notion that, as some experts have argued (Marx 1995:329; Nadelmann 1993:466), the theme of international police is too wide and varied to be captured by one simple proposition. Parallel to observations on the multidimensional nature of international processes in general (Kettner 1997), international policing covers many different dimensions – from bilateral and temporary practices to multilateral and relatively stable organizations; from developments during the 19th-century formation of national states to the present high-tech age of cyberspace – that may defy a single propositional explanation.

I hope that this analysis has demonstrated the value of a sociological approach that transcends narrow perspectives of police in terms of the enforcement of laws or the control of crime. Gary Marx (1981) once astutely described such legalistic outlooks as "trampoline-models" that view social control exclusively in reaction to violations of formal laws and that thus fail to account for the many sociologically relevant complexities of social control. Whereas much of Marx's work unravels the ironic nature of social control in terms of the characteristics of the situational interaction between rule-violator and rule-enforcer (e.g., Marx 1988), the study presented here argues for a similarly inherent dynamic at the organizational level of police institutions and the relationships among them. The bureaucratic model of police that I developed in this article shows that international police cannot indeed be viewed primarily in terms of an enforcement of legal norms. On the contrary, the international police organizations I reviewed relied on expert systems of knowledge, formulated beyond the realm of state-proclaimed laws. A theoretically founded approach beyond formal legality is precisely, I believe, what should be emphasized by sociological perspectives of police and social control. Such an approach is readily counterintuitive to an everyday understanding of police (as law enforcement) and rectifies scholarly accounts that are dominated by such a misconception. The task for sociologists of social control is to develop and test theories that are analytically rooted in the sociological imagination in order to show the specific role played by police institutions in the reproduction of social order.

Notes

1. Relatedly, the gradual delineation of social control as a separate theme of reflection has been the central development in sociological theorizing on the matter over the past decades (Coser 1982; Deflem 1994; Liska 1997). Although the 19th-century concept of social control was virtually synonymous with social order, since the 1950s it has come to be conceived more narrowly in relation to deviance and crime. Social control has become a mainstay in the more-restricted meaning, referring to social processes and structures that – corresponding to the three dominant sociological theory groups – redress, create, or reproduce more than crime and/or deviant behavior (see Cohen 1985; Cohen & Scull 1985; Marx 1981).

2. My reading of Weber's perspective of bureaucracy relies on the relevant sections from the posthumously published *Wirtschaft und Gesellschaft* (Economy and Society) (especially Weber [1922]:551–79, 815–37) and some additional writings on bureaucracy in

Germany ([1918]) and the political profession ([1919]). English translations can be found in Weber 1958, 1978.

3. Weber himself introduced the conception of police as bureaucracy when he discussed as a condition favorable to bureaucratization "the increasing need, in a society accustomed to pacification, for order and protection ('police') in all areas" ([1922]:561).

4. This statement resonates with a central theme addressed in the work of organizational theorists. Mary Douglas (1986), for instance, argues that an institution acquires legitimacy by showing how its own rules and practices are the only answer to a problem it had itself formulated. In the case of police bureaucracies, Jerome Skolnick (1966:238) similarly speaks of "organizational interests" and "official innovation" to indicate the tendency of modern police to set its own agenda of activities.

5. In the period before 1848, there had also been attempts – largely unsuccessful – to structure European-wide systems of international political policing. Mention can be made of attempts to organize European police systems during the Napoleonic reign in France and the Metternich regime in the Hungarian-Austrian monarchy (Fijnaut 1979:798–43; Liang 1992:18–19, 33–34).

References

Albrow, Martin (1970) *Bureaucracy.* New York: Praeger.

Anderson, Malcolm (1989) *Policing the World: Interpol and the Politics of International Police Cooperation.* Oxford, England: Clarendon Press.

Archiv für Kriminologie (1925) "Zeitschriften (*Internationale Öffentliche Sicherheit*)," 77 *Archiv für Kriminologie* 72–73.

Bayley, David H. (1975) "The Police and Political Development in Europe," in C. Tilly, ed., *The Formation of National States in Western Europe.* Princeton: Princeton Univ. Press.

―――― (1985) *Patterns of Policing.* Newark, NJ: Rutgers Univ. Press.

Beck, Friedrich, & Walter Schmidt, eds. (1993) *Die Polizeikonferenzen deutscher Staaten, 1851–1866: Präliminardokumente, Protokolle und Anlagen.* Weimar, Germany: Hermann Böhlaus Nachfolger.

Benson, Bruce L., David W. Rasmussen & David L. Sollars (1995) "Police Bureaucracies, Their Incentives, and the War on Drugs," 83 *Public Choice* 21–45.

Bittner, Egon (1970) *The Functions of Police in Modern Society.* Chevy Chase, MD: National Institute of Mental Health.

Black, Donald (1980) *The Manners and Customs of the Police.* New York: Academic Press.

Blau, Peter M. (1955) *The Dynamics of Bureaucracy.* Chicago: Univ. of Chicago Press.

―――― ([1964] 1976) "Social Exchange Among Collectivities," in W. M. Evan, ed., *Interorganizational Relations.* Hammondsworth, England: Penguin Books.

Blau, Peter M., & Marshall W. Meyer (1971) *Bureaucracy in Modern Society.* 2d ed. New York: Random House.

Boli, John, & George M. Thomas (1997) "World Culture in the World Polity: A Century of International Non-Governmental Organization," 62 *American Sociological Rev.* 171–90.

Bresler, Fenton (1992) *Interpol.* Weert, The Netherlands: M & P.

Busch, Heiner (1995) *Grenzenlose Polizei? Neue Grenzen und polizeiliche Zusam-menarbeit in Europa.* Münster, Germany: Westfälisches Dampfboot.

Clegg, Stewart R. (1994) "Max Weber and Contemporary Sociology of Organizations," in L. R. Ray & M. Reed, eds., *Organizing Modernity.* New York: Routledge.

Cohen, Stanley (1985) *Visions of Social Control.* Cambridge, England: Polity Press.

Cohen, Stanley, & Andrew Scull, eds. (1985) *Social Control and the State.* Oxford: Basil Blackwell.

Coser, Lewis A. (1982) "The Notion of Control in Sociological Theory," in J. P. Gibbs, ed., *Social Control: Views from the Social Sciences.* Beverly Hills, CA: Sage.

Deflem, Mathieu (1994) "Social Control and the Theory of Communicative Action." 22 *International J. of the Sociology of Law* 355–73.

——— (1996a) "Borders of Police Force: Historical Foundations of International Policing Between Germany and the United States." Ph.D. diss., Dept. of Sociology, Univ. of Colorado.

——— (1996b) "International Policing in 19th-Century Europe: The Police Union of German States, 1851–1866," 6 *International Criminal Justice Rev.* 36–57.

——— (1997) "Surveillance and Criminal Statistics: Historical Foundations of Governmentality," 17 *Studies in Law, Politics, and Society* 149–84.

——— (1999) "The Boundaries of International Cooperation: Human Rights and Neo-Imperialism in U.S.-Mexican Police Relationships." Paper presented at a conference on International Institutions: Global Processes-Domestic Consequences (April 9–11), Duke University, Durham, NC.

Douglas, Mary (1986) *How Institutions Think.* Syracuse: Syracuse Univ. Press.

Dunn, Timothy J. (1996) *The Militarization of the U.S.-Mexico Border, 1978–1992.* Austin, TX: CMAS Books.

Eisenstadt, S. N. ([1956] 1971) "Tensions and Conflicts in Bureaucratic Societies," in M. T. Dalby & M. S. Werthman, eds., *Bureaucracy in Historical Perspective.* Glenview, IL: Scott, Foresman & Company.

Enright, Richard E. (1925) "The Significance of the International Police Conference," 3 (3) *Police Magazine* 21–22, 88–89.

Ethington, Philip J. (1987) "Vigilantes and the Police: The Creation of a Professional Police Bureaucracy in San Francisco, 1847–1900." 21 *J. of Social History* 197–227.

Fijnaut, Cyrille (1979) *Opdat de Macht een Toevlucht Zij.* 2 vols. Antwerp, Belgium: Kluwer.

——— (1987) "The Internationalization of Criminal Investigation in Western Europe," in C. Fijnaut & R. H. Hermans, eds., *Police Cooperation in Europe.* Lochem, The Netherlands: Van den Brink.

——— (1997) "The International Criminal Police Commission and the Fight against Communism, 1923–1945," in M. Mazowar, ed., *The Policing of Politics in the Twentieth Century: Historical Perspectives.* Providence, RI: Berghahn Books.

Finger (1914) "Der Erste Internationale 'Congrès de Police Judiciaire' in Monaco" 1 *Deutsche Strafrechts-Zeitung* 268–69.

Foucault, Michel ([1975] 1977) *Discipline and Punish.* New York: Pantheon.

——— ([1978] 1991) "Governmentality," in G. Burchell, C. Gordon & P. Miller, eds., *The Foucault Effect.* Chicago: Univ. of Chicago Press.

Gamson, William A., & Ephraim Yuchtman (1977) "Police and Society in Israel," in D. H. Bayley, ed., *Police and Society.* Beverly Hills, CA: Sage.

Garland, David (1990) *Punishment and Modern Society.* Oxford, England: Clarendon Press.

——— (1997) "'Governmentality' and the Problem of Crime: Foucault, Criminology, Sociology," 1 *Theoretical Criminology* 173–214.

Gilboy, Janet A. (1997) "Implications of 'Third-Party' Involvement in Enforcement: The INS, Illegal Travelers, and International Airlines." 31 *Law & Society Rev.* 505–29.

Goldstone, Jack A., & Bert Useem (1999) "Prison Riots as Microrevolutions: An Extension of State-Centered Theories of Revolution." 104 *American J. of Sociology* 985–1029.

Greilsamer, Laurent (1986) *Interpol: Le Siège du Soupçon.* Paris: Alain Moreau.

Habermas, Jürgen (1985) *Der philosophische Diskurs der Moderne.* Frankfurt, Germany: Suhrkamp.

Hart, Errol E. (1925) "International Police Conference, Characters and Ideals," 3 (1) *Police Magazine* 54–55, 105–7.

Heindl, Robert (1914a) "Internationale Kriminalpolizei," 1 *Deutsche Strafrechts-Zeitung* 647–52.

——— (1914b) "Bericht über den I. Internationalen Kriminalpolizeikongress in Monaco; Bemerkungen zum I. Internationalen Kriminalpolizeikongreâ in Monaco," 58 *Archiv für Kriminal-Anthropologie und Kriminalistik* 333–53.

Heindl, Robert (1924) "Der Internationale Polizeikongreß in Wien," 76 *Archiv für Kriminologie* 16–30.

Herbert, Steve (1998) "Police Subculture Reconsidered," 36 *Criminology* 343–69.

Heyman, Josiah M. (1995) "Putting Power in the Anthropology of Bureaucracy: The Immigration and Naturalization Service at the Mexico–United States Border," 36 *Current Anthropology* 261–77.

Hochstetler, Andrew L., & Neal Shover (1997) "Street Crime, Labor Surplus, and Criminal Punishment, 1980–1990," 44 *Social Problems* 358–68.

Hubert, Rainer (1990) *Schober: "Arbeitermörder" und "Hort der Republik." Biographie eines Gestrigen.* Wien, Austria/Köln, Germany: Böhlau Verlag.

Huggins, Martha K. (1998) *Political Policing: The United States and Latin America.* Durham, NC: Duke Univ. Press.

International Police Conference (IPC) (1923) *Report of the Proceedings of the Third Annual Meeting, International Police Conference, New York City, New York, U.S.A., April 30 to May 5, 1923.* New York: Police Department, City of New York, Bureau of Printing.

Internationale Kriminalpolizeiliche Kommission (IKK) (1923) *Der Internationale Polizeikongreß in Wien (3. bis 7. September 1923).* Wien, Austria: "Öffentliche Sicherheit" Polizei-Rundschau.

——— (1928) *Resolutions Passed by the International Criminal Police Commission in Vienna. At the 5th Ordinary Meeting at Berne on September 10th–12th, 1928.* Wien, Austria: Internationale Kriminalpolizieliche Kommission.

——— (1934) *Die internationale Zusammenarbeit auf kriminalpolizeilichem Gebiete. Handbuch herausgegeben von der Internationalen Kriminalpolizeilichen Kommission (Zweite umgearbeitete und vermehrte Auflage).* Wien, Austria: Internationale Kriminalpolizeiliche Kommission.

Jacobs, David, & Ronald E. Helms (1997) "Testing Coercive Explanations for Order: The Determinants of Law Enforcement Strength over Time," 75 *Social Forces* 1361–92.

Jacobs, David, & Robert M. O'Brien (1998) "The Determinants of Deadly Force: A Structural Analysis of Police Violence," 103 *American J. of Sociology* 837–62.

Jacoby, Henry ([1969] 1973) *The Bureaucratization of the World.* Berkeley and Los Angeles: Univ. of California Press.

Jensen, Richard B. (1981) "The International Anti-Anarchist Conference of 1898 and the Origins of Interpol," 16 *J. of Contemporary History* 323–47.

Kettner, Matthias (1997) "Thesen zur Bedeutung des Globalisierungsbegriffs," 45 *Deutsche Zeitschrift für Philosophie* 903–18.

Lacombe, Dany (1996) "Reforming Foucault: A Critique of the Social Control Thesis," 47 *British J. of Sociology* 332–52.

Leibig, P. (1936) "XII. Ordentliche Tagung der Internationalen Kriminalpolizeilichen Kommission in Belgrad von 25. Mai bis 4. Juni 1936," 33 *Die Polizei* 266–70.

Liang, Hsi-Heuy (1992) *The Rise of the Modern Police and the European State System.* New York: Cambridge Univ. Press.

Liska, Allen E. (1997) "Modeling the Relationships Between Macro Forms of Social Control," 23 *Annual Review of Sociology* 39–61.

Manning, Peter K. (1977) *Police Work: The Social Organization of Policing.* Cambridge, MA: MIT Press.

Marabuto, Paul (1935) *La Collaboration Policière Internationale en Vue de la Prévention et de la Répression de la Criminalité.* Nice, France: École Professionnelle Don-Bosco.

Marx, Gary T. (1981) "Ironies of Social Control," 28 *Social Problems* 221–46.

——— (1988) *Undercover: Police Surveillance in America.* Berkeley & Los Angeles: Univ. of California Press.

——— (1995) "Undercover in Comparative Perspective: Some Implications for Knowledge and Social Research," in C. Fijnaut & G. T. Marx, eds., *Undercover: Police Surveillance in Comparative Perspective.* The Hague: Kluwer Law International.

Marx, Gary T. (1997) "Social Control Across Borders," in W. F. McDonald, ed., *Crime and Law Enforcement in the Global Village*. Cincinnati, OH: Anderson Publishing.

McDonald, William F., ed. (1997) *Crime and Law Enforcement in the Global Village*. Cincinnati, OH: Anderson Publishing.

Melossi, Dario (1990) *The State of Social Control*. Cambridge, England: Polity Press.

Meyer, John W., & Brian Rowan (1977) "Institutionalized Organizations: Formal Structure as Myth and Ceremony," 83 *American J. of Sociology* 340–63.

Meyer, John W., John Boli, George M.Thomas & Francisco O. Ramirez (1997) "World Society and the Nation-State," 103 *American J. of Sociology* 144–81.

Mommsen, Wolfgang J. (1989) *The Political and Social Theory of Max Weber.* Chicago: Univ. of Chicago Press.

Nadelmann, Ethan (1993) *Cops Across Borders: The Internationalization of U.S. Criminal Law Enforcement.* University Park, PA: Pennsylvania State Univ. Press.

National Archives, College Park, MD. *Military Intelligence Division Correspondence, 1917–1941*. Records of the War Department General and Special Staffs, Record Group 165.

——— *Records of the Reich Leader of the SS and Chief of the German Police.* Collection of Foreign Records Seized, 1941–, Record Group 242.

Ng-Quinn, Michael (1990) "Function-Oriented and Functionally Indirect Expansion as Bureaucratic Responses to Modernization: The Case of the Royal Hong Kong Police," 10 *Public Administration & Development* 101–17.

O'Reilly, Kenneth (1987) "Bureaucracy and Civil Liberties: The FBI Story," in R. M. Glassman, W. H. Swatos & P. L. Rosen, eds., *Bureaucracy Against Democracy and Socialism*. New York: Greenwood Press.

Page, Edward C. (1985) *Political Authority and Bureaucratic Power.* Knoxville: Univ. of Tennessee Press.

Palitzsch, Hans (1927) "Internationale Verbrecher und ihre Bekämpfung," in A. Daranyi & O. Daranyi, eds., *Große Polizei-Ausstellung Berlin in Wort und Bild.* Wien: Internationale Öffentliche Sicherheit.

Reiner, Robert (1985) *The Politics of Police.* New York: St. Martin's Press.

Roux, Jean-André, ed. ([1914] 1926) *Premier Congrès de Police Judiciare Internationale, Monaco (Avril 1914): Actes du Congrès.* Paris: G. Godde.

Sheptycki, James W. E. (1995) "Transnational Policing and the Makings of a Postmodern State," 35 *British J. of Criminology* 613–35.

——— (1998a) "The Global Cops Cometh: Reflections on Transnationalization, Knowledge Work, and Policing Subculture," 49 *British J. of Sociology* 57–74.

——— (1998b) "Policing, Postmodernism, and Transnationalization," 38 *British J. of Criminology* 485–503.

Simon, Jonathan (1988) "The Ideological Effects of Actuarial Practices," 22 *Law & Society Rev.* 771–800.

Skolnick, Jerome H. (1966) *Justice Without Trial: Law Enforcement in Democratic Society.* New York: John Wiley & Sons.

Skubl, Michael (1937) "Völkerbundidee und Polizei," 17 (1) *Öffentliche Sicherheit* 1–3.

Smelser, Neil J. (1998) "The Rational and the Ambivalent in the Social Sciences," 63 *American Sociological Rev.* 1–16.

Stenson, Kevin (1993) "Community Policing as a Governmental Technology," 22 *Economy & Society* 373–89.

Theoharis, Athan (1992) "FBI Wiretapping: A Case Study of Bureaucratic Autonomy," 107 *Political Science Quart.* 101–22.

Useem, Bert (1997) "The State and Collective Disorders: The Los Angeles Riot/Protest of April, 1992." 76 *Social Forces* 357–77.

Van Houten, M.C. (1923) "Internationale Zusammenarbeit auf kriminalpolizeilichem Gebiet," 75 *Archiv für Kriminologie* 41–46.

Walker, Samuel (1977) *A Critical History of Police Reform: The Emergence of Professionalism.* Lexington, MA: Lexington Books.

Walther, Hans (pseudonym for Hans Walter Gaebert) (1968) *Interpol auf Verbrecherjagd: Die Internationale Kriminalpolizeiliche Kommission im Einsatz.* Würzburg, Germany: Arena.

Weber, Max ([1918] 1988) "Parlament und Regierung im neugeordneten Deutschland: Zur politischen kritik des Beamtentums und Parteiwesens," in M. Weber, *Gesammelte Politische Schriften.* Tübingen, Germany: J.C.B. Mohr (Paul Siebeck).

———— ([1919] 1988) "Politik als Beruf," in M. Weber, *Gesammelte Politische Schriften.* Tübingen, Germany: J.C.B. Mohr (Paul Siebeck).

———— ([1922] 1980) *Wirtschaft und Gesellschaft: Grundriss der verstehenden Soziologie.* Tübingen: J.C.B. Mohr (Paul Siebeck).

———— (1958) *From Max Weber: Essays in Sociology*, H. H. Gerth & C. Wright Mills, eds. New York: Oxford Univ. Press.

———— (1978) *Economy and Society: An Outline of Interpretive Sociology*, G. Roth & C. Wittich, eds. Berkeley & Los Angeles: Univ. of California Press.

Welzel, Albrecht (1925) "Die New Yorker Internationale Polizeikonferenz," 4 *Deutsches Polizei-Archiv* 147–48.

8

The Emergence of the Police –
The Colonial Dimension

Mike Brogden

"Modern police history begins not in Britain itself but in Ireland, with the passing of the Irish Peace Preservation Force Act in 1814, when Peel was Irish Secretary". (Jeffries, 1952, p. 53).

Introduction

The Irish legislation is as arbitrary a debut of the professional police as the normative references to the Metropolitan Police Act 1829. Other organised forces had been in existence for many years prior to that date. Salaried state-appointed policing was hardly an invention of the Anglo-Saxon race. Ethnocentricity, inadequate comparative knowledge of policing, and a-historicism are the hallmarks of the Anglo-American sociology of the police. Chauvinism still prevails, among today's Reithians (Pike, 1985), as well as the Bunyanesque camp-followers (Scraton, 1985). The failure to consider the wider contours of the emergence of the professional police has been near-total.

In the radical case, there is a particular irony. In one recent British public order incident, the type of police tactics used were described as "... imported direct from Hong Kong" (*The Listener*, 31.10.1985). The Hong Kong practices in turn derived initially from the same medley of experimentation that gave rise to both the Metropolitan Police and to the Royal Irish Constabulary (successor to the Peace Preservation Force and the ancestor of the Royal Ulster Constabulary). In Manchester, in March 1985, with the visit of the then Home Secretary, the wheel had turned full circle.

Source: *The British Journal of Criminology*, 27(1) (1987): 4–14.

The tunnel vision of students of British policing has frustrated an adequate account of police origins and functions. Explanations have been bound by context and by an insular historiography. One gap in that literature can be plugged. The imperial circumstances of professional policing in Britain need to be explored. Before entering that field, there are, however, two preliminaries.

There are rival versions of the emergence of Anglo-American policing. Each of these interpretations has been subject to considerable individual criticism. However, they suffer from a common defect. They contain the *idée fixe* that salaried policework was, like the spinning jenny, a British invention. In fact, there are *competing* models of professional policework, in terms of practices – whatever duties were eventually assumed – and designated functions – whatever those who paid the law enforcement bills actually wanted. There is no inexorable law that made the British style and organisation of policework (as conventionally portrayed) the norm from which to assess critically the functions of the professional police in Western societies.

An appreciation of the imperial context permits a fresh appraisal. More sense can be made of the police public order role in present society by inserting the material omitted from most police histories – the centrality of colonial conquest and of imperial legitimation to institutional development in Victorian England. "The history of England is also the history of our colonies ..." (Sumner, 1982, p. 8).

Orthodox Explanations and Critique of Police Emergence

There are several conventional explanations of the origins of professional policing in Britain in the 1820s and 1830s. The early histories emphasised the importance of the "mob". Alternatively, crime fears were viewed as the catalyst. Thirdly, accounts of the development of policing in the United States have centred upon the more complex features of the urbanisation and migration process. Fourthly, a law of inexorable administrative proliferation has been detailed. Finally, there have been more radical commentaries, with debts variously to Foucault and to more materialist histories, and relating the rise of professional policing to the conjunctural crisis of early capitalism.

Critchley, for example, assumed that riots were the precipitating factor in the formation of the New Police. More recently, several American studies have followed Silver (1967) in elaborating on the riot theme (for example, Walker, 1977). Tolerance of public disorder waned, as its manifestations were transformed from symbolic protest to material destruction. Urban property owners called increasingly for organised protection. As the social protests of the slum dwellers spilt over the boundaries, the traditional form of lower class political articulation collided with the new bourgeois standards of the industrialising city. This clash brought forth a reaction in the form of the professional police, as one element in the new disciplinary order.

The criticisms of the "riot" explanation are well established. Several writers have argued (Monkkonen, 1981; Field, 1981; Emsley, 1983) that there were few such precipitating riots, and often a long interval between those conflicts and police formation. It is a mistake to over-emphasise the cause and effect relationship between mob violence and the creation of the New Police. In any case, violent street disorder continued to be a prominent feature of Anglo-American city life long after the arrival of professional policing.

Rising crime levels featured in many of the earlier accounts. A concern with crime dominated the original Parliamentary debate (Stead, 1977). Chadwick's (selective) production of witnesses to the 1839 Royal Commission emphasised the fear of crime. Many of the Reithian historians have taken it for granted that the creation of police was due to criminal threats to persons and to property, and was a natural concomitant of urban growth. More recent studies (e.g. Johnson, 1979) have explained police modernisation in the nineteenth century in terms of rising crime. They assumed that the traditional watch/constable system could not handle the rising wave of crime, which was produced by urban population growth.

Dismissal of the "crime explanation" has several components. It is doubtful whether crime was actually rising in London prior to the development of the Metropolitan Police (Phillips, 1980) or in United States cities before they established police forces (Monkkonen, 1981). For Harring (1983), social deviance was a product of the changes imposed upon the working class of the period, rather than a cause of police reform. Crime control was one way in which the new institutions of industrial capitalism could be legitimised. There was no necessity for a rising crime rate to be responded to by a uniformed and preventative police when, traditionally, other methods had been the conventional response: temperance campaigns for those who blamed the demon drink, educational reform where crime was blamed on illiteracy (Johnson, 1979), or variations in penal measures (Monkkonen, 1981).

Crime and the mob have latterly been merged in the accounts of writers in the social disorganisation tradition; linking together the processes of immigration and of urbanisation (Lane, 1967; Richardson, 1970). Police departments were not established to reduce crime or control riots. They were organised on behalf of urban elites to supervise the migrant poor, who were increasingly seen as a potentially "dangerous class" (embodied in the United States in the tramping phenomenon of the early Industrial Revolution: Levett, 1975). People control rather than crime or riot control was the primary cause. Until the lower orders could be socialised by the institutions of education and democracy into the practices of industrialism, they had to be regulated.

There are evident problems here. Like the previous explanations, they contain a causal flaw. They confuse what the police ended up actually doing with the reason for their coming into existence. Police duties are conflated with intended police functions, the latter being deduced from documentation of the former. As Monkkonen (1981) phrases it sardonically, it is equally plausible to argue that the police were created to look for lost children because that was what they ended up doing.

Other writers have developed ideas associated with the Weberian tradition. The older accounts (Radzinowicz, 1955) suggest that the New Police arose as part of the general administrative "tiding-up" of the disorderly edges of society. The same model of organisation that apparently served well in times of external conflict, with its apparent predictability, impartiality, and efficiency, could similarly be utilised as the major agency for "ordering" and regulating the city. Local elites considered that a "... regular force of patrolmen answering to a central office and on duty round the clock was a conveniently flexible instrument of administration" (Lane, 1980, p. 8). As an instrument of city government, the new police were the most convenient municipal agency.

The most forcible representative of this thesis is Monkkonen (1981). American cities adopted uniformed police as part of the shift from class-based politics to liberal pluralistic and professional urban administration, based on formal social control bureaucracies. When urban elites abandoned positions of power, and class-based political representation was replaced by ethnic representation, the administration of city business could no longer work on a particularistic basis, and the modern bureaucratic notion of rule-based, universalistic standards became the urban goal. Ideas of policing and policing organisation were "contagiously diffused" from large cities to small as a gradual form of innovation. The critical factors in police reform were demography and city size. Police organisation developed when a critical limit was reached.

This account suffers from epistemological and empirical defects. As Monkkonen himself argued in relation to earlier explanations, it imputes a remarkable causal awareness to city officers prior to the event. City elites are attributed a more far-sighted view of their own interests than nineteenth century history suggests. Further, as Harring argues (1983), there was no inevitable innovation process. Some United States cities reduced force establishments after the first few years. Others emphasised alternative forms of city regulation, from the appointment of municipal garbagemen in Chicago to technological innovations (such as the telegraph), instead of increasing police manpower.

Finally, more critical writers have located professional police emergence within the conjunctural crisis of the onset of industrial capitalism. The nascent working-class had to be disciplined by new forms of coercion and legitimation. A New Police, combining both those elements, was to be a major weapon in that victory (Harring, 1979), ensuring the stability of the social relations of production. As private policing increased in cost to the new manufacturers, property owners and merchants, the police institution was socialised and its cost transferred from the private to the public sector (Spitzer and Scull, 1977). Professional policing was one of several forms of social organisation that emerged to maintain and strengthen the position of the new city ruling classes, and hence to regulate the nascent class struggle.

All these accounts are insufficient. In the first place, they assume that because the professional police in Anglo-American societies developed in the form that they did, such development was inevitable. This deterministic history denies any contingent social contribution to that change (Emsley, 1983). Secondly, many explanations of the *origins* of the professional police are based on the duties assumed after their formation. There is a confusion between what the police actually did and the causes that brought them about. The fact that they "may" have been effective against social disorder, crime, migrant workers, and working-class people does not, of itself, prove that was why they were created. Nor does the diffusion model tell us why a particular form of policework arose in London at the outset.

The Emergence of Alternative Forms of Policework

The major reason for the inadequacy of the orthodox explanations is their ethnocentricity. They commence from the domain assumption of the early Metropolitan model of professional policework. It is presupposed that the London Metropolitan model, as conventionally portrayed, was the only possible prototype. None of the above explanations disputes the authenticity and inevitability of that particular form or organisation. Anglo-American police history fails to recognise alternative formulations of policework. A wider reading offers many possibilities.

The first is a *preventative police*, a model whose midwives were the Ministers of Louis XIV (Brodeur, 1983). "High policing" (police concern with the affairs of state) from Louis XIV, through the times of Fouché, to the present Sureté, has a history of its own. From this perspective, policing in relation to the "low crime" of the streets may be perceived of as an aberration from the primary police commitment to the defence of the realm. In this view of the police function, the Prevention of Terrorism Act 1974, would be the proper descendant of professional policing, and community policing merely a peculiar deviation. In high policing, the police function as the early-warning system of the despotic or corporate state.

A second model is the traditional European practice which regarded policing as the *administration* of the affairs of state. Donzelot notes that Enlightenment thought saw the "... science of policing (as) regulating everything that relates to the present condition of society, in strengthening and improving it, in seeing that all things contribute to the welfare of the members that compose it." (Donzelot, 1979, p. 7). Similarly in France by the eighteenth century, the term police had come to mean the administration of a city and the social order which that administration was meant to bring (Emsley, 1983). In the Victorian city, police work was shorthand for a form of local administration. It often had minimal connection with the preventative Rowan-and-Mayne

model. (We only have to recall Charles Reith's reference to agricultural ferti-
liser as "police-manure" to appreciate some of those functions).

Thirdly, there is the neglected influence *of commercial policework* on police
development. Apart from Spitzer and Scull (1977), some older references to
Colquhoun's experiments with the River Thames Police, and critical assessments of the hue-and-cry and thief-taking (Klockars, 1985), the history of
private policing as a profit-making activity is usually by-passed, and its influence on the functions of the public police ignored. However, recent accounts
have suggested the value of considering the private sector. In England, private bodies such as the Associations for the Prosecution of Felons survived
long into the nineteenth century (Phillips, 1977). In public police detective
departments, private rewards remained common (Klockars, 1985). More
importantly, in the United States, private policing actually expanded com-
mensurately with state policing. For example, until the founding of the F.B.I.
in 1924, public police forces were confined to city and state territories with
only the private agencies able to ship presumed offenders across jurisdictional boundaries (Kakalik and Wildhorn, 1977). Private policing, despite
its complementarity to the state sector (Shearing and Stenning, 1981), is
notable only by its absence in the literature.

An ethnocentric explanation of police emergence and functions also
ignores those various *democratic* types of policework and of police organisation
that have dotted a more authoritarian plain. There are latter-day examples
such as Bittner's (1975) account of a "team-based" and decentralised model
of police organisation in the context of advanced capitalism. One historical
experiment rarely receives as much as a foot-note (Emsley, 1983). In the
French Revolutionary context of 1848, a transient police agency guarded
the streets of Paris under Minister Caussidiere. That body of "montagnards"
elected its own officers, and recruited and promoted members on the basis
of their political commitment to the new revolutionary state. Police priorities
were directed against those who committed crimes against property or
persons, not against public disorder. Critically their function was to conciliate
on the street, not to repress on behalf of the state. Brady has described a
contemporary version of such a policing system in Cuba (Brady, 1981).

Finally, taking nineteenth century history seriously entails paying some
attention to the *colonial police work* that originated in response to the same
manifest imperatives of riot, crime, social disorganisation, ordering, and
class control. Colonial policing functioned to legitimate central rule from
Westminster. Colonial policework, and perhaps in turn British police work,
was pre-eminently missionary work to legitimise external governance.

Principally the traditional histories miss one major salient feature of the
policing of early nineteenth century Britain: its growing importance as an
imperial power. Orthodox accounts of police emergence have resulted in the
treatment of other forms of policing as simply aberrations from the English: a

kind of academic imperialism. But there is another kind of imperial tradition in the study of police origins and functions.

There are in reality only marginal differences between the colonial police and nineteenth century British policing; not the sharp polarities often depicted in the orthodox comparisons between the Metropolitan Police and the Royal Irish Constabulary (Tobias, 1972). Conventional representations of the Royal Irish Constabulary as the direct ancestor of the colonial police ignore the areas of congruence between the former and the Metropolitan, and the specific contribution of the Westminster model to the colonies.

The Relevance of Colonial Policework

In a major overview of the sociology of policing, Cain (1979) pointed to the lack of consideration of the colonial police. Davis (1985) noted the failure of those studies which have grasped the comparative dimension to recognise the centrality of colonial conquest and incorporation in the development of the British police. (George Orwell's first encounter with the British style of policing was as an Inspector in the Burmese colonial police.)

This lacuna, the failure to acknowledge the imperial commitment, has been acknowledged in one study of Victorian institutional development. Johnson (1982), in an original account of the professionalisation of medicine, argued that the search for "professional" standards of conduct, and for controls over occupational membership, was inextricably linked to the growth of the imperial state. One way that British rule was imposed or legitimised in the colonies was through the imposition of occupational standards and criteria derived from the British national context. Throughout the Empire, local particularistic rules over the practice of medicine and over the qualities of the practitioners were used to eliminate local competition and, more importantly, to incorporate the colonial territory within the imperial institutional domain. Local medicine was either incorporated as a subsidiary version of the imperial constructions, or delegitimated. Indigenous definitions of medical need and supply were displaced by imperial professional formulations. This thesis on the medical profession gives a major clue to understanding the use of law in the Empire.

Jeffries (1952) documented one problem of the early rulers of the colonial territories. Faced with the quandary of ruling by coercion or consent, they achieved a compromise in a system of law that incorporated some local practices while delegitimising others. The police forces were of the people, but insulated from them and not governed by them. Legal discourse was reconstructed in imperial terms. The continuing dilemma was to persuade the indigenous population that it was not sufficiently advanced to sustain its own judicial practices and law enforcement procedures until it had absorbed the colonial legal construction.

Several authors have acknowledged the critical links between the origins of the English police system and the development of colonial institutions. Bayley (1969) recounted the influence of the British police system in Asia, Africa, and the Middle East. Others made an indirect connection, by comparing the original Irish and Metropolitan forces (Tobias, 1972).

In sum, there is evidence of an immediate link between British policing and colonial practices. British institutions, from medicine to law enforcement, were transplanted to the Empire: to delegitimise indigenous customs; to impose centralized social control; and to incorporate local society as a branch of imperial society.

Colonising through Law

The central predicament of the early imperial state, both in relation to the mainland provinces, and to the new colonies of Africa, Asia, and the West Indies, was to legitimise its authority not only externally but also internally. The rule of London was spread by a variety of devices. Cultural imperialism succeeded coercion (taking, as G. B. Shaw has described it, the territory as a grateful gift from God). This ranged from the imposition of imperial measures of time, the official language of imperial rule, official criteria for professional practice in medicine, and accounting (central to the affairs of the colonial trading companies), and principally through images of law.

In the colonial policing literature, there is ample evidence of imperial arrogance in relation to indigenous law and legal practices, as they imposed British criteria. In the Sind, Sir Charles Napier denied any legitimacy to native institutions (Jeffries, 1952, p. 31). In Hong Kong, the first British governors regarded local law enforcement as non-existent (Crisswell & Watson, 1982, p. 8) no matter how coherent some contemporary civil servants might regard those social norms (Falconer in Ceylon, quoted in Griffiths, 1971).

According to a study of the early Royal Canadian Mounted Police, this delegitimation process together with the installation of imperial rule by the colonial police served varied economic, social and political functions (Morrison, 1975). In the Yukon, the entry of the Mounties to the settlements of gold-diggers disrupted the evolving democratic communal decision-making process, and established a particular capitalist notion of social order in determining that rules were based on property rights. Law was a weapon to ensure imperial rule.

Policing the Provinces, Policing the Colonies

In several ways, early colonial policing paralleled and reflected less-noted features of Metropolitan policing. In the use of alien rank-and-file, the recruitment of officers, the provision of task forces for outside excursions, the style of policing, the commitment to a preventative function, and even in the stated rationale for formation, the colonial police had a filial relation not just to the Royal Irish Constabulary, but to the practices and organisation of the London Metropolitan Police. Diffusion of ideas between British and colonial policing encompassed the period from Colquhoun (Edwardes, 1923) to the Palestine mandate (Bowden, 1975). Underpinning all these relations was the assumption that colonial police officers drew on the same body of common law powers as did the Metropolitan police (no matter how alien they were to the native tradition).

The original London recruitment of "alien" patrol officers is acknowledged, if given inadequate emphasis (Miller, 1977, pp. 26–7). This imperial policy of "policing strangers by strangers" was conducted throughout the colonial domains: in India (Cox, n.d., p. 147), in Ceylon (Dep, 1979), in Hong Kong (Jeffries, 1955), throughout the African colonies (Cramm, 1969; Jeffries, 1952; Foran, 1962), and in the West Indies (Cramm, 1969; Jeffries, 1952). Further insulation from the local populace was guaranteed at command level. In England and Wales, the officer ranks were predominantly filled at the outset by ex-soldiers who had already been alienated from the local habitat (Miller, 1977; Steedman, 1985). Throughout the colonies, the officers were predominantly of British stock (Jeffries, 1952; Bowden, 1978). Policing practices were diffused by officers who started their careers in the Metropolitan Police or the Royal Irish Constabulary before being promoted to the supervision of a colonial force (Jeffries, 1952), even taking the original training manual with them (Foran, 1962).

Colonial police forces had a major reserve function: available in emergency to be rushed to squash distant disorder. In the United Kingdom, the big city forces provided manpower reserves for troubled provinces (Critchley, 1978; Brogden, 1982). That facility was not as pronounced as in Ireland and in the colonies, where police officers commonly lived in barracks, in the form of a gendarmerie, to respond to external emergencies. But the differences were ones of degree rather than absolutes; although some colonial police forces adopted a punitive, para-military function as in the case of the British South African Police (Godly, 1935).

The relationship between the "home" police and the colonies ranged from the trivial (the Columbo force was at one time clad in Metropolitan uniform: Cox, n.d.) to more serious policing practices. The summary justice that characterised the policing of the lower classes in Victorian England was commonly followed in the colonies. Prostitutes were herded into the ghetto areas, and suspicious characters requested to leave town (in the Yukon – Morrison, 1975; in Bombay – Edwardes, 1923; and in Nairobi – Foran, 1962). Notions of preventative policing (supposedly a unique feature of the mainland British style) justified the creation of colonial forces long before the Metropolitan Police Act 1829. A preventative patrol police was introduced into Columbo as early as 1806 (Pippet, 1938) and at slightly later dates in Bombay (Edwardes, 1923) Jamaica and in British Guiana (Cramm, 1969).

Similar rationales paved the way for a paid police in colonies and in Victorian England. Riot was a common justification. In Jamaica, the emancipation of the slaves created a proletariat deemed threatening by their betters (Jeffries, 1952). In Madras, the first police were developed after a mutiny (riot) and intended to "keep vigilant observation over the community and to prevent secret plots" (Griffiths, 1971). In Bombay, levels of crime and the incursion of rural migrants were the primary catalysts (Edwardes, 1923).

But most commonly, professional policing was directly linked to the commercial interests of an expanding capitalism in search of new markets and resources. Colonial police history is essentially the history of that socialisation of police work. The British South Africa Company, the Royal Nigeria Company, and the Imperial British East Africa Company, amongst others, established policing systems. The East Indian Company spread its police tentacles as far as Singapore. The primary justifications for the new police were the exigencies of trade and company profit (Jeffries, 1952; Foran, 1962).

Most of the future British colonies commenced their imperial connection as the private domains of limited companies based in London. Colonial ventures were profit-motivated. Like the Liverpool merchants and shopkeepers (Brogden, 1983) committed to the cheap reproduction of labour and to distraints on competitors, the colonial governments saw the economic imperative as foremost in establishing a professional police.

In several ways therefore, colonial policing replicated the policing of Victorian society. There were differences of degree rather than in intent and organisation. This is not to deny that there were certain distinctions between the policing of Britain and the policing of the colonies, rather to suggest that the two types of policing are not separate categories but ranged on a continuum, in which some features are more heavily weighted towards the extremes than are others.

The Unique Features of Colonial Policing

There remain some discontinuities, situations in which the model for the colonies was clearly and absolutely the Royal Irish Constabulary, with few obligations to Rowan and Mayne. Principal amongst these similarities (and leaving the question of armaments aside) were the form of control, the physical location of the police, and their link with the military (Bayley, 1969).

In Ireland, the Royal Irish Constabulary was a national force controlled from Dublin Castle (Tobias, 1972). Similarly, in Hong Kong and the Indian provinces, the police were under the control of a civil official who was normally subordinate to the Governor. The colonial police were directly at the service of the civil power, not maintained at some distance as with the mediating common law powers of the English police. However, not too much should be made of this difference. In the first place, the relationship between the local police commanders and civil authorities in England and Wales arguably was less clear-cut than the common law view suggests (Brogden, 1982).

Secondly, as colonial policing evolved, in many colonies a similar structure of law enforcement developed as in the imperial state; with the separation of the enforcement arm from the judicial function (Jeffries, 1952).

The second key difference between Westminster-model forces and the colonial police lies in their physical location and their close proximity to the military. Like some Continental forces today (for example, the Guarda Civil, the Gendarmerie Nationale, and the Bereitschaftpolizei), the colonial police were often accommodated in barracks separate from the civil population. The Hong Kong Police in particular followed the Royal Irish Constabulary directly in this practice, as in the carrying of armaments, and in the form of control. The British South African Police had the clearest link with the military. In the African colonies generally, in emergencies (such as during World War I), the colonial police forces were conscripted as an arm of the military (Foran, 1962). But not all colonial forces had such a relationship: the important Indian Police Act 1861 attempted to distinguish between policing and military functions in that country.

Incorporation and Delegitimation

Internal colonisation, like external colonisation, is faced with a strategic problem in relation to its legitimacy (Brogden, 1987). The imperial state can impose its own arbitrary institutions. Alternatively, it can seek to incorporate existing features of the society within a larger construction defined in terms of imperial interests, practices which are re-shaped while maintaining their traditional connection with the indigenous society.

In British society, the second strategy developed, principally through a re-construction of the "citizen-in-uniform" and "original powers" theme. Police officers could justify their practices by reference to the "reconstructed" images of the pre-industrial tythingman and parish constable (Hall *et al.*, 1978). Internal police colonialism drew heavily on this connection between provincial working-class cultures and the new dominant ideology of industrial capitalism. In many of the Asian colonies, a similar structure was pursued (Griffiths, 1971, p. 56; Jeffries, 1952).

However, in colonies that had been acquired by conquest, from the Sind to Rhodesia, the indigenous legal system was ignored and a new imperial system imposed from above. In Hong Kong, in most of the African colonies and in the West Indies, local institutions, including the legal system and its appendages, were largely delegitimised. Local law enforcement practices were invalidated and imperial structures imposed.

The exploration of facets of colonial policing, such as the processes of incorporation and the delegitimisation of existing legal structures, permits a fresh consideration of policing in mainland Britain. Robert Storch's domestic missionaries (Storch, 1970) were in fact just that: apostles of the Westminster law enforcement gospel in provincial England (despite their coercive exaggeration in some radical citations of that author's work).

References

Bayley, D. H. (1969). *The Police and Political Development In India,* London: Sage.
Bowden, T. (1978). *Beyond the Limits of the Law.* Harmondsworth, Middlesex: Penguin.
Brodeur, J. P. (June 1983). "High Policing and Low Policing: Remarks about the Policing of Political Activities." *Social Problems,* 30: 5, pp. 507–20.
Brogden, M. E. (1982). *The Police: Autonomy and Consent,* London: Academic Press.
Brogden, M. E. (1983). "Policing a Mercantile Economy", *4th European Conference on Critical Legal Studies,* University of Kent.
Cain, M. E. (1979). "Trends in the Sociology of Policework", *International Journal of the Sociology of Law,* 7.2 143–67.
Cox, E. C. (n.d.). *Police and Crime in India,* London: Stanley Parks & Co.
Cramm, J. (1969). *The World's Police,* London: Cassell.
Crisswell, C. and Watson, M. (1982). *The Royal Hong Kong Police,* Hong Kong: Mannela.
Critchley, T. A. (1978). *A History of Police in England and Wales,* (2nd. ed.) London, Constable. [1st ed.: 1967]
Davis, J. (1985). "Review of Emsley: Policing and its Context". *International Journal of the Sociology of Law,* 13, 3.
Dep, M. (1979). *A History of the Ceylon Police,* Vol. II, Columbo: n.p.
Donzelot, J. (1979). *The Policing of Families,* New York: Pantheon Books.
Edwardes, S. M. (1923). *The Bombay City Police 1672–1916.* London: Oxford University Press.
Emsley, C. (1983). *Policing and its Context 1750–1870.* London: Macmillan.
Field, J. (1981). "Police, Power, and Community in a Provincial English Town, 1815–75", in V. Bailey (Ed.) *Policing and Punishment in 19th century Britain.* London: Croom Helm. 42–64.
Foran, W. R. (1962). *The Kenya Police 1877–1960,* London: Robert Hale.
Godley, R. S. (1935). *Khaki and Blue.* London: Dickson & Thompson.
Griffiths, P. (1971). *To Guard My People – The History of the Indian Police,* London: Ernest Benn.
Harring, S. L. (1979). "Class Conflict and the Suppression of Tramps in Buffalo, 1892–1894." In Messinger, S. I. and Bittner, E. (Eds.), *Criminology Review Yearbook.* Beverley Hills: Sage.
Harring, S. L. (1983). *Policing a Class Society,* New Brunswick: Rutgers U.P.
Jeffries, C. (1952). *The Colonial Police,* London: Max Parrish.
Johnson, D. R. (1979). *Policing the Urban Underworld,* Philadelphia: Temple U.P.
Johnson, T. (1982). "The State and the Professions," in A. Giddens & G. Mackenzie (eds.): *Social Class and the Division of Labour,* Cambridge: Cambridge U.P. 186–209.
Kakalik, J. S. & Wildhorn, S. (1977). *The Private Police.* New York: Crane Russak.
Klockars, C. B. (1985). *The Idea of Police,* London: Sage.
Lane, R. (1967). *Policing the City.* Cambridge, Mass: Harvard U.P.
Lane, R. (1980). "Urban Police and Crime in Nineteenth Century America." In N. Morris & M. Tonry (eds.): *Crime and Justice: An Annual Review Research.* Chicago: Chicago University Press. 1–44.
Levett, A. E. (1975), *Centralisation of City Police in the Nineteenth Century United States.* Ph.d. dissertation, Ann Arbor: University of Michigan.
Miller, W. R. (1977). *Cops and Bobbies.* Chicago: Univ. of Chicago Press.
Monkkonen, E. H. (1981). *Police in Urban America, 1860–1920.* London: Cambridge U.P.
Morrison, W. (1975). "The North West Mounted Police and the Klondike Gold Rush." In G. Mosse (ed.): *Police Forces in History.* London: Sage, 263–76.
Phillips, D. (1980). "A New Engine of Power and Authority: the Institutionalisation of Law Enforcement in England 1780–1830." In V. Gatrell, B. Lenman, and G. Parker (eds.): *Crime and the Law,* London: Europa. 155–89.

Pike, M. (1985). *The Principles of Policing.* London: Macmillan.

Pippet, K. (1938). *A History of the Ceylon Police,* Vol. I, Columbo: n.p.

Radzinowicz, L. (1955). *A History of English Criminal Law and its Administration, Vol. III,* London: Stevens.

Richardson, J. F. (1970). *The New York Police: Colonial Times to 1901.* New York: Oxford U.P.

Scraton, P. (1985). *The State of the Police.* London: Pluto.

Silver, A. (1967). "The Demand for Order in Civil Society" in D. Bordua (ed.): *The Police.* New York: Wiley. 1–24.

Spitzer, S. and Scull, A. (1977). "Social Control in Historical Perspective." In Greenberg, D. (ed.) *Corrections and Punishment,* Beverley Hills, Sage. 265–286.

Stead, P. J. (1977). "The New Police." In D. H. Bayley (ed.) *Police and Society,* London: Sage. 73–84.

Sumner, C. (1982). *Crime, Justice, and Underdevelopment.* London: Heinemann.

Toblas, J. J. (1972). "Police and the Public in the *U.K." Journal of Contemporary History.* 7–1, 201–220.

Walker, S. (1977). *A Critical History of Police Reform.* D. C. Heath, Lexington.

Theory: Sociology, Politics and International Relations

9

The Global Cops Cometh: Reflections on Transnationalization, Knowledge Work and Policing Subculture

James Sheptycki

Introduction

The notion of subculture has suffered greatly from overuse. It is not that the term cannot be used with precision more that, most often, it is evoked in a lazy and imprecise manner. Echoing David Downes (1966) we can say that it is not at all illuminating to label as 'subcultural' well known differences between different sectors of complex societies. In trying to think within a transnational frame of reference this problem is compounded if we take as our starting point 'world society' (Burton 1972) or 'world culture' (Featherstone 1990). By thinking about various types of global 'sub'-cultures merely through such theoretical abstractions the sociologist invariably sacrifices precision for theoretical breadth. In what follows the term subculture is constructed around a specific problem, that is: the emergence of a transnational police enterprise. It involves a word inversion which establishes a cognitive space; that space lying between the notions of the transnational subculture of police and the subculture of transnational policing. The goal is to illuminate this complex sociological phenomenon; one which is of such recent vintage that we have not yet developed a theoretical schema that is capable of doing so. In such circumstances it is possible that the sociologist can profit by 'retooling' old terms and applying them to new circumstances.

Source: *The British Journal of Sociology,* 49(1) (1998): 57–74.

Subculture Revisited

In retooling the term subculture, I take as my starting point not only the sub-culturalist approaches to deviance, but also the important contributions of Skolnick (1966) and other sociologists of the police organization. In developing his notion of the police officer's 'working personality', Skolnick, in common with the subcultural theorists more generally, viewed it as a set of 'learned problem solutions'. In the case of the police officer these problem solutions are said to be embedded in the routines of 'the job'. Conceptualizing cop culture in this way allows the sociologist to avoid the pitfall of visualizing the occupational subculture as a concrete entity (reification) to which various attributes (overt masculinity, racism or clannishness, for example) are attached. Such oft mentioned attributes of police subculture, it must be said, are not confined to the police organization, indeed they are far more widespread than the notion implies. A more profitable way to construct an understanding of police occupational subculture is to build up the concept from basic, and observable, features of police work. Skolnick did so by reference to notions of danger, authority and the need to get something done. In so doing he focused attention on certain specific features, notably the role of the symbolic assailant, police suspiciousness and solidarity and the concomitant social isolation that characterizes the archetypal police officer.

Skolnick's field work focused attention on police patrol and, to a lesser extent, detective work. More recent analyses of public police institutions have focused on police as 'knowledge workers'. Chatterton, for example, noted that field researchers on the lookout for 'real police work' are tempted to 'switch over to someone else who is remaining out on patrol' when a police officer under observation announces her intention to spend time in the police station writing reports' (Chatterton 1989: 108).

This skews our understanding of police work. Sociologists of the police organization have reported that detectives spend approximately one-half their time doing reports and even more reporting on their investigations than in the conduct of investigations *per se.* (Ericson 1981). Further, by managing calls for service the computer aided dispatch systems have so converted the job of uniformed police patrol that there is nothing *but* knowledge work (Manning 1988). Sociologists have paid scant attention to the large numbers of personnel, both uniformed and civilian, within the police organization devoted to knowledge production and management at every level. Strategic planning units, media liaison offices, environmental scanning units, quality assurance teams, community involvement teams, criminal intelligence specialists and a whole range of other sub-specialisms are devoted to the creation and dissemination of knowledge without which the modern police institution would cease to be. In the information age police officers of both staff and line spend far less time directly protecting persons and property from crimes than is commonly supposed and far more time processing and exchanging knowledge about crime and insecurity. For Ericson, knowledge work, particularly processing of pre-formatted knowledge for other 'risk institutions' (insurance companies, regulatory agencies the automobile industry and the like) has become the preeminent *raison d'être* for police (1994a). This may somewhat overstate the influence of actuarial justice on public policing, however, there is no denying that knowledge work has come to dominate the structure of the organization to such an extent that to conceptualize the occupational sub-culture of police purely around high speed car chases, pub brawls, and the apprehension of 'good prisoners' is to mistake the jam for the bread (cf. Holdaway 1983). Instead, I want to suggest that we shift our attention away from the danger/ authority nexus and on to policing as knowledge work.

This shift in our conception of the occupational sub-culture of policing is, in many ways, analogous to Riesman's classic discussion of the characterological transformation that people in various occupations undergo when, on promotion, they take up management positions (Riesman 1950). 'To sit at his big new desk' Riesman notes 'he has to learn a new personality-oriented speciality and un-learn or at least soft-pedal his old skill orientation' (p. 134). The characterological transformation of which Riesman wrote was not so much about occupational advancement within institutional hierarchies as it was about an overall characterological shift (from 'inner directed' to 'other directed') in response to the changing social structure of society. That shift was seen as the result of a move from a production oriented society to a consumption oriented one. In the terms developed in this essay, the shift is seen as a response to the creation of informated space (Zuboff 1988), the resultant information revolution (Castells 1989) and the creation of the knowledge society (Giddens 1979; Ericson and Shearing 1986; Stehr 1994).

Looking at policing as knowledge work produces a different matrix of problem-solutions than the danger/authority frame put forward by Skolnick. In the wake of the information revolution, the degree to which police work has shifted away from that which was described by Skolnick and others is striking. It is almost as if every police officer, bar those few who are left in specialist departments directly marshalling coercive power (public order police, firearms units, siege management units and the like) has been swept into the knowledge society. Indeed, even in units which are expressly dedicated to the co-ordination of coercive force, the amount of time devoted to knowledge work far outweighs that of actual 'hands on' danger time.[1] The vectors of danger and authority have been elided; they no longer constitute the primary space within which the problem-solutions of the occupational subculture of policing emerge. A characterological transformation analogous to that which Riesman talked of almost fifty years ago has become general to all those professions where knowledge work has become the primary preoccupation. Policing, and certainly transnational policing (as will become apparent), has been no less affected by this societal shift.[2]

The Correlates of Police Subculture in the Knowledge Society

We can begin by identifying four correlates which lie along two axes and which describe the space in which the occupational subculture of policing takes its form. Those correlates are: the technological and legal infrastructures and the political and managerial regimes, all of which are forms of knowledge production. The intersection of these vectors creates a space of tension requiring collective response. It is that collective response which counts as an occupational subculture.

The Technological Infrastructure

Taking the first of these correlates we might begin by noting the striking degree of technological innovation within the police organization in this century. In our current time developments in that technological infrastructure include the rapid deployment of information technology, especially software capable of handling large scale data sets pertaining to suspect populations. (Colton 1978; Doney 1990; Egger 1990; Leonard 1980). A classic historical example is the development of fingerprint technology (Hannant 1995).[3] A technical development that has generated considerable discussion amongst sociologists of police revolves around radio dispatch of car patrols (Manning 1980, 1983, 1988; Waddington 1993). Another area of technological innovation which has captured the imagination of police, police watchers and public alike is the latest development in forensic medicine: DNA profiling (Alldridge et al. 1995) Taken as a whole, what the literature on technological innovation within the police organization in this century reveals is an almost constant reconfiguring of police work as each new wave of technology is adapted for use. Each generation of police officers has been compelled to reform the parameters of 'the job'; the occupational routines are recast as the new tools are brought to bear on the police task. As the drama of police work is changed by technological innovation, the occupational subculture shifts along one dimension.

When we examine the literature on what is variously described as cross-border police 'co-operation' (Anderson et al. 1995), the 'internationalisation' of policing (Fijnaut 1993; Nadelmann 1993) or its 'transnationalisation' (Sheptycki 1995a) the role of information technology is recurrent. Particularly problematic is the expanding surveillance capacity of police in the transnational realm (McLaughlin 1992). Police officers at the transnational level are intimately wedded to this technology, as practically everything that they do is done in informated space (PRSU 1992; Sheptycki 1995b). Thus, the central place that information processing plays in transnational policing ensures that this correlate plays a significant part in the working personality of the police officers who take on this role. This is not to understate the place of such technology at the more local level that sociologists and criminologists are used to studying, merely to emphasis that, in the absence of 'policing cyberspace', the transnational sphere would be all but out of reach.

The Legal Infrastructure

The correlate on the opposite pole of this vector is the legal infrastructure. Contemporary jurisprudence conventionally holds that policing is bound up with the application of criminal law and, for the most part, it is. However, this view of the relation between policing and the law creates tensions for the way police operate, as Goldstein's (1960) classic, if somewhat idealistic, jurisprudential reasoning demonstrates. These legal tensions have been described by others as being established by the opposition between law as a vehicle for 'crime control' and law as adherence to 'due process' (cf. McConville et al. 1991; Packer 1968). Whatever the ideal relation between police and the law might be deemed to be, it seems clear that policing takes place *under* the law, but is not *driven* by it (see, for example, *R vs. Metropolitan Police Commissioner ex parte Blackburn* (1968); *R. vs Metropolitan Police Commissioner ex parte Blackburn* (1973)). In the terms developed here we might say that legal knowledge provides a rhetorical form in which police practice is discursively constituted. Practical mastery of that type of knowledge production is an occupational survival skill which is learned in close association with others who also have to contend with the ambiguities and tensions of the (criminal) law itself. This facet of the police occupational subculture is well known (cf. McCabe and Sutcliffe 1978; Chan 1996).

The complexities of (criminal) law at the purely national level have given rise to some ambiguities in policing and, hence, have lent a certain complexion to the occupational subculture, and sociologists, at least since Skolnick's work, have been well aware of this. This complexity is manifold at the transnational level where overlapping jurisdictional boundaries and a welter of treaties of both a bi-lateral and multi-lateral nature have built up a kaleidoscope of legal rules. The exchange of Memoranda of Understanding that facilitate the smooth operation of policing in specific cross-border situations is one type of legal instrument, as is the Extradition Treaty; more involved still are Mutual Legal Assistance Treaties. Police operating in the transnational realm are expected to master the legal rules that pertain to the sovereign ground that they police, as well as know the framework of transnational law which aims to facilitate cross-border policing initiatives. Lastly they need more than a passing familiarity with criminal and procedural law in other police jurisdictions with which they might seek to co-operate. A practical example of this are the Policing and Frontier Protocols and the Security and Defence Protocols incorporated into British and French Law under the provisions of the Channel Tunnel Act. These protocols are intended to deal with all aspects of policing and security that emanate from a unique transnational location:

the Channel Tunnel. They provide the legal framework through which police officers and officials from various other enforcement type agencies exercise their law enforcement powers on foreign soil (but within defined 'control zones'). This legal framework allows police actions such as arrest and seizure of property by French and UK police authorities on their respective territories; it also allows the French police to operate armed, as they are accustomed to, on the British side of the Channel and it allows the British police to maintain a Police National Computer (PNC) terminal on the French side. In effect, these legal instruments return policing from the transnational realm to the national by the reciprocal constitution of sovereign territory in the domain of the other. Other transnational legal instruments, such as the series of treaties between the Benelux countries (that facilitate such police actions as the 'right of hot pursuit' or the mounting of surveillance operations and arrests on each other's territories) are even less concerned to symbolically uphold sovereignty. In the North American context, Mutual Legal Assistance Treaties have provided for the routine and wide ranging exchange of crime data and criminal intelligence between a myriad of police agencies as well as other operational capacities. In general in order for police to operate they require familiarity with the law. Such knowledge is all the more hard won in the transnational setting. This specialist knowledge is part and parcel of the subculture of transnational policing, without it movement between the transnational and national realms cannot be negotiated.

Tensions between the Legal and Technological Infrastructures

The seemingly ever widening vistas opened up by continual technological innovation create lacunae and areas of ambiguity in the law, while creating at least the appearance of an increased capacity for control. This produces a dynamic tension which gives rise to the sorts of collective solutions which, in part, circumscribe police occupational subculture. Technology tends to develop and be employed within the police institution prior to adjustments of the legal framework in which police operate. The extent of this tension is evident with each wave of technological innovation, but the historical example of the adaptation of fingerprint technology is most instructive with regard to this point. The campaign for fingerprinting was one of the first truly international efforts made by the public police (in contradistinction to 'private police' – i.e. Pinkerton Agency etc.). The International Association of Chiefs of Police urged all police forces to adopt the technology and promoted the idea of universal fingerprinting at a conference held in New York City in 1925 (Hannant 1995: 52). To the frustration of police officials in Canada, Britain and the USA, laws pertaining to the use of the technique remained restrictive. As one might expect, J. Edgar Hoover was one of the most zealous promoters urging American police forces to fingerprint everyone who they thought it 'desirable to fingerprint'.

Under Hoover the technology became an overtly political tool. In 1933 the FBI established its Civil Identification Section 'receiving as a down payment the fingerprints of more than 140,000 US government employees' (ibid.: 53). By 1939 that collection had burgeoned to over 10 million fingerprints about half of which belonged to individuals with no criminal label as such. Hannant quotes a writer in *Good Housekeeping* who, upon seeing the scale of the Bureau's collection felt moved to write

> To me it was symbolic – that little (sic) file of fingerprints of public-spirited Americans with nothing in their pasts to hide, who trusted their Federal law-enforcement officers and were thankfully accepting their protective care. No communism in the minds of these individuals. No red revolution. Simply old-fashioned American faith in American institutions, (ibid.: 54)

Nor was this political edge to the application of the technology limited to the USA. Greg Marquis (1993) has noted that the need to scientifically collect, store and disseminate information on the 'criminal class' led to the creation of the Canadian Criminal Identification Bureau in 1911. In the inter-war years this fingerprinting system was extended to the role of 'security vetting', but 'no Canadian government brought it [security vetting] to the public's attention, let alone sanctioned it by legislation' (Hannant 1995: 79). During the period of the War Measures Act this system was both widened and deepened. Eventually approximately 20 per cent of Canada's working population were brought under surveillance using this system. The question as to why the Canadian Federal Government never legally sanctioned the build up of large scale security screening remains something of an enigma, but non-criminal fingerprinting did remain extra-legal up until 1946 and security screening itself was never approved by elected politicians. It is commonly believed that the Canadian state introduced security screening only in 1946 in the wake of the defection of Igor Gouzenko. However, 1946 does not mark the inception of such policing in Canada, but merely the point at which some 'rudimentary operating rules' for the operation of the screening system were introduced (Whitacker and Marcuse 1994: 253). Regarding our central theme, this history reveals that the tension between the promise of technical innovation and the brake of legal prescription create a space wherein subcultural modes and practices particular to the police occupation reside. It is this space which most often exercises our darkest imaginings about the police organization, and not without reason.

The Political Régime

In the transnational knowledge society it can come as no surprise that foremost amongst the legal instruments within the police domain are those that deal with data protection. This is certainly so in Europe where the increased

surveillance capacity of police agencies fostered by the simultaneous information revolution and the coming together of the European Union have
created quite widespread concerns about civil liberties (Bunyan 1993, Raab
1994). In so far as police work is transnational it is virtually pure knowledge
work; yet it is a standard proposition in the sociology of policing that police
work is 'results' oriented (Reiner 1985: 88) very often expressed in terms of
'clearance' rates (Skolnick 1994: 162–8) or 'clear-ups' (Young 1991: 281).
This is so often repeated in the literature that it is uncritically absorbed;
so much so that there is a tacit expectation that all police work is geared
toward this end. In looking at the role of policing in the transnational realm,
what is striking is that, there being no 'operational' transnational police
officer, virtually every task undertaken is pure knowledge work. What
we find is an almost exclusive concern with information or 'intelligence'
exchange and the lack of operational capacity is compensated for, to an
extent, through the various legal instruments previously mentioned which,
as was explained, bind transnational policing efforts to national or sub-
national police agencies.

The situation of Europol is particularly informative in this regard, since,
according to the Treaty of European Union (TEU), the tasks of Europol are
to be restricted to collecting and analysing information and intelligence, preparing situation reports and crime analyses, and maintaining a central data
base for specific crime areas, namely money laundering, international arms
and drugs trafficking, counterfeiting of money and credit cards, and abduction. While some politicians, notably Chancellor Helmut Kohl, have argued
that Europol should have an operational role, before this could come to pass
a number of other institutional developments would have to take place.
Present legal conventions would have to be extended, Europol would have
to be extended the power of arrest and there would have to be developed
some kind of European Prosecutors Office to process charges for court. In
addition, the remit of the European Court of Justice, based in Luxembourg,
would have to be extended (a development which is further complicated
by the overlapping interests it shares with the European Court of Human
Rights based in Strasbourg) and, lastly, there would need to be a European
wide police complaints system established. Given the political complexity
of establishing these institutions it seems likely that transnational policing
in Europe will continue to be virtually pure knowledge work, as the present
remit of Europol and the practices of other transnational police initiatives
reveals it to be.[4] The complexities of the political régime create very real
limitations for transnational policing which, in turn create space for learned
problem-solutions. Symptomatic of this are the sub-terranean networks of
police officers in the transnational realm (Sheptycki 1995a). We could say,
with a slight degree of irony, that networks such as the International Police
Working Group (a network of undercover police operatives in Europe that is

fostered under the Europol system) do not constitute a subculture so much as a police club.

The Managerial Régime

Casual observers of the police may not realize the fragmented nature of the enterprise but the managerial space within which policing takes place must be seen in all its complexity. Consider the USA with its welter of police agencies at local, state and national levels (Walker 1977). One study conducted in the USA which looked at 1,827 agencies providing police 'services' noted that informal interagency assistance is common (Ostrom et al. 1978). This informal networking is inherently labyrinthine and some commentators have pointed out that overlapping legal jurisdictions may lead to competition and/or 'linkage blindness'. (Egger 1990). Nor need this view of the managerial régime be restricted to large scale states like the USA. For example, this fragmentation was a feature of policing in the Netherlands until the early 1990s which, prior to that time, had 148 municipal police forces, a National police force, a waterways police, a specialist traffic police, an aviation police and a military police force (Jones 1995). This fragmented managerial régime might have had negative effects for policing in the Dutch context, but despite that manifest 'administrative confusion' (Mawby 1990) it was the process of Europeanization (a sub-species of transnationalization) that yielded the real impetus for the administrative reform that resulted in the present structure of twenty-four regional police forces and one national organization exercising its control through the CRI (Criminal Intelligence Agency). Prior to that restructuring it was the subcultural 'ways and means' approach which served as a social lubricant to ease the operation of this exceedingly complex machine.[5] In my own observations of policing in the English Channel region, it is evident that co-operation between police and other police type agencies (Immigration, Customs, Private Security etc.) create a tremendously complex inter-agency form. (Sheptycki 1995b)

In terms of transnational policing, the managerial régime offers something of a counterweight to the problems inherent in the political régime. While the latter is a product of the requirements of state sovereignty, the former is produced by the exigencies of policing in an inter-agency frame. It is important to stress, however, that the managerial régime is not reducible to this role of counterweight in the transnational realm. For example, the Combined Law Enforcement Unit (CLEU) which operates in the greater Vancouver area on the west coast of British Columbia, brings together RCMP and municipal police forces. This hybrid organization only incidentally facilitates cross-border policing initiatives. Its primary *raison d'être* is, as its name suggests, to combine the efforts of police agencies that are administratively distinct. The practice of forming 'task forces' for particular police operations in the US context is another management technique for overcoming adminis-trative fragmentation. In the transnational context, the Cross Channel Intel-ligence Conference (CCIC), which operates in the English Channel region, was formed in 1968 expressly to facilitate policing initiatives between the Belgian and UK police in the absence of a political régime capable of doing so. Any of these managerial régimes will require subcultural understanding (a *lingua franca*) sufficient to facilitate their smooth operation, as the notable failure of some 'task forces' in the USA amply, if negatively, demonstrates. The degree of balance along the managerial/political vector establishes an additional dimension along which the correlates of the occupational subcul-ture of policing can be said to lie (cf. Verbruggen 1995).[6]

Coercive Force, Overdetermination and Police Subculture

In addition to the four correlates of police subculture noted above we will have to add one final element and that is Bittner's (1970) observation that coercive force lies at the core of the police role. We can incorporate Bittner's insight into our analysis of police subculture, and avoid the essentialism of which he is often accused, by making use of the concept of 'overdeter-mination'. Garland (1990) defines the term succinctly as the convergence of a range of conflicting and connecting forces that produce a given social phenomenon (op. cit.: 124–5, 280–1). Even when police work is primarily knowledge work it is multidimensional. Thus the correlates of the subculture so far outlined can be seen both as independent effects each of which make up facets of the police subculture and as contradictory forces which open up the space within which this subculture can be said to lie.

Having said this, it is equally important to stress that police work is bound up with the orchestration of the state's capacity to muster coercive force. Many kinds of work in the knowledge society have become knowledge-based. As a consequence, surveillance has become a dominant modality in virtually every professional occupation. Here we might draw a deliberately remote analogy with the practice of medicine. While it is true that physicians have been increasingly affected by the production of knowledge in infor-mated space – so that diagnosis is now done in dialogue with 'expert systems' and treatment is prescribed with reference to the knowledge criteria based in economics, the law and risk management – it is meaningless to suppose that we could conceive of the occupational subculture of the healing professions without reference to disease, pain and death. Just as any formulation of the occupational subculture of the hospital and the medical profession must take account of the multiple effects brought to bear by the 'core' task of healing and the complexities of the institutional arrangements constituted by the knowledge society, and within which medical practice is precariously negoti-ated, so too must our understanding of policing be shaded by reference to the role of coercive force. Only when we take into account all of the relevant correlates have we adequately grasped the overdetermined nature of either occupational subculture.

Styles of Policing

This essay is not merely concerned with subculture as defined from the standpoint of major political institutions like the state, or from the standpoint of the sub-institutions, groups and language games (legal and otherwise) into which the state (and other forms of political institution) can be divided for the purposes of formal analysis. While the formal approach is both useful and necessary to understanding the constitution of an abstract analytical category like 'police subculture' our interest must also turn to the process by which people become related to this abstraction. Obviously an abstraction like police subculture cannot be neatly drawn. This is one reason why, in speaking of the consequences of police subculture for those who give it life on a daily basis, I use the impressionistic term 'style'. To paraphrase Riesman (1950), if the drama of policing is a ballet on a stage set by history, style tells us neither whence the dancers come nor whither they move but only in what manner they play their parts.

The police occupation as it exists within the transnational knowledge society gives rise to four styles that can be adopted by individuals they are: the technocrat, the diplomat, the entrepreneur and the enforcer. There is one other residual style that can be identified, what Reiner (1978, 1985) termed the 'uniform carrier', that is: the completely cynical and disillusioned time server. This residual category is unknown in the transnational domain because, in order to get into such a position, officers must pass muster. This category need not exercise us much anyway for its expressions have been well described elsewhere in the literature. Another reason for fleeting past this style of work, if one can call it that without being contradictory, is that it is not limited to the police organization and can be found readily in most human organizations, including the halls of *academe* – our intimate acquaintance with this style renders it analytically uninteresting. Of the four that are of analytical interest the first three are stylistic adaptations that are intended to facilitate the *bridging* of the multiple contradictions inherent in the relationships between the technological and legal infrastructures and the political and managerial régimes. The latter aims to *cut through* them.

The technocrat appeals to the apparent capacity for control seemingly inherent in the new information technology and technologies of surveillance. For the technocrat it is the efficient gathering and management of data and the constant patrolling of the informated security field that offers the promise of overcoming the problems of disorder conceived of both externally, out there in the 'real world', and internally, within the complex and fragmented police system. It was the technocrat who spoke for Interpol as that organization dodged the provisions of the French Data Protection Act;

'if we were governed by French law, we could only enter pure statistics – how many drug seizures were made last year or whatever – and that would hardly be of the greatest value' (Bresler 1992: 172).[7] What the technocrat needs is access to data about actual persons. Access to 'nominal data', not only on police computers, but also on civilian computers like those operated by telephone companies, credit card companies and the like, lends police a powerful tool with which to pursue the project of social ordering. The logic pursued here is reminiscent of Orwell's *1984*: complete infiltration, total surveillance and perfect knowledge on behalf of a Ministry of Truth that puts everything in order. However, it has been pointed out, and my own observations confirm this (see footnote 7, above), that this growth of information systems is so great that even the bureaucratic and professional custodians of it do not have this kind of control and, ultimately, their poor grasp curtails the reaches of the system (Ericson, and Shearing 1986). Nevertheless, the mere existence of this style of policing has given rise to legitimate concerns about the implications of the new technologies of surveillance for the institution of privacy. This style will persist as long as the technologies currently being applied in the policing organization offer the promise of control and the legal frame for its application remains ill-suited to the task required.

The diplomatic style offers another role for the police officer and one that can attempt to bridge the contradictions of the police world. The reader might be tempted to confine this character to an Embassy office. Indeed, many liaison officers do operate out of their countries' embassies attending to both their recognizable 'police duties' and to the diplomatic circuit. However, there are many institutions and situations that occur within the variegated institutional terrain inherent in the political and managerial régimes described above where such a style can be usefully displayed. The diplomat police style is one calculated to overcome the problem of 'turf battles' between different police organizations and, further, one which is attuned to the nuances of legal, bureaucratic and political differences embodied in the many institutional settings in which policing takes place. The diplomatic style might be tactfully employed to bridge the gap between different Federal police agencies and local police agencies that are brought under the umbrella of a 'task force' established to deal with a specific problem in the US context. This style is no less attractive to the truly transnational police officer who finds herself working in a liaison capacity in a foreign country. This is the most difficult and, hence, the rarest stylistic adaptation; it entails not only a wide-ranging appreciation of bureaucratic and legal rules and, very often, skill in two or more languages, it also requires a skill shared by sociologists: the capacity to step outside one's own narrow cultural frame of reference and appreciate another way of viewing issues that come to hand. This capacity for what Giddens (1976) refers to as 'reflexivity' is hard won and one not a little at odds with a police mission – very often narrowly construed in terms of 'law n' order' – nevertheless, it is a style that, through its great utility, continues to surface from time to time.

Another style which police officers might adopt is that of the entrepreneur. Successful policing is about the application of technique, and techniques are continually evolving. From Edward Henry's fingerprint classification system to new database management techniques for tracking serial offences, each technique had to be sold to a police consumer. Here again the historical example of fingerprint technology is illuminating since it had a rival, the Bertillion System. Indeed, for some years both systems were successfully 'marketed' to police agencies.[8] Two excellent examples of the entrepreneurial style emerge from my field notes. The first such example concerned an officer working on the Police Speak Project (Police Speak 1993) who, after successfully using the institutional competition between the two national police agencies in Belgium, the Gendarmerie and the Judicial Police, to sell what amounts to an e-mail terminal and network facilities to the latter force, confidently claimed that he 'could sell Bovril in a Marmite factory'. The second concerned RCMP officers involved in the development of the Violent Crime Linkage Analysis System (ViCLAS) data management software for handling information pertaining to serial murder and other forms of serial crime. This technology, based on networked desk top computers, is in market competition with an older American system, the Violent Criminal Apprehension Program (ViCAP) which is a centralized automated computer information system. These officers informed me that they had not only sold the software to police forces in the Commonwealth (New Zealand and Australia), but had also sold it to several European police forces including: Belgium, Holland and Austria. It is evident that the marketing of technical solutions to police problems provides a way of bridging the gaps between and within police agencies. The entrepreneurial style smooths over the tensions inherent in the structural form of the contemporary police organization. It is a successful adaptation to the dynamic tension established by the correlates of the police subculture since it is predicated on the discovery and selling of techniques calculated to overcome those very tensions.

The final style open to the police officer is the enforcer. This is a classic term from the literature on police occupational subculture defined most succinctly by William Ker Muir Jr. (1977). For Muir the enforcer style is predicated on an enhanced belief in the efficacy of coercion, in effect the enforcer takes Bittner's assertion about the 'core task' of policing and runs with it, forgetting the caveat placed upon it – that the skill in policing consists in finding ways to avoid the use of coercion. In the transnational realm this style is most evident in the actions of US law enforcement officers pursuing the 'war on drugs' (Sheptycki 1996). It is clear in the words one DEA official used to describe the 'puny' efforts of US law enforcement in their struggle to deal with the 'menace' of the Colombian cocaine cartels: 'Think of an ant, crawling up an elephant's leg [pause] with rape on its mind' (BBC 1991).

This style differs from the three previously mentioned in that it seeks to cut through rather than bridge the complexities of the police institution as it is constituted within the transnational knowledge society. In Muir's words, the enforcer style is symptomatic of a loss of contact with the complexity of reality and a tendency to grow ever more reliant on the exercise of force, all ideas of restraint are jettisoned and all that is left is a standing temptation to use violence (1977: 294–5). This style is as evident in the legacy left the LAPD by Daryl Gates as it is in the transnational declaration of war against the *pax Mafiosi*. It will persist as long as the metaphor of the 'war on crime' continues to have popular political appeal.

These, then, are the adaptive styles observable within the occupational subculture of policing. A caveat is in order. These 'styles' are ideal types and no one individual police officer conforms to one type. Real people are blends, more complicated and various than any scheme can encompass. A particular police officer may, on the whole, adopt a diplomatic style but certain situational determinants may prompt him to adopt an entrepreneurial cloak. Similarly, one type of police work, say having to do with drug smuggling, may trigger the adoption of the attitude of an enforcer, whereas car theft or credit card fraud will signal a shift to the technocratic mode. But these 'chameleonings' of character are not the only brake on our application of this particular schema. Perhaps more importantly, the crisis mood of much contemporary thinking, not only about the police but more generally, which is brought about by the apparently constant shifting and revolutionizing of our social world characteristic of the post-industrial knowledge society, may in itself be enough, or virtually enough, to explain the lack of development of new styles of policing (or again, more generally, new political modes of governance) based on collective tolerance and social difference. Any such developments that may come await the freeing up of human imagination; sociological reflection is one path towards that end.

Conclusion – The Hollowing Out of Character

Implicit throughout this discussion has been the notion of a cataclysmic characterological shift symptomatic of the knowledge society. With recourse to Riesman's terminology, we have moved along a continuum of characterological development from tradition-directed, through inner-directed to other-directed and beyond. Finally we reach the current stage where character no longer resides in individuals, whether it be in the pre-scripted and learned tradition-direction, the inner-direction based on a metaphorical 'internal gyroscope', or the other-direction of the, again metaphorical, internalized 'radar'. Rather character, the capacity to ensure individual social conformity through the internalization of the precepts of a mode of conformity, has been *externalized* – embedded in the surveillance capacity of the technologically grounded knowledge society. This externalization implies the hollowing out of character. Policing in this era is dominated by the rationalization of surveillance practices already firmly in place. Surveillance, in the sense used here, denotes simply the bureaucratic production of knowledge about suspect populations. One of the ironies of surveillance inherent in the concept of the transnational knowledge society is that police themselves constitute a suspect population; since the crime control system is already structurally arranged to give police access to legal, scientific, electronic and personal/confessional knowledge about suspects and suspect populations (that is: 'system rights have displaced suspect's rights'), the only recourse to control over the process of police investigation is to turn surveillance back on the system (Ericson 1994b). The result is the further development of rules and technologies that foster criminal justice agents' surveillance of each other. Sociologists may be forgiven an initial sense of foreboding here, since this trend is evident across the whole range of social institutions, the university not excepted. But surveillance can be no more endlessly recursive than Escher's *Drawing Hands*. As the political cartoonist Walt Kelly aptly put it: 'We have met the enemy and he is us'.

Notes

1. Consider the Football Intelligence Unit at the National Criminal Intelligence Headquarters (NCIS). The main hub of this enterprise is a wall of video display terminals. Personnel in this unit spend an incalculable amount of time (re)viewing video footage (processing knowledge) taken of crowds and individuals in and around football grounds and other public places in order to identify 'known trouble makers'. Photographs of such individuals are collated and disseminated to officers whose job it is to 'spot' known faces at strategic places; pubs near football grounds, train and subway stations and, especially given the interests of this paper, at ferry terminals and airports. The goal is to attempt to prevent these individuals from travelling to football matches where they might cause trouble, thereby pre-empting the need for large scale public order operations. Officers who work in this unit maintain that the video camera itself has a deterrent effect; knowledge work itself is credited with producing a crime control effect over and above any coercive force that may come in its wake.

2. It might be argued that this shift to knowledge work in policing is merely a product of new paradigms in sociology, rather than actual changes in police practice. While police work has always had knowledge as an important component (contained, for example, in the police adage to 'know the ground'), knowledge work conceived of as the collection, collation and dissemination of bureaucratically framed knowledge is something rather different and is a relatively recent development. The first kernel of this new way of policing was planted during the Progressive Era in the USA by August Vollmer who argued that policing needed to be made more 'scientific'. He characterized police in the pre-knowledge work phase as 'frequently unintelligent and untrained; they were distributed through the area to be policed according to a hit-or-miss system and without adequate means of communication; they had little or no record system; their investigative methods were obsolete ...' (Douthit 1975). The innovations he wrought on some, few, police forces carried tremendous implications but they were by no means general to policing prior to World War Two. Indeed, it was not until the advent of the computerization, especially for records and communications systems and other social scientific techniques for evaluating police efficiency and

effectiveness that this process attained a critical mass. Policing as knowledge work, in the sense employed here, is thus relatively recent. These changes have given rise to a new set of questions for sociologists of the police organisation.

3. In its earliest phase of use, in India, fingerprinting exemplified the application of scientific knowledge to attain greater political control on the shifting and politically volatile populations of the sub-continent. It subsequently became known as a criminal procedure and the mythology of its technical infallibility largely came on the back of this, but the technology 'did not entirely lose its political character' (Hannant 1995: 43). It was Sir Edward Henry, a high ranking bureaucrat in the Indian Civil Service, who initiated the perfection of the fingerprint classification system that today bears his name. In 1897 the Indian government adopted the Henry classification system as a criminal investigation method. In 1901, the year of Henry's appointment as Assistant Commissioner of the London Metropolitan Police, it was adopted for the same purposes in England and Wales. Significantly, one of Henry's first jobs was to maintain surveillance of Indian revolutionaries in England.

4. Police work that goes on under the rubric of the Schengen Convention has an operational edge insofar as it allows for the exchange of information on criminals and criminal activity, the mounting of proactive criminal investigations by means of covert cross-border surveillance (including the technique of 'controlled delivery'), the right of hot pursuit across borders and the stationing of liaison officers in other Schengen Member States. NB: such action is only sanctioned in the case of serious, that is extraditable, crimes.

5. One Dutch police officer recounted to me a story from early in his career, prior to the relaxation of border controls in the Low Countries. This involved an accident along the narrow corridor at the far southern tip of the Netherlands leading into the Limburg region, a strip of the country barely five kilometres wide. A lorry carrying several tonnes of steel crashed into a highway overpass, bringing the bridge down constraining traffic into Maastricht, the region's principal city. Through professional acquaintances in Belgium my informant was able to create a cross-border traffic diversion which bypassed Customs procedures. This informal arrangement was maintained for three days until the wreckage could be cleared and the traffic re-diverted back on to Dutch roads. My informant described this as 'totally illegal, but effective'.

6. Verbruggen provides a *tour de force* of comparative analysis between US and European federal police structures that clearly and comprehensively illuminates the tensions between what I am calling the managerial and political régimes.

7. Interpol is not constituted by formal treaty or any other legal instrument so there is little recourse in formal (i.e. international) law for data protection. Complicated legal manoeuvring ensured that the organization avoided coming under the umbrella of the French Data Protection Act. The 1985 Headquarters Agreement provided some internal and administrative controls, however, it is not clear that this squarely addressed issue of data protection and this may account for at least some of the problems that the organization has in maintaining its monopoly on 'criminal intelligence' in the Europe. On the other hand, my own observations of the Interpol NCB in London confirm that the system is overloaded with data, much of it going back many years, making well targeted and systematic surveillance difficult.

8. The Bertillion system was a complex identification method based on a variety of measurements of the human body invented during the latter part of the nineteenth century. Perhaps the most successful 'sale', certainly the most famous, was when it was adopted as a way to identify the criminals who were expected to prey on the World's Trade Fair in Chicago in 1893. Fingerprint classification was manifestly superior however. Among its benefits was the simple fact that criminals do not leave their Bertillion figures at the scene of a crime.

Bibliography

Alldridge, P., Van Poelgeest, B.S., Williams, K. 1995 'DNA Profiling and the Use of Expert Scientific Witnesses in Criminal Proceedings', in *Criminal Justice in Europe; A Comparative Study*, Oxford: Clarendon Press.

Anderson, M., den Boer, M., Cullen, P., Gilmore, W.C. Raab, C. and Walker, N. 1995 *Policing the European Union: Theory, Law and Practice*, Oxford: Clarendon.

BBC 1991 *DEA; The War Against Drugs*, broadcast Nov. 13, 1991.

Bittner, E. 1970 *The Functions of Police in Modern Society*, Chevy Chase, Maryland: National Institute of Mental Health.

Bressler, F. 1992 *Interpol*, London: Sinclair-Stevenson.

Bunyan, T. (ed.) 1993 *Statewatching the New Europe*, London: Statewatch.

Burton, J. 1972 *World Society*, Cambridge: Cambridge University Press.

Castells, M. 1989 *The Informational City*, Oxford: Blackwells.

Chan, J. 1996 'Changing Police Culture' in the *British Journal of Criminology* 36(1): 109–34.

Chatterton, M. 1989 'Managing Paperwork' in M. Weatheritt (ed.) *Police Research: Some Future Prospects*, Aldershot: Avebury.

Colton, K. W. 1978 *Police Computer Technology*, Lexington: D.C. Heath and Co.

Doney, R. H. 1990 'The Aftermath of the Yorkshire Ripper: The Response of the United Kingdom Police Service' in S. A. Egger (ed.) *Serial Murder; An Elusive Phenomenon*, New York: Praeger.

Douthit, N. 1975 'August Vollmer, Berkeley's First Chief of Police and the Emergence of Police Professionalism', *California Historical Quarterly*, LIV (Spring): 101–24.

Downes, D. 1966 *The Delinquent Solution; A Study in Subcultural Theory*, London: Routledge and Kegan Paul.

Egger, S. A. 1990 'A Taxonomy of Law Enforcement Responses' in S. A. Egger (ed.) *Serial Murder; An Elusive Phenomenon* New York: Praeger.

Ericson, R. V. 1981 *Making Crime: A Study of Detective Work*, Toronto, Butterworths.

——— 1994a 'The division of expert knowledge in policing and security', *British Journal of Sociology* 45(2): 149–76.

——— 1994b The Royal Commission on Criminal Justice System Surveillance', in M. McConville and L. Bridges (eds) *Criminal Justice in Crisis* Aldershot, Hants: Edward Elgar.

Ericson, R. V. and Shearing, C. 1986 'The Scientification of Police Work' in G. Böhme and N. Stehr (eds) *The Knowledge Society; The Growing Impact of Scientific Knowledge on Social Relations*, Dordrecht: Reidel.

Featherstone, M. 1990 *Global Culture: Nationalism, Globalisation and Modernity*, London: Sage.

Fijnaut, C. 1993 *The Internationalization of Police Co-operation in Western Europe*, Deventer: Kluwer Law and Taxation Publishers.

Garland, D. 1990 *Punishment and Modern Society*, Oxford: Clarendon Press.

Giddens, A. 1976 *New Rules of the Sociological Method*, London: Hutchinson.

——— 1979 *Central Problems in Social Theory*, London MacMillian.

Goldstein, J. 1960 'Police Descretion not to invoke the criminal process; low visibility decisions in the administration of justice', *Yale Law Journal* 69; 543–94.

Hannant, L. 1995 *The Infernal Machine; Investigating the Loyalty of Canada's Citizens*, University of Toronto Press, Toronto.

Holdaway, S. 1983 *Inside the British Police*, Oxford: Basil Blackwell.

Jones, T. 1995 *Policing and Democracy in the Netherlands*, London: Policy Studies Institute.

Leonard, V. A. 1980 *The New Police Technology; Impact of the Computer and Automation on Police Staff and Line Performance*, Springfield, Illinois: Charles C. Thomas.

Manning, P. K. 1980 'Organisation and Environment: Influences on Police Work' in R. V. G. Clarke and J. M Hough (eds) *The Effectiveness of Policing* Farnborough: Gower.

Manning, P. K. 1983 'Organisational Control and Semiotics' in M. Punch (ed.) *Control in the Police Organisation*, Cambridge Mass: MIT Press.

—— 1988 *Symbolic Communication: Signifying Calls and the Police Response*, Cambridge Mass: MIT Press.

Mawby, R. I. 1990 *Comparative Police Issues*, London: Unwin Hyman.

Marquis, G. 1993 *Policing Canada's Century: A History of the Canadian Association of Chiefs of Police*, Toronto: University of Toronto Press.

McCabe, S. and Sutcliffe, F. 1978 *Defining Crime, A Study of Police Decisions*, Oxford: Basil Blackwell.

McConville, M., Saunders, A. and Leng, R. 1991 *The Case for the Prosecution*, London: Routledge.

McLaughlin, E. 1992 'The Democratic Deficit: European Union and the Accountability of the British Police', *British Journal of Criminology* 34(4): 473–88.

Muir, W. K. Jr. 1977 *Police; Street Corner Politicians*, Chicago: University of Chicago Press.

Nadelmann, E. 1993 *Cops Across Borders; The Internationalization of US Law Enforcement*, University Park, Pennsylvania: Pennsylvania State University Press.

Ostrom, E., Parks, R. and Whitacker, B. 1978 *Patterns of Metropolitan Policing*, Cambridge Mass.: Ballinger Publishing.

Packer, H. 1968 *The Limits of the Criminal Sanction*, Stanford, CA: Stanford University Press.

Police Speak 1993 *Police Communications and Language and the Channel Tunnel Report*, Cambridge: Cambridge Research Laboratories.

PRSU 1992 'From Morse Code to E-mail in a Decade – Communications at Interpol London', London: *Police Requirements Support Unit Bulletin* No. 42 January 1992.

Raab, C. 1994 'Police Co-operation: the prospects for privacy' in M. Anderson and M. den Boer (eds) *Policing Across National Boundaries*, London: Pinter.

Reiner, R. 1978 *The Blue-Coated Worker*, Cambridge: Cambridge University Press.

—— 1985 *The Politics of the Police*, Brighton, Sussex: Harvester Wheatsheaf.

Riesman, D. 1950 *The Lonely Crowd*, New Haven: Yale University Press.

Sheptycki J. W. E. 1995a 'Transnational Policing and the Makings of a Postmodern State' in the *British Journal of Criminology* 35(4 Autumn): 613–35.

—— 1995b 'A Workload Analysis of the Kent Police European Liaison Unit' a paper presented to the British Society of Criminology July 1995 (published in the *Nuffield Foundation Annual Report 1994*).

——. 1996 'Law Enforcement, Justice and Democracy in the Transnational Arena; Reflections on the War on Drugs', *International Journal of the Sociology of Law* 24(1): 61–75.

Skolnick, J. H. 1994 *Justice Without Trial; Law Enforcement in a Democratic Society* (3rd edition), New York: Macmillan.

—— 1966 *Justice Without Trial; Law Enforcement in a Democratic Society*, New York: John Wiley and Sons.

Stehr, N. 1994 *Knowledge Societies*, London: Sage.

Verbruggen, F. 1995 'Euro Cops? Just Say Maybe; European Lessons from the 1993 Reshuffle of US Drug Enforcement', *European Journal of Crime, Criminal Law and Criminal Justice* 3(2): 150–201.

Waddington, P. A. J. 1993 *Calling the Police*, Aldershot: Avebury.

Walker, S. 1977 *A Critical History of Police Reform*, Lexington Mass.: DC Heath.

Whitaker, R. and Marcuse, G. 1994 *Cold War Canada: The Making of a National Insecurity State, 1945–1957*, Toronto: University of Toronto Press.

Young, M. 1991 *An Inside Job, Policing and Police Culture in Britain*, Oxford: Clarendon Press.

Zuboff, S. 1988 *In the Age of the Smart Machine: The Future of Work and Power*, Oxford: Heinemann.

10

Reasonable Force: The Emergence of Global Policing Power

Barry J. Ryan

Introduction

Police power, this article argues, is innovating in the international sphere, emerging to become a complex arterial force which flows through people and territory to secure the interstate system. This article explores the rise of police power as an emergent habitus of global governance. It traces this rise through an analysis of the practice of reasonable force, proposing reasonable force to be ontological to police power. This is to suggest that reasonable force inhabits the activity of policing. Broadly defined, reasonable force is encountered when an actor is confronted with the choice to succumb to reason or succumb to violence – to 'come quietly', as it were. It is treated here as a mode of persuasion where force stands as a defensive line behind the progress of a reasonable argument. The study thus contains an implicit assumption that police power is not solely derived from the institutions of law enforcement. Certainly, police power concerns the enforcement of law, but it also concerns the management of disorder. Therefore, police power is revealed whenever the reasonable force of administrative, legal, and military modalities of power is being brought to bear on a problem. This implies that policing as a mode of order produces relational power in the functional distribution of tasks found among a wide range of actors. At the micro level this might describe relations between the police officer, the social worker, the psychiatrist, the probation officer, and so on. Globally, police power becomes ever more complex and multi-layered and is produced

Source: *Review of International Studies*, 39(2) (2013): 435–457.

between coordinating actors involved in the pursuit of global security. These actors constellate a security architecture which engages with global disorder in a manner that is led by the strategies of domestic law enforcement. Thus, a policing rationality shapes and gives coherence to a constellation that includes states, international organisations, UN agencies, NGOs, academia and, arguably, global civil society.[1] The focus of this study is to identify these strategies of law enforcement and to scrutinise the rationality that promotes their increased deployment in the post-Cold War environment.

In its originary sense, police power expressed the sovereign activity of coordinating all aspects of order. It concerned maintaining a balance between the expansion of sovereign power and the maintenance of good order within the state. This understanding is the originary form of *polis*, the etymological source of the verb 'to police', and it referred to key tropes such as happiness, comfort, welfare, and hygiene.[2] In its late modern usage, police power is encountered as a constabulary body whose referent object of security is disorder and whose ends are preventative and developmental.[3] It is generally accepted that the emergence of Britain's New Police in the early nineteenth century introduced innovative practices to the historical understanding of police. New values, norms, and practices were introduced as police was redefined in terms of it describing a professional body concerned with crime and disorder.[4] While it is accepted that 'police' in early modern Europe had 'a completely different meaning to the one it has today',[5] it is plausible to suggest that the contemporary understanding of police emerged from the historical meaning.[6] New policing exhibited a break from and maintains continuity with earlier forms of police. In this sense the new emphasis on police as agents of law enforcement supplemented earlier patriarchal modes of police with a utilitarian liberal rationality.[7]

From this break and continuity, it will be argued, emerged the practice of reasonable force. As we shall see, reasonable force is constituted by a synthesis of elemental tactics associated with the shift between old and new police practices. One such element is military discipline. Thus, reasonable force is the site where late modern policing maintains its continuity with earlier more martial and authoritarian forms of power. Another element is the law. Police power operates sometimes beyond law in order to secure the norm; sometimes beyond norm to secure the law. This dynamism is the source of its political value, and particularly so when the norm being upheld is articulated as being progressive and reasonable. This attribute of police power has made it an elusive phenomenon to research. As a normative force, policing seemed to reveal itself everywhere, and nowhere. 'The police power' according to an early commentator, 'is the dark continent of our jurisprudence.'[8] Walter Benjamin described police power as something, 'formless, like it's nowhere tangible, all pervasive, ghostly presence in the life of civilized states'.[9] Benjamin's description, which might seem overstated, should not be dismissed. When Benjamin referred to its spectral quality he was alluding to the relationship between police and boundaries. Police, he was telling us, moves through boundaries as a ghost moves through walls. Policing, in other words, is something that cannot be confined. This insight informs us that policing cannot be confined by the law; that it is a limit unto itself, in many respects. Identifying reasonable force allows us therefore to give ontological form to a mode of power whose defining problematic has traditionally been the necessity of its formlessness.

Nowhere is the spectrality of police power more evident than in practices of global governance. Benjamin's description above reminds us that policing displays an intrinsic will to transcend limits. This means that police power cannot be simply understood as a derivative of sovereign power. Policing, it implies, in all of its formations is insatiably Universalist and expansive.[10] Policing is the force of reform. Operating as an equivalent force of reform to its domestic counterpart, the constellation that performs global governance is directed at increasing the power of the interstate system while maintaining good order. Consequently, this article treats local law enforcement strategies and global governance as being symbiotically related.[11] Together they form what Dillon and Reid refer to as a 'relational order'. The analysis presents reasonable force as the 'generative principle of formation' of this relational order.[12] At issue is a set of practices, norms, beliefs, and structures around which reasonable force is a governing imperative. This moves us beyond a definition of police power and into an analysis of the operating conditions in which reasonable force targets turbulence to maintain and progress a sense of order.

Prior to introducing reasonable force, we first need to appreciate the productive dynamic that exists within the late modern conceptualisation of police. This dynamic is presented through an elucidatory example taken from one of numerous (interrelated) police reform projects that occurred in the Balkans after the dissolution of Yugoslavia. The example utilised its representative of the security-first approach to post-conflict management adopted by various international organisations and government agencies in the late 1990s. The security-first agenda meant that responsibility to shepherd post-socialist and post-Soviet states through to their liberal future was, by and large, a policing chore.[13] The argument that the security-first doctrine animated the growth of police strategies can be found in the work of Mark Duffield.[14] It observes that as economic development became more biopolitical and focused upon premises such as good governance, its implementation required a more strategic deployment of force than previously. Duffield argues that international economic development, the epitome of reasonable progress, has become a matter of securing a population for the purposes of governance. This article suggests that this agenda has largely been delivered through policing practices that flow from the operationalisation of reasonable force.

Policing as Limit and as Link

At the turn of the twenty-first century, an ex-British police officer, working on behalf of the Organization for Security and Cooperation in Europe (OSCE), was dispatched to make recommendations that would lead to the liberalisation of internal security controls in the Federal Republic of Yugoslavia (FRY). The report he produced found that, post-Milošević, Serb 'police had become isolated from the community they serve'.[15] The report also found that the police lacked expertise to fight crime, in particular organised crime. The police required an intelligence network and needed to engage in community policing to build up contacts with civil society. Borders needed to be strengthened and it was recommended that a new Border Police Service be created to replace the existing military one. This had little to do with 'threats to sovereignty ... and more to do with resisting trans-national crime and illegal immigration'.[16] Later on the report clarifies that the rationale behind this recommendation:

> the principal threat to the security of Yugoslavia and for that matter from Yugoslavia to the rest of Europe is not incursion but crime – serious and substantial. The military do not deal with crime. The police do. It would therefore make more sense for the new border service to consist of a totally integrated police force.[17]

The irony here is ripe as FRY was in the process of recovering from what has been described as a policing intervention by NATO,[18] concerning the rights of ethnic Albanians to secede from the Federation. Nevertheless, the passage is quite revealing. Here, an ex-British police officer is radically redefining the meaning of FRY's state sovereignty. Borders no longer represent a legal limit, but a criminological one. The borders of Serbia for the OSCE are henceforth to be considered as objects of risk management and constitute a policing, or governance problem. Demilitarising the border is to detach it from the problem of sovereignty, to make it less an impenetrable fence or wall and more a dynamic and useful marker. As such, the function of the international border is turned inside-out. For the purposes of global governance the border does not face outwards as a physical line that protects those living within its confines from external threats. The border is now inward-facing; it protects the external environment by ensuring the problems of the state do not migrate beyond its confines. That which once afforded some protection from invaders and foreign occupation now serves to confine the population. The limit is permeable or 'dimorphous',[19] insofar as an effectively equipped border police will be capable of filtering the desirable from the undesirable.[20] The proposal for a 'totally integrated police force' meant that paramilitary police units would henceforth patrol FRYs borders. Policing power, having transgressed FRY's sovereignty in the form of NATO in order to uphold the human rights of Kosovars, therefore serves to transform the *limits* that uphold FRY's new post-sovereign order.

The other notable aspect of Monk's recommendations is the manner by which the police officer is repositioned from an agent of state power to an agent of societal power.[21] The report found that Serb police needed to integrate itself within the 'community', that it needed to rebuild legitimacy, and that it had to situate itself as a hub amidst an intelligence network.[22] Here we see the ex-British police officer reforming the strategy of internal controls so that police can operate as an arterial force, acting from society, rather than on society.[23] This is the strategy of consensus-oriented policing which was, as we shall see, developed in Britain in the nineteenth century. It taps into the potential for police to exercise relational power; to operate between bodies as a normative mediator. Positioned thus, the police may exercise normative power between individuals, communities, institutions, or states. Policing in this sense reforms, gains intelligence from and brings coherence to the lines which *links* all relations.

The capacity of policing to turn limits into links (and *vice versa*) enables us to understand the properties that transcend police from legal and military modes of operation. It shows that the reformation of limits is virtually indistinguishable from the reformation of links. In other words, performing as a border between states the police demarcate one category of population from another; while at the same time facilitating cooperation, information sharing, and consensus. Because police reform is a strategy that attempts to reconstitute a police so that it can produce power, this purposive limit and link is also found at the level of relations between individuals and communities. As Marenin has described it, 'The goal of reform is to have the people doing policing think, talk and act in specific ways, and the measure of success of reforms is whether they do or not.'[24] Reform aims at creating a unity of purpose, a common discourse of local and global security. This article seeks to reveal policing as an emergent strategy of global security wherein the goals of state and society, the community and individual are aligned and made coherent with a globalised *raison d'état*.

It is this curious interaction of limits and links that alerts us to the importance of Foucault's commentary on sovereignty and governmentality when analysing police power. Foucault's historical account of power argued that while sovereignty, the originary source of power, concerned protecting the rims of a ruler's territory, governmentality emerged in the eighteenth century as a power that concerned the welfare of the population within the confines of that territory. Governmentality is the rationalisation of administration. Through people and things, it exercises power through law, custom, force, and ethics to produce calculable, rational, governable subjects.[25] Whereas governmentality disciplined the *links* between men and things, sovereignty traditionally protected the *limits*. Foucault's analysis examines how an emphasis on population as a source of power tended to subordinate sovereignty. As Singer and Weir point out, 'The character of the sovereign, symbolized by the sword, is warlike in its defense of the realm; by contrast the character of the governmental ruler, variously symbolized, is patience and industry.'[26] Police, it goes without saying, has always been central to the emergence of governmental technologies of rule.[27]

The 'governmentalisation' of FRY's sovereignty was introduced with a security imperative through which wider police power could emerge centrifugally. Through a law and order discourse, the military sword that once protected the rims came to be replaced by the administrative force of a police agency. Thereafter, the sovereignty of FRY's borders became dependent upon its ability to regulate and rationalise the behaviour of its citizens. The emphasis on building links, incorporating societal and state actors into a common purpose internally, aimed to bring reasonableness to the space once occupied by the sovereign diktat of Slobodan Milošević. Externally the sovereign limits also served as a link, as points of cooperation in trade and security with other police agencies recently established along the borders that emerged from the break-up of Yugoslavia. Physical force, of course, persists in this strategy, but it is a force of last resort, an exceptional recourse to violence only utilisable in the name of protecting the new (globalised) *raison d'état*. Police reform seeks to admit a reasonable, calculable, and consensual sort of force.

This article builds on previous studies[28] of global police power by identifying reasonable force at the nexus of legal and military power. Moreover, it moves the empirical focus from Continental models of police power associated with Foucault. Instead it aims to isolate the singularity brought to police power by British liberalism to garner a greater understanding of the *rationale* behind its operation in the international sphere. At issue therefore is how the emergence of 'reasonable force' from nineteenth-century British liberalism can be understood to be a constituent attribute which now undergirds the global delivery of Anglo-American policing power. To capture the inherent shapelessness and the dynamism of police power, this article presents a conceptual genealogy of reasonable force. It presents this genealogy by utilising the most ubiquitous conceit in policing – the line. Lines are elemental to a policing discourse that draws on thin blue lines, police lines, lines of duty, and lines of enquiry to explain itself. It is thus through the line, and the capacity of the line to simultaneously bind and divide bodies, that we propose to critique reasonable force as a principle that generates global police power.[29]

Policing as Reasonable Force

The very evolution of reasonable force from military force is expressed in Anglo-American police mythology in terms of a line. The origins of the phrase 'thin blue line' illustrates the continuity between the traditional role of military power and new liberal police established in Dublin and London in the early 1820s. This phrase derives from a battle during the Crimean War when in 1854 an outnumbered British force successfully deterred a stronger Russian cavalry unit. By spreading itself out thin the British troops created an optical illusion of strength that fooled the Russians into retreat.[30] Termed the 'thin red line', this anecdote created a political metaphor denoting a small band of men outnumbered by an enemy, a force that would need to draw on strategy and illusion, a force whose mere presence could deter threat. Unlike the 93rd Highland regiment at Balaclava, an advancing police line does not seek to secure and hold territory. It aims instead to secure those it finds upon this territory. Policing arrives once the conditions for order have been violently established by the military so that the reason of state can be implemented. Policing is the continuation of military actions by other means. The emergent phenomenon of global policing and its colonisation of the space once inhabited by military forces points to a competitive interaction between military and police power. Evidentially, police has displayed itself as a more efficient and effective conduit through which state and societal power can merge.

The thin blue line metaphor imagines police to be an agent of reform, a civilising instrument of consensus through which policing binds (and separates) disparate phenomena; as a hyphen that seeks to mediate between 'I' and 'other', order and *dis-order*, rationality and *ir-rationality*. This attribute of linking and limiting materialises in the strategy of 'reasonable force', a quasi-legal construct that enables police to function as 'a mechanism for the distribution of situationally justified force'.[31] Reasonable force forms the distinctive technical-rational architecture of decision-making for police. The phrase is given to the continuum that serves to map the process of reasoning which informs every decision a police officer must make during his or her daily duty. Commencing with the issuance of a firm request for the suspect to submit, it progresses through a sequence of reasonable methods of physical and psychological violence that culminate in the use of lethal force. Along a spectrum that begins with the officer identifying her authority and exhibiting her capacity to deploy force there is a range of intermediary tactics available prior to the use of deadly force. Kleinig lists but a few;

> nightsticks, clubs, saps and batons, handcuffs and Velcro straps, hogtying, nets, armlocks, chokeholds, stun and Taser guns, tear gas and pepper spray, nutcrackers, nunchakus, water cannons, dogs, firearms and high speed pursuits.[32]

Those who write about the ethics of violence usually tend to concentrate on its direct application in an attempt to evaluate 'objectively' if its use was excessive or reasonable given 'the totality of circumstances'.[33] Violence however begins in the very arrival of an individual within whom the capacity to inflict death resides. It begins in the identification of authority as this authority is based upon threat. The existence of a continuum testifies to the inhabitance of the same reason in the issuance of a command as is present in the pulling of a trigger. Thus at issue is a spectrum of violence along which rationality and violence cohabitates, and in which Weberian violence is bound to Durkheim's view of the police officer as a moral-symbolic functionary.[34] Police use of violence has to be strategically deployed, regulated, and constantly legitimated if it is to function effectively. As one study suggests, the use of force forms the paradox of police governance.[35] Adopting the writings of Clausewitz, Salt and Smith present violence as a strategic technique, a calculation between 'what you want to do to the enemy as opposed to what you achieve by doing so'.[36] In this sense reasonable force is the governmentalisation of the sovereign use of force previously deployed by military power. What marks the police from the military is its moral and political capacity to combine such strategic reasoning with immediate violence, and to possess jurisdiction over both word and action. Reason is a phenomenon that traditionally did not concern the soldier (unless that soldier is performing a policing function). As Immanuel Kant once pointed out, military power is about obedience – soldiers are expected to act on command, not to question their orders or to argue with their superiors – 'do not argue (reason), obey'.[37] On other hand, policing gains its power by conferring upon the police officer the prerogative of discretion.

The power exercised by police officers in conjunction with other actors not only represents an evolution from the practices of military power, it also creates a complex political affect which has proven impossible to be confined by the law.

Essentially an interpretative prerogative, political ambiguity surrounds the legality surrounding any decision as to what is reasonable to affect an arrest, prevent the escape of a detainee, or quell a riot or insurrection. Thus, distinguishing between what is reasonable and what is excessive has proven difficult to define. Numerous studies have wrestled with making objective the inherent subjectivity of reasonableness.[38] The question seems to rest on whether an officer can illustrate that she reasonably believed force was necessary.[39] As one US study of judicial decisions on reasonable force has concluded, 'what is reasonable has become what is necessary'.[40] Such a finding implies that reasonable force and necessary force are equivalent techniques of expressing state power in a manner that is framed as being principled.[41] More pertinent to this study, the ambiguity between reasonable and necessary force reminds us that the police power is more attuned to what is right and wrong than what is legal and illegal. It is this moral necessity – this need to secure and promote a specific version of order – that permits policing to slide along a cartography in which principle is mapped onto contingency.

Carl Schmitt assists us to understand the political relationship between necessary police power and legal power when he points out that all law is situational. Political order, Schmitt observes, must be established for juridical order to make sense.[42] In other words, police power can be deployed where legal power does not yet exist. Police action occurs on both sides of the thin blue line that divides order and disorder. It not only marks the limit of legal power but it links the legal jurisdiction with space that does not yet admit legal order. This distinction embedded within the law between what is rational and what is irrational is also drawn out in Giorgio Agamben's writings as being core to the relation between interiority and exteriority, *nomos* and *physis*.[43] The external 'other', which defies the rational order, is included by the law's tendency to suspend itself and condone violence so that order can be (re)established. When order is to be (re)established the law retreats only to assert itself once again when the new order requires legitimation. This potent ambiguity of law constitutes, for Agamben, the 'force of law' as embodied by 'the capacity of law to maintain itself in relation to exteriority'.[44] Law survives by allowing its (apparent) antithesis – violence – to subsist within it. Jacques Derrida deconstructed this problematic when he observed that the 'force of law' maintains 'a more internal, more complex relation with what one calls force, power or violence'.[45] Derrida observed that the law cannot function without force, that the law is always an authorised force. Schmitt helps us to understand how this modern binding of authority, rationality, and force enables us to reconsider the 'age-old Aristotelian opposites of deliberation and action ... as two distinct forms', whereby the legal form is approached through deliberation while action is approached by technical formation.[46] By maintaining that violent action is inherent within the form of law, a sense of continuity is more readily evincible between reasoning and enforcing. And it is in this continuum between reason and force, embedded in governmental strategies of power, which this article illustrates as being foundational to strategies of global police power.

In order to account for the emergence of global police power we need to investigate the development of police from its origins in the domestic state. While Foucault has produced the most insightful account of this phenomenon, his analysis focused on continental Europe.[47] Britain however has played a key role in the evolution of police power. Elites in this liberal political economy displayed such great hostility to what was considered to be an illiberal, continental mode of rule that the cameralist, or welfare police state model was never fully developed.[48] Its first institutionalised modern police in London was established in 1829. The 'Peelers', as they were known, resulted from British antipathy to the existence of centralised armed body of men allied to the state.[49] The archetypical rule of law model of police force, British policing emerged from blueprints that by necessity required a police force that would be society rather than state oriented.[50] It was a police force that emerged as a liberal response to the military tradition of internal order and was founded on the premise that freedom was a form of security. Therefore, only by understanding the intentions behind the production of legitimation for the British bobby can we come closer to understanding how police power has expanded as a device to secure the globe.

The Emergence of Reasonable Force

Reasonable force emerged as a technique to distribute power in the utilitarian blueprints of early British policing. The values of new policing shifted the modality of power from the sovereign right to decide over life and death towards a governmental distribution of power whose emphasis was on the 'value and utility' of human productivity.[51] Peel's London Metropolitan Police represents the culmination of a century of reform during which ideas about public order, moral order, crime prevention, and crime detection evolved into a new frame; policing understood narrowly, as law enforcement.[52] Colquhoun's 1796 *Treatise on the Police of the Metropolis* draws upon both meanings of the word police.[53] Moreover, Colquhoun explicitly links 'the correct administration of whatever is related to the morals of the people' to 'the prevention of crimes'.[54]

Police was presented to the resistant middle-classes in England as a vehicle to improve society by improving the behaviour of the poor. Peel pointed to the threat posed to the economy by a criminal organised underclass[55] and advocated for the regulation, inspection, and guardianship of society to be based on a preventative model funded by churches and businesses.[56] The police, as Ericson and Haggerty conclude, was to be a superintending agency of risk management, brokering and monitoring the policing efforts of all the agencies involved in maintaining order.[57] Moreover, the conceptualisation of policing as a preventative force added other values. As O'Malley and Hutchinson observed, the discourse of prevention bestowed upon policing a prescient reasoning, charging it with intelligence gathering and surveillance capacities.[58] The need to construct legitimacy for these experimental propositions more or less consigned police as a 'domestic missionary, charged with bringing civilization and decorum' to the moral turpitude of vagabonds, drunken women, and prostitutes.[59] The normative model of police as law enforcement was from the outset inspired by the tenets of *laissez-faire* and envisaged policing as a form of security which would be bound with human development. Police in this sense is associated with moral and cultural progress. As a force it not only maintains order but it improves order – it is an agent which gives coherence to reformist ambitions.

The capacity of a police to reform is however entirely dependent on its ability to construct societal legitimacy.[60] To wit, the strategy behind British policing was to produce security by positioning the police officer as a common citizen, integrated and at one with the community. The key to the success of the model is the manner by which police act in the relations between individuals as a *primus inter pares*, as a neutral expert and as a model moral citizen respectful to the law but cognisant that morality often exceeds the rule of law. Community and consent are core themes in its legitimating discourse. Being seen to act *from* society rather than *on* society is therefore critical for police to realise Whittaker's aspiration that 'a trusted policeman can be the chief human regulator of our adult conduct'.[61] Police was constructed as a positive force, an agency through which state and societal power was harnessed and directed in the name of progress. Reasonable force has never simply been a defence mechanism; it is a force for progression.

Police power in the United States in the nineteenth century, as Markus Dubber's survey exhibits, was a vague and arterial phenomenon that was concerned with the administration of people and things with a view to the general welfare of the population.[62] The US was slow to abandon the early modern conceptualisation and the idea of police as a mode of governance which held a tense relationship to the law remained extant up until at least the 1930s, when it gave way to the narrower British understanding. The arrival of the narrower law enforcement understanding is associated with the direct importation of the police officer from the United Kingdom to the United States in the mid-nineteenth century.[63] Contemporary police power in the US is thus marked by the establishment of the New York police in 1844.[64] Histories of policing in the United States point to a continuous tension between radically different concepts of police – one Continental and cameralist and the other limited and British.[65]

Nevertheless, from its earliest inception, policing was both a domestic and an international technology of power. For Britain, it was Robert Peel's Peace Preservation Force, established to enforce the state of emergency declared in Ireland in 1814, which had first provided evidence of the worth of a civilian-military constabulary force. The Dublin Metropolitan Police, set up in 1796 to patrol the 'lawless city' paved the way for the establishment of the London Metropolitan Police. Once Ireland gained independence in 1922, Palestine became Britain's site of experimentation for police tactics that would, with some tinkering, eventually be brought to bear on its domestic population. It is perhaps valid to suggest that the capacity of British policing to utilise the entire continuum of reasonable force was gained in the colonies, in exceptional sites of policing practice. For the United States, it would seem that the inverse occurred. The effectiveness of policing the exceptional situations at home motivated its use as a tool of foreign policy.

While serving as president on the Board of Commissioners of the New York Police, Theodore Roosevelt came to see police power as a distinctly more effective way to achieve security than was presented by law. Roosevelt admired the continental police model of governance, seeing police power as necessary for a government to exercise its sovereignty.[66] Moreover he regarded police power as a means to influence and civilise regions within the United State's proximity that suffered from 'chronic wrongdoing' or from an 'impotent government'.[67]

Christopher Tomlins has keenly observed that Roosevelt 'stands at the point of convergence of domestic with international police discourse ... and embodies police's ultimate seamlessness'.[68] Roosevelt's conceptualisation of international police also marks a continuity between historical and contemporary understandings of police. A declaration of interventionism as a last resort, Roosevelt's foreign policy was to 'speak softly and carry a big stick' – which is, as we have seen, the essence of the reasonable force tactic upon which policing distinguishes itself as a moral and just force for progress. Police strategies were viewed therefore as a means by which civilised nations could secure the welfare of foreign state, 'by ensuring that they are well orderly and well-administered in their domestic affairs'.[69] Roosevelt's imperialism was not of the European sort. In foreign policy, he eschewed amassing territory in favour of an approach that was based on regulating foreign populations. It was in the dispatch of police units to America's near abroad that we can see US sovereign power interacting with an early attempt to spread governmental rationality. Under Roosevelt, gendarmerie units were dispatched *inter alia* to Cuba, Panama, Haiti and the Dominican Republic to establish or reform internal security structures in a quest to create self-governing jurisdictions that were bound to a regional political economic order.[70]

Reasonable Force and the Cold War

In Britain, by the middle of the twentieth century, police work had become a self-evident truth, an elemental aspect of the apparatus of state security. By pushing military power beyond the sovereign boundaries, the unarmed 'bobby' had gradually gained a monopoly on the legitimate use of force. This legitimacy had been primarily gained through a functional division of power. During the nineteenth century and up until the 1920s police operated through mainly reasonable methods while the military was called upon to violently confront striking workers.[71] By the 1950s, police authority had been assured, during the so-called golden age of legitimacy.[72] It was as this was occurring, and as the military role in domestic affairs was diminishing, that British police began gradually building its capacity to operate along the more forceful end of the spectrum of reasonable force.[73] As this was happening British policing power began to play a more important role in the manage-ment of Britain's colonies, which experienced a shift from a more coercive to a consensual based strategy at this time. Faced with the loss of territorial possessions, decolonisation effectively meant that colonial administrators had to ensure an order that was loyal and economically cordial to its former coloniser. A move towards the governmental mode – the notion that more rea-sonable methods of policing the 'other' assisted in the accumulation of neces-sary intelligence – alerted senior British police in the Palestine Mandate in the late 1940s that in the face of Arab-Jewish tension, 'while it was a police responsibility to fight ... by an intensification of their normal procedure and operation ... the intelligence gathering aspect of policing required the police to 'establish friendly relations with the public'.[74] Transferring responsibility for internal security to the newly independent governments was seen to be the most important and sensitive of political issues affecting successful decolonisation. Once the transition to independence had been made, the colonial power maintained its influence by sending police 'advisors' whose task was to advise on police reform. Reform of the Cypriot police, for instance, was directed from London throughout the 1950s. One study of decolonisation in British Malay in the early 1950s outlines Britain's 'Operation Service', which aimed to transform the Malayan Police from a 'force' to a 'service' by winning the hearts and minds of the local inhabitants. 'Operation Service' initiated multiracial recruitment policies, improved the pay and conditions of officers, provided the police with equipment (armoured cars), and emphasised 'normal policing'.[75] 'Operation Service' ultimately failed to bring reason to the force of decolonisation due to the necessity to draw on exceptional powers to counter the Communist threat. Nonetheless, it is clear that the policing strategies to manage an orderly retreat from the colonies contained the germ of strategies that would be used to consolidate the expansion of liberal internationalism a few decades later.

Reasonable force as a form of international administration, as a global arterial power which secures the populace, the state and the interstate system, emerged from decolonisation. It was given form with the birth of the United Nations, the 'most ambitious organic entity ever created by states'.[76] Tellingly, Franklin D. Roosevelt's blueprint for the United Nations was premised on an extension of the 'good neighbor' policy that had been practiced by the US in Latin America during the 1930s.[77] Roosevelt envisaged world order being maintained by 'four policemen; the US, China, Britain and Russia'.[78] Imagining humanity to be 'one neighbourhood', Roosevelt placed great emphasis on the preventative role that would be played by the UN to ensure against the 'germs of another world war'.[79] To Debrix,[80] the UN acquired for itself a policing position, one which could induce on states a 'conscious and permanent visibility'.[81] Notably, the Charter that affirms the legal basis of the United Nations can be interpreted as a codification of reasonable force. According to its preamble, the UN deploys 'international machinery' that aims to unite reason and force for the common good of all humanity. The machinery operates around forming consensus against certain activities that are seen to be contrary to international security and peace. When faced with a deviant actor, Articles 39 to 42 outline how the actor's behaviour ought firstly to be criminalised, secondly arrested, and then reformed. The Charter commences by requiring the UN to produce a universal condemnation of actor's behaviour – this might be seen as the police officer exhibiting her authority. This institutionalises the deviancy of the act, and establishes it as criminal against a set of universal principles. The deviant actor is then isolated while the UN issues a command for the behaviour to cease. Upon non-compliance the UN will generate sanctions and embargoes prior to having recourse to more forceful means. The Charter gets more blurred and open to interpretation the further one travels along the spectrum, gradually distancing itself from legal certainty. Tellingly, it is from this zone that the 'moral wars', which came to define international police activity, emerged in the mid-1990s.

Throughout the Cold War (with one or two notably unsuccessful exceptions) the UN remained firmly at the lawful end on the spectrum reasonable force. The ideal was that of a watchful, politically neutral force that was ever-ready to intervene to prevent global instability. Impressed by the 'police action' undertaken by the US-led UN mission to Korea in 1950, Lestor Pearson with the support of UN Secretary General, Dag Hammarsköld, proposed peacekeeping as a solution to the Suez crisis in 1956.[82] Peacekeeping was from its inception articulated by Pearson as a policing activity based on the maintenance of global order.[83] Consequently, peacekeeping adopted a domestic model that was based on the core characteristics of the domestic British bobby: impartial, legitimate, lightly armed mediators and monitors. On the ground peacekeepers remained a transparent, consent-seeking force dutifully respectful of the international law of sovereignty. UN peacekeepers, generally, did not transcend the border. The horizon was long-term evidently, as a statement in 1963 by the Secretary General U. Thant explains;

> I have no doubt that the world should eventually have an international police force which will be accepted as a part of life in the same way as national police forces are accepted. Meanwhile, we must ensure that developments are in the right direction.[84]

Writing in the same year as U. Thant spoke about his aspirations for an international police force, Hans Morgenthau opined that such a force was unlikely due to the 'lack of an automatic commitment to a particular legal order and political status quo'.[85] Thus, he argued, the requisite continuity of authority found in a domestic police force could not be replicated in the international sphere because global commitment needed to be reproduced for each security event. An international police would always be 'threatened with partial or total disintegration' as it would remain subject to fluctuating national interests.[86] Morgenthau, ever the theorist of sovereign power, was somewhat justified in his view that police legitimacy at the time rested on a coherency across time and space that transcends national interest towards a normative supranational order. Indicatively, during the Cold War international police activity was piecemeal and tenuous.

By the time the Berlin Wall collapsed police power had been consigned to a very marginal role in global politics. There were very few blue helmets on duty and only a handful of relatively symbolic missions. The use of law enforcement officers had all but vanished. In 1988, the year in which the Nobel Prize was awarded to UN Peacekeeping, there were only 34 UN police officers on global duty – all of whom were based in Cyprus.[87] Historical tensions within the United States, between a judicial and limited definition of police power and a political and expansive understanding, resulted in human rights activists successfully curtailing the use of US police power abroad in the mid-1970s. Section 660 of the 1974 Foreign Assistance Act prohibited (with certain exceptions) the provision of police training, advice or funding to foreign governments, or law enforcement agencies.[88] Prior to the passage of this Act the Truman and Kennedy administrations had made extensive use of police power through the Office of Public Safety (OPS).[89] Under the cover of liberalising, the internal security sectors of states susceptible to Communist influence, the Central Intelligence Agency was able to maintain the legitimacy of governments, provide intelligence, and suppress insurrection.[90] Operating along the entire spectrum of reasonable force, US ally police institutions were trained how to move seamlessly from normal operational policing through to paramilitary tactics to the use of torture and other extra-juridical tactics of order maintenance. US policing abroad promoted methods that were deemed *necessarily* reasonable in the existential war being waged against its irrational 'other'. The exception pertaining to the 1974 Act became normalised during the 1980s when the Communist threat in Central America and the Caribbean resurfaced during the Reagan's administration. An Anti-terrorism Assistance Programme was authorised to train foreign police in 1983, whereby foreign police were trained on US soil. In 1984, a waiver was granted that would pave the way for the creation of the International Criminal Investigative Training Assistance Program (ICITAP) when judicial reform projects were authorised for El Salvador. By 1985, the judicial reform project was looking at the need to improve criminal investigation techniques and the number of exemptions increased, as projects in Costa Rica, Honduras, and the Caribbean were added to the El Salvador project.[91] The project in El Salvador centred on investigating human rights abuses and led to the establishment of the El Salvador Commission of Investigation.[92] Hailed by the same human rights lobby which had tried to scupper the OPS, the project to liberalise El Salvador provided legitimacy to US international policing activity by aligning it firmly to judicial and limited police practices. In January 1986, ICITAP was created as a purely technical agency to improve criminal investigation techniques for human rights purposes.

Reasonable Force after the Cold War

The re-emergence of US policing power through human rights discourse might be viewed as a harbinger for the birth of global police activity as an arterial and dominant form of power in the post-Cold War period. By restricting US activity to the legal end of the spectrum of reasonable force (and by precluding access to more forceful methods) police power was rejuvenated as a legitimate conduit through which would pass the primary themes of post-Cold War international politics. Henceforth all policing activity would occur to progress freedom. This trajectory was observable in the speech made in 1987 by Ronald Reagan at the Brandenburg Gates in Berlin. Telling Gorbachev to 'tear down the wall'.

Reagan declared that in the West, 'we believe that freedom and security go together'.[93] For Reagan, the Berlin Wall symbolised a rigid sovereign barrier, a limit to progress. Once it fell all limits were open for contestation and the early nineteenth-century proposition of police power as a force of improvement was endowed with global meaning. From 1989, through borders suddenly permeable, police power steadily advanced into the populations of the former Soviet and socialist sphere. The year 1989 might therefore be understood as a critical juncture in the evolution of global police power. Starting with projects that aimed to reform the *modus operandi* of police institutions in the former Soviet or socialist sphere, police power expanded centrifugally, transforming institutions such as the EU, the OSCE, NATO, and the UN through which it passed. As we will see, police power affected the military and the legal practices of these organisations and gave coherence to the means by which they operated in the international sphere.

It was in 1989 that the US, during its invasion of Panama, realised the value of an international police force which could legitimately restore order following the military phase of intervention.[94] Consequently between 1991 and 1993, returning to its former sphere of interest in Guatemala and El Salvador, the US worked closely with the UN to construct human rights compliant, consent-oriented local police. The idea was that police force, if constructed around the discourse of freedom and human rights, could attain sufficient legitimacy to strengthen these states by transforming their modality of rule from military to civilian.[95] In Haiti operating within UNCIVPOL, 829 US police officers, armed with full executive authority and under martial law conditions, were tasked with recreating the Haitian police force. Between 1988 and 1992, the number of police officers on UN missions increased one hundred fold. While reconstituting state controls in Cambodia in 1992, UNCIVPOL awarded itself executive authority to conduct investigations and make arrests.[96] This, in effect, opened up to international police the full spectrum of reasonable force.

The Balkans, however, marks the birth site proper of international policing as an arterial power. The violent dissolution of Yugoslavia produced 5000km of new borders.[97] The ubiquitous discourse of ancient ethnic hatreds [98] meant that Yugoslavia would be interpreted as a place wherein an infinitude of 'interface' zones needed to be secured. As we saw with FRY, the approach was thus to construct antithesis forces (that is, 'services') by reducing the numbers of officers, decentralising operations, making police accountable to a reformed rule of law, instilling transparency and managerial accountability, and demilitarising their ethos while training and equipping new gendarmerie units.[99] The elevated moniker given to this process of embedding the methodology of reasonable force (through strategies of reasonable force) was that it was 'democratic policing'.[100]

In six years, between 1993 and 1999, the capacity of international actors to deliver this antithesis force increased at an exponential rate. Conceptually, this might be expressed as the incorporation of gendarmerie capacity to the reasonable expansion of human rights. When the UN first entered Eastern Slavonia in 1993 they were merely monitors who, alongside ICITAP, provided training in the ethical use of force. During the implementation of the Dayton Agreement post-1996 the UN together with SFOR (NATO Stabilisation Force in Bosnia-Hercegovina), ICITAP and the European Union were far more muscular in their approach to transformation. Military peacekeeping managed by NATO worked alongside the UN civilian administration together with a host of NGOs, state aid agencies, and human rights groups. Faced with a population slow to reform and intransigently tied to 'irrational' practices, a far more coercive approach is evincible in Bosnia than in previous missions.[101] Bosnian reform efforts were assisted by the introduction of international gendarmerie units called MSUs (multinational strategic units). Introduced by NATO ostensibly to protect international police as they travelled the territory, MSU's more importantly addressed the so-called 'enforcement gap'.[102] This problem related to the time it took to train local police to use force and the legitimacy problem created by the usage of military used in their stead. The identification of an 'enforcement gap' opened up military operations to police power. More than exhibiting a lacking in the capacity of law enforcement it highlighted the need for military operations to incorporate reasonable force, to seek license to use lethal force.

Looking back at the Bosnian mission the former EU High Representative Paddy Ashdown described the emergent strategy as being one where an internationalised *raison d'état* is firstly forged through military force and thereafter cemented by police power and the rule of law;

> So what this means is that your troops have to be fighting 'hot war' at one minute to midnight, and be part policeman, part aid worker, part community friend at one minute past midnight – and by the way be able to shift between one and the other until the police forces arrive. That may be weeks, it may even be months. But that is what they have to do ... And then you have to bring in the rule of law. Unless you have the rule of law, you cannot have decent democracy, you cannot have a growing economy, you cannot give people security. So priority number one, day one, is security. Priority number 'one A', day one or day two, is bring in the rule of law as quickly as possible.[103]

Robert Mandel[104] has contextualised this strategy. He observes that contemporary victory provides the protagonist leverage to activate a 'normalisation' process. This means that a modern victory does not result in sustained occupation or the annexation of a defeated enemy. Instead it means that the adversary reasons in the manner desired by the victor. This is, as we saw, the strategy that Theodore Roosevelt had in mind at the turn of the twentieth century during US interventions in Latin America. The UN mission in Kosovo presents most clearly the strategic confluence of administrative, legal, and military force that produces the sort of reasonable force most conducive to persuading hearts and minds. From its inception, full executive authority was bestowed upon the international police who arrived in Kosovo. At the height of the mission the UN Special Representative, the sovereign authority in Kosovo had access to approximately 7,200 Kosovo Police, 16,300 NATO KFOR troops and 3,300 UNMiK police.[105] Support was delivered by 'a system-wide UN response' that 'subsumed various actors and approaches within an overall political-strategic crisis management framework'.[106] It was a security-oriented project described by its adherents to be 'a political project that changes relationships in a society'.[107] The very pursuit of policy coherence around the definition and application of these norms, marks not only the construction of a project called Kosovo, but the emergence of a constellation of governance that would project itself from the Balkans into the wider global security domain.

Brightest in this constellation of global governance, policing agencies such as the UN, the OSCE, and the EU can be found. Both the OSCE and the EU were entirely transformed by the principle of reasonable force as they worked to transform power relations in the Balkans. Merlingen has observed how the EU's failure to negotiate the siege of Sarajevo in the mid-1990s convinced EU policymakers that the Union's ability to exercise power in the international realm depended on its capacity to draw upon force as an *ultima ratio*.[108] By 2003, the role of policing in the civilian aspect of the Common Security and Defence Policy (CSDP) was affirmed when member states were requested to contribute to a police rapid reaction force. At subsequent summits further commitments were agreed that supplemented the Union's access to police officers with a European Gendarmerie force. These moves were made in the light of the European Security Strategy, published in 2003, which framed its conception of security on a correspondence between domestic and international law and order.[109] Police was more conducive to soft power and between 2003 and 2009 the EU launched 23 missions, all but four of which were policing and rule of law-led missions.[110] In 2004, missions were launched beyond the Balkans. It has established a presence in Georgia, Iraq, the Democratic Republic of Congo, and more recently it entered Afghanistan.[111]

Working alongside, within and sometimes in competition with the EU, the *raison d'etre* of the OSCE was also reinvigorated by the application of reasonable force during and after the Balkans conflict. Reinterpreting its Cold War mission as a neutral mediator between East and West, the OSCE pronounced itself in the early 1990s to be a soft power organisation committed to the spread of liberal norms.[112] By doing this the OSCE successfully redirected its skills in the macro politics of Cold War confidence building strategies towards the micropolitics of community building in south-eastern Europe.[113] As an unarmed global police officer, it relies on its voice of reason to persuade, while conscientiously building close partnerships with more force-oriented organisations such as NATO. This functional division of power that generates reasonable force was first established during the OSCE's Kosovo Verification Mission. While the OSCE undertook consensual surveillance and gauged compliance with UN resolutions, NATO waited in the wings, preparing itself for intervention.[114] As Bellamy and Griffin have pointed out, 'this mission should be viewed as a wider nexus of policy instruments used by states, one that acted as a tripwire for enforcement measures by other organizations'.[115] Here we see the classic community policing tactic at work with the deliberating, participatory ethos of the OSCE exhibiting itself as commensurable with the norm-enforcing violence of NATO.

And yet these organisations represent but one strata of global policing. Other international organisations, such as the International Organisation for Migration, the World Bank, the International Monetary Fund and the Inter-American Development Bank have also invested in the development of global police development programmes. Interspersed between these international organisations there moves a stratum of state actors which have come to identify policing as a focal aspect of foreign policy.[116] The United States for example, through the State Department, the Department for Homeland Security, the Drug Enforcement Administration, the Federal Bureau for Investigation, private security companies, and a multitude of other state agencies, intelligence networks, and liaison channels is the most dominant bilateral provider of foreign police assistance.[117] The level of transnational policing activity emanating from the United States is incalculable – estimates of $750 million per year made by Bayley intuitively seem conservative.[118] Similarly, the United Kingdom through its Home Office, its Foreign and Commonwealth Office, and its state aid agency, DFID, funds reform, promotes values and dispatches trainers, advisors, and private consultants to various strategically important sites in all four continents. The state aid agencies of Norway, Sweden, Canada and Australia, to name but a few have also embedded security objectives within socioeconomic developmental aims and dispatched domestic police and security experts to implement foreign strategic security interests. Gravitating around this activity one can find a multitude of local and international non-governmental organisations and academic and policy research institutes. Constituting another stratum of the constellation, this transnational epistemic community, brings together bodies such as the Organization for Economic Cooperation and Development (OECD), UNDP, Saferworld, South Eastern and Eastern Europe Clearinghouse for the Control of Small Arms and Light Weapons (SEESAC), Geneva Centre for the Democratic Control of Armed Forces (DCAF), the Rand Corporation, and the International Peace Institute. These global civil society organisations have specialised in producing knowledge, evaluating, and promoting the use of security-mediated development. They are according to Marenin, 'the link and liaison between transnational regimes and structural and operational reforms of policing at the local level; between theorizing about policing and governance and the craft of implementing good policing'.[119]

A shared ontology of reasonable force also structures policing activities that stem from the global war on terror. Moreover it has provided the constellation with a coherent imperative. In the performance of global security certain sites serve as hubs of risk around which the constellation tends to settle, constructing networks through which a myriad of international organisations, NGOs, and state agencies can channel police power. Typically, borders have become the primary interlocking site of practice through which global terrorism, migration, and organised crime can be managed through themes such as 'democratic policing' and good governance. The fascination with transforming limits into links, which we observed with the Monk Report in FRY, persists as a methodology to secure the expansion of global governance.

Notably, there is a tendency for policing power, having established its legitimacy through reason, to gradually move towards the more violent end of the spectrum upon which it operates. This tendency is discernible in contemporary practices of global policing. We view it in the increased use of gendarmerie in the northern hemisphere,[120] the training objectives of NATO in Afghanistan,[121] or the manner by which the UN has become increasingly reliant on the paramilitary capacities of Formed Police Units.[122] It is marked by the necessity of police power to enter zones more resistant, more exceptional, and thus less inclined to succumb to reasonable methods of persuasion. The necessity of progress would appear to be inscribed within the instrumental rationality that impels police force. Violence will always be necessary to a global order where, in the words of Dillon and Reid, the 'cry of unfair' must succumb to the reply, 'it works'.[123]

Conclusion

This article has presented reasonable force as an emergent governmental technique designed to produce power through reforms that are deemed necessary for global order. Tracing the development of reasonable force through the phenomenon of policing has allowed us explore how traditional practices of sovereign power have percolated through to the Universalist pretensions of global governance. Notwithstanding the productive tension evincible between the narrower legal and a wider political interpretation of police power, the key attributes of early British policing persist in the performance of global governance. The concept of police as a superintending agency whose monopoly of force coordinates and facilitates the policing actions of (reasonable) civil society actors in response to disorder persists. Moreover, so too does the monopoly of police to name this disorder – awarding policing power (prescient) dominion over public order, moral order, and the prevention of crime.

Fortified by a rationality which admits the necessary duress of progressive change, police power ultimately aims to produce coherent, self-governing rational actors who perform productively in what this article has termed a globalied *raison d'etat*. Reasonable force presents us with the calculus that binds this coherency. The quality of force exerted will always be derivative of the perceived irrationality of the 'other'. The force ought not to defeat the 'other', but should be sufficient to demonstrate that she has a stake in reforming. As a mediating force, police power forms a link and a limit with its object of improvement, binding otherness into an asymmetrical power relationship. Conversely, the actions of the 'other' will be measured along the spectrum of reason that forecloses any use of force. Police power holds the monopoly on the legitimate use of violence. The use of force by the 'other' will be always judged irrational or unreasonable. The greater the level of illegitimate force exerted against police, the more reasonable it is for police power to move up the scale of violence in its reaction.

Policing, with its will to reform, has from its inception sought to signify the boundary between things and people. Like a chain, policing is a series of links which forms a dynamic relational limit. It emerged by challenging boundaries. It challenged sovereign power by incorporating legal power and simultaneously challenged legal power by being more attuned to a contingent sense of what is right and wrong than what is legal and illegal. It challenged military power at the domestic and at the level of the international. Its reason seeped into military power and transformed the nature of modern victory by elevating the winning the hearts and minds of the subject population above territorial conquest. One need only look at the doctrine of COIN adopted by US military as being illustrative of a new formation of military power that aims for an interagency approach that fuses military operations and intelligence gathering/sharing capabilities.[124] Military strategies that aim to integrate political, economic, and military force are essentially based upon networking techniques that underpin policing power. As the links between police and military actions are continually reinforced, the importance of distinguishing between the two is insisted upon. The boundaries of military and police are becoming undecidable.

The multilayered constellation of global policing actors cannot but return us to Benjamin's 'nowhere tangible, all pervasive, ghostly presence'. As a strategy that aims to strengthen the state system through society this constellation secures and reforms relationships, managing coherence between individuals, communities, institutions, and states. And yet, the emergence of late modern policing power reveals far more than simply the wax and wane of reason around purposeful violence. Dillon's description of modern power as something which moves productively and intrusively through space and time by synthesising and radically exceeding juridical and territorial modes of power is apposite to our understanding of police power.[125] It reveals reasonable force as a spectrum of action, a normative force for progress that is expansionary and instrumental, fluid and contingent, rather than principled and constant.

Notes

1. Louise Amoore, and Paul Langley, 'Ambiguities of Global Civil Society', *Review of International Studies*, 30 (2004), pp. 89–110.
2. Michel Foucault, *Security, Territory and Population: Lectures at the College de France 1977–78*, ed. Michel Senellart (Basingstoke, Hampshire: Palgrave, 2007), p. 312.
3. Mitchell Dean, 'Military Intervention as "Police Action"?', in Markus D. Dubber and Marianna Valverde (eds), *The New Police Science: The Police Power in Domestic and International Governance* (Stanford: Stanford University Press, 2006), pp. 193–5.
4. J. M. Beattie, *Policing and Punishment in London, 1660–1750* (Oxford: Oxford University Press, 2001).
5. Foucault, *Security, Territory and Population*, p. 312.
6. For studies of early modern understandings see Markus D. Dubber, *The Police Power: Patriarchy and the Foundations of American Government* (New York: Columbia University Press, 2005); Pasquale Pasquino, Pasquale, 'Spiritual and Earthly Police: Theories of the State in Early Modern Europe', in Markus D. Dubber and Marianna Valverde (eds), *The New Police Science: The Police Power in Domestic and International Governance*, pp. 42–72.
7. Mark Neocleous, *The Fabrication of Social Order: A Critical Theory of Police Power* (London: Pluto Press, 2000).
8. John William Burgess cited by Cook, Walter, and Wheeler, 'What is Police Power?', *Columbia Law Review*, 5 (1907), pp. 322–36.
9. Walter Benjamin, 'Critique of Violence', in Walter Benjamin (ed.), *One-Way Street* (London: Verso, 2006), p. 142.
10. Mark Neocleous, 'The Police of Civilization: The War on Terror as a Civilizing Offensive' *International Political Sociology*, 5:2 (2011), pp. 144–59.
11. Klaus Mladek, 'Exception Rules: Contemporary Political Theory and the Police', in Klaus Mladek (ed.), *Police Forces: A Cultural History of an Institution* (Basingstoke, Hampshire: Palgrave Macmillan, 2007), pp. 221–66.
12. Michael Dillon and Julian Reid, *The Liberal Way of War: Killing to Make Life Live* (London: Routledge, 2009), p. 74.
13. Barry J. Ryan, 'The EU's Emergent Security-First Agenda: Securing Albania and Montenegro', *Security Dialogue*, 40:3 (2009), pp. 311–31; Tor Tanke Holm, and Espen Barth Eide, 'Introduction', in Tor Tanke Holm and Espen Barth Eide (eds), *Peacebuilding and Police Reform* (London: Frank Cass, 2000), pp. 1–8.
14. Mark Duffield, *Development, Security and Unending War: Governing the World of Peoples* (Cambridge: Polity Press, 2007).
15. Richard Monk, *Study on Policing in the Federal Republic of Yugoslavia* (Belgrade: OSCE Mission to FRY, 2001), p. 5.
16. Ibid., p. 6.
17. Ibid., p. 28.
18. Howard Caygill, 'Perpetual Police; Kosovo and the Ellision of Police and Military Violence', *European Journal of Social Theory*, 4:1 (2001), pp. 73–80, at p. 77.
19. Detlef Nogola, 'Policing Across a Dimorphous Border: Challenge and Innovation at the French-German Border', *European Journal of Crime, Criminal Law and Justice*, 9:2 (2001), pp. 130–43.
20. Didier Bigo, 'Security and Immigration: Towards a Governmentality of Unease', *Alternatives, Global, Local, Political*, 27 (2002).

21. Barry J. Ryan, 'What the Police is Supposed to Do: Contrasting Expectations of Community Policing in Serbia', *Policing and Society*, 17:1 (2007), pp. 1–20.
22. Sonja Stojanović and Mark Downes, 'Policing in Serbia: Negotiating the Transition between Rhetoric and Reform', in Mercedes S. Hinton and Tim Newburn (eds), *Policing Developing Democracies* (Abingdon Oxon: Routledge, 2009), pp. 73–98.
23. Mark Downes, *Police Reform in Serbia: Towards the Creation of a Modern and Accountable Police Service* (Belgrade: OSCE Mission to Serbia and Montenegro, 2004).
24. Otwin Marenin, 'Implementing Police Reforms: The Role of the Transnational Policy Community', in Andrew Goldsmith and James Sheptycki (eds), *Crafting Transnational Policing* (Oxford: Hart Publishing, 2007), pp. 177–201, at p. 181.
25. Michael Dillon, 'Sovereignty and Governmentality: From the Problematics of the "New World Order" to the Ethical Problematic of the World Order', *Alternatives*, 20:3 (1995), pp. 323–68, at p. 329.
26. Brian C. J. Singer and Lorna Weir, 'Politics and Sovereign Power: Considerations on Foucault', *European Journal of Social Theory*, 9:3 (2006), pp. 443–65, at p. 446.
27. Mitchell Dean, *Governmentality: Power and Rule in Modern Society* (London: Sage, 1999).
28. See, for example, Michael Hardt and Antonio Negri, *Empire* (Cambridge, Mass.: Harvard, 2000); Giorgio Agamben, 'The Sovereign Police', in Brian Massumi (ed.), *The Politics of Everyday Fear* (Minneapolis: University of Minnesota Press, 1993), pp. 61–5; Giorgio Agamben, *Homo Sacer: Sovereign Power and Bare Life* (Stanford CA: Stanford University Press, 1998); Didier Bigo, 'Global (in)security: The field of the professionals of unease management and the Ban-opticon', in Jon Solomon and Sakai Naoki (eds), *Traces: A multilingual series of cultural theory*, 4 (Sovereign Police, Global Complicity) (Hong Kong: University of Hong Kong Press, 2004a).
29. Carl Schmitt identified linear thinking as a principle of modernist order. See Carl Schmitt, *The Nomos of the Earth in the International Law of Jus Publicum Europaeum* (New York: Telos Press, 2003), pp. 86–100.
30. Philip Warner, Philip, *The Crimean War: A Reappraisal* (London: Arthur Barker Ltd., 1972), pp. 66–7.
31. Egon Bittner, *The Functions of the Police in Modern Society* (Cambridge, Mass.: Oelgeschlager, Gunn & Hain, 1979).
32. John Kleinig, *The Ethics of Policing* (Cambridge: Cambridge University Press, 1996), p. 99.
33. Ibid., p. 99.
34. *Cf.* Emile Durkheim, *Professional Ethics and Civil Morals* (London: Routledge, 2001). For a discussion on the relationship between Weber and Durkheim see Jan Terpstra, 'Two Theories on the Police: The Relevance of Max Weber and Emile Durkheim to the Study of Police', *International Journal of Law, Crime and Justice*, 39:1 (2011), pp. 1–11.
35. James Salt and M. L. R. Smith, 'Reconciling Policing and Military Objectives: Can Clausewitzian Theory Assist the Police Use of Force in the United Kingdom?', *Democracy and Security*, 4 (2008), pp. 221–44.
36. Ibid., p. 225.
37. Immanuel Kant, 'Ideas For a Universal History With A Cosmopolitan Intent (1784), *Immanuel Kant, Perpetual Peace and Other Essays*, trans. Ted Humphrey (Indianapolis/Cambridge: Hackett Publishing Company, 1983), pp. 29–40, at p. 42.
38. William Terrill, 'Police Use of Force and Suspect Resistance: The Micro Process of the Police Suspect Encounter', *Police Quarterly*, 6 (2003), pp. 51–83; William Terrill, 'The Elusive Nature of Reasonableness', *Criminology and Public Policy*, 8:1 (2009), pp. 163–72; Kenneth J. Novak, 'Reasonable Officers, Public Perceptions and Policy Challenges', *Criminology and Public Policy*, 8:1 (2009), pp. 153–61.
39. Nicholas De Roma, 'Justifiable Use of Deadly Force by the Police: A Statutory Survey', *William and Mary Law Review*, 12:1 (1970), pp. 67–85.

40. Geoffrey P. Alpert and William C. Smith, 'How Reasonable is the Reasonable Man? Police and Excessive Force', *The Journal of Criminal Law and Criminology*, 85:2, (1994), p. 486.
41. Geoffrey P. Alpert and Roger G. Dunham, *Understanding Police Use of Force: Officers, Suspects, and Reciprocity* (Cambridge: Cambridge University Press, 2004).
42. Carl Schmitt, *Political Theology; Four Chapters on the Concept of Sovereignty*, trans. George Schwab (Chicago: University of Chicago Press, 2005), p. 13.
43. Giorgio Agamben, *Homo Sacer: Sovereign Power and Bare Life* (Stanford CA: Stanford University Press, 1998).
44. Ibid., p. 18.
45. Jacques Derrida, 'Force of Law: 'The Mystical Foundation of Authority', *Cardozo Law Review*, 11, trans. Mary Quaintance (1990), pp. 920–1045, at p. 941.
46. Schmitt, *Political Theology*, p. 28.
47. Michel Foucault, *Society Must be Defended*, trans. David Macey (London: Penguin Books, 2004); Foucault, *Security, Territory and Population*.
48. Philip Rawlings, *Policing: A Short History* (Devon: Willan Publishing, 2002).
49. Galen Broeker, 'Robert Peel and the Peace Preservation Force', *The Journal of Modern History*, 33:4 (1961), pp. 363–73.
50. Clive Emsley, *The English Police: a political and social activity* (London: Longmans, 1996).
51. Michel Foucault, *The History of Sexuality: Volume One* (London: Penguin, 1987), p. 144.
52. Beattie, *Policing and Punishment*.
53. Ibid., p. 78.
54. Patrick Colquhoun, A *Treatise on the Police of the Metropolis* (1796), p. iii.
55. Randall Williams, 'A State of Permanent Exception: The Birth Of Modern Policing In Colonial Capitalism', *Interventions*, 5:3 (2003), pp. 322–44, at p. 328.
56. David Garland, 'The Limits of the Sovereign State: Strategies of Crime Control in Contemporary Society', *British Journal of Criminology*, 36:4 (1996), pp. 445–71.
57. Richard V. Ericson and Kevin D. Haggerty, *Policing the Risk Society* (Toronto: University of Toronto Press, 1997).
58. Pat O'Malley and Steven Hutchinson, 'Reinventing Prevention: Why Did "Crime Prevention" Develop So Late?', *British Journal of Criminology*, 47 (2007), pp. 373–89.
59. Emsley, *The English Police*, p. 74.
60. Andrew Goldsmith, 'Police Reform and the Problem of Trust', *Theoretical Criminology*, 9:4 (2005), pp. 443–70.
61. Ben Whittaker, *The Police in Society* (London: Metheun, 1979).
62. Dubber, *The Police Power*, p. 81.
63. J. J. Tobias, 'Police and Public in the United Kingdom', in George L. Mosse (ed.), *Police Forces in History* (Beverly Hills, CA: Sage Publications, 1977), pp. 95–115.
64. R. I. Mawby, 'Variations on a Theme: The Development of Professional Police in the British Isles and North America', in R. I. Mawby (ed.), *Policing Across the World* (London: UCL Press, 1999), pp. 28–58, at p. 38.
65. S. Walker, *A Critical History of Police Reform* (Toronto: Longman, 1977), p. 81.
66. James Holmes, *Theodor Roosevelt and World Order: Police Power in International Relations* (Washington: Potomac Books, 2006).
67. Roosevelt cited by Tom Lansford, *Theodore Roosevelt: In Perspective* (Haupauge, NY: Nova Science Books, 2005), p. 70.
68. Christopher Tomlins, 'Necessities of State: Police, Sovereignty and the Constitution', *The Journal of Policy History*, 20:1 (2008), p. 54.
69. Roosevelt cited in Ron Levi and John Hagan, 'International Police', in Markus D. Dubber and Marianna Valverde, Marianna (eds), *The New Police Science*, p. 213
70. Robert M. Perito, *The American Experience with Police Operations* (Clemensport, Canada: The Canadian Peacekeeping Press, 2002).

71. *cf.* Roger Geary, *Policing Industrial Disputes* (Cambridge: Cambridge University Press, 1985); Norman Baxter, *Policing the Line: the development of a theoretical model for the policing of conflict* (Dartmouth: Ashgate, 2001).
72. Robert Reiner, *The Politics of the Police* (Oxford: Oxford University Press, 2000).
73. Phil Scraton, 'Unreasonable Force: Policing Punishment and Marginalization', in Phil Scraton (ed.), *Law, Order and the Authoritarian State* (Oxford: Oxford University Press, 1987), pp. 145–89.
74. Charles Wickham cited by Georgina Sinclair, 'Get into a Crack Force and Earn £20 a Month and all Found …: The Influence of the Palestine Police on Colonial Policing 1922–1948', *European Review of History*, 13:1 (2006), pp. 49–65, at p. 54.
75. A. J. Stockwell, 'Policing during the Malayan Emergency, 1948–1960: Communism, Communalism and Decolonisation', in David Anderson and David Killingray (eds), *Policing and Decolonisation* (Manchester: Manchester University Press, 1992), pp. 105–26, at p. 115.
76. Thoman Franck and Faiza Patel, 'UN Police Action in Lieu of War: "The Old Order Changeth"', *The American Journal of International Law*, 85:1 (1991), pp. 63–74, at p. 73.
77. Martha K. Huggins, *Political Policing: The United States and Latin America* (London: Duke University Press, 1998).
78. Susan Butler, Susan, *My Dear Mr. Stalin: The Complete Correspondence of Franklin D. Roosevelt and Joseph V. Stalin* (New Haven, CT: Yale University Press, 2008). p. 73.
79. Derek Chollet and James Goldgeir, *America Between the Wars: from 11/9 to 9/11* (New York: Public Affairs, 2008), p. 6.
80. Francois Debrix, 'Space quest: Surveillance, governance, and the panoptic eye of the United Nations', *Alternatives: Global, Local, Political*, 24:3 (1999), pp. 269–95.
81. Michel Foucault, *Discipline and Punish; The Birth of the Prison*, trans. Alan Sheridan (London: Penguin Books, 1991), p. 201.
82. Lestor Pearson, *Peace in the Family of Man. The Reith Lectures 1968* (London: British Broadcasting Corporation, 1969), p. 78.
83. Lestor Pearson, 'Force for UN', *Foreign Affairs*, 35:3 (1957), pp. 395–404.
84. U. Thant cited in UN Police Magazine, 3 (July 2009), p. 9, available at: {http://www.un.org/en/peacekeeping/publications/unpolmag/unpolmag_03.pdf} accessed 1 Aug. 2011.
85. Hans Morgenthau, 'The Political Conditions for an International Police Force', *International Organization*, 17:2 (1963), pp. 392–403, at p. 401.
86. Ibid.
87. Chuck Call and Michael Barnett, 'Looking for a Few Good Cops: Peacekeeping, Peace-building and CIVPOL', in Tor Tanke Holm and Espen Barth Eide (eds), *Peacebuilding and Police Reform* (London: Frank Cass Publishers, 2000), pp. 43–68, at p. 43.
88. Perito, *The American Experience*, p. 18.
89. Ethan Nadelmann, *Cops Across Borders* (Pennsylvania: Pennsylvania State University Press, 1993), p. 113.
90. Perito, *The American Experience*, p. 15.
91. Charles T. Call, 'Institutional Learning within ICITAP', in Robert B. Oakley; Michael J. Dziedzic, and Eliot M. Goldberg (eds), *Policing the New World Disorder* (Honolulu, Hawaii: University Press of the Pacific, 2002), pp. 315–98, at p. 319.
92. Nadelmann, *Cops Across Borders*, p. 121.
93. This speech is available online at: {http://www.ronaldreagan.com/sp_11.html} accessed 29 July 2010.
94. Perito, *The American Experience*, p. 25.
95. William Stanley, 'International Tutelage and Domestic Political Will: Building a New Civilian Police Force in El Salvador', in Otwin Marenin (ed.), *Policing Change, Changing Police* (New York and London: Garland Publishing, Inc., 1996), pp. 37–77.

96. Michael Doyle, 'Authority and Elections in Cambodia', in Michael Doyle, Ian Johnstone, and Robert C. Orr (eds), *Keeping the Peace: Multi-dimensional UN Operations in Cambodia and El Salvador* (Cambridge: Cambridge University Press, 1997), Pp. 134–64; Annika S. Hansen, 'Civil-Military Cooperation: the military, paramilitaries and civilian police in executive policing', *Executive Policing: Enforcing the Law in Peace Operations* (Oxford: Oxford University Press, 2002), pp. 67–84.

97. European Court of Auditors, *The Effectiveness of the Commission's Projects in the Area of Justice and Home Affairs in the Balkans; Special Report no. 12* (Luxemburg; European Court of Auditors, 2009), p. 12.

98. Misha Glenny, *The Balkans 1804–1999* (London: Granta Books, 2000).

99. M. Caparini, 'Police Reform: Issues and Experiences', paper presented to *Fifth International Security Forum*, Zurich (14–16 October 2002), p. 6.

100. David H. Bayley, *Democratizing the Police Abroad: What to do and How to do it* (Washington: US Department of Justice Office Programs, 2001).

101. Gemma Collantes Celador, 'Police Reform Through Democratic Policing?', *International Peacekeeping*, 12:3 (2005), pp. 364–76.

102. M. J. Dziedzic and A. Bair, 'Introduction', in R. B. Oakley, M. J. Dziedzic, and E. M. Goldberg (eds), *Policing the New World Disorder: Peace Operations and Public Security* (Honolulu, HI: University Press of the Pacific), 2002.

103. Foreign Affairs and International Trade Canada, 'Interview with Lord Paddy Ashdown, High Representative for Bosnia and Herzegovina until January 2006', recorded 14 February 2007, available at: {http://www.dfait-maeci.gc.ca/cip-pic/discussions} accessed 17 Nov. 2009.

104. Robert Mandel, *The Meaning of Military Victory* (Boulder, CO: Lynne Rienner, 2007).

105. Barry J. Ryan, 'Policing the State of Exception in Kosovo', in Aidan O'Hehir (ed.), *Kosovo, Intervention and Statebuilding* (London: Routledge, 2010), pp. 114–31.

106. Espen Barth Eide, Anja Therese Kaspersen, Randolph Kent, Randolph and Karen von Hippel, *Report on Integrated Missions: Practical Perspectives and Recommendations* (Independent Study of the Expanded UN ECHA Core Group. Oslo: NUPI, 2005), p. 3.

107. Renata Dwan (ed.), 'Conclusions', *Executive Policing: Enforcing the Law in Peace Operations* (Oxford: Oxford University Press, 2002), p. 126.

108. Michael Merlingen and Rasa Ostrauskaitė, *European Union: Peacebuilding and Policing* (London: Routledge, 2008), p. 37.

109. European Council, *EU Security Strategy: A Secure Europe in a Better World* (Brussels, 2003).

110. Giovanni Grevi, Damien Helly, and Daniel Keohane (eds), *European Security and Defence Policy: The First Ten Years* (Paris: The European Institute of Strategic Studies).

111. Luis Peral, 'EUPOL Afghanistan', in Giovanni Grevi, Damien Helly, and Daniel Keohane (eds), *European Security and Defence Policy: The First Ten Years*, pp. 325–38.

112. David Galbreath, *The Organization for Security and Co-operation in Europe* (London: Routledge, 2007).

113. Barry J. Ryan, *Police Reform and Statebuilding: The Freedom of Security* (London: Routledge, 2011).

114. Howard Caygill, 'Perpetual Police'.

115. Alex Bellamy and Stuart Griffin, 'OSCE Peacekeeping: Lessons from the Kosovo Verification Mission', *European Security*, 11:1 (2002), p. 1.

116. David H. Bayley, 'Police Reform as Foreign Policy', *The Australian and New Zealand Journal of Criminology*, 38:2 (2005), pp. 206–15.

117. Nadelmann, *Cops Across Borders*.

118. Bayley, 'Police Reform as Foreign Policy'.

119. Marenin, 'Implementing Police Reforms', p. 179.

120. Derek Lutterbeck, 'Between Police and Military: the New Security Agenda and the Rise of Gendarmeries', *Cooperation and Conflict*, 39:1 (2004), pp. 45–68.
121. *Cf.* Tonita Murray, 'Police-building in Afghanistan: A Case Study of Civil Security Reform', *International Peacekeeping*, 14:1 (2007), pp. 108–26; Robert M. Perito, 'The US Experience with Provincial Reconstruction Teams in Afghanistan: Lessons Identified, in the US Institute of Peace Special Report no. 152 (2005), available at: {www.usip.org} accessed 5 Aug. 2011.
122. Seven of the eighteen UNPOL missions currently deployed draw upon the paramilitary force capabilities of Formed Police Units. The majority of missions on the African continent are led by these paramilitary units.
123. Dillon and Reid, *The Liberal Way of War*, p. 38.
124. Colonel Dan Roper, 'Countering Insurgency in Complex Environments', presented at the Institute for Defense and Government Advancement (IDGA) Irregular Warfare Conference, Washington DC (May 2010), available at: {www.idga.org} accessed 1 Aug. 2011.
125. Dillon, 'Sovereignty and Governmentality', p. 334.

11

International Policing and International Relations

B.K. Greener

I n the last few years police personnel have become increasingly important players on the international scene. Demands for domestic civilian
police to become transnational actors have proliferated markedly. Police
are now expected to combat terrorism; respond to civil defence emergencies;
undertake liaison roles offshore; and to respond to the needs of post-conflict
peace support operations. The rise of different forms of international policing, particularly the use of police to undertake executive policing roles or to
reform, rebuild and restructure police services in post-conflict situations, is
part of broader developments in the management of international peace and
security. Put simply, the use of domestic agents abroad to respond to security issues and to help maintain law and order challenges the inside/outside
distinction at play in international relations.[1] More specifically, the simple
fact of increased international policing, combined with the types of norms
being promoted within policing paradigms, contributes to the consolidation
of a rules-based order as sought by those promoting liberalism's domestic
analogy.

This article outlines the rise of international policing, examining the
relationship between recent operational developments and broader political
changes at the international level. Beginning with an investigation of earlier conceptualisations of 'international policing', the article questions what
authority, which values and whose police are at the heart of moves towards
international policing today. In evaluating the 'new international policing'

Source: *International Relations*, 26(2) (2012): 181–198.

agenda, so-called as it differs considerably from earlier conceptualisations of a possible international police force (IPF), it is noted that operational problems remain significant and that critiques of the political agenda underpinning current policing trends have much salience. However, the new international policing is still promising in that it potentially provides an important additional instrument for achieving operational goals such as the protection of civilians and, more fundamentally, increases the possibilities of achieving an international order based on the rule of law.[2]

An International Police Force?

In the 1930s following the apparent failings of the League of Nations, Lord David Davies, founder of the New Commonwealth Society who also endowed the first chair in International Politics (the Woodrow Wilson Chair) in the University of Wales, Aberystwyth, lobbied for the creation of new, more robust forms of international institutions and structures. In particular he called for the creation of an impartial tribunal with its own international police force to enforce international justice.[3] Davies's suggestion was premised upon liberalism's 'domestic analogy' which essentially focuses on 'how, in domestic society, justice is upheld and order maintained by the courts and the police', and the concomitant notion that this system should be applied to international society too.[4] The IPF concept was intended to be a workable, enforceable solution to the problem of an anarchical state-centric system seemingly plagued by numerous insecurities. As Michael Pugh points out, then:

> Aggressors who failed to acknowledge international law and the Tribunal's decisions would have to confront the second pillar of the system, the IPF. Davies stressed that the IPF should embody the principles of rapidity and certainty in its effect ... [and he] favoured a mixed system, comprising both centralized forces and recourse to national contingents available for joint action.[5]

There was an initial flurry of interest in the topic at home and abroad and at least something of this plan was later borne out in Articles 42 to 45 of the United Nations Charter in which member states essentially agree to 'undertake to make available to the Security Council, on its and in accordance with a special agreement or agreements, armed forces, assistance, and facilities, including rights of passage, necessary for the purpose of maintaining international peace and security' (Art. 43).[6] The ongoing hope that this fledgling UN system might later evolve into something more was pursued further in 1963 by U Thant, then Secretary General of the United Nations, when he claimed that he had 'no doubt that the world should eventually have an international police force which will be accepted as an integral and essential part of life in the same way as national police forces are accepted'.[7]

However, there are two issues at play here that bear on our contemporary understanding of international policing. The first is that we have come to rely on a much more fluid and ad hoc system for maintaining international peace and security than was envisaged either by Davies or by those creating the UN charter. Member state contributions to UN peace operations are delivered on a much more makeshift basis than hoped for, and the current system has a number of attendant problems. Indeed, despite recent calls by Graham Day and Christopher Freeman for the creation of a 'blue force of gendarmes' to undertake international 'policekeeping' even these authors advocate that 'leadership should be exercised within the national remit to facilitate international frameworks' rather than a standing force per se.[8] There certainly is not, therefore, currently any standing IPF and 'no global sovereign claims universal policing authority'.[9]

The second issue at play is the fact that the ideas proffered above were actually referring primarily to the use of armed forces, particularly air forces manned by volunteers, thereby confusing this notion of 'international policing'.[10] Any notion of 'policing' international affairs has therefore in practice often been associated with the use of *military* forces in various efforts to attain increased degrees of peace and security. In particular, this conceptual confusion is tied up with the various efforts undertaken to try to operationalise some of Davies's IPF idea in practice. For example, as Chuck Call and Michael Barnett point out, throughout the Cold War years there had been a 'curious' neglect of civilian police in international peace operations and this reinforced the notion that military forces should and could 'police' conflict between and within states.[11] These broader developments in international affairs were further complicated by academic theses such as Morris Janowitz's notion that military forces should become 'constabulary forces'.

Janowitz claimed that 'the military establishment becomes a constabulary force when it is continuously prepared to act, committed to the minimum use of force, and seeks viable international relations rather than victory because it has incorporated a protective military posture'.[12] This use of the term added further confusion as to the distinctiveness of roles between police and military as the phrase 'constabulary forces' was and is in more common usage to describe forces that have both military capabilities and police powers.[13] Relevant examples of constabulary forces include the French *gendarmerie*, who were originally used in part for nation-building, and in more contemporary times provide a more robust, rapidly deployable policing capability to enforce public order, stem riots and respond to serious threats to law and order.[14]

Instead of a standing UN (military) force that enforces international law, or the applied use of military personnel as 'constabulary' forces in an apparently ever increasing number of roles, the new international policing agenda that has emerged in recent times differs markedly from these earlier conceptualisations of what might be termed 'international policing'. The new international policing is not the systematic use of an IPF (civilian or military) to enforce state behaviour. It is instead a phenomenon that involves much more fluid and varied responses to specific issues pertaining to international peace and security – responses that have brought civilian police increasingly into the international arena outside their national jurisdictions to perform particular functions.

Though at first glance purely an operational concern, in the carrying out of these particular functions this new international policing may well have much greater impact beyond the operational level in reinforcing trends towards a rules-based international order through, amongst other things, an increased standardisation of policing behaviour.

The New International Policing

To illustrate the new international policing agenda at work, numbers of UN police involved in peace operations have increased dramatically in recent years. UN police personnel in the field (called CIVPOL from 1964 to 2005, and since then called UNPOL) grew from 35 in 1988 to 1500 deployed during the Namibia peacekeeping operation in 1989–90, with numbers steadily increasing over time so that by February 2000 the UN was mandated to deploy 9000 CIVPOL around the world.[15] In more recent times numbers of UN police officers deployed on operations increased from 7300 in August 2006 to 8800 in January 2007 to 9600 in August 2007, while numbers since late 2008 have generally hovered around the 13,000 mark with higher numbers projected for the next few years.[16] There are, therefore, simply many more police undertaking policing tasks outside their home jurisdictions. Most of these are deployed to help police or mentor local police in post-conflict peace operations. Though not nearly as numerous as their military counterparts, this rise in numbers of police, combined with the changing roles being attributed to these personnel, is both spurred by and in turn contributes to a merging of international and domestic security spheres.[17]

Again using the UN example, the tasks assigned to UNPOL in these operations have broadened and deepened to include executive policing and democratic or human-rights-oriented police reform from the ground up. For many years UNPOL functioned under the SMART model of civilian policing abroad – 'SMART' meaning Support, Monitoring, Administering, Reporting and Training.[18] Since the later 1990s such personnel have been tasked with greater responsibilities according to needs and expectations.[19] Executive policing roles were allocated to police in missions, allowing for such police officers to have powers of arrest, search and detention in those states, while basic tasks such as 'monitoring' have changed from observation to more stringent reviews monitoring compliance with internationally accepted standards of human rights and the UN Criminal Justice Standards

(UNCJS).[20] The Brahimi Report of 2000 then called for a 'doctrinal shift' in the use of CIVPOL and other personnel involved in rule of law institutions to reflect an increasing focus on strengthening human rights and the rule of law in post-conflict situations, and asserted that CIVPOL should actively retrain and restructure local police, not just 'observe and scold'.[21] Perhaps even more fundamentally, UNPOL involvement in police reform has seen a move away from police reform that focuses only on technical and structural issues (size, organisational structure, equipment, etc.) to focusing on building the public's confidence in the police as a force for public safety and security that is independent of political agendas.[22]

Moreover such developments are not the sole preserve of the UN. Similar situations have occurred in bilateral or other multilateral policing operations around the world. The legal frameworks for the Regional Assistance Mission to Solomon Islands (RAMSI), for example, ensured a police-led mission, gave powers of arrest to the Participating Police Force and allowed for RAMSI personnel to help rebuild indigenous policing capacity.[23] Post-conflict stability and reconstruction missions as well as counter-insurgency operations have also witnessed a rise in the use of police as important actors in international affairs, though in these cases the basis for involvement can differ considerably as discussed later in this paper.[24] In order to be able to undertake such activities national and regional police deployment groups are increasingly the norm, with a number of countries creating standing international deployment groups or international policing capacities of different kinds and with varying capabilities within their existing police services.[25]

Although these changes in the field of international policing are very different to the type of international police force promoted in the visions of Davies and Thant, they are nonetheless significant. These developments not only allow for alternative instruments of response, but at the same time are the embodiment of changes in the conceptualisation of what constitutes an international security issue and how the international community should respond to such issues. The question of who can authorise such policing is therefore also of importance.

International Policing: What Authority?

For policing to occur an accepted authority must be in situ. As Mathieu Deflem and Suzanne Sutphin claim in reference to domestic jurisdictions, 'a society that has not attained a degree of pacification cannot afford a civilian police', as that authority is still contested.[26] This thesis can be extrapolated to the international level. Given that we still currently reside in a state of international anarchy, it could be said that any 'degree of pacification' is for the present somewhat deficient as we do not have a positivist legal framework at play. This also further helps explain any previous reliance on military forces, as these are forces that typically operate in situations where authority is contested, while police are more representative of an established order in that they uphold an existing form of authority.[27]

The legal status of instances of current international policing efforts is therefore highly significant. Who can authorise international policing? Despite advances in the institutionalisation of international law, there is no international tribunal that works in a systematic and comprehensive way regarding the management of international conflict in the sense envisaged by Davies. As there is no positive legal authority at play, each instance of international policing is at present negotiated on a case-by-case basis. In some cases legal frameworks to help legitimate an international policing presence are negotiated with host authorities if there is some form of functioning government. This occurred in the case of the Solomon Islands where a beleaguered government headed by Prime Minister Kemakeza requested foreign help and where the Pacific Island Forum has been the main partner organisation in responding to the government in situ.[28] A number of bilateral initiatives such as those undertaken between Papua New Guinea and Australia in providing long-term police mentoring, or in New Zealand, where Australian police were sworn in to help provide additional help in manning cordons and identifying victims in the wake of significant earthquakes in February 2011, also demonstrate this dynamic at work.[29]

Alternatively, the legal foundations for instances of international policing may be formulated within broader UN resolutions when the UN is effectively handed the administration of certain territories before a host government is formed – such as in the case of Kosovo and Timor-Leste.[30] In a related but different scenario, the US-led operations in Iraq and Afghanistan have involved attempts by the US to claim legitimate authority through the doctrine of pre-emption, though such claims to legality and legitimacy are highly contestable. These are operations that are problematic in both political and operational terms – particularly as the US military has at times been utilised in some policing roles due to both practical and constitutional restraints.[31] In these two cases the notion of there being a legal or legitimate source of authority at play is more tenuous, as is the notion of these constituting genuine cases of 'international policing'. The situations in Iraq and Afghanistan are relevant to the overall trajectory of international policing but remain 'hard' cases that intersect and diverge from the overall international policing agenda at different points.

There are, therefore, varying sites of authority that can work to help legitimate international policing efforts, though that legitimacy can also be lost through incompetence or a lack of engagement with local needs and priorities.[32] Central to *any* of these arrangements, and arguably vital to legal justifications for the very existence of international policing, is the assumption that these arrangements are to be temporary in nature. The very point of such international policing is always presented as an intention to 'police oneself out of a job', not to collapse into mere rolling deployments that control unruly parts of the world on behalf of wealthier states, as is feared by scholars critical of the nature of peace operations.[33] To that effect a stated key component of international policing is to support the development of local police services so that any intervening external police personnel can exit – although this development has occurred only along very particular lines.

International law has become less ad hoc and a growing web of global governance has emerged where sites of legal authority can potentially be vested in various institutions. However, it is arguable that the most signifi-cant authority at play rests *in ideas* rather than in one overarching sover-eign.[34] Different legal precedent or sites of authority can be claimed, but one constant throughout recent policing missions has been the underlying value set that has been promulgated. Thus the previous claim that 'no global sovereign claims universal policing authority' is only true in one sense of the term.[35] There is no one universally accepted agential source of policing authority, no supreme sovereign global authority in a solid corporeal sense, but there is a *type* of authority that has emerged in terms of the principles being espoused: the rule of law, and in particular its relation to upholding, protecting and promoting certain values.

International Policing: Which Values and Whose Police?

Police personnel are being deployed in increasing numbers to undertake a broad range of tasks under the umbrella of 'human-right-oriented' or 'demo-cratic' policing, and the development of these ideals as international norms can be seen through the example of the UN experience. The 1979 UN Code of Conduct for Enforcement Personnel, for example, encapsulated a number of liberal values, and although this Code did not really achieve the accept-ance that was sought for it among UN member states at the time, more con-crete policing guidelines have since been formulated.[36]

In 1995 UNCIVPOL defined seven principles for democratic policing to guide police reform efforts in Bosnia-Herzegovina, and these kinds of prin-ciples were to be mimicked in later operations in Kosovo, Timor-Leste and elsewhere.[37] As noted by David Bayley, in the 1990s 'the template for police reform and reconstruction in foreign countries was developed and codified for the first time. It is now universally referred to as "democratic policing"'.[38] Yet it was only in 2007 that the UN Police Division began developing doctrines and pre-deployment training curricula for all UNPOL personnel, with certain values being promoted as key guiding principles for action – an important emphasis being human-rights-centred policing.[39] At that time only 65 per cent of UNPOL officers received any form of general pre-deployment training to prepare them for international deployments and only 35 per cent received training and information on matters relevant to their duties in the international context.[40] A later 2008 Strategic Peacekeeping Training Needs Assessment similarly asserted that at least one-third of police officers being deployed to UN missions were believed not to have received sufficient training.[41] Work therefore began in earnest on developing standardised pre-deployment training with additional modules being created on a case-by-case basis, tailored for imparting knowledge about particular missions.

In 2009 a new module on 'UN Peacekeeping Training Standards for Pre-deployment Training of UN Police Officers' was created.[42] This material was sent out to member states in mid-2009 and special 'Train the Trainer' courses were conducted throughout the year in Sweden, Ghana, Argentina and Australia.[43] In late 2009 the UN Police Division also began work on an overarching strategic doctrinal framework to understand both the core business of UNPOL in the field (the outer limits of what should be taken on in a UN context) and also the types of values that needed to be inculcated – with particular focus here again being on the protection of civilians and the respect for human rights. There is some reservation about using the particular term 'democratic policing' within the UN context, with other phrases such as 'human rights' or 'the protection of civilians' taking precedence, but in essence many of the objectives remain the same.

The overall aim of this current agenda is to ensure that those undertaking policing roles in peace operations, under UN auspices at least, have had common training in issues such as human rights, due legal processes and, to a certain extent, ideal relationships between police, society and government in democratic societies. In explicating democratic policing principles, David Bayley argues that police can support democratic development but they are only a means to that end if they give top priority to individual citizens and private groups; are accountable to the law rather than the government; protect human rights; and are transparent in their activities.[44] Similarly Jones et al. provide the criteria summarised here that must be met to qualify as democratic police service provision:

1. equity: fair allocation of resources according to need as well as proportionate enforcement;
2. delivery of service: effective and efficient delivery of police services;
3. responsiveness: as government should reflect the wishes of citizens;
4. distribution of power: to ensure that police cannot become a force for repression;
5. information: freely available about the police and their powers;
6. redress: working complaints process, bad practices addressed and compensation offered;
7. participation: ability for members of the public to have input into policing policy.[45]

With such principles informing UN training modules, UNPOL would therefore not only become familiar with these kinds of ideals, but could potentially also *internalise* them to a certain extent. Thus 'policing' could potentially be following what has happened more narrowly in criminal justice where 'the rising tide of international collaboration on crime control has involved both the homogenization of criminal justice systems (and particularly criminal laws) towards a common norm and the regularization of criminal justice relationships across borders'.[46]

This argument is, admittedly, controversial. It has not yet been borne out in any evidential way given the recent nature of these developments. However, it is still possible that police training for UN missions and consequent deployment may change attitudes in those undertaking policing activities – particularly if a failure to demonstrate human-rights-oriented policing begins to see Police Contributing Countries (PCCs) being less favoured for deployment in the UN system. As many countries use UN deployments as significant revenue streams, selective use of PCCs seems a plausible method for pressuring for better policing. On the other hand, a number of relevant concerns about both the operational aspects and the political framing of the new international policing phenomenon have been raised, and these criticisms must be acknowledged.

The Salience of Critiques

In considering recent international policing efforts there are a number of criticisms at play. The first critique relates to the quality of policing offered. This then brings another criticism to bear: that is, that policing missions have also been insensitive to context in both carrying out policing roles, and in pursuing police reform programmes in the host country. The question of whose security is being served by the policing arrangement in place is also relevant. Last, there remains the question as to how the new international policing agenda is faring when utilising police personnel from significantly different backgrounds.

One of the problems with international policing efforts so far has been the quality of the policing provided. Experiences in Bosnia, Timor-Leste, Sudan and elsewhere have demonstrated that the ideals of human-rights-centred democratic policing where police 'protect and serve' the local population have often not been adhered to, with a number of charges of abuse of office, unwillingness to carry out policing tasks, or corrupt, immoral or illegal behaviour being reported.[47] Problems have occurred because police operating overseas may be getting paid very well, while at the same time feeling fewer ethical constraints and being less accountable to stringent internal oversight mechanisms. Operationally, then, recent international policing efforts have been somewhat mixed in terms of adherence to professional standards.

In addition to these questions about professionalism, relevant questions have also been asked as to how police personnel from outside a jurisdiction could possibly hope to successfully 'police' (when executive policing is part of their mandate) or to 'reform' a local police service in an area that they are not connected to nor necessarily very familiar with, with a lack of cultural sensitivity or language capability often causing difficulties on the ground.[48] Policing is highly contextual, reflecting as it does societal and political norms within a given area, and a number of commentators have therefore also questioned the application of standardised international police reform models in places such as the former Yugoslavia or the Pacific. In the latter, for example, it has been argued by a number of commentators that policing models advocated by international actors have been inappropriate as well as unsustainable.[49]

The purported suitability of particular policing models for application anywhere in the world, particularly the advocating of a centralised approach as part of state-building initiatives, has therefore come into question, particularly when those models have little resonance for local populations. Baker has therefore noted that, in post-conflict societies, 'governments and donors in post-conflict countries simply call for reform programmes with no regard to the issues of lack or resources to sustain them or popular demand for them'.[50]

This brings in another related critique that, in addition to these more general contextualisation problems, policing efforts in counter-insurgency or counter-terrorism contexts such as in the cases of Iraq and Afghanistan have created less than ideal policing capacities within the host state in order to help serve external rather than local security imperatives.[51] As David Bayley and Robert Perito have pointed out, local police training in such operations is 'debilitated by ad hoc planning, systematic lack of documentation, and weak accountability; it is also overly militarised, focusing on the technical skills of law enforcement rather than on community service and crime prevention'.[52] In Iraq:

> Any Iraqi policeman will tell you that the Iraqi people are not satisfied with security provision; and the strength of the militias is at least in part a response to the failure of the state to provide security. The key mission of the Iraqi police is seen as fighting terrorism. This may seem reasonable to an outsider, but it is essentially a state-centric priority established with the occupying coalition.[53]

The focus on counter-terrorism and counter-insurgency has resulted in a skewed approach to internal security whereby the liberalisation agenda noted above has been postponed in the light of external and potentially regime-only-oriented security interests. In such cases, external actors can counter-productively improve the capability of a major institution of potential repression, and thereby risk domestic order and their own reputations.[54] The question as to who such policing serves or secures therefore remains a relevant and underlying concern, raising the spectre that external agendas could also be driving other cases of international policing.

In addition to these issues, there is at times a discrepancy between the value sets being promoted and the original value sets held by those police personnel being deployed in such missions.[55] For example, at present some of the countries partaking in international policing missions have a mixed record of upholding or embodying liberal democratic human-rights-oriented policing models. Yet in UN deployments, and most others, they are being asked to help achieve an increasingly human-rights-centred society and, at times, to help reform, rebuild or restructure national police forces into ideal liberal democratic models of policing. UNPOL figures show that the top ten PCCs for 2010 were, in order: Bangladesh, Jordan, Pakistan, India, Nepal, Nigeria, Senegal, Ghana, Egypt and the Philippines.[56] Significantly, this constitutes a major change from the list of top PCCs for 2000 which included a number of Western countries such as the US (1), Germany (4), the UK (7), Portugal (9) and Spain (10).[57] The ability of such police personnel to adapt and absorb UN requirements regarding the use and promotion of liberal democratic human-rights-centred policing has not yet been tested, and this matter is discussed in more detail below. What can be argued is that the standardisation of value sets differs markedly between different PCCs, as does the interoperability of these personnel.

Combined with the effects of different political and social value sets that influence how these police personnel seek to carry out their tasks, more technical or operational challenges such as levels of interoperability are also problematic. The police, more than the military, are highly contextualised within their own societies. Military forces tend to be more interoperable in terms of a common language, rank structure and understandings of basic roles and responsibilities, helping to provide a level of international comparability. Police services, on the other hand, can be highly centralised or decentralised, highly militarised or unarmed, or can be of the Anglo model or European third-force model or regime-reinforcing types of police. This can create misunderstandings in carrying out various policing tasks.

These issues combined constitute significant problems with international policing as currently construed. However, there is reason to believe that there may still be merit in the new international policing agenda despite the relevance of these concerns.

Potential Merits

Underlying a number of the concerns expressed above, there are also legitimate worries about the possible misuse of international policing, as policing can be seen as 'an instrument of geo-political strategy', potentially supporting neo-colonial projects or serving external rather than local interests.[58] However the nature of the policing that is being promulgated through these mechanisms and processes requires, at least in ideal terms, that local police forces are responsive to their contexts. Key to policing in this tradition is the notion of legitimacy. As Goldsmith and Sheptycki note, then, 'good policing is undertaken with, and on behalf of, a community that both understands and *endorses* the police mission to secure social order'.[59] If the international policing agenda can remain true to the concept that policing must be legitimated by the very community that the police are supposed to protect and serve for this to constitute policing rather than occupation, this operational requirement could help to allay fears of international policing being wielded only for external agendas at the political or strategic level. It may become a *strategic* or political requirement of international policing that the concepts of consent and legitimacy must be in place for policing to take place at all, given that this is a key *operational* tenet.

Even in the hard cases of Iraq and Afghanistan the pursuit of overly militarised policing models that serve external interests are increasingly under fire for being both counter-productive and not really constituting 'policing' in the correct sense of the term. Thus:

> It is counter-productive to treat police as an auxiliary fighting unit in battling the insurgency, as has been happening with increasing frequency in the troubled south. Afghanistan, like any other democracy, requires police service more than police force … In countering an insurgency, the police are the first line of defence as the interface with the community. They have powers of stop and search, arrest and detention, and since they observe daily comings and goings, should be aware of the first signs of illegal activity. Yet, as the interior minister rightly said, 'it is not the responsibility of the police to fight [the insurgency]. The police are responsible for implementing the law, and we should not train our policemen with an inclination for war'.[60]

As evidence of the counter-productivity of militarised law enforcement mounts, and as pressure grows to provide policing that serves and protects the local community rather than external agendas, even the policing efforts underway in Iraq and Afghanistan must come to more genuinely reflect the policing norms discussed here.[61]

Moreover, in considering related critiques about power imbalances, the various police reform programmes, for example, need not be perceived as exercises in a one-way transmission of 'expertise', as they present important opportunities for policing improvements to shuttle between participants in a multi-directional manner. For example, countries such as New Zealand and Australia may themselves learn from smaller Pacific Island communities when it comes to alternative methods of community policing. In these cases it has increasingly been recognised that the type of policing assistance offered needs to be tempered better to fit local contexts, and critical commentary has directly impacted upon the policy of metropolitan policing powers, partly mollifying critiques of the neo-colonial aspect of such policing efforts.[62]

Perhaps most interestingly, these policing developments at a more operational level may potentially signal that groundwork is being laid for some general agreement between states on the types of basic values that are commendable both at home and in international society. The fact that there is an increasingly systematic approach to trying to ensure police personnel serving in peace operations are 'on the same page' in terms of seeing their role as protecting and serving the public through human-rights-centred or democratic policing offers an opportunity for some increased standardisation along these lines. This could mean certain key policing principles are adhered to, while less important principles may be adapted to different contexts to help avoid the problems with templating that have occurred in the past.

On this more general topic of value and norm dissemination creating a foundation for changing international society, Sheptycki surmises that 'the essential foundation of a constabulary ethic worthy of the name ought to be a politically, economically, culturally and socially inclusive global social order', that 'the principal structural barrier to achieving such an ethic is the fragmentary nature of the field of governance globally', and that transnational policing efforts will be inherently problematic until such broader issues are addressed.[63]

However, this argument may be putting the proverbial cart before the horse. If we are to achieve broader global governance, perhaps we can begin with sub-governance level shifts to help create the bedrock upon which these much grander aims may be built. If police norms and values become more standardised, in which the rule of law and human-rights-centred approaches are key, this feeds into (and could also temper) the overarching liberalisation agenda that is being pursued through various multilateral and bilateral peacebuilding and development programmes worldwide.

Indeed, it is important to note that there are some additional relevant developments that suggest that some of the standardisation themes highlighted above are not occurring in isolation. For example, when one considers the numerous democratically oriented police reform programmes underway in developing democracies, the standardisation of policing norms seems even more likely. Although the record is not yet established as to how these efforts are progressing, it is significant that such efforts are also underway in a wide variety of countries such as Turkey, Russia, Serbia, South Korea, India, Timor-Leste, Venezuela, Mexico, Brazil, Kenya, South Africa, Nigeria, Panama, Afghanistan, Iraq, Papua New Guinea and Tonga to name a few.[64] A number of different concurrent and converging processes are therefore occurring at the same time and, significantly, some of these processes of norm standardisation are beginning to incorporate certain enforcement mechanisms. In the UN case, for example, initiatives to create better record-keeping to note competent and valuable police personnel, as well as those that are incompetent, corrupt or abusive, are underway.

Though on the ground interpretation of basic democratic policing principles can result in somewhat different working models (variations can occur between continental and Anglo models; between community policing and models focused on law enforcement and risk management, and so on, though there appears to be some consolidation here in terms of an overriding focus on community policing), the basic principles of democratic or human-rightsoriented policing underlying such police services is the dominant agenda of the day. In one specific example, police are often uniquely placed to provide for the protection of civilians both in peace and in more volatile post-conflict situations. As the concept of 'POC' (protection of civilians) becomes central to UN peace operations, police are a vitally important instrument in attempts to provide for that protection, and discussions about international policing roles within the police policy community have centred on ways in which to achieve this key task.[65]

Finally, these micro-level shifts in the dissemination of particular policing norms in turn creates more fertile ground for a deeper sort of domestic analogy to develop – bringing stronger understanding and agreement on the centrality of the rule of law, the need to protect the vulnerable, and potentially to even support the development of a rules-based international order where the use of military force becomes even less likely if these values are internalised.

Conclusion

Although we do not have an international police force like that envisaged by David Davies or U Thant we are witnessing an era of new international policing in terms of scale, institutional arrangements, and roles and expectations attributed to civilian police in peace support and other such deployments. In thinking about the consequences of the rise of instances of international policing it is useful to call on David Bayley's suggestion that 'analytically, two questions may be asked about policing: first, what effect is it having upon society, and second, what effect is society having on the police'.[66] Bayley was talking about police in the domestic setting. Yet we can extrapolate these thoughts to the international stage by asking what effect changes in international policing can potentially have upon the shape of international society.[67] In this case operational changes in terms of the scope, conduct and intent of international policing have both been underpinned by and in turn contributed to broader political changes at the international level.

Efforts are underway to standardise international policing values and practices. Police deployed on international missions are now supposed to support the rule of law, protect and serve their communities, and ascribe to democratic or human-rights-centred models of policing. This promotion of certain policing norms is further reinforced by the broader adoption of doctrine that seeks to emphasise the protection of civilians in conflict or post-conflict settings.[68] In considering the prospects for overcoming tensions between global and local norms in security sector reform, Annika Hansen has noted:

> in short, the dual goals of establishing a democratically accountable security sector and of promoting local ownership are not easily reconciled. In many cases, though, the key lies in an iterative approach in which values are introduced gradually and in ways that are amenable to the local society. While local preferences may not correspond with Western models of governance and individual rights, international agencies can be far more tolerant of different ways in which human rights can manifest themselves or be operationalised in local security arrangements.[69]

Her work suggests that an 'iterative approach in which values are introduced gradually', and where the international community reflexively learns from the importance of context in tempering non-essential demands, may work in the more particular case of embedding basic but fundamental policing values across a range of police personnel.

This issue of norm dissemination – the possible internalisation of human-rights-centred policing values across contributing PCCs – may seem to be the most significant issue at hand when it comes to assessing the consequences of new instances of 'international policing'. After all, operational issues such as human-rights training within policing impact upon societal norms. However, this also hints at an even more fundamental issue: these developments may in turn lay the groundwork for the move towards a more systematic form of international policing that is closer to Davies's vision of calling rogue international actors to account for their actions.

Politically, the contemporary international policing agenda lends itself to a broader liberalisation agenda at play in international affairs.[70] As noted above, it is integral to that agenda at an operational level through the promotion of certain democratic or human-rights-centred policing norms. However, it is also central to that agenda at a political level in that it promotes the centrality of the rule of law and an awareness of and respect for human rights. The effects of these operational and political developments reinforce each other. If certain norms are internalised *both* by police personnel working in operations *and* by political actors considering the use of policing and the rule of law as instruments for managing aspects of international security, other more fundamental changes become possible. Such normative developments necessarily contribute to a respect for the rule of law and a rights-centred approach, impacting upon actors' outlooks, interactions and expectations. Through this process liberalism's 'domestic analogy' – a vision that would see domestic constraints and norms become internationalised – becomes more plausible as it resonates more readily with international actors.

This article has spoken to the interrelationship between ongoing operational developments in international policing and the potential for deeper political change. Despite there being no 'international police force' as envisaged by Davies and Thant, scholars may therefore still be well advised to look beyond the apparently technical function of international policing efforts in order to consider the political consequences of the recent moves to utilise police as international actors.

Notes

1. R. B. J. Walker, *Inside/Outside: International Relations as Political Theory* (Cambridge: Cambridge University Press, 1992).
2. There are legitimate concerns about the possible use of police for repressive purposes. In terms of international policing, the words of Michael Pugh, 'Peacekeeping and Critical Theory', *International Peacekeeping*, 11(1), 2004, p. 41, express a more general concern about the entire peacekeeping paradigm, suggesting that this is merely 'forms of riot control directed against unruly parts of the world to uphold the liberal peace'. Operational and strategic concerns about police as instruments of repression are salient and are discussed briefly in this article.
3. David Davies, *An International Police Force* (London: Benn, 1932), and *The Problem of the Twentieth Century* (London: Benn, 1930), as well as Clement Attlee, *An International Police Force* (London: New Commonwealth Society, 1934).
4. Brian Porter, 'David Davies: A Hunter after Peace', *Review of International Studies*, 15(2), 1989, p. 35.
5. Michael Pugh, 'Policing the World: Lord Davies and the Quest for Order in the 1930s', *International Relations*, 16(1), 2002, p. 99.
6. Porter, 'David Davies', p. 30, cites Peter Lewis's *Biographical Sketch of David Davies* to suggest there was at least one strong supporter of this idea, with the New Zealand government officially endorsing it in early 1937. Davies tried to persuade New Zealand's then Finance Minister (later Prime Minister) Walter Nash to return to Britain to lead the British Labour Party along the same lines. John Hillen, *Blue Helmets; The Strategy of UN Military Operations*, 2nd edn (Washington, DC: Brassey's, 2000), p. 11, points out that there was provision for the creation of a comprehensive Military Staff Committee in Articles 46–7 but that this was soon moribund.
7. UN Secretary General U Thant as cited in Gavin Brown, Barry Barker and Terry Burke, *Police as Peacekeepers: The History of the Australian and New Zealand Police serving with the United Nations Force in Cyprus 1964–1984* (Melbourne: UNCIVPOL, 1984), p. 6.
8. Graham Day and Christopher Freeman, 'Operationalizing the Responsibility to Protect – the Policekeeping Approach', *Global Governance*, 11, 2005, p. 141.
9. Peter Andreas and Ethan Nadelmann, *Policing the Globe: Criminalization and Crime Control in International Relations* (Oxford: Oxford University Press, 2006), pp. 252–3.
10. Porter, 'David Davies', p. 30.
11. Chuck Call and Michael Barnett, 'Looking for a Few Good Cops: Peacekeeping, Peacebuilding and CIVPOL', in Tor Tanke Holm and Espen Barth Eide (eds), *Peacebuilding and Police Reform* (London and Portland OR: Frank Cass, 2000), p. 64. Brown et al., *Police as Peacekeepers*, p. 2, suggested in their analysis of the Australian and New Zealand contributions to the Cyprus deployment, that it is a surprise 'that it took so long for the United Nations to call on professional police from member States to facilitate peace-keeping operations'.
12. Morris Janowitz, *The Professional Soldier: A Social and Political Portrait* (London: Free Press of Glencoe Collier-Macmillan Ltd, 1960), p. 418.
13. This reference to 'military capabilities and police powers' is taken from Robert Perito, *Where Is the Lone Ranger When We Need Him? America's Search for a Postconflict Stability Force* (Washington, DC: United States Institute of Peace, 2004), p. 46.

14. For an overview of some of the roles of the gendarme, see Clive Elmsley, 'Peasants, Gendarmes, and State Formation', in Mary Fulbrook (ed.), *National Histories and European History* (Boulder, CO: Westview Press, 1993), pp. 69–93. This reference to 'military capabilities and police powers' is taken from Perito, *Where Is the Lone Ranger*, p. 46.

15. David H. Bayley, *Democratizing the Police Abroad: What to Do and How to Do It* (Washington, DC: US Department of Justice, 2001), p. 4.

16. UN Police Presentation by Mark Kroeker, outgoing Police Advisor to UN Police Division, Third Meeting of the International Policing Advisory Council, 30–31 August 2007, National Museum of Australia, Canberra, and discussions with UN Police Division officials, Turin, Italy, November 2009. Numbers deployed in missions stood at around 14,000 in mid-2011.

17. This merging of domestic and international security spheres is noted by a number of authors. For one of the clearest expositions from an international relations perspective, see Peter Andreas and Richard Price, 'From War-Fighting to Crime Fighting: Transforming the American National Security State', *International Studies Review*, 3(3), 2001, pp. 31–52.

18. Halvor Hartz, 'CIVPOL: The UN Instrument for Police Reform', in Holm and Eide, *Peacebuilding and Police Reform*, p. 31.

19. B. K. Greener, 'UNPOL: UN Police as Peacekeepers', *Policing and Society*, 19(2), 2009, pp. 106–18.

20. Annika S. Hansen, *From Congo to Kosovo: Civilian Police in Peace Operations*, Adelphi Paper 343 (Oxford: International Institute for Strategic Studies, 2002), p. 18.

21. United Nations Secretariat, *Report of the Panel on United Nations Peace Operations*, UN Doc. A/ff/305, S/2000/809, 21 August 2000, available at: www.un.org/peace/report/peace_operations.

22. Hansen, *From Congo to Kosovo*, p. 13.

23. Solomon Islands Government, Facilitation of International Assistance Act (2003), available at: www.paclii.org/sb/legis/num_act/foiaa2003386. See also the RAMSI website at www.ramsi.org/ for more detail on this particular mission.

24. See, for example, T. Pfaff, *Development and Reform of the Iraqi Police Forces* (Carlisle, PA: Strategic Studies Institute US Army War College, 2007), and M. Sedra, 'Security Sector Reform in Afghanistan: The Slide Towards Expediency', *International Peacekeeping*, 13(1), 2006, pp. 94–110.

25. The UK, Canada, Australia, Norway, El Salvador, Samoa, New Zealand, Nigeria and a number of other countries have developed international policing capacities.

26. Mathieu Deflem and Suzanne Sutphin, 'Policing Post-War Iraq: Insurgency, Civilian Police and the Reconstruction of Society', *Sociological Focus*, 39(4), 2006, p. 279.

27. This is, admittedly, a contentious and somewhat generic statement but serves to illustrate a particular functional division between police and military.

28. Michael Fullilove, 'The Testament of Solomons: RAMSI and International State-Building', Lowy Institute Analysis, March (Sydney: Lowy Institute, 2006).

29. For commentary on the Solomon Islands and PNG cases, see Sinclair Dinnen, Abby McLeod and Andrew Goldsmith, 'Police-Building in Weak States: Australian Approaches in Papua New Guinea and Solomon Islands', *Civil Wars* 8(2), 2006, pp. 87–108. Local news media reported that 324 Australian police had been sworn in to help prevent looting, man cordons and undertake victim identification following major earthquakes in Christchurch, New Zealand, in February 2011.

30. For further commentary on these various cases, see B. K. Greener, *The New International Policing* (Houndmills; Palgrave Macmillan, 2009), ch. 3.

31. See David E. Keller, *US Military Forces and Police Assistance in Stability Operations: The Least Worst Option to Fill the US Capability Gap* (Carlisle, PA: Strategic Studies Institute US Army War College, 2011), for literature that promotes this role. See Cornelius

Friesendorf, *The Military and Law Enforcement in Peace Operations: Lessons from Bosnia Herzegovina and Kosovo* (Geneva: Geneva Centre for the Democratic Control of the Armed Forces, 2009), for an argument contesting this role.

32. Admittedly decisions emerging from these sites can be contested, as in the case of the aborted Enhanced Cooperation Programme in Papua New Guinea where a fledgling Australian police reform effort that would have seen Australian police granted both executive powers of arrest and immunity from prosecution under local law was found to be unconstitutional and hurriedly downgraded.

33. On such issues of local ownership, see Timothy Donais (ed.), *Local Ownership and Security Sector Reform* (Geneva: Centre for the Democratic Control of Armed Forces, 2008).

34. Ron Levi and John Hagan, 'International Police', in Markus D. Dubber and Mariana Valverde (eds), *The New Police Science: The Police Power in Domestic and International Governance* (Stanford CA: Stanford University Press, 2006), p. 233.

35. Andreas and Nadelmann, *Policing the Globe*, pp. 252–3.

36. John Kleinig, *The Ethics of Policing* (Cambridge: Cambridge University Press, 1996), p. 237.

37. David H. Bayley, *Changing the Guard: Developing Democratic Police Abroad* (Oxford: Oxford University Press, 2006), p. 8.

38. Bayley, *Changing the Guard*, p. 7.

39. Thanks to discussions at UN Police Division, UNDPKO, New York, November 2007.

40. International Policing Advisory Council, *Summary Meeting Report of the Third Meeting of the International Policing Advisory Council (IPAC)*, Canberra, Australia 30–31 August 2007, p. 12.

41. 'UN Reform in Progress', *UN Police Magazine*, 4th edn, January 2010, p. 17.

42. 'UN Peacekeeping Training Standards for Pre-deployment Training of UN Police Officers', available at: http://peacekeepingresourcehub.unlb.org.

43. 'UN Reform in Progress', p. 17.

44. Bayley, *Democratizing the Police Abroad*, pp. 13–15.

45. T. Jones, T. Newburn and D. J. Smith, 'Policing and the Idea of Democracy', *British Journal of Criminology*, 36(2), 1994, pp. 185–6.

46. Andreas and Nadelmann, *Policing the Globe*, p. 8.

47. See Greener, *The New International Policing*.

48. For example, Gordon Peake, 'Police Reform in Timor-Leste', in Mercedes S. Hinton and Tim Newburn (eds), *Policing Developing Democracies* (Milton Park: Routledge, 2009), pp. 154–7, points out how international police personnel often lack the basic skills required to get along, let alone have any major understanding as to how the more important informal or traditional aspects of the host society function.

49. Such as Dinnen et al., 'Police-Building in Weak States', p. 104.

50. Bruce Baker, 'Policing Post Conflict Societies: Helping out the State', *Policing and Society*, 19(4), 2009, p. 329.

51. For the challenges faced in Afghanistan, see International Crisis Group, *Reforming Afghanistan's Police*, Asia Report no. 138, 30 August 2007, available at: www.crisisgroup. org/home/index.cfm?id=5052&l=1. On some of the problems in Iraq, see Robert Perito, *US Police in Peace and Stability Operations*, USIP Special Report, no. 191, August 2007, pp. 10–11 (available at: www.usip.org/files/resources/sr191.pdf), who points out that the US military created 'heavy police units' made up of former soldiers (Public Order Battalion, Mechanised Police Unit and Emergency Response Unit composed of unvetted Sunnis with military weapons and counterinsurgency training), which were merged in 2006 to create the Iraqi National Police (INP), and which was engaged in death squad activities. In early 2011 there was a similar critique of British policing programmes in the Middle East as concerns grew that bilateral programmes

had contributed to police brutality in government responses to pro-democracy protests. Counter-arguments said that such training had restrained police, with some senior police in Egypt, for example, supporting crowds calling for political change.

52. David H. Bayley and Robert M. Perito, *The Police in War: Fighting Insurgency, Terrorism and Violent Crime* (Boulder, CO: Lynne Rienner, 2010), p. 4.

53. Alex Martin and Peter Wilson, 'Security Sector Evaluation: Which Locals? Ownership of What?', in Donais, *Local Ownership and Security Sector Reform*, p. 90.

54. Bayley, *Changing the Guard*, p. 13.

55. A related critique regarding the discrepancy between those who make the decisions and those that bear the risks in the UN system is relayed by Philip Cunliffe, 'The Politics of Global Governance', *International Peacekeeping*, 16(3), 2009, pp. 323–36.

56. UN Police Division, 'Top Contributing Countries December 2010', *UN Police Magazine*, 6th edn, January 2011, p. 35.

57. Andrew Carpenter, *UN Police Peacekeeping; It's Different from the Day Job*, 2010 Powerpoint Presentation UN Police Division, Office of Rule of Law and Security Institutions, UNDPKO.

58. Michael Hardt and Anthony Negri, *Empire* (Cambridge, MA: Harvard University Press, 2000), Pugh, 'Peacekeeping and Critical Theory', and Robert Rubenstein, 'Peacekeeping and the Return of Imperial Policing', *International Peacekeeping*, 17(4), 2010, pp. 457–70.

59. Andrew Goldsmith and James Sheptycki, 'Introduction', in *Crafting Transnational Policing: Police Capacity-Building and Global Policing Reform* (Oxford and Portland OR: Hart, 2007), p. 2, italics added.

60. International Crisis Group, *Reforming Afghanistan's Police*.

61. See, for example, Cornelius Friesendorf and Susan Penksa, 'Militarized Law Enforcement in Peace Operations: EUFOR in Bosnia and Herzegovina', *International Peacekeeping*, 15(5), 2008, pp. 677–94, and Cornelius Friesendorf and Jorg Krempel, *Militarised versus Civilian Policing: Problems of Reforming the Afghan National Police*, Peace Research Institute Report, no. 102 (Frankfurt: PRIF, 2011).

62. Dinnen et al., 'Police-Building in Weak States', pp. 87–108. For example, Dinnen, McLeod and Goldsmith were part of a major project funded by the Australian Research Council called 'Policing the Neighbourhood' that assessed the record of the Australian Federal Police (AFP) in policing in the Pacific. Their research resulted in definite changes in the way that the AFP does business. See Garth Den Heyer, 'Measuring Capacity Development and Reform in the Royal Solomon Islands Police Force', *Policing and Society*, 20(3), 2010, pp. 298–315.

63. James Sheptycki, 'The Constabulary Ethic and the Transnational Condition', in *Crafting Transnational Policing: Police Capacity-Building and Global Policing Reform*, p. 33.

64. On these particular cases, see the various chapters included in Hinton and Newburn, *Policing Developing Democracies*; Bayley, *Changing the Guard*, p. 8; Andrew Goldsmith and Sinclair Dinnen, 'Transnational Police-Building: Critical Lessons from Timor-Leste and Solomon Islands', *Third World Quarterly*, 28(6), 2007, pp. 1091–1109; Dinnen et al., 'Police-Building in Weak States', pp. 87–108.

65. See, for example, Report of the Secretary General on the Protection of Civilians in Armed Conflict, UNSC S/2010/5769 dated 11 November 2010, available at: www.un.org/ga/search/view_doc.asp?symbol=S/2010/579.

66. David H. Bayley, 'Policing: The World Stage', in R. I. Mawby, *Policing Across the World: Issues for the Twenty-First Century* (London: University College London Press, 1999), p. 8.

67. This use of the term 'international society' is not a direct reference to English School understandings of that term; rather it just mimics Bayley's phrase and seeks to relate this notion to the global community.

68. Global Centre of the Responsibility to Protect, *The Relationship between the Responsibility to Protect and the Protection of Civilians in Armed Conflict*, June 2009, available at: http://responsibilitytoprotect.org/files/GCR2P%20Policy%20Brief-%20 The%20relationship%20 between%20R2P%20and%20the%20Protection%20of%20 Civilians%20in%20Armed%20 Conflict.pdf.

69. Annika Hansen, 'Local Ownership in Peace Operations', in Donais, *Local Ownership and Security Sector Reform*, p. 47.

70. On the influence of the liberalisation agenda in the field of peacebuilding, for example, see Roland Paris, 'Saving Liberal Peacebuilding', *Review of International Studies*, 36, 2010, pp. 337–65, and a response by David Chandler, 'The Uncritical Critique of "Liberal Peace'", *Review of International Studies*, 37, 2010, pp. 1–19. For an assessment of the place of different liberal theories in contemporary theoretical debates, see Benjamin Miller, 'Democracy Promotion: Offensive Liberalism versus the Rest (of IR Theory)', *Millennium: Journal of International Studies*, 38(3), 2010, pp. 561–91.

12

The Possibility of Transnational Policing

Alice Hills

The idea that police officers share a distinctive outlook on the world and their job is well established. It was originally formalised by Westley, who, from research conducted in a US city in the 1950s, argued that the key to understanding the police was to see them as a social and occupational group (Westley 1953). A consensus has since emerged that, although there is no single culture in any one police organisation, police typically share a 'set of assumptions, values, modes of thinking, and acting' (Cancino 2001, Chan 2007, p. 148).

Perceptions of occupational commonality are nowadays reinforced by the widely shared conviction that police forces must co-operate if they are to respond effectively to the crime and insecurity facilitated by globalisation. Various forms of bilateral, multilateral and international co-operation are encouraged by intergovernmental organisations (IGOs) such as the EU and Interpol, as is the notion of shared professional standards. Donors such as the UK's Department for International Development (DFID), which sponsors police reform projects as a means of implementing liberal values, further strengthen the desire for commonality. The operational requirements of multinational peacekeeping deployments play a part, too, as the composition of UN police (UNPOL) missions emphasises: in August 2007, the top contributing countries included Bangladesh, Benin, Cameroon, China, France, Ghana, India, Jordan, Malaysia, Nepal, Nigeria, Pakistan, Philippines, Portugal, Romania, Senegal, Ukraine and the USA, none of which provided any form of standardised pre-deployment training.

The notion of transnational policing exemplifies this trend. It may, or may not, form part of an emerging system of global governance (Duffield 2001,

Source: *Policing & Society: An International Journal of Research and Policy*, 19(3) (2009): 300–317.

Dubber and Valverde 2006), but the promotion of a style of policing claiming to transcend territorial boundaries is influential, especially in the rich liberal democracies of Australasia, Europe and North America (hereafter democracies). As such, it receives systematic attention in Goldsmith and Sheptycki's (2007) edited *Crafting Transnational Policing*.

Based on the premise that a common ethic is part of the self-understanding of police in a variety of contexts, Goldsmith and Sheptycki's contributors explore the possibility of crafting a transnational 'constabulary ethic'.[1] Sheptycki's approach is particularly thought-provoking because he argues that such an ethic is driven not just by officers' self-interest or self-regard, or by 'a genuine structural continuity between the dynamics of security-threatening situations, across a broad range of national and transnational contexts', but by 'a real sense of the value of a common policecraft in repairing these situations' (Loader and Walker, cited in Goldsmith and Sheptycki 2007, p. 139).

This last statement marks my analytical point of departure, for I see no evidence of a common policecraft, or of a set of norms capable of fulfilling this requirement. I look to UNPOL operations for verification of a common ethic on the basis that, given the UN's codes, declarations and standards on policing, this is surely where they should be found; yet commonality on the lines proposed by Sheptycki is missing. Admittedly my assessment relies on anecdotal evidence, rather than a systematic evidential basis, but so, too, do the claims made on behalf of transnational policing. More to the point, the stream of well-documented reports on corruption and brutality involving police from the UN's contributing countries published by advocacy groups such as Human Rights Watch (HRW) and the Commonwealth Human Rights Initiative (CHRI) suggests that transnational ethics have more to do with what should be, than with what is. Admittedly, Goldsmith and Sheptycki (2007, p. 2) explicitly favour such an approach, but it does not help us understand why certain norms and processes travel across cultures and others do not. Goldsmith and Sheptycki (2007, p. 2) may argue that 'good policing is undertaken with, and on behalf of, a community that both understands and endorses the police mission to secure social order', but notions of good policing and community (to say nothing of the accountability often thought to link them) mean little in most of the world.[3]

The possibility of developing a genuinely transnational policecraft is accordingly slim. The immediate reason for this is political, and to do with power, but the deeper reason is that sub-state policing realities invariably outweigh the idealism and universalising tendencies of liberal commentators and organisations such as the UN. In particular, there is no transnational consensus on what is necessary for effective policing. Further, there is no consensus on the levels of force required for effective policing, and each country assumes that its own practices are appropriate. In other words, my explanation of transnational policing's limitations is based on the primacy of sub-state practice. It builds on Westley's (1953, p. 34) observation that police habitually legitimise their actions in terms of ends defined by their (local) colleagues to counter-balance Sheptycki's emphasis on fostering a collective ethic.

This argument is presented in five sections. First, I note the tendency of many commentators to idealise the notion of a transnational ethic while ignoring, second, the subjective nature of effective policing, and the role of force within it. These issues come to the fore in the artificial environment of UN peacekeeping, which the third section uses as a laboratory in which to examine the possibility of transnational policing. Fourth, the relationship between international and sub-state standards is illustrated by reference to Norwegian support for Nigerian peacekeepers. Fifth, I conclude that the chances of developing a transnational police ethic are minimal.

Fostering Transnational Policing

One of the foundational principles of police studies is that police must be seen within the context of the society that permits their operation, so it is ironic that transnational policing is increasingly popular. This situation has developed in response to the promotion by democracies of international human-rights legislation, humanitarian intervention strategies and cross-border security operations. The security strategies of specific agents play a part too. In order to achieve its political objectives, the EU, for example, must export its procedural standards and ideological ideals, both of which rely on a system of cross-border police co-operation. Similar imperatives apply to the Bush administration's attempted Americanisation of non-US criminal justice since 2001. The extensive literature on cross-border forms of policing that resulted (Anderson *et al.* 1995, Occhipinti 2003, Andreas and Nadelmann 2006) is not synonymous with transnational policing as defined by Goldsmith and Sheptycki, but it forms a basis on which the latter is to be built.

Just as the emphasis of such literature is on the transfer of specific forms of Western policing, so transnational policing is invariably presented in terms of liberal values, which are then universalised. These include accountability and responsiveness, and the use of ethnically representative and non-partisan officers. Yet the term says more about Western values than functional standards, and it is typically applied in societies where the prospects for democratic-style policing are negligible. Matters are further obscured by differences between democracies. Take the case of Israel, which arguably has had the greatest influence on police tactics around the world. The ideal of a police employing minimal force has made little progress amongst its security agents because Israel prioritises national security; reform is understood to mean greater functional effectiveness (Luethold 2004, Sayigh 2007). The enthusiasm with which Scandinavian democracies merge security and development introduces further ambiguities, though the

OECD at least is aware of the dangers associated with this. As its *Handbook* notes, 'many capacity development interventions have failed because the wider governance constraints (e.g., systematic corruption) have not been understood' (OECD 2007, p. 86). But this does not stop the OECD promoting 'international' standards and overestimating the value of change for the police concerned.

This situation provides the backdrop to transnational policing as presented by Goldsmith and Sheptycki. By this term they mean the various forms of engagement undertaken by donors, governments and foreign enforcement agencies in the policing concerns and programmes of recipient countries. The perspectives offered by their contributors are representative of the current debate, but Sheptycki's (2000, 2002) contribution deserves special attention here because it builds on earlier publications to discuss the possibilities for 'fostering a "constabulary ethic" capable of guiding (police) practices … towards social peace and good ends with just means' (Sheptycki 2007, p. 32).

Sheptycki (2007, p. 33) acknowledges the difficulties of creating such policing, and of making it accountable to 'the global commonwealth'. He knows that institutional fragmentation prevents 'concern for the global common interest into practical action', and admits that 'the transnational condition is not conducive to fostering an ethic of good policing', but argues that 'it is precisely because of this that choosing to foster a constabulary ethic is both desirable and necessary'. His proposed ethic is founded on a 'politically, economically, culturally and socially inclusive global social order'.

Sheptycki (2007, p. 34) is well aware that his proposals are based on 'hope', but argues that it is 'constructive not only to observe and critique how policing power is being manifest globally, but also to think positively about the possibilities for fostering a constabulary ethic'. This is laudable, but unhelpful. It advances arguments of universalism in the face of clashing cultural values (Donnelly 2007), but it does not help us understand the dynamics of either the police or policing (Goldsmith and Dineen 2007). Further, the principal barrier to achieving Sheptycki's (2007, p. 33) ethic is not structural issues such as 'the fragmentary nature of the field of governance globally', but the alternatives to liberalism that dominate in most of the world. Even if the transnational condition were conducive to fostering an ethic of 'good' policing practice based on 'social peace, and good ends with just means' (Goldsmith and Sheptycki 2007, p. 32), fostering a transnational ethic is unlikely to offset the realities of Southern policing's 'violence, discordance and studied ugliness' (Goldsmith and Sheptycki 2007, p. 33). More to the point, the effectiveness of 'good' policing (i.e., its functional utility) in fragile societies is as yet unproven. This suggests that we need to re-examine not only the balance between international and sub-state policing standards, but also the various national understandings of effective policing and the role played by physical force in it.

Explaining Effective Policing

Effective policing usually means one of two things: it is either policing that successfully achieves the political, technical, ideological or normative objectives of the actor concerned, or it is policing that achieves its goal in a shorter time (Klockars 1985). Anecdotal evidence suggests that the most effective police operate in rich democracies with high levels of institutional capacity, such as EU member states, or in authoritarian countries such as China. In contrast, most police in the South (which is where UNPOL usually operate) lack bureaucratic skills and technical resources, and are notoriously ineffective. Nevertheless, it is difficult to avoid the conclusion that force always plays a key role in facilitating policing, effective or otherwise (Alpert and Dunham 2004, p. 18).

Liberal industrialised urban societies, for example, prize effectiveness even if their tolerance of overt violence tends to be relatively low. It could not be otherwise in, say, London where the Metropolitan Police's 31,000 officers police a multi-ethnic population of 7.2 million in an area of 620 square miles. Societies such as the UK's also tend to make ideological value judgements about effective policing. Thus, London's police authority defines effective policing as that which enables it to fulfil its objectives of 'equality and diversity within the police service', and fair and respectful treatment for London's inhabitants (MPA 2008). Similarly, the police authorities of South Yorkshire, Staffordshire and West Mercia constabularies claim a statutory duty to secure an effective and efficient police. Such statements are tautological in that the activities the authorities undertake are justified in terms of such goals, which are in turn legitimised on the grounds that they facilitate effective and efficient policing.

Ironically, many non-industrialised societies also claim to value effective policing. Take sub-Saharan Africa, whose 47 countries have police forces that are, by Western standards, as ineffective as they are brutal, corrupt, untrained and under-resourced. Their role involves regime representation, regulatory activities and static protection, rather than detection or crime prevention, but technical and institutional incapacity, combined with systematic under-funding, means that most are incapable of achieving such goals effectively. Yet even notoriously corrupt countries such as Kenya advocate effective policing. In 2004, the manifesto of Kenya's National Rainbow Coalition (NARC) stated that its aim was 'to build an effective community policing service' (Saferworld 2004).

In fact, there is no consensus on the meaning of effective policing outside achieving the objectives of specific mandates or goals. And without a general understanding it is difficult to know what can be used as a foundation for an operationally meaningful transnational policecraft. Admittedly, norms relevant to international policing exist in a formalised series of overlapping international declarations, codes and standards,[2] but they are not synonymous with effective policing. Indeed, starting with the UN's Universal Declaration on Human Rights of 1948, such declarations were formulated precisely because too many police thought that effective policing required the use of force. Hence the UN's conventions against torture, degrading treatment and summary execution. It is true that the UN's publications have been supplemented by guidelines such as the Council of Europe's 2001's recommendations for a European Code of Police Ethics, and the OSCE's (2006) *Guidebook on Democratic Policing*, all of which could in theory form the basis of a transnational policing ethic. Further, such publications use the terminology of 'international' policing, as does the OECD DAC's authoritative *Handbook* of 2007 (OECD 2007). This defines international policing as policing that uses minimal force, is relatively uncorrupt, and provides reasonably impartial assistance and redress within an accountable and known Western-style criminal justice framework.

Nevertheless, such guidelines are essentially descriptive or normative, so working definitions of effective policing must be extracted from specific projects. Even then, caution is essential because donors and IGOs treat effective and democratic policing as synonymous, as when in a paper on community policing in Russia, DFID stated that within the Ministerstvo Vnutrennikh Del (MVD; Russian Federation Ministry of Internal Affairs) 'there is a recognition that to be effective the police need to improve their working relations with other national and local government departments and civil society' (DFID 2002). The notion that a militarised and centralised police accountable only to the ruling party would willingly give up power is fanciful to say the least (Brogden and Nijhar 2005, pp. 193–196).

Clarity is further obscured by the tendency to conflate effectiveness with Western policing fashions. Hence DFID's statement that 'an effective and accountable community based police service that enjoys the confidence of the Russian people is a fundamental element in securing a safe and secure environment where sustainable economic and social development can take place' (DFID 2002). Similarly, in a submission to the International Development Committee, the NGO Saferworld (2004) insisted that 'Effective policing arrangements delivered by the adoption of Community based Policing is critical to achieving a safe and secure Kenya and wider region'.

In practice, effective policing is always defined as policing that achieves the political, technical, ideological or normative goals of the actor concerned, and it is difficult to get beyond the case studies, project assessments or anecdotal accounts to first principles. Even so, the debate about balancing police effectiveness with democratic-style norms and procedures is as longstanding amongst scholars (Ziegler and Neild 2001, Call 2003, Ellison 2007, p. 232) as donors neglect it.

Call's (2003, p. 2) analysis is therefore particularly useful because he identifies a range of reformist approaches offering insight into the meaning of effectiveness. Thus policing assessed from a human-rights perspective focusses on the extent to which internationally recognised rights are protected, while that from peacekeeping organisations emphasises limiting the role of foreign militaries, incorporating formerly excluded groups into a police, and conflict prevention more generally. Significantly, such approaches focus attention on the interests and experiences of international actors, rather than on the performance, effectiveness and conduct of, and popular support for, indigenous police organisations. Meanwhile, the law-enforcement perspective emphasises the need to strengthen local capacities to manage local and regional crime. This may or may not include broader democratic goals such as adherence to human rights legislation, but there is a commonality based on shared experience. This perspective also incorporates the views of officials from powerful organisations such as the US Federal Bureau of Investigation (FBI) and Drug Enforcement Administration (DEA), which define success in terms of national forces acting as proxies for US interests. Lastly, Call distinguishes a perspective that judges policing primarily in relation to its ability to facilitate economic development or democratisation. This has been especially powerful because it underpins the reform programmes implemented after many conflicts. It is also characterised by tension because the goal of international police reform usually includes both tactical effectiveness (as in combating crime) and accountability in terms of human rights.

Role of Force

Given the subjective nature of effectiveness, and the coercive nature of policing, the identification of acceptable levels of force was always likely to be problematic. Views polarise as commentators such as Fyfe argue that that a reduction in police violence does not lead to lower arrest rates and more crime (Chevigny 1995, p. 55), whereas anecdotal evidence suggests that many police believe human rights legislation prevents effective policing. Some police resolve the tension by prioritising results or organisational effectiveness at the expense of principles such as human rights (Herzog 2000, p. 434). Whatever the case, and despite the intense controversy surrounding the US-led war on terror, and the work of the 'Police Use of Force' research group (e.g., Policing: A Journal of Policy and Practice 2007; PUOF 2008), systematic comparative analysis is neglected.

This may be because the realities of police work have changed little since Westley and Bittner wrote. Officers are still expected to manage situations, rather than persons (Bittner 1967, p. 699), and to enforce order rather than the law, and physical force often achieves the required results (Bittner 1990). At the same time, however, liberal attitudes have changed. The sanctioned use of force arguably remains the defining characteristic of policing (Bittner 1970), but employing the minimal levels of force situationally justified is now held to be a mark of well-trained ('professional') police. The use in liberal democracies of non-lethal weapons such as Tasers (electroshock guns that stun with a 50,000-volt charge) is one manifestation of this trend. Yet liberal ideology is not in itself sufficient to act as an indicator of appropriately effective levels of force. The post-2001 controversy about interrogation methods involving American agents is evidence of this.

Given the significance of force in ensuring effective policing, how, then, should the use of force be analysed? Westley (1953, p. 34) argued that violence is a consequence of occupational experience and group sanction, whereas Alpert and Dunham (2004, p. 41) emphasise the explanatory value of a deference-exchange theory whereby the use of force is influenced by a suspect's demeanour. In contrast, Manning (1997, p. 156) argues that violence tends to result from a combination of social processes and cultural behaviours that create patterned actions and structures conducive to violence. Cancino's (2001, p. 157) research furthers this interpretation by arguing that the use of violence is 'situationally determined by informal values and norms ..., not formal training or departmental regulations that supposedly structure and define its use'.

Most commentators accept that, while organisational factors are probably the main external influence on the use of excessive force, they cannot provide a complete explanation (Uildriks and van Mastrigt 1991, Skolnik and Fyfe 1993, Klockars 1996, Jacobs and O'Brien 1998, Herzog 2000, Weisburd *et al.* 2000). After all, most police adopt hierarchical structures. Organisational structures (such as degree of centralisation) have no direct relation to policing styles, and the existence of police complaints commissions is no guarantee of accountability. Context matters, too. For example, Alpert and Macdonald argue that the relationship between agency characteristics and police behaviour offers a key to understanding the use of force, with the agency's properties operationalised to include structural and administrative means for dealing with the use of force, such as use of data and the existence of police unions (Alpert and Mitchell 2001, p. 397). But data and unions play little or no part in Southern policing.

Compare Herzog's study of deviant Israeli officers, which suggests that while personal pathology goes someway to explaining recourse to violence, 'for this potential to become manifest, interaction with external factors (situational, organisational, or environmental) has to take place' (Worden 1996, Herzog 2000, p. 416). Police violence is, according to Herzog, best understood as 'a group behavior and a developmental process ... directed by a variety of formal and informal occupational norms', both of the force in general and of the individual's work group. New officers undergo a complex process of organisational socialisation as they learn the behaviour and attitudes necessary for organisational membership (Herzog 2000, p. 417). Yet, Herzog's research may be equally misleading in that in much of the world the use of force is normal, rather than deviant.

Contrast the perspective offered by the PUOF group, which argues that intent is key:

> distinctions between force and violence is not material (based on their consequences), but moral (based on the purposes for which they are used). Force is physical intervention for justified reasons, such as the need to defend someone's life or to bring a law violator to justice. Violence is physical intervention without justification. Thus, when physical intervention by the police is unjustified, police use of force has been transformed into police violence. (PUOF 2008)

But this in turn fails to address the issue of justification, which is likely to depend on the training, resources and expectations of the police concerned.

It appears, then, that while the main external factors affecting police attitudes to violence are organisational and social, police attitudes to force are affected by situational variables. Indeed, I would go further and suggest that the analytical key to the role of force in both transnational and sub-state policing is to be found in behaviour that is perceived as 'normal' by the society concerned, with normal force being coercive behaviour that is regarded as 'necessary, appropriate, reasonable, or understandable' (Hunt quoted in Cancino 2001, p. 147). This helps to explain differences between police, and also why ineffective policing in the face of violent crime often leads to politicians and civil leaders calling for tougher policing. In Kenya in 2005, levels of violent crime were so high that an MP insisted that the police should be allowed to shoot to kill criminals (East African Standard 2005).

Two further points are noteworthy. First, cultural differences influence the use of force in everyday policing. Alpert and Dunham (2004, p. 39) may say that the use of force by US officers in 'police–citizen conflicts' is 'an infrequent event', but, as HRW and CHRI know, brutality is routine elsewhere. Similarly, Alpert and Dunham's (2004, p. 39) survey suggests that in the US violence is most frequently inflicted on those groups that are most unlike the dominant middle class, but this is not the case in, say, Zimbabwe.

Second, context is critical. No matter how harsh life in Ohio is, it does not compare to that in, say, Nigeria, where police violence is merely one manifestation of a wider acceptance of violence. This ranges from police beating motorists who fail to pay at road blocks to the systematic use of police by governments to crush political opposition. Indeed, there may be a close connection between armed violence by police and political competition, especially in countries like Nigeria where great value is 'attached to the utility of violence in politics, with political and electoral success often indexed to the capacity to threaten or unleash violence' (Ginnifer and Ismail 2005, p. 8). It is difficult to conceive of a transnational ethic capable of integrating such a range of practices and norms.

UN Policing

Integration is a major operational challenge for UNPOL in particular. Indeed, UN operations present the notion of a transnational policecraft with a real test: if it does not work in the artificial context of UNPOL then it is unlikely to work elsewhere.

Almost every problem associated with the rationale, recruitment, deployment and management of multinational police is evident in a UN context. UNPOL operations reflect changing expectations of transnational policing, the limits on what it can achieve, and the dominance of pragmatic and technical imperatives over ideology. The circumstances in which they are conducted represent a laboratory in which to investigate the obstacles in the way of crafting a common policecraft – and also the reasons why it should be promoted. They offer a discrete opportunity to assess the influence of sub-state policing standards on international operations.

If transnational policing means anything, it will surely be evident in UN operations. The need for agreed standards is evident from the number and variety of police involved, and the demands made on UNPOL's services in response to Security Council mandates and calls from regional organisations: UNPOL numbers increased from 2% of peacekeeping forces in 1995 to 12% in 2007, by which time 8000 officers were in the field. In the last six months of 2006 alone, new operations took place in Nepal, Chad, the Central African Republic and Somalia, and the Security Council authorised the deployment of more than 15,000 UNPOL officers.

Until recently, UNPOL's role was administering what were seen as the prerequisites of order: officers were restricted to monitoring, advising and training indigenous police on technical matters such as records management and public order. Such activities formed a relatively neutral basis on which consensus could be built. Public order units from Bangladesh, Jordan and Pakistan formed part of UNCIVPOL in Haiti, while gendarmerie units from Argentina, France, Italy and Spain operated in the Balkans, and the use of force was publicly debated only when officers stood by as crowds attacked former regime representatives. The utility of such policing was evident from UNPOL's expanded remit, which reached a peak in Kosovo and East Timor when officers were given executive authority to enforce the law. But Kosovo and East Timor were small territories with small populations, a majority of whom welcomed international intervention. Significantly, UNPOL's role in Afghanistan and Iraq – where violence and torture are policing realities – is negligible.

UNPOL encourages the perception that it provides a public good on behalf of the international community. Its strategic mission is developing institutional police capacity in post-conflict environments, and its role is supporting the reform, restructuring and rebuilding of local police. The mandates of 11 of the 12 missions authorised since 1999 refer to monitoring, reforming and rebuilding local police, all of which the UN understands in

terms of democratic-style policing, which it presents as international policing. But this does not represent the equivalent of a transnational policecraft.
UNPOL's contribution is uneven and temporary by virtue of its nature: UNPOL
are the equivalent of temporary, miscellaneous, civilian (though increasingly
paramilitary in nature) and comparatively cheap fire-fighters, most of who
are unfamiliar with liberal-style policing. The major contributing countries
in April 2007 were Jordan, Bangladesh and Pakistan, whose domestic police
routinely employ high levels of force; countries employing a civilian police
that adheres to notions of minimal force, such as Canada, Germany and
Norway, are a minority. Cultural assessments of the application of force vary
enormously, and the blanket categorisation by the then UNPOL adviser of 'all
UN police officers, no matter where they come from (playing) a vital role in
assisting the UN to build institutional police capacity' is, given the explicitly
liberal objectives of UN peacebuilding, misleading (Smith *et al.* 2007, p. 26).

The two most pressing challenges confronting UNPOL throughout the
1990s and for the foreseeable future – the recruitment and training of officers, and their performance – make this explicit. Additionally, both are linked
to effectiveness, and to the place of force within it. The role of paramilitary-
style formed police units (FPUs) make this explicit.

Personnel contributions are usually based on time-sensitive political decisions, but police are in demand at home, and (unlike the military) are normally unavailable for deployment abroad. Nonetheless, UNPOL needs some
form of specialist rapid response capacity. Various solutions have been proposed, with the use of FPUs of 120–140 armed officers trained in skills such
as crowd control and close protection being especially popular. Heavily influenced by the paramilitary models of countries such as Argentina, France and
Italy, FPUs were originally authorised for UN operations in 1999 in Kosovo,
where they were known as specialised police units. They became a regular
feature of UN missions from Liberia in 2003 onwards, and, by mid 2007,
35 FPUs (approximately 4000 strong) were deployed in Côte d'Ivoire, DRC,
Haiti, Kosovo, Liberia and Timor Leste.

FPUs make sense: they work. They are used for crowd control when local
police are unprepared, unwilling or overwhelmed, and they have propaganda value; they can make it seem that local police can cope, just as they
can make it seem that transnational policing has utility. Indeed, 'it is intended
that FPUs will be a "role model" to the local police' (DPKO 2006). FPUs have
logistical value, too, because they expand the number of countries providing
police, and establish the equivalent of a standing cadre of experts for rapid
deployment in insecure conditions; they represent a module that facilitates
planning and deployment. Also, they are cheaper than military or individual
officers, and their cost-effectiveness makes them an attractive option for the
Security Council; it costs around $5 million to set up an FPU, whereas a regu-
lar military unit can cost up $30 million (*UN Police Magazine* 2006, p. 4). And
the 2007 contribution of an all-female Indian FPU to Liberia (albeit one with

a reputation for repressive counter-insurgency operations in northern India) allowed UNPOL to conform to the UN's political proprieties, for Resolution 1325 calls for the equal and full participation of women in peace operations. But whether FPUs can provide the basis for a transnational policecraft is more questionable.

UNPOL's inability to provide an unequivocally transnational form of police craft is evident from the way in which it must rely on robust par-amilitary skills even as its advisers emphasise the importance of civilian policing. The UK's FCO argues that FPUs reinforce the distinction between police and military, but this is disingenuous: FPUs have functional utility, but they are paramilitary and their composition and operations blur police/military boundaries. Meanwhile, senior UNPOL officers stress their differences from military peacekeepers. According to the current (Australian) UNPOL adviser, Andrew Hughes, the use of (legitimate) lethal force is a military task, whereas police apprehend criminals, escort children to schools and calm rioting mobs: 'For us the use of force is absolutely the last option ... Our police are trained much more extensively to defuse the situation, and negotiations are by far and away the biggest tool we have' (IHT 2007).

More generally, UNPOL's promotion of transnational standards is undermined by the behaviour of many of its officers. Not only is criminal misconduct problematic in most operations (some national contingents are notorious for corruption and sexual predation), but also most UNPOL have little knowledge of the democratic norms and procedures on which transnational policing is to be based. Poor quality applicants, high turnover and rotation rates exacerbate the problem. It could not be otherwise, for although applicants now undergo a two-week pre-deployment training course, the top contributing countries in August 2007 included Bangladesh, Benin, Cameroon, China, France, Ghana, India, Jordan, Malaysia, Nepal, Nigeria, Pakistan, Philippines, Portugal, Romania, Senegal, Ukraine and the USA. Inevitably, some UNPOL have less professional experience and competence than the police they are advising. Officials may refer to 'international' policing standards but national perspectives ensure that the parameters of policing, its transitional points, and rules of engagement differ according to national experience and special interests. When confronted with food riots, one contingent may prefer to use firearms whereas another may favour non-lethal weapons (e.g., rubber bullets) or physical force (e.g., pushing crowds apart).

In order to understand the interface between national and international practices we need to know more about what police do when they co-operate, why they do it and how their actions reflect or influence sub-state practices.

Norway, Nigeria and Peacekeeping

Peacekeeping provides a good test of the possibility of developing a transnational policecraft because it require forces with markedly styles practices to co-operate, or, more commonly, to establish some form of working relationship. Anecdotal evidence suggests that the often strained relationship between Australian Federal Police, Portuguese Guarda Nacional Republicana and Malaysian officers in Timor Leste illustrate the multiple operational and procedural difficulties involved.[4] These ranged from differences over the use of force to time keeping and attitudes to Australian female officers. The more straightforward example of Norwegian training assistance to Nigerian police en route for Darfur is used here on the basis that it is less controversial yet indicative of the relevant issues.

In October 2007, the Nigerian government requested that Norway assist in training 250 Nigerian police for UN deployment.[5] The first batch of 70 completed a course directed by five senior Norwegian officers (and one Batswana) at the Nigeria Police Staff College, Jos, in February 2008. In addition to including an overview of the UN's history, organisation and legal framework, the course introduced the elements underpinning policing in an international context. These included human rights law versus host nation law, standard operational procedures, cultural awareness, humanitarian assistance, negotiation and mediation, ethics, the UN's policing standards and code of conduct, and the consequences of their violation (National Daily 2008, Nigerian Tribune 2008).

Whether such elements represent the foundations for transnational policing is debatable. Nigerian police evidently appreciate Norwegian assistance, aspire to the international status it promotes, and are aware of the occupational commonalities UNPOL share. Yet appreciation does not necessarily represent commitment to a transnational ethic: governments value UN operations for the public-relations opportunities they offer, while officers like them because of the allowances they provide. In fact, peacekeeping operations are, like transnational policing itself, an inherently artificial exercise divorced from the realities of everyday domestic policing. This may not be a significant factor for Norwegian police, whose standards are relatively consistent across a range of environments, but it is for Nigerians whose international and domestic practices diverge. The different understandings of effective policing are evident when contextual issues affecting domestic policing and the use of force are taken into account.

Norway

In Norway, effective policing is that which manages the country's rich, ethnically homogenous, and politically and socially consensual society with minimal disruption. The police play a generalist role in which crime prevention and social welfare concerns feature strongly, and surveys over the last 20 years suggest that public confidence in the police is strong, with around 85% of respondents reporting confidence in the police (UNODC 2000, Burke and Mikkelsen 2005, Larsson 2006).

It is, perhaps, too easy to present an idealised version of Norwegian policing. Force is most commonly used against young males (often drunk or drugged) resisting arrest and is typically divided into two categories. The first is where 'legal' use of physical force (e.g., handcuffing) occurs during arrest in an excessive or unnecessary fashion. The second includes beating or kicking (Larsson 2005). But it seldom goes beyond this. The Norwegian Organisation for Asylum Seekers has in recent years accused Oslo's police immigration unit of systematic harassment of asylum seekers, but this cannot be compared to the policing that the Iraqis or Pakistanis concerned have fled from.

Consensus, co-operation and a preference for using minimal force shape Norway's attitude to many regional issues, too. This usually works because Nordic police share a history and worldview regardless of their markedly different attitude towards the meaning of real police work (i.e., catching criminals), the categorisation of crime (Larsson 2005, pp. 461, 462), and the carrying of guns (Norwegian officers are unarmed whereas Swedish and Danish police carry guns). The extent to which this approach influences international operations is debatable, but some 800 Norwegian police have contributed to UN operations since 1989.

Nigeria

The situation in Nigeria is very different. Like Norway, Nigeria is proud of its peacekeeping tradition and is familiar with the international standards UNPOL advocates. In addition to Norwegian support, Nigeria receives technical aid from France, which donated a language laboratory to the peacekeeping centre at Abuja's police headquarters, and support for capacity building from the Canadian Government through the Pearson Peacekeeping Centre. But UN-style standards have yet to influence domestic policing.

The gulf between Nigeria's international and everyday policing styles is best measured in terms of the number of people killed by officers. In 2007, official statistics indicated that police had shot and killed more than 8000 Nigerians over the preceding five years. Indeed, as HRW notes, the true number of people killed probably exceeded 10,000, given that the police killed half as many armed robbers as they arrested during the first three months of the then inspector general's tenure alone (casualties are usually described as armed robbers). The dependent variable used by Alpert and Macdonald (2001, p. 400) may be the rate of force reported by police for a specific year, but this has little relevance in Nigeria. Not only is bureaucratic capacity low, but also there is no incentive for police to report incidents. Further, senior officials seem to regard the number of killings as a point of pride (HRW 2007). In the words of the UN special rapporteur on torture, torture and extrajudicial killings by police appear to be 'an intrinsic part of how law enforcement services operate' (HRW 2007).

Armed robbers kill dozens of badly trained and poorly paid Nigerian officers every year, and abuse is sometimes a response to this. Other cases result from public and political pressure on the police to address Nigeria's high levels of violent crime. Hence the language used by officials who told HRW that between January 2000 and March 2004, police killed 7198 'armed robbers' in 'combat' (HRW 2007). Some officers extract confessions through torture, or kill suspects in their custody who they believe to be guilty precisely because they lack the skills or resources to carry out effective investigation. Suspects held in the custody of agencies such as the Economic and Financial Crimes Commission (EFCC) receive similar treatment (HRW 2007, p. 3).

Official investigations into the disproportionate use of force are rare. People were surprised when in 2005 the then inspector general publicly investigated the arbitrary execution of six innocent market traders (the 'Apo Six') in Abuja, not least because the police concerned had been openly abusive for several years. But the murders were far from atypical even if the manner of their resolution was not. More common was a case in August 2006, when the bodies of 12 men (previously paraded by the police as armed robbers) were found in the town of Umuahia. No investigation was carried out.

An extreme version of this approach to effective policing is documented in HRW's (2005) report 'Rest in Pieces', which describes torture routinely inflicted by, and with the knowledge of, mid- to senior-level officers. The majority of victims were young males from low socio-economic backgrounds who were arrested for crimes ranging from petty theft to armed robbery. Police also arrested, detained and tortured the friends or relatives of suspects they were unable to find. This was seen as an effective way to bring the suspect forward, though it was also used for extortion. But extortion is usual, as is payment for bail or release without charge. After years of military rule, the use of violence by police and other state institutions is accepted with resignation[6]; few complaints are registered (compare Thomassen 2002).

Peacekeeping Operations

What, then, happens when officers from such a system receive a brief training in international standards by Scandinavian officers, which they are expected to implement in a violent environment. Do Nigerian officers take the UN's formal standards seriously? Or do they sympathise with the situation indigenous police find themselves in? In Darfur, the Janjaweed militia responsible for much of the government sanctioned displacement and killings have been incorporated into the Darfur police who are themselves responsible for torture, extortion and sexual violence.

Systematic hard evidence is not available. However, anecdotal evidence from previous operations suggests that some educated mid-ranking young officers do take UN standards seriously,[7] and Nigeria's record in Liberia and the DRC since 2003 is suggestive of its general approach; 163 Nigerian police and prison officers served in Liberia, 2003–2006, as part of 1100 UNPOL officers from more than 38 states. Nigerian military on checkpoint duty in Liberia were considered arrogant, but when there was fighting to be done they were usually the ones who did it, even if they were not too fussy about the finer points of their mandate, and some UN officials thought the same of Nigeria's police. But this approach was arguably appropriate, for many Liberians thought that the UN was the only organisation in the country capable of providing security (Mehler and Smith-Höhn 2007, p. 54). The peace agreement of 2003 left Liberians feeling vulnerable to street boys, ex-fighters, political militias, secret societies and machete gangs, while the ineffectual Liberian police (who were disarmed for three years after the 2003 agreement) were dependent on UN forces.

In practice, corruption was – and is – more problematic for the UN than the use of force. Publicly, UNPOL ideals guided Nigerian behaviour: in 2006, UNMIL police commissioner Mohammed Alhassan said that the Nigerian contingent served in Liberia with 'dignity and professionalism ... courage, tolerance, understanding and respect for others' (UNMIL 2006). But complicity and sexual exploitation were common. To its credit, Nigeria withdrew its 120-strong police contingent from Kinshasa in September 2005 after the UN launched an investigation into sexual harassment by 10 members of the unit. This had nothing to do with effective policing as such, but it was indicative of the contingent's general approach: the operation had been plagued by allegations of sexual abuse, with peacekeepers being accused of rape and giving food or money in exchange for sex.

In the event, the unit was withdrawn on the basis that its actions contaminated all Nigerians. A spokesman said: 'We have contingents in about 19 countries right now and we want to send a message to all other contingents that if one finger collects oil, the whole hand is stained'. But corruption probably went right to the top. Some senior Nigerian military officers were accused of dubious business dealings with Liberian leaders, and this was presumably true of police too (BBC 2003). Also, it was alleged that senior officers (including the inspector general) extracted the UN duty allowances of officers and men in Liberia (Daily Trust 2007).

Some officers undoubtedly value their exposure to UN norms and procedures. But it is not clear what this amounts to; no follow-up studies are known. Given the state of policing in Nigeria, it seems reasonable to conclude that adaptation to UN standards is an essentially temporary response to financially attractive opportunities. UNPOL operations are an artificial construct, and the norms and behaviour encouraged or tolerated during them bear little resemblance to those shaping routine policing in Nigeria. UN operations do not provide evidence of a transnational constabulary ethic.

Conclusion

Despite Nigeria's uneven record, a degree of occupational commonality exists within the artificial environment of UN operations, just as it exist outside, too; organisations such as UNPOL (and Interpol) could not otherwise function. However, understanding is built on functional issues and technical jargon, rather than the norms emphasised by Sheptycki. Further, the accommodation and networking that undoubtedly exists between officers is not synonymous with a transnational ethic. If anything, it suggests that personal relations and networks are important precisely because of the strength of cultural differences between police (compare Larsson 2006).

Occupational commonalities and differences are particularly evident when it comes to working definitions of effective policing and the levels of force required to achieve it, for this is determined not by international pressure but by the role force plays in an officer's home environment. Contra Alpert and Dunham, violence is not rare, and training will not ensure that officers respond effectively using minimal violence. Force is assessed in a culturally specific manner, and the prospects for developing a liberal-style transnational policecraft are low.

This is mainly because transnational policing seeks to promote a specific philosophy and normative approach as much as techniques and procedures, and the transfer of its preferred models is overlaid with political assumptions about the right 'professional' trajectory. The goal is restructuring and rebuilding indigenous police 'to an acceptable level of democratic policing' (UN Police Division 2007, p. xi), and the perspective of its advocates is that of the European centre-left. Policing is a means to promote conflict resolution, and to facilitate or manage a new order consistent with liberal principles. Indeed, its objectives appear to include strengthening or facilitating a rights-based universalising order, which requires the modification or replacement of existing forms of social order. Functional effectiveness is therefore judged according to its alignment with Western notions of good policing.

On the other hand, liberal consensus is often outweighed by disagreement on what constitutes effective policing. For policing is always understood from national perspectives and officers regard the practices and norms of their home force as appropriate. It could not be otherwise when British, Iranian, South African and North Korean police trained the Uganda police (New Vision 2007), Chinese riot police joined a Brazilian-led UN force in Haiti's capital, Port-au-Prince, and Indonesian police were committed to Darfur.

In practice, global interdependence (and the less controversial process of internationalisation) encourages Western academics and organisations such as UNPOL to assume that liberal structures and standards apply whereas they may not. Police in developing regions may reflect rationalities and causalities that are different to those of Europe or North America, and their definitions of effective policing may be disconnected from individual morality and the shortcomings of state institutions. Also, transnational policing has potential disadvantages. Democratic policing models may, for example, contribute to ineffectual policing by imposing inappropriate or unsustainable schemes. They may even constitute 'a new form of exploitative, entrepreneurial neo-colonialism' (Murphy 2005, p. 143), structuring change in ways that are favourable to the geostrategic interests of key Western states. This may benefit senior Southern officers sent on training courses in France, the UK and USA, but it rarely improves the lot of ordinary officers, and its influence on domestic policing is at best superficial.

This suggests that current modes of transnational policing are not primarily intended as a means for ensuring effective policing. Neither are they concerned with creating police capable of dealing with organised crime, trafficking or armed robbery *per se*. Enhancing accountability and responsiveness may, of course, ensure that the police concerned gain public support, and therefore do not need to rely on force, but transnational policing, like reform projects more generally, ignores the nature and purpose of police institutions in the South, downplays the underlying causes of insecurity (Fayemi 2001), and assumes that international agents can manipulate political and social forces (Luckham 2003). For such reasons, developing a transnational policecraft presents significant intellectual and empirical challenges.

Notes

1. This is separate from traditional English constabularies and the gendarmerie-style constabularies advocated by Perito (2004).
2. Similar reservations apply to Shetpycki's argument that a constabulary ethic might be possible 'if predicated on a Neo-Kantian, existentialist ethic of the individual' (Goldsmith and Sheptycki 2007, p. 21). The value attached to the individual by different societies varies.
3. Available through www.ohchr.org
4. Compare Goldsmith (2008).
5. This section is based on private conversations with Nigerian and Norwegian officers in Abuja and New York, January and May 2008. See also TfP (2008).
6. Compare Shari'a law, which, as applied in northern Nigeria, allows the death penalty, amputations and floggings.
7. Comment based on private conversations with mid-ranking Nigerian officers in Nigeria and the UK, 2007–2008.

References

Alpert, G. and Dunham, R., 2004. *Understanding police use of force: officers, suspects, and reciprocity*. Cambridge: Cambridge University Press.

Alpert, G. and MacDonald, J., 2001. Police use of force: an analysis of organizational characteristics. *Justice Quarterly*, 18, 393–409.

Anderson, M., *et al.*, 1995. *Policing the European Union*. Oxford: Oxford University Press.

Andreas, P. and Nadelmann, E., 2006. *Policing the globe: criminalization and crime control in international relations*. Oxford: Oxford University Press.

BBC, 2003. *The perils of Liberian peacekeeping*. 4 August. Available from: http://news.bbc.co.uk/1/hi/world/africa/3113009.stm [Accessed November 2008].

BBC, 2007. *Terror police 'shot' man in coma*. 15 November. Available from: http://news.bbc.co.uk/1/hi/england/west_yorkshire/7096456.stm [Accessed November 2008].

Bittner, E., 1967. The police on skid-row: a study of peace keeping. *American Sociological Review*, 32 (5), 699–715.

Bittner, E., 1970. *The functions of police in modern society.* Rockville, MD: NIMH.

Bittner, E., 1990. The police on skid row. *In:* E. Bittner, ed. *Aspects of police work.* Boston, MA: Northeastern University Press.

Brogden, M. and Nijhar, P., 2005. *Community policing: national and international models and approaches.* Cullhompton: Willan.

Burke, R. and Mikkelsen, A., 2005. Burnout, job stress and attitudes towards the use of force by Norwegian police officers. *Policing: An International Journal of Police Strategies and Management,* 28 (2), 269–278.

Call, C., 2003. *Challenges in police reform: promoting effectiveness and accountability.* New York: International Peace Academy.

Cancino, J., 2001. Walking among giants 50 years later: an exploratory analysis of patrol officer use of violence. *Policing: An International Journal of Police Strategies & Management,* 24 (2), 144–161.

Chan, J., 2007. Police stress and occupational culture. *In:* M. O'Neill, M. Marks, and A-M. Singh, eds. *Police occupational culture: new debates and directions.* Oxford: Elsevier.

Chevigny, P., 1995. *Edge of the knife: police violence in the Americas.* New York: New Press.

Daily Trust, 2007. Corruption and the police. *Daily Trust,* 27 June. Available from: http://allafrica.com/stories/200706270723.html [Accessed June 2007].

DFID, 2002. *Russia: safety, security and access to justice. The development of police and community partnerships – community policing.* Available from: http://dfidweb.dfid.gov.uk/prismdocs/EMAD/292543132p1.doc [Accessed May 2008].

Donnelly, J., 2007. The relative universality of human rights. *Human Rights Quarterly,* 29 (2), 281–306.

DPKO Policy, 2006. *Functions and organization of formed police units in United Nations peacekeeping operations.* New York: UNPD.

Dubber, M. and Valverde, M., eds., 2006. *The new police science: the police power in domestic and international governance.* Stanford, CA: Stanford University Press.

Duffield, M., 2001. *Global governance and the new wars: the merging of development and security.* London: Zed.

East African Standard, 2005. Crime by the numbers. *East African Standard,* 10 April. Available from: http://allafrica.com/stories/200504110177.html [Accessed April 2007].

Ellison, G., 2007. Fostering a dependency culture: the commodification of community policing in a global marketplace. *In:* A. Goldsmith, and J. Sheptycki, eds. *Crafting transnational policing police capacity building and global policing reform.* Oxford: Hart, 203–242.

Fayemi, K., 2001. *Comments on the human security aspect of the poverty reduction guidelines.* Lagos: Centre for Democracy and Development.

Ginnifer, J. and Ismail, O., 2005. *Armed violence and poverty in Nigeria: mini case study for the armed violence and poverty initiative.* Bradford: Centre for International Cooperation and Security, University of Bradford.

Goldsmith, A., 2008. 'It wasn't like normal policing': voices of Australian police peacekeepers in Operation Serene, Timor-Leste 2006. *Policing and Society,* 18 (4), 1–14.

Goldsmith, A. and Dineen, S., 2007. Transnational police building: critical lessons from Timor-Leste and Solomon Islands. *Third World Quarterly,* 28 (6), 1091–1109.

Goldsmith, A. and Sheptycki, J., eds., 2007. *Crafting transnational policing police capacity-building and global policing reform.* Oxford: Hart.

Herzog, S., 2000. Deviant organizational messages among suspect police officers in Israel. *Policing: An International Journal of Policing Strategies and Management,* 23 (4), 416–438.

Human Rights Watch (HRW), 2005. *'Rest in pieces': police torture and deaths in custody in Nigeria.* New York: HRW.

Human Rights Watch (HRW), 2007. *Nigeria: investigate widespread killings by police. Police chief boasts of 785 killings in 90 days.* 18 November. Available from: http://hrw.org/english/docs/2007/11/16/nigeri17361.htm. [Accessed November 2007].

International Herald Tribune (IHT), 2007. Historically eclipsed by blue helmets, UN police force prepares for major expansion. *International Herald Tribune*, 31 October. Available from: http://www.iht.com/articles/ap/2007/11/01/news/UN-FEA-GEN-UN-Police.php?WT.mc_id=rssap_news [Accessed November 2007].

Jacobs, D. and O'Brien, R., 1998. The determinants of deadly force: a structural analysis of police violence. *American Journal of Sociology*, 103 (4), 837–862.

Klockars, C., 1985. The dirty Harry problem. *In:* F. Elliston and M. Feldberg, eds. *Moral issues in police work*. New York: Rowman & Allenheld, 55–71.

Klockars, C., 1996. A theory of excessive force and its control. *In:* W. Geller and H. Toch, eds. *Police violence: understanding and controlling police abuse of force*. New Haven, CT: Yale University Press, 23–51.

Larsson, P., 2006. International police co-operation: a Norwegian perspective. *Journal of Financial Crime*, 13 (4), 456–466.

Luckham, R., 2003. Democratic strategies for security. *In:* G. Cawthra and R. Luckham, eds. *Governing insecurity: democratic control of military and security establishments in transitional democracies*. London: Zed, 3–28.

Luethold, A., 2004. *Security sector reform in the Arab Middle East: a nascent debate*. Geneva: DCAF.

Manning, 1997. *Police work: the social organization of policing*. 2nd ed. Prospect Heights, IL: Waveland Press.

Mehler, A. and Smith-Höhn, J., 2007. Security actors in Liberia and Sierra Léone: roles, interactions and perceptions. *In:* T. Debiel and D. Lambach, eds. *State failure revisited II: actors of violence and alternative forms of governance*. Duisberg: Institute for Development and Peace, University of Duisburg-Essen, 50–66. Available from: http://inef.uni-due.de/page/documents/Report89.pdf [Accessed December 2007].

MPA, 2008. *Home page*. Available from: http://www.mpa.gov.uk/default.htm [Accessed July 2008].

Murphy, C., 2005. Police studies go global: in Eastern Kentucky? *Police Quarterly*, 8, 137–145.

National Daily, 2008. Norwegian police varsity trains Nigerian officers. *National Daily*, February. Available from: http://www.nationaldailyngr.com/1law11.htm [Accessed March 2008].

New Vision, 2007. Uganda: Iranian police to train Ugandans. *New Vision*, 28 September. Available from: http://allafrica.com/stories/200709290018.html [Accessed November 2007].

Nigerian Tribune, 2008. Nigeria police excel in UN operations. *Nigerian Tribune*, 8 February. Available from: http://www.tribune.com.ng/08022008/news/news20.html [Accessed February 2008].

Occhipinti, J., 2003. *The politics of EU police cooperation: toward a European FBI*. Boulder, CO: Lynne Rienner.

OECD, 2007. *OECD DAC handbook on security sector reform (SSR): supporting security and justice*. Paris: OECD.

Perito, R., 2004. *Where is the lone ranger when we need him? America's search for a post conflict stability force*. Washington, DC: USIP.

Policing: A Journal of Policy and Practice, 2007. Use of force. *Policing: A Journal of Policy and Practice*, 1 (3), Special issue.

PUOF, 2008. *A joint transnational research on justification of use of force by police*. Available from: http://www.policeuseofforce.org/members_new.htm [Accessed June 2008].

Saferworld, 2004. *Submission to International Development Committee*. Available from: http://www.saferworld.org.uk/images/pubdocs/DfID%20CAP%20-%20UK%20SCID%20submission%20-%20Feb%2004.doc [Accessed March 2008].

Sayigh, Y., 2007. *Security sector reform in the Arab region: challenges to developing an indigenous agenda*. Amman: Arab Reform Initiative.

Sheptycki, J., ed., 2000. *Issues in transnational policing.* London: Routledge.

Sheptycki, J., 2002. *In search of transnational policing: towards a sociology of transnational policing.* Aldershot: Ashgate.

Sheptycki, J., 2007. The constabulary ethic and the transnational condition. *In:* A. Goldsmith and J. Sheptycki, eds. *Crafting transnational policing police capacity building and global policing reform.* Oxford: Hart, 31–72.

Skolnik, J. and Fyfe, J., 1993. *Above the law: police and the excessive use of force.* New York: Free Press.

Smith, J., Holt, V., and Durch, W., 2007. *Enhancing United Nations capacity for post-conflict police operations.* Washington, DC: Stimson Center.

TfP, 2008. Available from: http://www.trainingforpeace.org [Accessed March 2008].

Thomassen G., 2002. Investigating complaints against the police in Norway: an empirical evaluation. *Policing and Society,* 12 (3), 201–210.

Uildriks, N. and van Mastrigt, H., 1991. *Policing police violence.* Deventer: Kluwer.

UNMIL, 2006. *UNMIL's Nigerian police contingent decorated with UN peacekeeping medals.* 16 February 2006. Available from: www.un.org/Depts/dpko/missions/unmil/pr21.pdf [Accessed December 2008].

UNODC, 2000. *Seventh United Nations survey of crime trends and operations of criminal justice systems, covering the period 1998–2000.* Vienna: United Nations Office on Drugs and Crime, Centre for International Crime Prevention.

UN Police Division, 2007. *Portfolio of police and law enforcement projects 2007.* New York: UN DPKO.

UN Police Magazine, 2006. India pledges to send 125 female police officers for UN peacekeeping. *UN Police Magazine,* 4 December.

Weisburd, D., *et al.,* 2000. *Police attitudes toward abuse of authority: findings from a national study.* National Institute of Justice. Available from: http://www.ncjrs.gov/txtfiles1/nij/181312.txt [Accessed November 2008].

Westley, W., 1953. Violence and the police. *American Journal of Sociology,* 59 (1), 34–41.

Worden, R., 1996. The 'causes' of police brutality: theory and evidence on police use of force. *In:* W. Geller and H. Toch, eds. *Police violence: understanding and controlling police abuse of force.* New Haven, CT: Yale University Press, 31–60.

Ziegler, M. and Neild, R., 2001. *From peace to governance: police reform and the international community.* Conference report. Available from: http://www.gsdrc.org/go/display/document/legacyid/648 [Accessed March 2009].

The Future of Global Policing

13

Past, Present, and Future Trajectories

Peter Andreas and Ethan Nadelmann

While terrorists, drug traffickers, migrant smugglers, money launderers and other transnational law evaders provoke enormous attention and concern, far less noticed and even less understood is the growing global reach of law enforcers. In this book, we have examined the historical expansion and more recent dramatic acceleration and intensification of criminalization and crime control in international relations, from past campaigns against piracy and slavery to contemporary campaigns against drug trafficking and transnational terrorism. We have shown how and why states have criminalized particular cross-border activities and attempted to transcend the limitations imposed by national sovereignty on the task of deterring and apprehending transnational law evaders, seizing their assets, and confiscating contraband.

We have evaluated the rise and transformation of international crime control from three distinct angles. The first is from a global angle, focusing on the evolution and spread of prohibition norms across the world. The second is from a regional angle, focusing on Western Europe, the region of the world where cross-border law enforcement relations are the most intensive, advanced, and institutionalized. And the third is from the angle of a single country, the United States, and its emergence as a hegemonic policing power and leading global crusader against transnational crime. Taken together, these three angles account for much of what has been significant in the internationalization of crime control.

We have emphasized growing cooperation amid enduring conflict. On the one hand, our story has been about a rising tide of international collaboration

Source: *Policing the Globe: Criminalization and Crime Control in International Relations* (USA: Oxford University Press, 2006), pp. 223–253 and 313–318.

in policing transnational crime. The negotiation of bilateral and multilateral law enforcement agreements; the creation of bilateral and multilateral law enforcement organizations, working groups, and conferences; the inclusion of foreign police agents in training programs; the stationing of liaison officers in foreign countries – all represent efforts to extend the reach of law enforcement systems beyond borders, to achieve a greater regularization of international law enforcement relations and homogenization of criminal law norms, and to minimize the frictions that result when sovereign law enforcement systems interact. On the other hand, our story has been about persistent international tension and conflict: the coercive practices and contentious politics involved in defining crime and determining the procedures and tools to combat such crime.

We have stressed the dominant role of major Western powers and Western-based transnational moral entrepreneurs in aggressively exporting favored prohibition norms and in initiating and determining the content and intensity of international crime control campaigns. Many of these campaigns have been driven not just by the narrow political and economic interests of powerful states but also by moral and emotional factors. Indeed, many leading international crime control initiatives have not simply been about enhancing control but about signaling moral resolve and collectively stigmatizing particular cross-border activities. Thus, contrary to the conventional wisdom, the internationalization of crime control is far from simply a natural, functional response to a growing global crime challenge. The complexity and diversity of international crime control across time, place, and issue area defy any single or simple explanation. Instead, they call for a more analytically eclectic approach that selectively combines multiple perspectives.[1] In this concluding chapter, we bring together the central themes in our story, assess popular arguments regarding the growing transnational crime challenge to state power in an age of globalization, and evaluate what past and present trajectories may tell us about the future.

The Primacy of Criminalization

The globalization of crime control, we have emphasized throughout this book, cannot be explained entirely or even primarily in terms of the functional need to respond to the globalization of crime. It is equally valid to turn this common explanation on its head. The underlying impetus of all international criminal law enforcement activities is the initial fact of criminalization by the state. New laws turn once legal cross-border activities into criminal activities, resulting in a sudden and sometimes dramatic overall increase in transnational crime. And new criminalizations often inspire and justify the creation of new international law enforcement capabilities, which in turn can invite additional laws and other initiatives. Thus criminalization has been a powerful motor for state expansion – and based on current trends, we can expect it to be an even more important source of growth in the years ahead. The policing face of the state is becoming more and more prominently displayed, with its gaze increasingly extending beyond national borders.

As we contemplate the future of international criminal law enforcement and recollect its historical evolution, we do well to keep in mind the potential for today's laws to be repealed, for new criminal laws to emerge, and for policing priorities to shift. Although it may be easy for some to perceive the criminal law as essentially immutable, and to believe that what is regarded as criminal in one's own society has always been regarded as such both within and without, this is readily undermined by any historical or comparative examination.[2] One need only compare the "opium wars" of the mid-nineteenth century, in which the British deployed military force to maintain the legal trade in opium and reverse China's short-lived effort to criminalize it, to the "drug wars" of recent decades, in which the United States has used military force in the name of drug criminalization and even invaded Panama and arrested its leader, General Manuel Noriega, on drug trafficking charges (no doubt the most expensive drug bust in history). Thorsten Sellin long ago observed that the "crimes of yesteryear may be legal conduct today, while crimes in one contemporary state may be legal conduct in another."[3] It is important to recall, for instance, that the origins of international law enforcement in Europe were intimately connected with the efforts of European governments to surveil and apprehend military deserters, vagabonds, and political dissidents resident in other countries, and that many of the crimes for which they were sought are no longer regarded as criminal. Conversely, we do well to keep in mind that much of international criminal law enforcement in recent decades has been preoccupied with investigating and prosecuting activities that were not regarded as criminal a century ago. This is particularly true of transnational trafficking in cannabis, cocaine, heroin, and other drugs as well as other corollary activities such as money laundering that were criminalized principally to aid drug law enforcement efforts. But it is also true of insider trading and other violations of securities and commodities laws, new sorts of tax law violations and export controls, environmental depredations, trafficking in cultural artifacts, animals, ivory, and other products of endangered species, intellectual property theft, and transnational migrations of peoples.

Homogenization and the Future of Global Prohibitions

It is difficult to understand the evolution of international law enforcement without recognizing the historical trend toward ever more homogeneous criminal law norms among countries. Criminal law norms around the world are far more similar today than they were at the beginning of the twentieth century, just as criminal law norms then were far more similar than they were at the start of the nineteenth century. But this trend toward greater homogeneity is inherently limited in global society. As long as the power to make and unmake criminal laws remains in the hands of states rather than supranational institutions, laws and their enforcement will always vary from one state to another depending on different and ever-changing moral notions and perceptions of foreign and domestic risks and threats.

The reasons for the current level of homogenization of criminal law norms across the world are many, but certainly the principal explanation is the global triumph of Western political power, with the result that Western criminal law norms have been imposed, imported, imitated, and/or adopted across much of the globe. Violent acquisitions on the high seas were redefined as acts of piracy and suppressed by the British Royal Navy and other naval forces. During the nineteenth century, Her Majesty's government focused its attentions on the global criminalization and abolition of the slave trade and the institution of slavery. During the twentieth century, the U.S. government promoted the globalization of a host of prohibitions. And during the first decade of the twenty-first century, Western powers have collaborated in internationalizing common rules and standards to more intensively police travel, cargo, and financial flows as part of a global antiterrorism campaign.

The capacity of a state to suppress transnational criminality depends greatly on the extent to which its criminal law norms conform with or vary from those of other states. The fact that one state views as legal that which another state views as criminal provides a substantial impediment to international crime control. During the mid-nineteenth century, for instance, the British government's efforts to eliminate the transatlantic slave trade were undermined by the persistent legality of slavery in Cuba, Brazil, and the United States. During the 1920s and early 1930s, U.S. efforts to curtail the illicit influx of alcoholic beverages were fatally handicapped by the fact that most foreign governments shared neither its zeal nor its taste for alcohol prohibition. The U.S.-sponsored global drug prohibition regime has long been hobbled not just by the dynamism of the illicit market and the ease of smuggling relatively compact, hardy, and profitable commodities but also by variations in local prohibition laws, enforcement capabilities, and enthusiasm for the laws themselves. In more recent years, efforts by U.S. law enforcement officials to investigate the extraterritorial dimensions of money laundering and securities law violations have been hindered by the uneven implementation of comparable criminal laws in foreign countries.

In the coming years, this pattern is likely to continue to repeat itself in other realms of international criminal law enforcement, perhaps most notably in the global policing of intellectual property theft, in which much of the developing world does not share the advanced industrialized world's enthusiasm for copyright and patent protection.[4] Securing international cooperation in this area is partly limited by charges of hypocrisy. Pat Clioate points out that as a newly industrializing country in the nineteenth century, the United States engaged in the kinds of practices it is now asking developing countries to prohibit and crack down on. The U.S. Patent Act of 1793, for example, did not protect foreign inventors, meaning that an American could steal a foreign invention and legally develop it for commercial applications. Similarly, the U.S. Copyright Act of 1790 did not protect the copyright of foreign nationals. The United States was a hotbed of copyright piracy during the nineteenth century – just as China is today. Other industrializing countries, such as Germany and Japan, similarly engaged in intellectual property theft.[5] We can expect this historical pattern of theft-aided development to continue, but in a more contentious context of global efforts to criminalize violations of intellectual property rights.

As we have seen, the relatively few criminal law norms that evolve into global prohibition regimes typically have two features in common: they tend to mirror the criminal laws of countries that have dominated global society to date (i.e., European powers and the United States) and they target criminal activities that in one way or another transcend national borders. The transnational dimension of the proscribed activity provides both much of the incentive for states to devote efforts toward constructing a prohibition regime as well as the justification typically required to provoke and justify external intervention in the internal affairs of other states. Many global prohibition regimes are promoted not just by states but by transnational moral entrepreneurs who mobilize popular opinion and political support and lobby governments both within their host country and abroad.

Global prohibition regimes are more likely to involve moral and emotional considerations than are most other international regimes. Like many criminal laws, they seek not to regulate but to ban; the underlying assumption is that certain activities must be prohibited because they are evil. Transnational moral consensus regarding the evil of a particular activity is not, however, sufficient to ensure the creation of a global prohibition regime, much less its success in effectively suppressing a proscribed activity, even when it complements the political and economic interests of hegemonic and other states. If states are unable or unwilling to conform to the regime's mandate in practice and if deviant or dissident states and groups within individual states persistently refuse to conform to the regime's demands, they can significantly undermine the global prohibition regime, particularly if their capacity for involvement in the criminal activity is great. Examples include the disruptive impact of the Barbary pirates in the early decades of the nineteenth century, the U.S. and Brazilian slave markets in the middle of that century, the coca producers and cocaine refiners and exporters in South America during recent decades, and Japanese consumers of whale meat and ivory products in recent years.

The ultimate success of a global prohibition regime inevitably depends on the vulnerability of the targeted activity to enforcement efforts. Most difficult to suppress are those activities that require limited and readily available resources and no particular expertise to commit, those that are easily concealed, those that are unlikely to be reported to the authorities, and those for which consumer demand is substantial, resilient, and not readily substituted for by alternative activities or products. If the past is any guide to the future, we can expect that technological changes will continue to strongly influence the success or failure of prohibition regimes. Recall that piracy succumbed to enforcement efforts in good part because technological developments at sea strengthened the capacities of governments to project their naval forces wherever pirates sought refuge, and that recent technological developments now facilitate a limited resurgence of piracy. The regime directed at the suppression of currency counterfeiting has proven relatively successful to date because governments have managed to remain a technological step ahead of potential counterfeiters – but that, too, could change. The global drug prohibition regime will certainly undergo changes in future decades as both the technology of manufacturing synthetic psychoactive drugs and other stimuli and the technology of drug interdiction and drug testing evolve. And a new frontier of crime and crime control – cyberspace – is by its very nature defined by technological change, presenting distinct law enforcement and law evasion challenges and opportunities. The success of the antislavery regime, by contrast, was less a consequence of technological developments than of the peculiar vulnerability of slavery to changes in its legal status. As for efforts to eradicate prostitution, it is unlikely that any developments, technological or otherwise, will significantly improve the prospects of the prohibition regime directed at the suppression of what has been termed the "oldest profession."

But the failure of a global prohibition regime does not necessarily signal its future demise. Regardless of effectiveness, part of the appeal of a global prohibition regime is its symbolic allure and usefulness as a mechanism to express disapproval. Regime proponents seek not just to suppress undesirable activities but also to create and maintain moral boundaries between acceptable and unacceptable behavior in international society. This is particularly true of the global drug prohibition regime. Open defection from the regime is highly unlikely anytime soon. It would place the defecting country in the category of a pariah "narcostate," generate material repercussions in the form of sanctions and aid cutoffs, and deeply damage the country's moral standing in the international community. But moderate reforms are clearly under way, such that the 1988 antidrug convention may one day be seen as the high point of criminalization in international drug control.[6] The inclusion of cannabis in the drug prohibition regime is increasingly in dispute as a growing number of countries follow in the footsteps of the Dutch by decriminalizing the plant and exploring ways to regulate its production and sale. The global ban on international commerce in coca teas, tonics, and other low-potency products of the coca plant has no basis in science or public health; Bolivia and Peru historically lacked the political will and power to challenge the United States on this point.[7] But the election in 2005 of a former head of the coca growers union, Evo Morales, as president of Bolivia has shifted the political equation. Most significant, the global AIDS pandemic is undermining U.S. efforts to enforce its zero tolerance view of global drug prohibition. Whereas until recently the United States could count on governments in Asia, Africa, and Scandinavia to bolster its claim that "harm reduction" principles and practices were inconsistent with international antidrug conventions, that is no longer the case. Latin America and much of Asia and Africa increasingly endorse the European Union's view that needle exchange and other harm reduction measures are essential to stem the spread of HIV/AIDS and that the antidrug conventions must be interpreted accordingly.[8] A new generation of transnational moral entrepreneurs has played an important role in these developments, grounding their advocacy in science, compassion, health, and human rights.[9]

Can and will a global terrorism prohibition regime emerge in years to come? This would seem particularly plausible given the high prioritization of terrorism concerns on the security agendas of the most powerful states in international society. Hijacking of airplanes already is the target of a successful global prohibition regime, and activities such as facilitating terrorist financing and providing weapons of mass destruction to groups labeled as terrorists are the targets of nascent regimes. International cooperation to secure global travel, trade, and financial channels from terrorist penetration is increasingly globalized and standardized. Yet creating and maintaining a comprehensive global prohibition regime against terrorism is an inherently elusive objective given the fundamental political differences over what constitutes terrorism. Thus, UN member states have collectively condemned terrorism in public pronouncements without actually agreeing on what exactly it is that they are condemning. The UN has traditionally shown great reluctance in prioritizing terrorism.[10] Even though this reluctance has eroded noticeably in the aftermath of September 11, the organization's embrace of counterterrorism remains ambivalent and may prove difficult to sustain.

Just as few people during the eighteenth century could have imagined the emergence of a global antislavery regime, and few in the nineteenth century could have envisioned a global ban on ivory, so, too, is it difficult to imagine any activities that are entirely legitimate today evolving into targets of global prohibitions. One worth contemplating is the international traffic in tobacco. The economic interests and cultural traditions underlying this traffic are almost as powerful as were those underlying the slave trade. Yet the consumption of tobacco is the single greatest cause of preventable deaths in dozens of countries; it is indisputably linked to the premature deaths of millions of people each year. Norms with respect to tobacco consumption, especially in public, have changed rapidly in the United States and some other countries in recent years. We can well imagine that some countries will choose to ban production and sale of tobacco and thereafter propagate their prohibitions to others, and that transnational moral entrepreneurs will proselytize and lobby for a global tobacco prohibition regime. Whether these efforts will follow in the footsteps of the stillborn alcohol prohibition regime promoted by the United States in the 1920s or be incorporated into the broader global drug prohibition regime is hard to say. Far preferable would be a global consensus in favor of regulation rather than prohibition, which is the thrust of the World Health Organization's Framework Convention on Tobacco Control.[11] Indeed, there is much to be said for the entire global drug prohibition regime evolving in the direction of the WHO's regulatory framework for tobacco.

Regularization and the Fate of International Police Cooperation

Even as the European Union, the Council of Europe, and the United States have sponsored and advocated multilateral efforts to make the criminal laws and criminal justice systems of states more alike, law enforcement officials have focused their efforts on regularizing their contacts, relationships, and exchanges across borders. In this respect at least, the proliferation of police liaisons and joint training programs in recent decades differs little from the international police efforts of their nineteenth-century forebears. Then, as now, police have sought to cut through red tape, to avoid diplomatic imbroglios, and to obtain more and better assistance from foreign colleagues. Their cumulative progress has been substantial. No longer do police plead in vain, as they did just a few decades ago, to be allowed to communicate directly across borders instead of via foreign ministries and consulates. Transgovernmental enforcement networks are more expansive and intensive than ever before, encouraging and facilitating a thickening of cross-border policing relationships.

One significant outcome of the regularization of law enforcement relations across borders has been the emergence of an international law enforcement community, with its own distinct expertise, understandings, and subculture.[12] The common sentiment that a cop is a cop no matter whose badge is worn, and a criminal a criminal regardless of citizenship or where the crime was committed, serves as a form of transnational value system that can override both political differences and formal procedures. It provides the oil and glue of international law enforcement. This certainly helps to explain the current expansion and durability of U.S.-European law enforcement cooperation in a period otherwise defined by a highly contentious transatlantic diplomatic divide over the Bush administration's foreign policies in Iraq and elsewhere.

Transnational criminality of a political sort has provided the impetus for many of the most vigorous and unprecedented collaborations in the history of international crime control.[13] Until well into the nineteenth century, most international law enforcement initiatives focused on the surveillance and

immobilization of political offenders. This preoccupation with political policing (or high policing) provided the impetus for most early extradition treaties, most transnational police interactions, and even the first multilateral
efforts among governments to collaborate in the suppression of land-based
crime. The desire of autocratic governments in Europe during the nineteenth
century to surveil, harass, and apprehend political refugees and agitators
beyond their borders inspired the first delegations of police attachés to foreign countries; anarchist assassinations of tsars, empresses, prime ministers,
and presidents provided the sparks required to convene the first multilateral
law enforcement conferences; and shared concern over transnational terrorism resulted in the creation of the first consultative body composed of interior ministers representing democratic states. In each case, the combination
of sovereign jealousies and governmental complacence that had previously
impeded effective international law enforcement efforts was overcome by
fears, concerns, and outrage over politically motivated crimes. Those states
most threatened were stirred to action, and those with little at stake were
obliged to accommodate. This historical pattern has repeated itself most
recently on an unprecedented and truly global scale in the aftermath of the
terrorist attacks on September 11, 2001.

What most distinguishes the contemporary era is the relatively greater
transnational nature and reach of some terrorist networks and the growing
fear of catastrophic criminality involving the use of weapons of mass destruction by nonstate actors. As the technologies to create such weapons become
more diffused, responsible governments have little choice but to coordinate
their control and enforcement efforts ever more effectively. As with other
types of transnational criminality, deviant or "outlaw states" and government
agents represent a major part of the law enforcement challenge.[14]

Yet it is important to remember that the very political motivations for the
crimes that so shocked states into action in past eras ultimately also imposed
limits on their cooperation. Central to the success of multilateral law enforcement initiatives from the 1898 antianarchist conference to the creation of
TREVI in the 1970s was the willingness of governments with quite disparate political perspectives and interests to acknowledge that certain types
of violent political action could not be justified by either their motivation or
their target. The same was true of the globally subscribed prohibition against
piracy, the murder of diplomats, and the hijacking of airplanes. But the scope
of such acknowledgment has always been limited by the persistence of differences of opinion among governments regarding the legal treatment of those
individuals who engage in politically motivated violence. Even where many
governments agree in principle, the strength of the consensus is often less
than it appears.

We examine the past not only because it helps to explain why the present is the way it is but also because it suggests the possible way of the
future. Based on past patterns, future international police cooperation will

substantially depend on the degree to which law enforcement issues can be depoliticized. We do well to recall that only when governments in the twentieth century began to focus greater attention on the transnational dimensions of more "common" criminality did the possibility for more permanent and comprehensive agreements and institutions emerge. The success and intensity of international law enforcement cooperation directed at counterfeiting, for example, can be explained not just by the powerful and mutual interests of governments, but also by the capacity of anticounterfeiting efforts to in some sense transcend politics. That same capacity also explains the unprecedented reach and intensity of international law enforcement efforts directed at illicit drug trafficking. Although the United States has provided the impetus for collaborative policing action, the criminalized activity itself is widely perceived as bereft of any legitimate political justification and offends the moral sensibilities of powerful nations. International drug enforcement efforts are thus readily perceived as transcending the parochial political interests of any one state – a perception that opens the door to relatively intensive forms of international police cooperation as well as relaxations of sovereign prerogatives that are a necessary precondition to such cooperation. The same dynamic has been evident in the case of international anti – money laundering measures, such as the evaluation mechanisms developed by the Financial Action Task Force. This initiative, although established and backed by the United States and other major powers, gained credibility "by the fact that the process was driven by neutral, technocratic analysis rather than politics, with decisions and recommended targets of sanctions taken largely by career civil service bureaucrats rather than by more politicized senior policymakers."[15]

Can counterterrorism efforts be similarly depoliticized? "While ideological sentiments on terrorism are very divided in the world of international diplomacy," Mathieu Deflem writes, "the target of terrorism at the level of police bureaucracy is defined in a language that can be shared among police institutions across the world. Indeed, indications are that police institutions have 'de-politicized' terrorism and stripped it of its (divisive) ideological justifications."[16] His perhaps overly optimistic conclusion is that "criminalization of terrorism – calling it a crime matter – enables police across the globe to rally around a common cause."[17] Malcolm Anderson, by contrast, believes that "effective and continuing cooperation in the field of counterterrorism is almost impossible to achieve because the basis of this cooperation must be agreement between governments on political rather than criminal law enforcement objectives."[18] The maturation of the international criminal law enforcement community provides support for Deflem's view, and Anderson's skepticism is well grounded in the realpolitik of power politics. We venture two predictions: that efforts to build a global counterterrorism regime will increasingly incorporate new prohibitions on specific tactics, analogous to hijacking, that even the most hostile of states agree must be deterred and delegitimized; and that political pressures to collaborate more closely on counterterrorism will provide the impetus and architecture for improved cooperation in other areas of crime control, such as curtailing cargo theft, tracking "conflict commodities," detecting suspect financial transactions, and policing the Internet. Just as the contemporary era of international crime control was powerfully shaped by U.S. insistence on international antidrug cooperation, so the emerging era of crime control will reflect the new emphasis on improving collaboration against terrorism. The result may well be far greater international police cooperation than was previously thought possible.[19]

Securitization and Desecuritization

The domains of counterterrorism, counterespionage, and other areas of international crime control (such as enforcement of export control laws) directed principally at transnational political threats to a regime's security straddle the often antagonistic worlds of criminal justice and national security. It is in this respect that the continuities between our account of contemporary international law enforcement efforts and those of the nineteenth century are most apparent. International law enforcement efforts directed at terrorism, espionage, and other security threats are most likely to involve informal unilateral and bilateral operations. Many of the normal legal constraints on police activities often do not apply; prosecutors are often kept in the dark; high-level political considerations often descend to interrupt routine cooperative relationships among law enforcement authorities or to authorize the sharing of highly sensitive intelligence; and formal multilateral relationships often prove to be less productive given the intense need for discretion and confidentiality with respect to sources and methods. Now, as in the past, terrorism is a crime in which intimate bilateral relationships between counterterrorism officials are key, and in which discreet unilateral activities, including state-sponsored assassinations and other "black bag" operations, play an important role.

The growing fusion of criminal justice and security concerns in recent decades also reflects the highly malleable nature of the concept of security.[20] A remarkably wide range of international policing issues have been securitized, desecuritized, and resecuritized over time. For instance, in the case of the United States, the contemporary securitization of many prominent criminal law enforcement issues represents a partial throwback to the early years of the nation's history, when security and law enforcement concerns overlapped at sea, where naval patrols sought to suppress piracy, and along U.S. borders until World War I, where posses, law enforcers, and military forces were often deployed. With the quieting of borders, the two sets of concerns were more or less disentangled. By World War II, the U.S. involvement in international law enforcement was far less reliant on navies and armies (not to mention posses and vigilante gangs, private police and bounty hunters) and, like that of many other countries, increasingly demilitarized and professionalized. During the decades following World War II, espionage and high-tech smuggling were virtually the only issues implicating both law enforcement and national security concerns.

But the desecuritization of U.S. law enforcement concerns was not irreversible. Changing markets and morals, and new laws and definitions of security, transformed international crime control in ways both new and familiar in the last decades of the twentieth century. During the 1980s, extraterritorial terrorism, traditionally a national security concern, was placed on the U.S. criminal law enforcement agenda by congressional statutes, and drug trafficking, traditionally a criminal justice matter, was formally elevated to the national security agenda by a national security directive. U.S. military and the intelligence agencies were directed to reorient their missions and priorities to devote greater attention to drug trafficking, money laundering, and other criminal activities. By the end of the twentieth century, this shift had progressed substantially, driven by the quest for new agendas and objectives to fill the vacuum left by the disintegration of the Soviet Union and the lifting of the Iron Curtain. The refusion of criminal justice and national security concerns in the post–cold war era was especially visible along the U.S.-Mexico border, where substantial efforts were under way to enhance the presence of federal law enforcement and even the military. The integration of security and border policing concerns was further accelerated and institutionalized through the creation of the Department of Homeland Security in the aftermath of the terrorist incidents on September 11, 2001. More broadly, security and law enforcement institutions are increasingly intertwined in the global counterterrorism campaign. As Peter Raven-Hansen has suggested, "Although federal antiterrorist law enforcement's self-transformation is well-advanced, the fusion of intelligence and military operations into law enforcement has barely begun. We are observing the early stages of a possible trend, not the end-points."[21]

These securitization trends have been equally evident in Western Europe, though in a less militarized and more multilateralized and institutionalized fashion. Old distinctions between high and low policing have become less and less meaningful. As one team of European police researchers has described it, at the EU level there has been a post–cold war ideological merging (with crime problems increasingly relabeled as security problems), an instrumental merging (as police agencies increasingly borrow instruments and tactics from the security and intelligence apparatus), and an institutional merging (with law enforcement and security institutions having increasingly overlapping missions).[22] These shifts began well before September 11, 2001, but have accelerated sharply. As articulated in the European Security Strategy (adopted in Brussels in December 2003), the cross-border dimensions of organized crime are now considered to be a leading security threat that can be tied to terrorism.[23]

Given the historical malleability of the concept of security, the day may come when international crimes such as those against the environment[24] are officially redefined as security issues while some other international crimes, such as drug trafficking, are desecuritized and redefined as public health rather than criminal justice concerns. It is also possible that the threat of global pandemics will lead to public health issues being redefined as priority security concerns.[25] The result may well be a new and uneasy integration of public health, security, and law enforcement missions and institutions.

The Europeanization of International Crime Control

It is in Europe where we have seen bilateral and multilateral dimensions of international policing and other aspects of international law enforcement proceed the furthest. The degree of convergence in crime control policies[26] and intensity of cross-border collaboration among criminal justice systems in Europe today would appear remarkable to all but the most optimistic of officials just a few decades ago. The reasons are multifold: nowhere else is such a large number of states grouped together in a territory so small; nowhere else is the process of crossing national borders so unencumbered by either geographic or political impediments; nowhere else is the frequency and intensity of transnational interactions so great, or the interdependence of societies, economies, and states so complex and multidimensional; and nowhere else has the shared consciousness of belonging to a partly supranational political community developed to such a high level. Police relations in Scandinavia and the Benelux countries increasingly resemble the quality of interstate police relations within the United States; those within an enlarging "Schengenland" are following suit. As Western Europe's neighbors have discovered, the politics of integration are intimately linked to the politics of embracing EU-wide policing standards.

To be sure, Europol cannot yet compare to the federal police agencies and multiagency strike forces that have proliferated in the United States, and the prospect of supranational police agencies with international arrest powers still seems chimerical. But the maturation of police relations in the European Union has certainly loosened the constraints of national sovereignty to a degree never before achieved and until recent decades unimaginable. The result is that even as the police agencies of EU members have followed the hegemonic lead of the United States in certain areas, they have very much been at the forefront of cross-border efforts to reduce the frictions that impede international cooperation in criminal justice matters.[27] The internationalization of policing by European states is far more intensive, even if not nearly as globally expansive, as U.S.-led international law enforcement efforts. Its development and influence today are felt much more at the regional than the global level, as evident in the EU's aggressive efforts to export "European standards" to the Balkans and elsewhere in its immediate periphery.

EU members recognize that their own claims to internal sovereignty depend increasingly on their capacity to control transnational interactions, and that this capacity in turn depends on the ability and willingness of other states to collaborate in control efforts. Conceding a right to hot pursuit to foreign police agents, revising municipal criminal laws and procedures to better accommodate foreign criminal justice systems, even acknowledging the legitimacy of supranational regulatory criminal justice agencies – all represent concessions of the traditional prerogatives of "external" sovereignty vis-à-vis other states in return for greater gains in preserving "internal" sovereignty over one's territory in an interdependent world. Though still feeling much discomfort, EU members have accepted this sovereignty trade-off to an unprecedented and globally unrivaled degree. This has involved a partial "unbundling of territoriality," but it has been carried out in the name of the traditional objective of enhancing the policing of territorial access.[28]

Can this remarkable development not only be sustained but deepen and expand in the coming years and decades? These questions are part of a much larger ongoing debate regarding the future of the European integration project, with Euro-optimists pointing to the remarkable progress that has been made in a relatively short period of time and Euro-skeptics emphasizing the limits of greater integration, the enduring primacy of intergovernmental relations, and the perils of continued expansion (including a potential political backlash and even rollback of the integration process). Signs of fatigue include the French and Dutch rejections of the proposed EU Constitution in 2005 and a slowdown in the process of EU enlargement. It remains unclear whether this is merely a bump in the road or a major turning point.

Although obviously difficult to predict, it is not unimaginable that in a decade or two the EU will have some kind of common external border guard force, Europol will more closely resemble a European FBI, most EU member states will require their citizens to carry a uniform EU identity card with biometric identifiers, and the European arrest warrant will have survived its difficult birth and become an integral and even taken-for-granted part of European criminal justice cooperation. In this regard, the EU may behave more and more like a federalized territorial state, with many international crime control practices, in turn, treated as de facto domestic crime control matters. Although the European Union has been described as both "neo-Medieval" and a "post-Westphalian polity," in some policing realms such as border control it may in fact behave more and more like a traditional state, perhaps even coming to resemble interstate cooperation in criminal justice matters within the United States. This would, in effect, represent a quasi-federalization of international criminal law enforcement at the regional level.

The other big question, of course, is whether Europe's highly institutionalized and multilateralized level of cross-border police cooperation and homogenization of criminal justice systems can be exported and adopted elsewhere. In writing about the transformation of border controls in Europe,

Malcolm Anderson cautions that although ideas of state sovereignity and territoriality have in the past been diffused from Europe to the rest of the globe, "it is far from inevitable that European precedents will have the same trajectory in the future."[29] Asia seems unlikely to follow Europe's lead. As Peter Katzenstein points out, "All governments perceive terrorism, illegal immigration, the smuggling of drugs and narcotics, and armed insurrection as increasingly important security threats. In sharp contrast to Europe, however, Asian governments remain largely uninterested in political solutions at the regional level."[30] Prospects are somewhat better in North America. The heated policy debates following the September 11 terrorist attacks included discussions of creating a "security perimeter" around the NAFTA partners, which would represent a substantial deepening – and indeed a "Europeanization" – of the North American integration project. But to truly "Schengenize" North American borders would require a level of formal institutionalization, multilateralism, and policy convergence that is difficult to imagine in the present political context. Based on current trends, the most likely scenario is not a full-scale "fortress North America" mirroring "fortress Europe," but a series of incremental, piecemeal initiatives, involving a mixture of enhanced cross-border police coordination and collaboration, partial and uneven policy convergence, and innovative new inspection methods and technologies. This may eventually develop into a less formal, less bureaucratized, quasi-continental security perimeter that selectively borrows from the European model.[31]

Thus, although it may be tempting to look at the direction of international law enforcement developments in Europe and assume that there, in time, will go the rest of the globe, the more modest conclusion that can and should be drawn is that the future of international law enforcement outside of Europe will consist of a wide variety of outcomes, almost all of which have already occurred within Europe. The impoverished regions of the world remain substantially underdeveloped in international law enforcement. This reflects the uneven state of law enforcement, particularly criminal investigation, in nations where military and paramilitary forces have played a more prominent role in police matters (often preoccupied with securing the state from internal threats and subversion). Perhaps most important, most states with relatively limited financial resources are prone to view much of international law enforcement as a luxury. Like the major European states of earlier centuries, many poor countries are likely to react with relief to the flight of fugitives abroad; the expense of extradition, and of sending police agents abroad to conduct extraterritorial investigations, figure in their calculations in a way that they do not for more affluent states. At the same time, less developed countries are under increasing pressure to embrace the international law enforcement priorities and join the interrational policing campaigns of wealthier states. In this regard, EU relations with many of its eastern and southern neighbors share some of the characteristics of

292 The Future of Global Policing

U.S. relations with many of its neighbors in the Americas. Policing matters promise to be an increasingly pivotal dimension of richpoor relations in coming years.

The Americanization of International Crime Control

Among the features that differentiate U.S. international policing actions from those of European powers and most other states are the relatively higher number of endeavors in which U.S. officials act unilaterally and coercively. No other government behaves so aggressively in obtaining evidence from foreign jurisdictions, apprehending fugitives from abroad, indicting foreign officials in its own courts, and compelling foreign governments to change their criminal justice norms to conform to its own. Nor does any other government allocate comparable diplomatic energy and resources to carrying out its international criminal law enforcement priorities. The U.S. government is more willing than any other to intrude on the prerogatives of foreign sovereigns, to confront foreign political sensibilities, and to override foreign legal norms.

These aggressive activities have helped to convince foreign governments to modify their laws, set up law enforcement working groups and other cooperative arrangements with U.S. law enforcement officials, enter into extradition and mutual legal assistance treaty negotiations prompted by U.S. officials, and generally play a more active role in vicariously representing U.S. criminal justice interests. U.S. law enforcement agencies play an especially pivotal role in shaping a transnational police community and thickening intergovernmental law enforcement networks,[32] providing technical assistance and training for many foreign police officers, advocating for more intensive and systematic bilateral and multilateral cooperation, and prompting new initiatives in both criminal procedure and criminal legislation.

There are a number of reasons for the relative U.S. success in extending its law enforcement reach and priorities abroad. First, and most obvious, is U.S. hegemonic power. Foreign governments recognize that the cost of defying the United States may be substantial, especially if they represent relatively vulnerable and less developed countries. Foreign banks and corporations know that ignoring U.S. court orders for documents can lead to their exclusion from U.S. territory and markets. The second factor is the rapid rise of criminal justice officials, objectives, and concerns to the upper tier of U.S. foreign policy formulation and implementation, a phenomenon that can be substantially explained by the prominence of "law and order" issues in U.S. national politics since the late 1960s and the securitization of these issues in more recent years. The third factor is the ever present and seemingly ever more strident and pervasive sense of moralism associated with criminal justice efforts both domestically and internationally.[33]

Foreign governments have reacted to U.S. pressures, inducements, and examples in recent decades by creating new criminal laws targeting drug trafficking, money laundering and terrorist financing, insider trading, and organized crime and by reforming financial secrecy laws as well as their codes of criminal procedure to better conform to U.S. legal needs. Some foreign initiatives, moreover, are motivated by other governments' wishes to preempt U.S. criticism and unilateral action or win diplomatic favor from Washington. Foreign police have incorporated U.S. investigative techniques, and foreign courts and legislatures have followed up with the requisite legal authorizations. The internationalization of law enforcement is thus far from equal or reciprocal. For the most part, the United States provides the models and sets the priorities, and other governments do the accommodating. International agreement often require the adoption of new laws in foreign countries that reflect legislation already in place in the United States – evident, for instance, in the 1988 Vienna antidrug convention and the 2000 Palermo Convention on Transnational Organized Crime. At the same time, the U.S. government sometimes pushes other governments to adopt measures that it itself is unwilling to adopt, including providing aid and training to foreign militaries to direct and carry out frontline policing tasks that the U.S. military is prohibited from engaging in at home.

Thus, although the European Union plays an activist role in creating regional and international law enforcement institutions, it would not be too much of an exaggeration to say that much of the internationalization of crime control has in practice meant Americanization. The global reach of U.S. criminal law enforcement is likely to extend further in the immediate years ahead. Other countries' law enforcement systems may therefore increasingly reflect U.S. examples and norms, thereby enhancing the vicarious enforcement of U.S. laws, representing, in essence, a continued outsourcing of crime control. Although far more often overlooked than U.S. military power, in the realm of policing power the United States very much retains the title of global hegemon.

The exercise of U.S. hegemonic policing power can often be subtle, such as playing the lead role in setting the policing priorities of international institutions and providing much of the legal and technical expertise necessary to hammer out and implement bilateral and multilateral agreements. The charge that the United States has neglected and even subverted international institutions in favor of unilateralism in recent years has only limited validity in the realm of international law enforcement. When one digs beneath the surface of UN and many other multilateral crime control initiatives, one inevitably finds U.S. funds, personnel, model legislation, and diplomatic endeavors. Thus, far from taming and constraining U.S. power, in this policy realm international institutions extend, obscure, and legitimate it.

Both the United States and the weaker countries that it pressures on law enforcement issues have incentives to understate the power imbalance and coercive aspects of the relationship by framing the issue as conforming to international standards and obligations. For many states, it is politically more palatable to portray their behavior as meeting their international commitments rather than as caving in to U.S. demands. The appearance of consensus not only saves face for weaker states, but has the added advantage of projecting an image of being a good citizen in the international community, giving new meaning to the term "community policing." For the United States, exercising policing hegemony through international institutions enhances legitimacy, is easier and less costly than the raw exercise of power, and reduces reliance on brute force. This is a striking illustration of what Andrew Hurrell calls "coercive socialization."[34] It reaches its most institutionalized form in U.S.-sponsored global prohibition regimes, which, as Richard Friman argues, provide a mechanism for the United States to externalize many of the costs of law enforcement. He notes that even as U.S. influence over trade and monetary relations may be in decline, "the United States continues to dominate the structure and normative content of global prohibition regimes. To date, there is little indication that the United States is likely to reverse criminalization within existing national or global prohibition regimes or halt the proliferation of new prohibition regimes."[35]

The question is how long U.S. policing hegemony will last and who will emerge as the most likely challengers. In other words, at what point will we no longer be able to characterize the internationalization of crime control as Americanization? When will the fingerprints of U.S. negotiators fade in the creation of international agreements, and the footprints of U.S. law enforcement officials overseas become less pronounced? Will there be a counter-process of de-Americanization? The EU may be a viable challenger in some international law enforcement arenas, especially if member states can strategically behave as a collective bloc. But for the most part, EU efforts are likely to complement more than challenge U.S. policing hegemony. At least in the short term, we can expect that the U.S.-European law enforcement relationship will continue to be based on a mixture of competition and collusion, reflecting an uneasy combination of political tension and regional divergence amid broader policy convergence and cooperation at the global level in policing transnational flows of people, goods, and money. As we have suggested, a new kind of transatlantic security community is arguably emerging through the expansion and institutionalization of these policing arrangements.[36]

Based on past historical patterns and trajectories, we can expect that as power centers shift, so too will international crime control priorities and practices. The diffusion of power away from the United States is likely to have important consequences for international crime control as policing preferences become more varied, priorities change, and coordination becomes more cumbersome. In this regard, the rise of China and other potential regional challengers in coming decades may erode the hegemony of U.S.-sponsored international crime control initiatives and approaches. For instance, China is likely to continue to place far greater emphasis on policing the Internet to enforce its strict censorship laws (aided by security tools, firewalls, and information provided by U.S. companies)[37] rather than enforcing intellectual property rights laws.[38] This, in turn, may become a growing source of international friction as China flexes its policing muscle and uses market access as a powerful leverage to pressure foreign governments and companies to cooperate in carrying out its own law enforcement agenda.

At the same time, U.S. influence may outlast its waning power in coming decades.[39] Some U.S.-backed international initiatives, such as the anti–money laundering monitoring efforts of the Financial Action Task Force, have generated their own momentum. Major international agreements that the United States played an instrumental role in creating have built on and reinforced each other and provided models for future agreements. For example, the Palermo Convention Against Transnational Organized Crime very much built on the Vienna Convention Against Illicit Traffic in Narcotic and Psychotropic Substances, and the more recent UN Convention Against Corruption, in turn, has built on the Palermo Convention (and is being ratified at a speed surpassing all others). If this pattern continues, we can expect future multilateral crime control agreements to at least partly borrow from these earlier models regardless of the level of U.S. sponsorship and influence.

State Power, Globalization, and Transnational Crime

Our examination of the historical and contemporary internationalization of crime control provides a corrective to the common perception – reinforced and perpetuated in media reports and policy debates – that states are somehow "losing control" in the face of ever growing transnational crime challenges in an era of globalization. There is certainly an enormous gap between stated policing goals and actual outcomes. More law enforcement can also simply prompt more sophisticated and geographically dispersed law evasion techniques; this, in turn, can make law enforcement more difficult and complicated, providing a rationale to further empower, fund, and expand the international reach of crime control efforts. Law enforcement pressure can perversely turn disorganized crime into more organized crime, as evident in the transformation of professional migrant smuggling in recent years. It can also exacerbate problems of corruption by creating incentives for criminals to spend more on bribes and payoffs. There are certainly built-in limits to how much states can deter certain criminalized transnational activities, especially if they wish to maintain open societies and keep their borders open to high volumes of legitimate cross-border exchange.[40]

But to then jump to the conclusion that states are losing control is highly misleading because it falsely implies that states were "in control" in the past. As we have seen, the limits of state controls and the challenges posed by transnational criminal activity are nothing new. Contrary to popular mythology about crime and globalization, there never was a golden age of state control.[41] Cross-border crime is as old as the creation of national borders and the imposition of state controls. Arguments that imply otherwise suffer from historical amnesia. Borders have always been far more permeable than the Westphalian ideal of the sovereign state would indicate.

Viewed from a broad historical perspective, state capacities to detect, deter, and detain transnational law evaders have, if anything, grown substantially. The number of safe havens for criminals across the globe has dramatically shrunk over time as the law enforcement reach of the state has expanded (consider, for example, the proliferation of extradition and mutual legal assistance treaties in recent decades). And it should be remembered that some key control tools, such as the universal adoption of the passport, arrived relatively late in the development of the modern state.[42] Moreover, one should not lose sight of the fact that it is the very existence of state controls that makes it necessary for smugglers and other criminalized transnational actors to try to devise such creative and elaborate means to evade and circumvent them. Transnational crimes such as drug trafficking and migrant smuggling are so enormously profitable precisely because states impose and enforce prohibitions. Transnational criminal organizations attempt to bully and buy off state officials, but in most cases this is primarily because they lack the capacity to bypass them. Corruption reflects state weakness, but also state power: most transnational criminals, after all, would prefer to evade state controls entirely rather than have to pay for state protection and nonenforcement of the law. Some governments "profit" from crime by informally taxing criminal earnings.[43] Some even offer "protection" to criminals, not only from agents of foreign governments but also, in the true style of mafiosi, from their own agents. This practice was as true of governments' treatment of pirates in the eighteenth century and slave traders in the nineteenth as it is true of drug smugglers and embargo busters today.

Regardless of effectiveness in combating transnational crime, it should also be emphasized that many international policing efforts and prohibition regimes have politically useful perceptual effects and symbolic uses that are too often taken for granted or overlooked. As one criminologist has put it in the case of drug control, "Drug police, like priests, are more important for what they symbolize and stand for than for what they do."[44] Thus to judge the expansion of international prohibition regimes and policing practices strictly in terms of whether or not their stated instrumental goals are attained partly misses the point. Criminalizing and policing undesirable transnational activities is not only about apprehension and deterrence but also about employing the powers of the state to express moral resolve. This can have substantial payoffs for both political leaders and law enforcement practitioners by impressing and appeasing various domestic and international audiences.

It is commonly asserted that the forces of globalization are empowering nonstate transnational actors (both licit and illicit) and making borders and state controls increasingly antiquated, with the rapid spread of transnational criminal organizations viewed as a particularly extreme challenge to the state. For example, in the 1990s, Susan Strange boldly proclaimed transnational organized crime to be "perhaps *the* major threat to the world system,"[45] and more recently, Moises Naim has provocatively characterized the conflict between states and transnational crime as "the new wars of globalization," with states increasingly on the losing side.[46] There are elements of truth in these often sweeping claims. After all, illicit cross-border flows take advantage of the same transformations in global communication and transportation that facilitate licit flows. And some economic policies designed to encourage and facilitate the globalization of licit flows can unintentionally aid illicit flows.[47] The stakes are also certainly higher today given the potential for violent nonstate actors to gain access to nuclear material and other weapons of mass destruction through transnational smuggling channels. More generally, it is reasonable to conclude that transnational crime has grown as the amount of transnational activity in general has grown. But as an overall percentage of cross-border activity, it is probably no more (and possibly much less) today than in past eras. The dramatic liberalization of trade in recent decades has certainly reduced the incentives to engage in smuggling practices based on evading tariffs and export/import duties, which historically has been the basis of a significant proportion of global smuggling.

Moreover, many of the same transformations that facilitate the globalization of crime, including revolutions in transportation and communication, also greatly facilitate the globalization of crime control. Globalization therefore both challenges and empowers the state. For instance, even as new information technologies enable transnational criminal activities (and indeed create new categories of crimes such as cybersmuggling and cyberpiracy), these technological advances also greatly increase tracking and surveillance capacities and even create new forms of policing (such as cyberpolicing). Technology has dramatically lowered the costs and increased the intensity and frequency of transgovernmental law enforcement networks, allowing state actors to interact with their foreign counterparts more rapidly and frequently.[48]

New technologies will continue to enhance the ability of states to collaboratively police the cross-border movement of cargo, information, money, and people. In this regard, the emerging "virtual borders" touted by U.S. law enforcement strategists are essentially electronic borders.[49] As we have seen, the digitization of border enforcement has ranged from the use of more expansive and sophisticated databases for data mining and computer tracking systems to the development of more tamper-resistant travel documents and "smart" IDs with biometric identifiers (such as digital fingerprints and facial and retinal scans). Border controls are thus being reconfigured, redefined, and deterritorialized, even as the traditional objectives of apprehension, territorial exclusion, and control of the domestic realm endure. This is an old story, as technological innovations have long played a key role in the development of travel documents[50] and in enabling cross-border police investigations (such as the invention of photography and fingerprint systems).[51] At the same time, police agencies have long pointed to the crime-facilitating role of new technological developments as a rationale to further internationalize their policing efforts, and we can expect this to not only continue but to intensify in the future.[52] Cutting-edge technologies enabling future crimes such as DNA theft and illicit cloning may have equally significant policing applications, such as new types of DNA mapping and testing and other forms of identification (with profound implications for privacy protection).

Furthermore, leading private sector agents of globalization that are typically viewed (by both critics and proponents) as challenging and even circumventing the state, such as major financial institutions and multinational corporations, are being creatively enlisted and deputized by governments to help police transnational crime. Shipping companies and airlines are increasingly being compelled through both negative and positive inducements to more carefully track and screen cargo and passengers. The same is true for banks and other financial institutions in the monitoring and reporting of suspicious monetary transactions. And some communications companies have facilitated efforts by intelligence agencies (most notably the U.S. National Security Agency) to eavesdrop on and "data mine" international phone calls. These and other mechanisms make it possible to "monitor, surveil, or analyze data and behaviors beyond the reach or capacity of traditional state surveillance or monitoring power."[53] Although still very much in its infancy, one can see the makings of a global surveillance and monitoring system that increasingly relies on the private sector for tracking, documenting, reporting, and analyzing cross-border flows. This is not to deny the substantial limitations and shortcomings,[54] or that the privatization trend can be a double-edged sword that both subverts and bolsters state power.[55] Some aspects of privatization also raise serious concerns about transparency and accountability, concerns that some governments view as advantages and that indeed are part of the political motivation for subcontracting.[56]

In a few countries, most notably the United States, the multinational corporation even provides a vicarious means of extending the state's sovereign powers extraterritorially. Not just U.S. multinationals but foreign ones as well find that their affiliates and other contacts within the United States render all their operations outside the United States susceptible to court orders and sanctions imposed by U.S. courts as well as other requirements of U.S. laws. Foreign companies find themselves subject to U.S. antitrust laws and export control laws, and foreign banks can be ordered to hand over to U.S. criminal justice authorities financial documents stored in branches outside the United States, often in the face of financial secrecy laws and blocking statutes to the contrary. The capacity of the U.S. government to make the most of these options reflects not just the fact that almost all major multinational firms maintain affiliates and other contacts on U.S. soil but also the fact that those contacts are sufficiently important that these firms are willing to tolerate and accommodate U.S. extraterritorial assertions as a necessary cost of doing business.[57] The broader point, however, is that even as the proliferation of transnational interactions challenges the state's control of its territory, the same process also provides a rationale and opportunity for expanding its jurisdictional reach.

Our account of the internationalization of crime control thus suggests that the state is not, as some have alarmingly claimed, simply retreating and decaying in the face of ever more intensive transnational interactions. Quite the contrary, as Wolfram Hanrieder argued decades ago: "It is precisely the domestication of international politics which sustains (and demonstrates) the vitality of the nation-state. By extending domestic political processes and their corresponding attitudes into the international environment, the nation-state has eroded traditional aspects of international politics."[58] This domestication process is readily evident in the realm of international criminal law enforcement.

Lessons and Implications

The international orientation of policing priorities and international extension of policing practices have reached unprecedented levels. Though still far from forming a globetrotting international police force with sovereign authority, states now agree and collaborate on more cross-border policing matters than ever before. Substantially driven by the interests and moralizing impulses of major Western powers, a loosely institutionalized and coordinated international crime control system based on the homogenization of criminal law norms and regularization of law enforcement relations is emerging and promises to be an increasingly prominent dimension of global governance in the twenty-first century.

States have developed a broad range of collaborative tools to manage the challenges posed by transnational crime, but along with the advantages of international crime control we should recognize and confront the substantial downside. This includes growing problems of accountability and transparency (a widening "democratic deficit" as police functions become more internationalized and privatized), troubling civil liberties and human rights implications of the securitization of policing and the spread of more invasive laws and surveillance technologies in the wake of September 11,[59] the emergence of an international crime control industrial complex, and the rising costs for developing countries of complying with ever more stringent law enforcement expectations and demands of wealthy states. Many governments have also latched on to high-profile global policing campaigns not only to impress and appease various audiences but also to further other political agendas, including providing a thinly disguised cover and legitimizing instrument to suppress domestic dissent and tighten their grip on power.

Some leading international law enforcement efforts have generated enormous collateral damage. Take, for instance, the efforts to curb the smuggling of people and drugs. The tightening of U.S. and European immigration controls has prompted migrant smugglers to turn to more daring and dangerous border-crossing strategies, leading to hundreds of migrant deaths per year. The global antidrug campaign has been a driving force in forging cooperative links among criminal justice systems, but has also generated extraordinary levels of crime, violence, corruption, disease, and other ills. The U.S. approach to suppressing the trafficking of women and children has been far more focused on criminalizing the traffic than helping to protect the human rights of those being trafficked. Supply-side law enforcement initiatives abroad often endlessly chase the international symptoms rather than the source of the problem at home. Blaming and targeting international drug traffickers and migrant smugglers is politically easier than dealing honestly with the enormous consumer demand for psychoactive substances and cheap migrant labor. Criminalizing and targeting the supply side of these problems masks the fact that they are first and foremost public health and labor market regulation issues.[60]

More generally, criminalization and international crime control have too often substituted and distracted attention away from the need for more fundamental political, social, and economic reforms. Across much of the world, a punitive policing state increasingly overshadows and substitutes for a retreating welfare state, even as the social dislocations that result fuel further calls for more policing. It is perhaps no coincidence that the United States, the most enthusiastic promoter of criminalization at the global level, is also the world's leading incarcerator. With roughly 5 percent of the world's population, the United States claims roughly 25 percent of the world's incarcerated population.[61] Indeed, it incarcerates more people for drug law violations than Western Europe incarcerates for all offenses combined.[62] Unlike Great Britain's nineteenth-century campaign to prohibit slavery worldwide, which sought essentially to extend freedom by abolishing the legal institutions that permitted slavery, the U.S. antidrug campaign has resulted in millions of people being deprived of their freedom. There is surely something perverse about international crime control policy being so powerfully shaped by a nation that applies criminal sanctions to diverse activities with such striking alacrity. Most governments that look to the United States for leadership in international crime control matters would do well to examine the broader costs and consequences of U.S. criminal justice policies both within its borders and beyond.

We should also take care not to overstate the internationalization of crime control. The vast majority of policing remains largely insulated from foreign affairs. Attempts to further internationalize policing face considerable political resistance, provoke familiar turf battles and age-old concerns about infringements on national sovereignty, and are limited by enduring problems of mistrust. Moreover, cross-border law enforcement cooperation is too often treated as the end point rather than a means to an end.[63] Measuring the effectiveness of internationalization is frustratingly elusive, with the favored indicators easy to manipulate and often having more of a perceptual effect than substantive meaning. Conformity with international criminal law enforcement standards, ranging from the protection of endangered species to curbing money laundering and the trafficking of persons, often represents little more than "paper compliance," especially in less developed countries with anemic enforcement capacity. Major powers collaborate in devising and promoting standardized international rules and regulations to more carefully police cargo, travel, and financial flows, but actual implementation and capacity building remain at a relatively early stage of development.

We should be similarly wary of overstating how new and different the contemporary era is from past historical experience. Bold pronouncements regarding the emergence of a "postmodern state" and the "erosion and diminution of the state system" in the realm of cross-border policing seem exaggerated and premature.[64] Such proclamations of fundamental change may be intellectually fashionable, but we should recognize that there is a strong element of "back to the future" in current policing trends. Much of today's preoccupation with counterterrorism is in some respects a modern variant of what political policing meant in continental Europe more than a century ago. The growing privatization of policing can similarly be viewed as a modern-day variant on the reliance on posses, privateers, and private detective agencies such as the Pinkertons in earlier eras. And the contemporary process of securitization, in which military and intelligence agencies are increasingly utilized to confront acts defined as criminal (i.e., terrorism, drug trafficking, migrant smuggling), is in some ways a throwback to earlier centuries, when navies were deployed to eradicate piracy and the slave trade and troops were sent to crack down on border bandits and other transnational law evaders. In short, the contemporary period provokes a certain sense of déjà vu. The past may be prelude more than is typically recognized.

Finally, we should stress that, amid ever growing levels of global cooperation, international crime control will remain defined by persistent conflict and turbulent change. Continued heterogeneity is inevitable. No global sovereign claims universal policing authority. Criminal laws, procedures, and norms are constantly changing, at different rates, within different states, as a consequence of political, cultural, and technological transformations. Conflict is inevitable so as long as transnational moral entrepreneurs and the most powerful states seek to promote and impose their criminal norms on others. Just when it appears that a new level of common understanding and cooperation is reached and an unprecedented diminishing of frictions is achieved in international crime control, new criminalizations and criminal law enforcement initiatives emerge to generate new conflicts and tensions. Such is the dialectic of criminalization and crime control in international relations.

Notes

1. See Rudra Sil and Peter J. Katzenstein, "What Is Analytic Eclecticism and Why Do We Need It? A Pragmatic Perspective on Problems and Mechanisms in the Study of World Politics," paper presented at the annual meeting of the American Political Science Association, Washington, DC, September 2005.
2. Chambliss, "The Criminalization of Conduct," 45.
3. Thorsten Sellin, *Culture Conflict and Crime* (New York: Social Science Research Council, 1938), 22.
4. On China, see Mertha, *The Politics of Piracy*.
5. Pat Choate, *Hot Property: The Stealing of Ideas in an Age of Globalization* (New York: Knopf, 2005).
6. See the special issue *of International Journal of Drug Policy* 14, no. 2 (April 2003); David R. Bewley-Taylor, "Harm Reduction and the Global Drug Control Regime: Contemporary Problems and Future Prospects," *Drug and Alcohol Review* 23, no. 4 (December 2004): 23, 483–489. Also see Martin Jelsma and Pien Metaal, "Cracks in the Vienna Consensus: The UN Drug Control Debate," *Drug War Monitor*, Washington Office on Latin America, January 2004.
7. See Transnational Institute, Debate Paper No. 10, April 2004; Transnational Institute, Drug Policy Briefing No. 5, April 2003, available at http://www.tni.org.
8. See Transnational Institute, Drug Policy Briefing No. 13, April 2005, available at http://www.tni.org.
9. See, for example, http://www.drugpolicy.org; Ethan Nadelmann, "Challenging the Global Prohibition Regime," *The International Journal of Drug Policy* 9, no. 2 (April 1998): 85–93. Available at http://www.drugtext.org/library/articles/98921.htm.
10. See Edward Luck, "Another Reluctant Belligerent: The United Nations and the War on Terrorism," in Richard Price and Mark W. Zacher, eds., *The United Nations and Global Security* (New York: Palgrave, 2004).
11. For more information, see http://www.who.int/features/2003/08/en.
12. Criminologists have long pointed to the importance of police subcultures but have rarely extended this to the international realm. An exception is James Sheptycki, "The Global Cops Cometh: Reflections on Transnationalization, Knowledge Work and Police Subculture," *British Journal of Sociology* 49, no. 1 (March 1998): 57–74.
13. All international law enforcement endeavors are, in a sense, political, but the degree of politicization varies dramatically. At one extreme are counterespionage, counterterrorism, and export control activities. All these implicate traditional notions of national security, invite the involvement of the intelligence and military agencies, and provide substantial latitude for explicitly political and discretionary interventions into routine criminal justice processes. At the other extreme are extradition and other international law enforcement efforts directed at apprehending common murderers, rapists, and thieves; these are handled primarily by criminal justice personnel with minimal political input by foreign ministry and diplomatic officials. In the middle are a variety of activities that range from unilateral state efforts to enforce states' own tax, customs, and immigration laws to multilateral efforts to deter and investigate drug trafficking and other activities criminalized through international conventions.
14. See, for example, Charles D. Ferguson and William C. Potter, *The Four Faces of Nuclear Terrorism* (New York: Routledge, 2005).
15. Winer, "Tracking Conflict Commodities and Financing," 77.
16. Mathieu Deflem, "Law Enforcement 9–11: Questioning the Policing of International Terrorism," *Pro Bono* 9, no. 1 (Fall 2002): 8.
17. Deflem, *Policing World Society*, 230.
18. Anderson, "Counterterrorism as an Objective of European Police Cooperation," 227.

19. As Mathieu Deflem reminds us, international cooperation in crime control at the turn of the nineteenth century was "facilitated by prior practices of cooperation that had been initiated for political reasons." Mathieu Deflem, "Wild Beasts without Nationality?, The Uncertain Origins of INTERPOL, 1898, 1910," in Philip Reichel, ed., *Handbook of Transnational Crime and Justice* (Thousand Oaks, CA: Sage), 276.

20. On the process of securitization, see Barry Buzan, Ole Waever, and Jaap de Wilde, *Security: A New Framework for Analysis* (Boulder, CO: Lynne Rienner, 1997).

21. See Raven-Hansen, "Security's Conquest of Federal Law Enforcement," 227.

22. Anderson et al., *Policing the European Union*, 165.

23. This document is available on the European Union Web site: http://www.eu.int.

24. Environmental issues have already become partly securitized. See Daniel H. Deudney and Christopher A. Mathew, eds., *Contested Grounds: Security and Conflict in the New Environmental Politics* (Albany: State University of New York Press, 1999).

25. See the collection of articles on "The Next Pandemic?" in the July/August 2005 issue of *Foreign Affairs* 84, no. 4.

26. For example, Cyrille Fijnaut and Letizia Paoli write that the "internationalisation of policy on organized crime well explains why changes that have taken place on several fronts in individual countries are so similar." "Comparative Synthesis of Part III," in Cyrille Fijnaut and Letizia Paoli, eds., *Organized Crime in Europe: Concepts, Patterns and Control Policies in the European Union and Beyond* (Dordrecht, The Netherlands: Springer, Kluwer 2005), 1037.

27. This has been greatly facilitated by the development of personal contacts and professional relationships between representatives of national police agencies. See especially Didier Bigo, "Liaison Officers in Europe: New Officers in the European Security Field," in Sheptycki, *Issues in Transnational Policing.*

28. On "unbundling territorially," see John Gerard Ruggie, "Territoriality and Beyond: Problematizing Modernity in International Relations," *International Organization* 47, no. 4 (1993): 139–174.

29. Malcolm Anderson, "The Transformation of Border Controls: A European Precedent?," in Andreas and Snyder, *The Wall around the West*, 26.

30. Katzenstein, *A World of Regions*, 136–137.

31. This vision is articulated in a May 2005 Council on Foreign Relations–sponsored Independent Task Force Report, "Building a North American Community," which includes proposals for creating a common security perimeter by 2010, introducing a biometrics-based "North American border pass," and the development of a unified border action plan and expanded border customs facilities. The report is available at http://www.cfr.org/publication.html?id=8102.

32. Anne-Marie Slaughter has noted that although we might expect the EU to "support the creation of global government networks," it is actually "the United States that has led the way in supporting these networks at the global level." Slaughter's general point very much applies to the realm of policing. *A New World Order*, 265.

33. For a historical account of the powerful moralizing impulses in U.S. politics, see Morone, *Hellfire Nation.* Although not Morone's focus, the "politics of sin" that he identifies as a catalyst for state expansion at the domestic level also extends to the international realm through U.S.-promoted crime control campaigns.

34. Hurrell, "Power, Institutions, and the Production of Inequality," 53. Also see G. John Ikenberry and Charles Kupchan, "Socialization and Hegemonic Power," *International Organization* 44, no. 3 (1990): 283–315.

35. Friman, "Globalization's Poster Child," 18.

36. On security communities, see Emanuel Adler and Michael Barnett, eds., *Security Communities* (Cambridge, UK: Cambridge University Press, 1998).

37. Tina Rosenberg, "Building the Great Firewall of China, with Foreign Help," editorial, *New York Times*, 18 September 2005, sec. 4, 11.

38. In September 2005, for example, the Chinese government stepped up its policing of online information by imposing much tighter controls on the scope of content allowed on Web sites. Joseph Kahn, "China Tightens Its Restrictions for News Media on the Internet," *New York Times*, 26 September 2005, A9.

39. There is certainly much historical precedence for this. Consider, for example, the continued legacy of colonialism.

40. More generally, as Herbert L. Packer long ago argued, there are inherent limits to what criminal sanctions can accomplish. *The Limits of the Criminal Sanction* (Stanford, CA: Stanford University Press, 1968).

41. Janice E. Thomson and Stephen D. Krasner, "Global Transactions and the Consolidation of Sovereignty," in Ernst-Otto Czempiel and James N. Rosenau, eds., *Global Changes and Theoretical Challenges: Approaches to World Politics for the 1990s* (Lexington, KY: Lexington Books, 1989), 198.

42. John Torpey, *The Invention of the Passport: Surveillance, Citizenship, and the State* (New York: Cambridge University Press, 2000); Mark Salter, *Rights of Passage: The Passport in International Relations* (Boulder, CO: Lynne Rienner, 2003).

43. See, for example, Hans Van der Veen, "Taxing the Drug Trade: Coercive Exploitation and the Financing of Rule," *Crime, Law, and Social Change* 40, no. 4 (December 2003): 349–390.

44. Peter K. Manning, *The Narc's Game* (Cambridge, MA: MIT Press, 1980), 253.

45. Strange, *The Retreat of the State*, 121. For a thoughtful critique, see H. Richard Friman, "Caught in the Madness? State Power and Transnational Organized Crime in the Work of Susan Strange," *Alternatives* 28, no. 4 (2003): 473–489.

46. Moises Naim, *Illicit: How Smugglers, Traffickers and Copycats Are Hijacking the Global Economy* (New York: Doubleday, 2005); Moises Naim, "The Five Wars of Globalization," *Foreign Policy* (January/February 2003): 29–37.

47. See Peter Andreas, "Transnational Crime and Economic Globalization," in Mats Berdal and Monica Serrano, eds., *Transnational Organized Crime and International Security* (Boulder, CO: Lynne Rienner, 2002).

48. On the role of technology in enhancing transgovernmental networks, see Raustiala, "The Architecture of International Cooperation," 21–22.

49. On the turn to new information technologies in state control efforts, see Flynn, "The False Conundrum"; Rey Koslowski, "International Migration and Border Control in the Information Age," unpublished paper, Rutgers University, Newark, NJ, 12 April 2002.

50. See Jane Kaplan and John Torpey, eds., *Documenting Individual Identity: State Practices in the Modern World* (Princeton, NJ: Princeton University Press, 2001).

51. For a fascinating historical account, see Cole, *Suspect Identities*.

52. See especially Mathieu Deflem, "Technology and the Internationalization of Policing: A Comparative Historical Perspective," *Justice Quarterly* 19, no. 3 (September 2002): 453–475.

53. K. A. Taipale, "Transnational Intelligence and Surveillance: Security Envelopes, Trusted Systems, and the Panoptic Global Security State," draft paper prepared for the conference "Beyond Terror: A New Security Agenda," Watson Institute for International Studies, Brown University, Providence, RI, 3–4 June 2005, 4.

54. In the case of cargo tracking, see Stephen E. Flynn, "Addressing the Short-comings of the Customs-Trade Partnership against Terrorism (C-TPAT) and the Container Security Initiative," testimony before the hearing of the Permanent Sub-Committee on Investigations, Committee on Homeland Security and Governmental Affairs, U.S. Senate, 26 May 2005.

55. A particularly extreme illustration of this is the practice of subcontracting customs work to multinational security firms. In Ghana, a Swiss-based corporation, COTECNA, has essentially become the country's customs service. The company is

involved in customs work in fourteen countries in Africa and Latin America, and its Japanese partner carries out similar functions in many Asian countries. Brenda Chalfin argues that "the multinationalization of Customs operations simultaneously compromises and shores up state power." She concludes, "This is a situation where the state is abrogating its exclusive territorial control – to a foreign body, no less – in order to strengthen its capacity to regulate and oversee that territory." "Working the Border in Ghana: Technologies of Sovereignty and Its Others," Occasional Papers No. 16, School of Social Science, Institute for Advanced Study, Princeton, NJ, November 2003, 3–5.

56. On the growth of private policing, see Johnston, "Transnational Private Policing."

57. See Michael Schroeder and Silvia Ascarelli, "Global Cop – New Role for the SEC: Policing Companies beyond U.S. Borders," *Wall Street Journal*, 30 July 2004, 1A. The authors note that the Securities and Exchange Commission is gaining a reputation as "the cop on the beat for the world's securities markets."

58. Wolfram F. Hanrieder, "Dissolving International Politics: Reflections on the Nation-State," *American Political Science Review* 72, no. 4 (1978): 1276–1287.

59. Some observers have provocatively pointed to the possible emergence of a globalized variant of Jeremy Bentham's panopticon, a design for prisons and other institutions that makes it possible to watch the inhabitants without their knowing if or when they are being watched. See Kirstie Ball and Frank Webster, "The Intensification of Surveillance," in Ball and Webster, *The Intensification of Surveillance*.

60. In the case of Mexican migration to the United States, see Douglas Massey, *Beyond Smoke and Mirrors: Mexican Immigration in an Era of Economic Integration* (New York: Russell Sage, 2003).

61. See Marc Mauer, *Comparative International Rates of Incarceration: An Examination of Causes and Trends* (Washington, DC: Sentencing Project, 2003), available at http://www.sentencingproject.org/pdfs/pub9036.pdf; Roy Walmsley, "Global Incarceration and Prison Trends," *Forum on Crime and Society* 3, nos. 1–2 (December 2003): 65–78, available at http://www.unodc.org/pdf/crime/forum/forum3_Art3.pdf.

62. See Roy Walmsley, *World Prison Population List: Research Findings No. 88* (London: Home Office Research, Development and Statistics Directorate, 1999); Vincent Schiraldi, *Poor Prescription: The Costs of Imprisoning Drug Offenders in the United States*, (San Francisco: Center on Juvenile and Criminal Justice, 2002).

63. For a critique, see M. R. Chatterton, "Reflections on International Police Cooperation: Putting Police Cooperation in Its Place – An Organizational Perspective," in Koenig and Das, *International Police Cooperation*.

64. See James Sheptycki, "Transnational Policing and the Makings of a Postmodern State," *British Journal of Criminology* 35, no. 4 (autumn 1995): 616.

14

Conclusion: The Global Cops Have Arrived

Ben Bowling and James Sheptycki

In the global networked society, police power is no longer constrained by the borders of the nation-state. The idea of the hapless detective standing impotent at the airport cursing in frustration as 'Mr Big' jets off to an untouchable retirement on a distant 'Costa Del Crime' is as anachronistic as the image of Bonny and Clyde driving triumphantly over the state line to escape the local sheriff in depression-era America. Policing today is connected around the world by mobile phone and email, shared databases and personnel exchanges. Thousands of police have global mobility or are stationed permanently overseas.

Policework now extends in a complex global web that enables surveillance of suspect movements and the use of coercive power to disrupt and arrest criminal and terrorist suspects around the world and to render them overseas for trial or detention. With well developed mutual legal assistance treaties, fast-track extradition, regional arrest warrants and a growing number of people working to administer the system, transnational policing is emerging as a new specialism with its own unique subculture. Explaining global policing is made possible through empirical research on how transnational policing works in practice but that research needs to be understood in the context of theories about emerging systems of global governance. Since the power to govern means little, if anything at all, without being able to marshal coercive power, no theory of global governance can be complete without a theory of global policing.

Source: *Global Policing* (London: SAGE Publications Ltd, 2012), pp. 128–136 and 168.

As a mechanism for distributing legitimate coercive force to resolve conflict and secure the ends of safe and peaceful communities, policing is an integral element of all systems of governance.[1] As a set of practices and beliefs, policing is tightly linked to the defining nature of the social system within which it is embedded. Pre-modern policing was tied closely to locality – the village constable and night watchmen are examples of policing in tightly knit communities. Modern policing systems in many parts of the world were constructed within 18th- and 19th-century systems of public administration focused on cities, counties and other sub-national units. In some countries city police chiefs, county chief constables, sheriffs and regional superintendents are supplemented with national police forces, some of which were bequeathed to them by former colonial masters. In the late 20th century, countries without centralised state police forces created new national criminal intelligence services, serious crime agencies or other national policing hubs to link the local and global policing networks.

As we explained in Chapter 2, in the mid-20th century, governance began to evolve from an inter-national to a transnational-state-system, a process that has continued to develop to this day. The institutions of global governance created since the mid-20th century include *political* (e.g. UN, G8), *economic* (e.g. WTO), *legislative* (e.g. UN and ILO), *judicial* (e.g. ICC) and *policing* organisations (e.g. Interpol). What characterises the transnational-state-system is that in addition to relationships between actors operating on behalf of national governments, there are connections and interactions among actors operating 'above', 'below' and 'beyond' the nation-state.[2] As systems of global governance have evolved, police power has begun to fly from its original nesting place within the nation-state-system. Today's 'global cops' could work for a city police force, a private company, a national intelligence hub or a supranational policing agency.

The sociology of policing defines police as being concerned with the maintenance of social order through two distinct means: surveillance and coercion. In Chapter 1 we described the boundaries of the policing field drawing analytical distinctions between 'high' and 'low' forms of police power; 'public' and 'private' security providers and surveillance and control of 'territory' and 'suspect populations'. In Chapter 5 we illustrated these theoretical distinctions by describing new policing practices as emerging in the attempt to secure transnational spaces (e.g. border zones, airports, skies and seas) and to conduct surveillance on flows of people (e.g. migrants and suspect populations) and flows of things (e.g. drugs, money, guns).

These surveillant and coercive practices, while not entirely new, have expanded massively and changed shape dramatically in recent decades. They require continuing close empirical and theoretical scrutiny. Research in the sociology of policing has developed from its initial focus on local beat policing to explore other forms of policework, most recently documenting transnational policing including the practices of customs, immigration, airport security, financial intelligence and private security agencies. By definition, all of these policing agencies have surveillance and coercive powers. All of them are 'knowledge workers' with systems to store and share intelligence collected by technical surveillance, informers and undercover officers. Many also have the power to use physical force to search and seize property, arrest and question suspects, impose travel restrictions and freeze financial assets. A crucial empirical research finding is that police powers now transgress and transcend the boundaries of the nation-state. We have shown that the subculture of transnational policing is no longer anchored by national sovereignty but is writing a new script for policing sovereignty. The evidence suggests that transnational policing constitutes, and is constituted by, the nature of the emerging transnational-state-system.

In Chapter 1, we set out a theory of police legitimacy based on the notion of the social contract.[3] As enlightenment philosopher John Locke put it, because human beings have certain inherent moral rights, any use of coercive power by the state is morally suspect.[4] The power of policing cannot simply be taken for granted: the onus lies with the wielder of coercive power to justify any interference with individual liberty. In terms of classical liberal theory, state power is constrained by reference to democratic relationships within a state that describe a rational and principled separation of governmental power. What distinguishes policing from a mere 'protection racket' is that the people who are policed know, understand and endorse the police mission.[5] That is, the police have legitimate authority. In a democracy, this legitimacy is secured through mechanisms of accountability by which police are answerable to the public whom they both serve and are members of. In Geoffrey Marshall's terms, democratic police should go about their work in ways that are explanatory, co-operative, obedient and subordinate to the will of the people.[6]

It is an axiom of liberal democratic theory that when policing agents abuse their power, they can be called to account by bodies representing the will of the people for the purposes of sanction. These systems of accountability can be legal, political or administrative. A serious problem for any theory of policing beyond the boundaries of the nation-state is in defining who 'the people' are when considered in a global context. In the world system, there is no global *polity* (i.e. an organised world government or representative political organisation) nor a global *demos* (i.e. a common people constituting a democratic state). The problem of global policing then becomes a Gordian knot about the accountability for coercive and surveillant policing power authorised and originating transnationally.

Policing in the world system is not under 'rule-of-law', nor is it 'rule-by-law' but rather 'rule *with* law'. Law is like a tool in the hands of transnational policing actors whose occupational subculture, examined in detail in chapter 4, provides a worldview and rhetoric of justification that largely leaves global policing to be defined in terms of its own script. The resulting insecurity exacerbates a democratic tug-of-war between Rousseauian punitive populism and Hobbsean authoritarianism creating the dangerous possibility of a global social contract torn asunder. In the extreme, transnational paramilitary police power has been used to facilitate assassinations, kidnap, and the illegal rendition by chartered aircraft of 'terrorist suspects' to face torture in other countries.[7] Fortunately such Machiavellian moments are rare. Nonetheless a central problem for the use of global policing power is the absence of a global social contract that could hold global policing to account or provide it with legitimating authority.

This book obliquely confronts calls for a global police force – a supranational investigative body with enforcement powers – an idea which has shown remarkable resilience despite being highly problematic.[8] The 'vision' of a global police force first mooted by UN officials in the 1960s is once again being touted by transnational technocrats. In October 2009, the *New York Times* reported on an Interpol and UNPOL-hosted meeting of justice and foreign ministers from 60 countries (including the USA and China) coming together as a first step in creating a 'global policing doctrine'. It reported that Interpol and the UN were 'poised to become partners in fighting crime by jointly grooming a *global police force* [which] would be deployed as peace-keepers among rogue nations driven by war and organised crime' (emphasis added).[9] Ron Noble, secretary general of Interpol, said that among the most critical tasks were combating illegal arms, drug trafficking and peacekeeping. 'We have a visionary model', he said, 'The police will be trained and equipped differently with resources. When they stop someone, they will be consulting global databases to determine who they are stopping.'[10]

Our analysis of the architecture of global policing sketched out in Chapter 3 shows that UN policing capacity has grown exponentially since the 1960s, a growth that has accelerated during the past decade. At the same time, other global policing agencies – Interpol, the WCO and the FATF – have also grown in capacity, scope and ambition. In our view, a world police force is problematic and is probably destined to remain a law enforcer's dream. It is certainly undesirable in the absence of a global polity based on a principled separation of governmental powers and a demos created out of a widely inclusive system of cultural meaning enshrined with human rights and human security ideals. The essence of the problem for liberal democratic policing theory is the lack of any prospect of a social contract upon which to base the legitimacy claims of such an entity and the absence of an authoritative and representative body that could hold a global police force to account.

While there is no global police force, there is global policing. It seems probable that global policing will continue to play a significant part of the global governance project and seems likely to grow rather than shrink. Every hour of every day, ILOs and a global network of Interpol NCBs, alongside a web of corporate security expertise will probably continue to facilitate policing talk and information exchange, often in the 'transnational space between'. UNPOL will almost certainly carry on with their overseas missions. Regional police bodies will most likely continue to meet, make policy, train and network. Various national intelligence officers will continue to act as agents for the transnational traffic in messages. Overseas liaison officers will go on doing their work stitching together the patchwork quilt of global policing. In a networked society, global policing power can be felt at borders, ports and airports and behind the scenes of national policing bureaucracies. In domestic contexts, local police are increasingly 'globally aware' and seem set to become even more so. The experience of Derek Bond, described in Chapter 1, shows that transnational policing power can extend down to the policing of rural areas as remote as the game parks of KwaZulu-Natal. This is just one illustration of how global policing can affect anyone, in most instances without attracting the attention of the world's media, public scrutiny or democratic accountability mechanisms.

Global policing is an integral component of global governance and one of its defining features. In our view the simple functionalist notion that global policing has arisen because of a need to chase after the global bad guys does not provide a very satisfactory account of the observable transformations. Neither theories of insecurity nor theories of global governance can be complete without a theory of global policing. Any such theory must put the dualistic view of the world divided into good and evil to one side while remaining cognizant that this simplistic functional explanation creates powerful cultural expectations that have real consequences for policing.

In much the same way as domestic policing, transnational policing reflects and reinforces inequality. Priorities, politics and practices are skewed in the interests of the powerful. The policing mission and its patterns of action and justificatory rhetoric are based on the 'usual suspects' being targeted as 'suitable enemies'. And there is no shortage of these: serious organised travelling criminals, suspected terrorists, global protesters, money launderers, fugitives from justice as well as economically marginal migrants more generally. These 'folk devils' legitimate the development of new institutions and the inauguration of new powers. However, not all that is policed causes grave harm (e.g. the production and consumption of marijuana) and some extremely harmful things (e.g. environmental destruction) go un-policed.

Seen in a planetary context, the gulf between the police and the policed is very wide. The existing subculture of transnational policing is dominated by a world view that pits 'enforcers' against 'folk devils'; consequently, it often fails to foster peaceful and safe communities. It is therefore important to challenge the taken for granted assumptions of the transnational-state-system as a container for insecurity. In some places, particularly those where social exclusion and poverty are most entrenched and policing governance

weakest, serious violence is endemic and police are often powerless to protect and are themselves sometimes abusive themselves. While some people
are confined to insecurity hot-spots where violence and disorder are a fact of
everyday life, others inhabit gated enclaves or security bubbles, excluding,
or attempting to exclude, global insecurity. This exclusivity, let us not forget,
has given rise to what some scholars have called 'social junk' that is, people
who have fallen through the cracks – impoverished, economically and ultimately socially excluded.[11]

The construction of these outsiders tends to be couched in racialised
terms relegating the black and brown peoples of the global south to the
ranks of the permanently excluded. Around the world there are plenty of
examples of transnational policing power having iatrogenic effects that damage human well-being.[12] Such contradictions lead inevitably to a crisis of
legitimacy and exacerbate the security–control paradox: the more police are
empowered with legal tools, surveillance and coercive technologies in the
name of 'providing security', the less secure some people actually become.
Trapped in a cycle of insecurity, policing slides into a strategy of colonial
war and counter-insurgency in an attempt to enforce peace through superior
firepower. The result is 'social dynamite' and the socially excluded become
rebellious and violent.[13]

As policing becomes the dominant modality of global social ordering,
the destructive association of governance with enforcement power distorts
every other aspect of security governance including public health, education and public administration.[14] That is one reason why a theory of global
policing is so vital and rather more complex than the usual functionalist
thinking assumes. In this book we have concentrated on developing a theoretical language for talking about global policing that not only challenges
these functionalist assumptions but also provides a robust analysis based on
empirical research findings. In doing so, we show the continuity clearly in
the development of transnational police co-operation over the past century
and its acceleration at the end of the Cold War. The idea that global policing
is a reflexive response to changes in the external security environment – such
as the events of 9/11 – is incorrect.

Our theory allows for local subcultural variations in policing practice and
is attuned to the fragmentation of the division of policing labour including parts under both private and public auspices. This theory is historically
mindful that the roots of the policing idea are part of a conceptual system
concerning the nation-state-system. The theory seeks to take into account
the complex and often contradictory relations between policing and law as it
is played out in a global polycentric power system where a universally recognised source of authority is absent. Finally, this theory explains how a policing field that is practically or organisationally fragmented is held together
by the meanings inherent in its occupational subculture and how this system
of meaning impinges on the global system by imprinting pre-programmed

notions based on the transnational-state-system idea. Global policing arises out of a complex overdetermination arising from multiple factors.

Policing subculture is more important than the letter of the law because it is on the basis of culture that meanings regarding the application of law derive. In other words, legal discourse about policing makes sense of policing in the terms already actually present. We have a particular take on law that describes legal rules as tools and emphasises the discretionary responsibility of social actors in choosing how to rule with law. The symbolic content of law can have effects on cultural meanings and police are not the only social agents who have access to legal tools. However, simply put, the language for talking about transnational crime and insecurity was substantially scripted from within the subculture of transnational policing thus pre-shaping expectations about what policing law is for.

It is striking how the vocabulary of 'crime as business' prevalent in the circuits of UN governance in the early 1970s drew attention to terms like corruption and white-collar criminality by multi-national corporations and to novel types of crime such as environmental destruction. The analytical account of agenda setting presented in this book has shown that the hegemony of 'law enforcement' and 'national security discourse' leaves many lacunae in global policing practice. The shortcomings of global policing have palpable consequences for the overall health of the world system. These patterns are closely related to the continuing influence of high policing often, though not always, at the behest of military or security service agents acting within the circuits of transnational policing. The subcultural discourse of policing is shaped within a complex division of institutional labour and not all the participants have the same degree of influence. The language of insecurity that emerges, and the strategies of containment that come with it, act as a brake on the development of a global social contract or a democratic polity. Currently existing global policing practices call into question liberal democratic policing theory just as a tug-of-war intensifies between advocates of strong authority on the one side and advocates of people power on the other – the inheritors of Hobbes and Rousseau. Consequently, the possibility of a global social contract becomes ever more remote.

An important feature of the emerging transnational-state-system described in Chapter 2, is the 'hollowing out' of the Keynesian 'welfare state' and its gradual replacement with Schumpeterian ideas about a 'workfare state'. This shift in thinking, often referred to as the neo-liberal turn, has had profound consequences for policing. The theory of global policing developed here has stretched to accommodate the hybrid forms of security governance that have emerged between public and private types of policing networks which, we hasten to add, encompass the entire panoply of policing functions including both high and low forms and everything from the militarised policing of border zones to policing drugs, money, guns or fish.

Before all of the global nodes of policing and security governance can be harnessed to the language of human rights and human security, rather than the elimination of enemies, a massive cultural shift in policing would have to take place. The signs are not hopeful, least of all when it comes to observations concerning the privatisation of security functions. Studies of private security companies, private military companies and 'in-house' security in the corporate 'resource extraction industries' show an almost reckless disregard for disempowered communities. Privatised security in urban contexts reflects social class differences patterning the mixed geography of the global south in the global north. Keeping in mind the preponderance of private security and private interest in the production of the global policing apparatus, the predominant preference for private capital accumulation precipitates further insecurity. Private interest provokes public insecurity and then retreats behind walls and security barriers.

The transgressive effects of corporate power in a global system predicated on neo-liberal ideas makes the transnational-state-system fundamentally different from the nation-state-system that preceded it. This transforms the linguistic possibilities for articulating a global social contract and the terms of its legitimacy. Ideas about a global social contract between all individuals are considerably challenged in an age where corporations have become legal persons. The extent and nature of corporate organisation and the ways in which it co-articulates with the global structures of governance in the late modern age are challenges to a just and equitable global social contract.

Our analysis makes this claim on the basis of a social constructionist perspective. It is controversial for many, perhaps most, people to learn that phenomena like 'transnational organised crime' and 'terrorism' are socially constructed. This is no denial on our part of the very real violence associated with illicit markets and political extremism. Of course the violence associated with both phenomena have real consequences. The death and destruction caused by armed violence – irrespective of where in the world it takes place and whether it is carried out by 'criminals', 'gangsters', 'terrorists', 'corporations', 'states' or any other kind of organisation – is a major social and political problem. It is only right that scholars think about solutions to violence whether it is instrumental, expressive or political. The constructivist approach challenges the presumptions that the 'real threats' posed by 'suitable enemies' are enough to justify the construction of a global policing architecture. Still, there can be no doubt that there are people who will kill for an idea or ideological commitment, and who will exploit the economic weakness of others ruthlessly through the means of illicit market transactions. Obviously, we condemn such acts.

It is equally important to acknowledge that appearances can be deceptive and it is not always the case that the social actors claiming to be 'good guys' and pointing fingers at the 'bad guys over there' have anyone's best interests in mind other than their own. Indeed, we would even go so far as to say that it is more important to unmask the taken for granted assumptions, because the rhetoric of 'war on terror' and 'war on crime' have well documented harmful effects. If the solution to the problem of terrorism or drugs trafficking exacerbates the harm associated with the phenomenon at hand, we simply have to reconsider the terms of discourse used to describe the problem. Thinking as police researchers who have spent many years working and researching inside police organisations, we hold an appreciation of policework, especially when it comes to violence.

Sometimes there will be people who can only be prevented by coercive means from doing real harm to others. Police action will therefore feature in any social order; the point is to prevent it from becoming oppressive. Other commentators in this field may eschew normative contemplations in favour of a 'strict examination of empirical developments' along realist assumptions, but we have tried to challenge Manichean thinking while remaining pragmatically engaged with the idea of global policing.[15] There are many authors who provide technocratic analyses prioritising the enforcer's role. In our view it would be better if the diplomats, field-operators and problem solvers moved centre-stage because we firmly believe that one of the most important virtues of good policing is to minimise the use of coercive solutions to social problems.[16] The enforcer role-type will obviously continue as a player in the drama of global policing, but a welcome sign of improvement would be that this role moved from centre-stage to the margins in the theatre of police operations.

In this book we have attempted to describe the forms of transnational policing, their historical genesis and future trajectory so as to raise key theoretical and practical questions about the emerging global system. We have sought to make global policing theoretically visible. In our way of thinking, policing is an essential aspect of any social order but it cannot live up to its normative claims – to maintain the health of the social body and to ensure a generalised state of prosperity – without the legitimacy and accountability that spring from a social contract widely experienced as just. As policing moves into the transnational realm, there will likely evolve a supranational system to regulate its power within and beyond national borders 'from above' and an active globally connected civil society to engage police accountability 'from below'.[17] Developing global policing with the capacity to maintain peace and order and to contribute to good governance means strengthening the democratic ethos or 'constabulary ethic'.[18] Such an ethos would be imbued with notions and principles such as responsiveness to the global commonwealth, adherence to international human rights norms and the values of 'human security'. Accountability would run through its entire blood stream in delivering a service to the public as well in the democratic functioning within policing institutions in order to ensure that global policing reflects the communities that it serves.[19] We hope that making global policing *visible* – empirically and theoretically – will facilitate this process.

In these pages we have engaged with one of the most pressing questions of our time – how peaceful and safe communities be can sustained or created in a world in which the sources of insecurity and the forces of 'law and order' originate beyond the boundaries of the nation-state. This conclusion is therefore a kind of ending, but also a beginning for new thinking about the provision and regulation of good policing in the global system.

Notes

1. Robert Reiner, *The Politics of the Police*, see fn 63.
2. Ian Loader (2002) 'Governing European Policing: Some Problems, and Prospects', see fn 233.
3. John Kleinig, *The Ethics of Policing*, see fn 43.
4. Ibid., see fn 43.
5. Charles Tilley (1985) 'War-Making and State-Making as Organized Crime', see fn 50, pp. 169–86.
6. Geoffrey Marshall, 'Police Accountability Revisited', see fn 400.
7. Philippe Sands, *Lawless World: America and the Making and Breaking of Global Rules*, see fn 159; A. Goldfarb and M. Litvinenko (2007) *The Poisoning of Alexander Litvinenko and the Return of the KGB*. New York: Simon & Schuster.
8. S.D. Brown (2008) *Combating International Crime: The Longer Arm of the Law*, see fn 7, p. 5.
9. 'Interpol and UN back "Global Policing Doctrine"'. *New York Times* 11 October 2009.
10. Ibid.
11. Steven Spitzer, 'Toward a Marxian Theory of Deviance', see fn 113.
12. Stan Cohen, 'Western Crime Models in the Third World …', see fn 42. Ben Bowling, 'Transnational Criminology …', see fn 42.
13. Spitzer, see fn 113.
14. Paul Gilroy, *After Empire*, see fn 84, p. 47.
15. M. Deflem, *The Policing of Terrorism*, see fn 494, p. 29.
16. Ben Bowling (2008) 'Fair and Effective Police Methods: Towards 'Good Enough' Policing'. *Scandinavian Studies in Criminology and Crime Prevention*, 8(1): 17–23.
17. Ben Bowling, *Policing the Caribbean*, see fn 12, pp. 311–5.
18. James Sheptycki, 'The Raft of the Medusa', see fn 549.
19. Ben Bowling, Coretta Phillips, Alexandra Campbell and Maria Docking (2004) *Human Rights and Policing: Eliminating Racism, Discrimination and Xenophobia from Policework*. United Nations Institute for Social Research and Development.